I0147925

PRAISE FOR *RAGE AND THE REPUBLIC*

"Jonathan Turley has written a masterpiece for the 250th anniversary of the Declaration of Independence. *Rage and the Republic* sheds new light on the foundation of our country, including a riveting account of Thomas Paine's journey through both the American and French Revolutions. Turley brings out the essential elements that created the oldest and most successful democratic system in history. He then explores the challenges to that system in the twenty-first century, from AI to global governance. In contrast to many legal experts today, Turley explains how the survival of our system will depend on our commitment (not our abandonment) of our core values, from the emphasis on individual rights to maintaining 'a liberty-enhancing economy.' It is a moving account on the very essence of liberty that should be on the shelf of every American."

—Mark Levin, host of Life, Liberty & Levin *and #1* New York Times *bestselling author*

"In this deft blend of two braided subjects, political history and constitutional reasoning, Jonathan Turley demonstrates a discomforting and painfully timely truth: The phrase 'democratic despotism' is not an oxymoron."

—George F. Will, Pulitzer Prize winner and Washington Post *columnist*

"Jonathan Turley's *Rage and the Republic* is a riveting account of the unique and uniquely enduring American version of democracy. Turley offers fresh insights into both the past and the future of American democracy, including the dangers of 'democratic despotism' that have plagued past revolutions. *Rage and the Republic* is a fascinating and inspiring account of the foundations of the American system. It is a must-read on the 250th anniversary of our Declaration of Independence."

—Nadine Strossen, former president of the American Civil Liberties Union

"Brilliant and riveting. The American Revolution comes alive, and so does the birth of the Constitution, with unexpectedly timely lessons for the perils we face today. Turley vividly reminds us how democracy can lead to tyranny and how America escaped that fate at the founding."

—Jed Rubenfeld, Yale Law School professor,
author, and constitutional law expert

"In his insightful book about the lessons of the American Revolution for our own fractious, disruptive times, Jonathan Turley astutely focuses on Thomas Paine, the fiery and flawed influencer of his day. Turley paints a compelling picture of Paine as disruptor in chief, helping to fuel the revolution as the righteous voice of the common man. But the story doesn't end there. Later in life, Paine abhors how rage and fervor lead to violence and extremism. While capturing Paine's many dimensions, Turley also describes one of America's great challenges on its 250th birthday: How to deal with broken, illiberal institutions without sabotaging stability and wrecking the American project.

"Clarity and insight for our own contentious times, *Rage and the Republic* is Jonathan Turley's birthday gift to America to mark its 250 years of independence, reminding us of Thomas Paine's evolution from fiery force for independence to wary critic of extremism. A wise guide to avoid wrecking the American project."

—Uri Berliner, contributing editor at Free Press *and*
former senior business editor at National Public Radio

"From ancient times to the present day, demagogues, fanatics, and mobs have threatened democratic republics. Jonathan Turley's absorbing narrative brings these dramas to life, from the Athenian agora to revolutionary Philadelphia to Jacobin Paris, in a scholarly tour de force that could not be more timely. Turley's arguments are bound to be controversial, but his plea for a renewed adherence to America's time-tested constitutional norms cannot—and should not—be ignored."

—Charles Lane, author of The Day Freedom Died *and*
nonresident senior fellow at the American Enterprise Institute

"In the spirit of Tocqueville, Jonathan Turley in *Rage and the Republic: The Unfinished Story of the American Revolution* examines the principles and practices of democracy in America. Looking backward to the American Revolution and then forward to a future in which our lives will be shaped by stunning developments in robotics and artificial intelligence, Professor Turley assesses the health and continuing relevance of our republic's constitutional principles and institutions. Although professional historians and scholars will learn from the book, it is not an academic tome but rather a work for general readers, and as such it is a valuable contribution to American civic life."

—Robert P. George, McCormick Professor of Jurisprudence and director of the James Madison Program in American Ideals and Institutions

"On the 250th Anniversary of the Declaration of Independence, will the fruits of the American Revolution be supplanted by another 'democratical' mobocracy like that which arose in parts of the U.S. before the adoption of our republican Constitution? Not if Jonathan Turley has anything to say about it. In this riveting book, he revisits the past—focusing particularly on the remarkable life of Tom Paine and how the democratic principles of the French Revolution differed from our own—to identify the nature of the current threats to our liberties and our constitutional order. History has never been put to a better use."

—Randy E. Barnett, Patrick Hotung Professor of Constitutional Law at the Georgetown University Law Center and director of the Georgetown Center for the Constitution

ALSO BY JONATHAN TURLEY

The Indispensable Right: Free Speech in an Age of Rage

RAGE
and the
REPUBLIC

THE UNFINISHED STORY OF THE AMERICAN REVOLUTION

JONATHAN TURLEY

SIMON & SCHUSTER

New York Amsterdam/Antwerp London
Toronto Sydney/Melbourne New Delhi

Simon & Schuster
1230 Avenue of the Americas
New York, NY 10020

First Simon & Schuster hardcover edition February 2026

SIMON & SCHUSTER and colophon are registered trademarks of Simon & Schuster, LLC
Simon & Schuster strongly believes in freedom of expression and stands against censorship in all its forms. For more information, visit BooksBelong.com.

For information about special discounts for bulk purchases, please contact Simon & Schuster Special Sales at 1-866-506-1949 or business@simonandschuster.com.

The Simon & Schuster Speakers Bureau can bring authors to your live event. For more information or to book an event, contact the Simon & Schuster Speakers Bureau at 1-866-248-3049 or visit our website at www.simonspeakers.com.

Interior design by Joy O'Meara

Manufactured in the United States of America

10 9 8 7 6 5 4 3 2

Library of Congress Cataloging-in-Publication data is available.

ISBN 978-1-6682-0502-0
ISBN 978-1-6682-0504-4 (ebook)

To my wife, Leslie,
who answered an advertisement for an antique dresser
and ended up with a husband,
four children, and a most improbable journey.

If revolution devours its own,
it is devotion that restores those you love.
That dresser, this book, and a still-smitten academic
belong entirely to you.

"Like Saturn, the Revolution devours its children."

—Jacques Mallet du Pan (1793)

Contents

RAGE
and the
REPUBLIC

Introduction

When in the Course of human events, it becomes necessary
for one people to dissolve the political bands which have
connected them with another . . . they should declare
the causes which impel them to the separation.

—The Declaration of Independence (1776)

Chronos and His Child, circa 1625–1650, by Giovanni Francesco Romanelli

Like Saturn, the Revolution devours its children." Those words from journalist Jacques Mallet du Pan during the French Revolution referred to the Roman God Saturn, or Kronos in Greek. The youngest son of twelve titans, Kronos was given an ominous prophesy by his mother that he would be overthrown by his own child. That made for a less than ideal family. Kronos would castrate his father and, after ascending to the throne, he defied the prophesy by eating each of his children upon their births. Hestia, Demeter, Hera, Hades, and Poseidon all became Daddy's digestives. Not surprisingly, his familial diet did not sit well with his consort Rhea so, when her son Zeus was born, she decided to trick Kronos by wrapping a stone in a swaddling blanket and handing it to him to devour. She then hid Zeus on Crete. Once he reached adulthood, Zeus returned and, fulfilling the prophesy, defeated his father.

The story of Kronos held obvious meaning for Mallet du Pan, who watched with alarm as the French Revolution devoured first its aristocratic foes and then its own supporters. The lesson of Saturn would also be raised in the American Revolution by none other than Thomas Paine. There is an aspect of the myth that has an added, if unintended, meaning. Zeus would force his father to regurgitate his siblings, who went on to populate Olympus as deities. Conversely, it was Kronos who was viewed as heralding the "golden age of mortals." Indeed, Kronos may have been all too human in allowing his ambition and rage to overwhelm every other emotion and consideration. He embodied an insatiable appetite that once unleashed would continue with inexorable and horrible consequences. It is a story played out over and over again in history as ambition becomes activism, activism becomes extremism, and extremism becomes authoritarianism. Call it the Saturn gene. We are all Saturn's children with an inherent impulse that rests within each of us: the capacity of all mortals to become monsters.

Most countries are the progeny of revolution, including the United States. Revolution remains the ultimate act of self-determination for a free people. It was a moment captured at the very start of the Declaration of Independence that "in the Course of human events, it becomes necessary for one people to dissolve the political bands which have connected them with another." All revolutions begin with noble aspirations of a people seeking "certain unalienable Rights." If civil society is based on a "social contract," revolutions reflect a terminal breach of that contract in the failure of a government to perform its most essential obligations. It is the farthest point of political discourse where reason becomes rage. It is a moment that is often motivated by the highest ideals of a generation, a pursuit of a new horizon for realizing the essential rights and potential of a people. In that act of separation, there can be not just the release from existing bonds but also the unleashing of pent-up anger, ambition, and avarice. As Napoléon Bonaparte observed, "a revolution is an idea which has found its bayonets."

The challenge is to put away the bayonets once the idea has taken hold. All too often in history, the rage has overwhelmed the reason for revolution as citizens are led forward at the tips of those very bayonets. As Hannah Arendt observed, "liberation and freedom are not the same." Revolution can just as easily become anarchy or authoritarianism as the freedom of action mutates into a type of license for violence. Once our "political bands" are dissolved with preexisting governing structures, the best and worst of human nature are laid bare. That is why revolutions are really the story of human exploration and exploitation, each with its own inherent virtues and vices. The problem with revolutions, Alexis de Tocqueville observed, is that, like writing a book, "the most difficult part to invent is the end." This book is about that quintessential human struggle and how a fleeting combination of factors can prove the difference between a stable democracy and a brutal despotism. A unique set of fortuitous circumstances produced the American Revolution, the moment when, as John Adams marveled, "thirteen clocks had struck as one."

With the 250th anniversary of the Declaration of Independence, the United States celebrates its own revolutionary moment. The American republic was born in rage. The Boston Tea Party is honored today but, at the time, was denounced by many as a violent, criminal act. Patriots and loyalists took up arms as a long, bloody war waged across the colonies. At the same time, the Declaration of Independence embodied a truly revolutionary concept beyond the rage of the moment. It spoke to the shared rights of all mankind. It claimed those rights not as Englishmen, but as human beings born to liberty. In 1,320 words, the Declaration of Independence shattered hundreds of years of not just British rule but the very rationale for British authority. A new American voice rose from that single page of parchment; a voice that was not just Thomas Jefferson's but an amalgamation of bold and enlightened writers. Liberty was embraced as the natural and undeniable state of all humanity. Democracy is not mentioned once in the declaration. It is liberty that defined the revolution. The system of government, whether a democracy or a republic, was the means of achieving that promise without smothering it in the process. It was, as described by the philosopher Rousseau, the "age of revolutions."

We are again living in revolutionary times. It is not just classic revolutions where governments are overthrown, but rather revolutions that can change countries from within. We refer to the Industrial Revolution and the Information Revolution to signify the transformative changes that they brought to society. Often those new realities produce countervailing political changes in government. The twenty-first century has seen the acceleration of new technology like artificial intelligence (AI) that is reframing every aspect of human existence. These changes will redefine not just the workplace but also the place of citizens in society at large. The question is whether American democracy can survive in the twenty-first century or collapse under the same forces of democratic despotism that brought down its contemporaries. It is the unfinished story of the American Revolution.

Democratic despotism can seem a contradiction in terms, but it was one of the central fears of the framers in seeking to create a system that protected individual rights. The threat of the rise of a tyrant can never be dismissed entirely in any system or in any century. However, the greatest threat to a democratic system in history has been the rise of majoritarian tyranny, the despotism of the many over the few. Fueled by economic unrest, uncontrolled democratic movements can produce a self-destructive cycle as both rights and wealth are curtailed to satisfy public demands. The resulting chaos can often produce the very antithesis of democracy in the form of an individual tyrant who assumes sweeping emergency powers. History shows this pattern repeating of tyrants emerging not from aristocracy but democracy. It is not the linear Marxist progression from feudalism through to a proletariat revolution. Rather, it has proven more circular than linear with systems moving at times from aristocracy to democracy to tyranny and back again. In looking at the past breakdowns of democracies, three conditions often emerged: economic stress, class divisions, and unrestrained majoritarian power. It is after such breakdowns that a free people can embrace a dictatorship.

The framers understood that the erosion of political rights can emerge from popular government and popular justice. There are various examples of such abuses from the Bolsheviks of Russia to the cultural revolutionaries of China to the Hutus of Rwanda. In any generation, there is a conceit that our problems are unprecedented and what we face is *sui generis*, or unique. There is no question that we are facing transformative changes on a global scale, including new technology that will bring both great benefits and costs for citizens. We have been here before. While the overall context can change in the marketplace and the workplace, the central issue remains basic human nature and human rights. The voices heard today calling for radical, even revolutionary, changes are the same voices that have echoed throughout history. They arise as economic and social conditions push our institutions and values to the breaking point. The striking similarities between the changes in the eighteenth and twenty-first centuries are ignored at our peril. If history is known to repeat itself, it may do so with a terrible vengeance in the years to come. This book details the struggle of central figures to harness the unlimited energy released by the Enlightenment to fuel a revolution and then, as equally challenging, to convert that revolution into a stable government. The Founders saw democracy as both the means and the menace of a free people. Some would come to recognize (and experience) the dangers of democratic despotism by the end of their lives.

The most influential voice of the American Revolution was an unlikely character who belatedly washed up on the shores of the New World, the wreckage of a life that found little but ruin in the Old World. He was Thomas Paine. While late to the cause, Paine saw the American Revolution for what it was, or at least what it could be. He told his new adopted nation that "we have it in our power to begin the world over again. A situation, similar to the present, hath not happened since the days of Noah until now."

The focus on Paine in this book may seem a curious choice, particularly on this milestone anniversary of the Declaration of Independence. Jefferson is viewed as the face of the Declaration and deserves every bit of acclaim that he received for his life and legacy. Paine did not participate in the Second Continental Congress in adopting the Declaration.

In fact, he was not even in Philadelphia when it was signed (Paine was with Washington and the militia facing the British in New York). Yet long before Jefferson put pen to parchment, it was Paine who would speak of the natural and inalienable rights as the basis for the American Revolution. It was Paine, in his pamphlet *Common Sense*, who made the case for "independency." At the time, there was no debate as to who was the "father of the American Revolution." Indeed, it was a recognition that left figures like John Adams fuming in jealousy and led figures like Washington to actively recruit Paine to help rally his troops. The later elevation of Jefferson over Paine is itself telling. Jefferson was a far better champion for many of the Founding Fathers. He was everything Paine was not: highly educated, refined, handsome, and sophisticated. A slaveholder, Jefferson was the image of a Southern gentleman. Conversely, Paine was a heavy-drinking reprobate and unabashed contrarian. He was unkempt, irascible, and impoverished. Yet Paine was arguably the truest revolutionary among them. Before the Revolution, many of the Founders sought reconciliation with England or the re-creation of much of the English system. Paine came to this country with revolution on his mind. He saw the new nation as an opportunity to truly start the world anew; a new civilization built by what a contemporary called a "new man" forged in the New World. Paine was also ardently antislavery. As on so many issues, Paine had the courage of his convictions and defied critics in denouncing this immoral institution. While Jefferson would seek to add antislavery language to the Declaration, he not only agreed to remove the language but lived a life of hypocrisy in retaining a large number of slaves at his estate at Monticello.

Paine has another distinction among his peers. He would play a significant role in two revolutions that took strikingly different paths in America and France. Among the best-known figures of the American Revolution, only the Marquis de Lafayette could make a similar claim. Despite not speaking French, Paine's voice would resonate with a rebellious people. One commentator in Paris noted that "the idea of a republic had previously presented itself to no one, but some of the seed sown by the audacious hand of Paine were now budding in leading minds." While Paine would eventually ally himself with the more moderate faction of

French revolutionaries, his model of government would be again dangerously untethered to limiting principles. This included his early rejection of the moderating influence of a monarchy and of structural elements like bicameralism. Paine would proselytize for a new understanding of government based on a new view of humanity.

The Declaration of Independence was forged in a miraculous moment of unanimity among men who came from different cultural, religious, and social backgrounds. Indeed, some, like John Adams and Thomas Jefferson, would become the most bitter of enemies after defeating their common foe, King George III. That transcendent moment in Philadelphia not only created something truly greater than themselves but also found a shared faith that was only just emerging. We may need to summon the same commitment in the years to come. Those same voices have returned with the same appeal to rage and revolutionary change. They include some of the very same ideas that were advanced by Paine and the French Jacobins in stripping away constitutional protections to unleash the "general will." Paine serves as a penetrating point of reference in this history in his own struggle with democratic despotism. Paine learned the dangers of unrestrained popular government in the hardest possible way. It came close to killing him. He would learn that what was lost in Paris was precisely what he had left in Philadelphia—a system that could channel tremendous political and economic pressures into a stable republic.

The significance of that moment in Philadelphia was lost on some, including those who sought a new world order. In a letter to Abbé Raynal, one of the key intellectual figures in the French Revolution, Paine disagreed with his understanding of the impetus for the American Revolution, including dismissing it as a mere taxation dispute. He objected that the influential Raynal had "misconceived and mis-stated the causes which produced the rupture between England and her then colonies." Paine stated that the true revolution was in the "new method of thinking" and that "we see with other eyes, we hear with other ears; and think with other thoughts, than those we formerly used." Central to the Declaration of Independence was freedom of thought and expression. Paine wrote that "mankind are not now to be told they shall not think, or they shall not read; and publications that go no farther than to investigate principles of government, to invite men to reason and to reflect, and to show the errors and excellences of different systems, have a right to appear." Paine saw it as a new dawn, declaring not just independence but "a morning of reason rising upon man, on the subject of government, that has not appeared before." What was long discussed by the elite of the Enlightenment in Europe would be realized in America.

The Declaration echoed the same views advanced in Paine's *Common Sense* in defining the government as the protector of natural rights, not the source of those rights. Likewise, Jefferson's original draft condemning slavery was reminiscent of Paine's earlier writings denouncing slavery as a denial of natural rights and morality. Jefferson saw the Declaration as a break from the calcified mindset of many before it; "the monkish ignorance and superstition [that] had persuaded [citizens] to bind themselves." The model of self-government for Jefferson was grounded in reason and, by protecting individual rights, in the creation of a new type of citizen: "We believed that men, enjoying in ease and security the full fruits of their own industry, enlisted by all their interests on the side of law and order, habituated to think for themselves and to follow their reason as their guide, would be more easily and safely governed than with minds nourished in error and vitiated and debased . . . by ignorance, indigence and oppression."

There is a tendency of many judges and academics to treat the Declaration as an almost perfunctory act of separation from the Crown rather than the statement of a revolutionary set of principles. The Constitution is often treated as our defining moment. Yet the Constitution was designed to protect and advance the previously declared values; a declaration based on individual liberty and principles of the Enlightenment. It was in the Declaration of Independence that Yale president Ezra Stiles said Jefferson "[poured] the soul of the continent into the monumental act of independence." That "soul" embodied the transcendence of natural rights, reason, and immutable principles.

The natural right to self-governance and revolution had long been denounced as not just a destabilizing but a dangerous idea. It was viewed as an invitation to mobocracy. Sir William Blackstone, one of the most influential legal authorities of the time, rejected the very right to rebel. He saw an unbreakable bond and obligation to the sovereign: "No human laws will therefore suppose a case, which at once must destroy all law, and compel men to build afresh upon a new foundation nor will they make provision for so desperate an event, as must render all legal provisions ineffectual." The Declaration of Independence rejected this theory of binding loyalty for a theory of natural liberty. Still, the Founders knew that democracies could easily become anarchy or tyranny by popular demand. The Declaration refers to liberty, not democracy. The separation from Great Britain was due to the failure to honor natural or human rights that can be denied by no government because they are not derived from any government.

It was not just Paine who saw the Declaration of Independence as a new dawn for humanity. The most rapt audience was found 3,700 miles away from Philadelphia in Paris. It would inspire French revolutionaries who saw the Declaration as a birth of a new type of citizen. Ironically, the French monarchy offered key financial support for the American Revolution despite worsening economic conditions at home. After the "Flour War" in 1775, it was a bold and arguably destabilizing decision. It not only deepened the crippling debt crisis for France, but supplied an alternative to the ancien régime. Revolutionary calls were already being heard throughout Paris as the French contemplated sweeping democratic changes. The American Revolution seemed like the emergence of not just a new type of government but a new type of citizen. Frenchman Michel Guillaume Jean de Crèvecoeur, who later became an American citizen known as John Hector St. John, asked, "What then is the American, this new man?"

The full story of the American Revolution is captured in the story of two very different men: Thomas Paine and James Madison. The Declaration of Independence was the moment of true creation, a passionate statement of a new nation founded by a new political species described by Paine. It was followed by a document that sought to harness that passion and power into a stable republic. Where Paine was righteous rage,

Madison was pious reason. The two documents speak to the different roles that they played as well as the key figures associated with them. The Declaration is exhilarating in its language and declarations of liberty. The Constitution in comparison is more clinical in tone and focus. The Declaration focused on transcendent principles of liberty, while the Constitution focused on the nuts and bolts of democracy. The Constitution is neither poetic nor particularly inspiring. It was written by the ultimate political wonk. Madison was a true genius who viewed government as more of a science than an art. He saw the inherent dangers of democracy far more clearly than Paine; a more sobering reality taken from Madison's review of failed systems going back to ancient Athens. Human beings—not deities—run governments, and any government must be able to withstand the petty, corrupt, and pernicious motives of those in power. As C. Bradley Thompson observed, "American revolutionaries were not proponents of permanent revolution," but rather believed in a new foundation for government. In that sense, the Madisonian design was based on a less idyllic vision that came closer to David Hume's admonishment that "every man must be supposed a knave." While Madison did not necessarily subscribe to such a blunt and pessimistic view, he shared the view that government must be based on a frank assessment of human impulse and interests. That was most evident in his famous statement in Federalist 51 that "if men were angels, no government would be necessary. If angels were to govern men, neither external nor internal controls on government would be necessary." Even Paine, who was viewed as favoring robust democratic powers, acknowledged that "government, like dress, is a badge of our lost innocence." Paine would find few angels in power in Paris and come to recognize the necessity of some of Madison's "precautions."

Madison saw government as a type of superstructure in which majoritarian impulse would be directed toward compromise and moderation. A successful constitution had to be based on a sober appreciation of not only what unites us but also what divides us. Where many saw fellowship, Madison saw factions in democratic systems, including at the nadir of democracy in ancient Athens. He wanted a system that could force those factions to the surface where they could be addressed and defused. The pressures from factions would explode into the streets of Paris, but would implode into the political system in Philadelphia. The different trajectories taken in the two cities are telling precisely because they began on similar declarations based on the rights of man. While John Adams told Madison that "there was not a single principle the same in the American & French Revolutions," Madison disagreed. Both certainly overthrew royalty and initially embraced democratic principles. However, one evolved into a stable democratic republic, while the other devolved into democratic despotism. As shown by the abuses of the twelve-member Committee of Public Safety during the French Revolution, democracy often leads to nondemocratic concentration of authority in the few—tyranny exercised in the name of democracy. Ultimately, it included banning workers from forming their own unions or "trooping together" as a threat to the state. That mutation of democracy can then supply the perfect conditions for the emergence of a Napoléon or a Hitler—dictators who assume office to the applause of citizens tired of unrest and uncertainty. The chilling reality is that history has shown that a free people can willingly, even happily, surrender political and individual rights when the right conditions are present.

If American democracy is to survive in the twenty-first century, it must, again, break this cycle. The country—and the world—are facing profound economic and social changes. The causes may be different in the form of robotics or AI, but the challenge remains the same in maintaining political stability during a period of economic unrest with hard-stratified class divisions, subsistence income, and greater social separation. The answers may be found in what occurred 250 years ago and how revolutionary pressures were vented within a Madisonian system. We are witnessing the convergence of radical movements with ominous economic conditions developing in this century due to changes in technology and the workplace. The American Revolution was a revolution in political thought, as stated so eloquently by Adams, Paine, and others. However, the tipping point of the revolution was reached as a result of changes in economic conditions rather than political philosophy. After all, the Enlightenment works relied upon by the framers had appeared much earlier without a spontaneous or even contemporaneous demand for a new form of government. Locke's *Two Treatises of Government* was published in 1689, almost one hundred years before the American Revolution. Moreover, until shortly before the Revolution itself, figures such as Benjamin Franklin saw the tensions with Great Britain as economic in nature and believed that there was a basis for reconciliation with the Crown. Likewise, France was the very fount from which writers like Rousseau had written for decades before the Revolution, but there was no spontaneous revolt. Rousseau wrote his *Discourse on Inequality* in 1755 and *The Social Contract* in 1762, roughly four decades before the French Revolution in 1789. It was the highly inefficient and repressive economic conditions that sparked France's massive uprisings, as would later be the case with the bread riots in Russia. Paine himself made this connection when he wrote in *The Decline and Fall of the English System of Finance* that "it is worthy of observation that every case of failure in finances, since the system of paper began, has produced a revolution in government, either total or partial." We are seeing, in my view, the similarly extreme changes in economic conditions that produced earlier revolutions and the potential for a type of democratic despotism. If we wait for these economic conditions to grow more acute and destabilizing, it may prove too late to avoid the patterns of history in the erosion of individual rights and social order.

In the United States, the political divide has become deep and increasingly violent. At the same time, a soaring deficit, widening wealth disparities, and massive economic changes are creating a chillingly familiar environment. The country is facing what could be the most significant economic shifts since the Industrial Revolution with the increase in robotic manufacturing, AI, and widening wealth stratification. After the last industrial revolution, social upheaval and displacement were followed by political instability. Despite those initial impacts, the massive rise in production and wealth eventually brought prosperity to this and other nations. It is less clear that the new economic and technological advances will produce the same wealth infusion for the middle class, let alone the lower class. We are already seeing the signs of political atrophy as influential figures join the call for sweeping constitutional and institutional changes in the United States. The assumption that the Constitution can, once again, weather this period of unrest and uncertainty is a dangerous conceit. The coming storm will test again a system that has lost key allies in politics and academia. Rage also plays a role. We are living through what I have previously called "an age of rage." It is not our first. Righteous rage has long been the fuel of revolution. Those who rail against existential threats rarely accept limits on the means needed to defeat those threats. The enormity of a threat or the essentiality of a victory define the scope of acceptable action.

In the last ten years, we have seen radical voices on both the left and the right dismissing democratic traditions and safeguards to achieve immediate change. It seems, if "democracy is at stake," even democratic norms can be sacrificed to save it. Thus, many academics and activists fought to bar former President Donald Trump as well as other Republicans accused of "insurrection" from the 2024 ballot. Others point to climate change or extremism as threats that must be combated with extreme measures, including the censoring and blacklisting of citizens. There are growing calls among academics to radically change our constitutional and political systems. In a *New York Times* column titled "The Constitution Is Broken and Should Not Be Reclaimed," Harvard law professor Ryan D. Doerfler and Yale law professor Samuel Moyn called for the Constitution to be "radically altered" to "reclaim America from Constitutionalism." Georgetown University law professor Rosa Brooks warned the public not to become "slaves" to the U.S. Constitution if it stands in the way of real change. Harvard law professor Mark Tushnet and San Francisco State University political scientist Aaron Belkin called upon President Joe Biden to defy rulings of the Supreme Court in the name of what they called "popular constitutionalism." MSNBC commentator Elie Mystal called for the dumping of the U.S. Constitution as "trash." On the right, conservative activist Jack Posobiec at the 2024 Conservative Political Action Conference (CPAC) called for the "end of democracy" to better glorify God: "We are here to overthrow it completely. We didn't get all the way there on January 6, but we will endeavor to get rid of it and replace it with this right here. All glory is not to government. All glory to God." Both presidents Donald Trump and Joe Biden referred to their political opponents as "traitors" and threats to the nation.

These voices are having an impact on public opinion. Polls by the University of Virginia Center for Politics showed that a majority now views the opposing party as a threat to the nation and that violence is justified in combating their efforts. Leading up to the 2024 election, a virtual mantra was heard in politics that the election could be our last democratic election if Donald Trump were elected to a second term, including by Vice President Kamala Harris. It is a crisis of faith in a system that has survived every challenge from military attacks to economic meltdowns to social unrest. It is also being used to seek radical measures.

In his masterpiece *Democracy in America*, Alexis de Tocqueville wrote that "nothing is more wonderful than the art of being free, but nothing is harder to learn how to use than freedom." There is an art to living freely, but that is only made possible by what Madison referred to as "the science" of governance. If democracy is to survive in the twenty-first century, democratic institutions will have to adjust to the new technological and economic challenges facing citizens. Madison designed a government not for the best of times, but the worst of times. That system may soon again be stress tested by unprecedented social and economic changes.

In part I, this book explores the American vision of liberty through the eyes of the quintessential American revolutionary, Thomas Paine. His fascinating story in coming to our shores captures the essence of the struggle for a new concept of governance. It was a transformation of a man from a corset maker to a privateer to a tavern philosopher to a revolutionary. His story offers a telling, and at times chilling, insight into our own times. As a significant figure in both the American and French revolutions, Paine worked through the contradictions of liberty and democracy at his own peril.

In part II, this history is taken forward to how revolution unfolded in two countries, France and the United States, in the eighteenth century. We follow the same figure, Paine, as he tries to make actual what was theoretical for Enlightenment writers in both nations. It is a tale of two cities:

Philadelphia and Paris. These cities would see the same inexorable pattern emerge as free people struggled with political and economic forces that swept over them. It was, as Charles Dickens described, "the best of times, it was the worst of times, it was the age of wisdom, it was the age of foolishness, it was the epoch of belief, it was the epoch of incredulity." For these cities, it was the age of revolution, but each city took a strikingly different path. Historian Barbara Tuchman once wrote that "every successful revolution puts on in time the robes of the tyrant it has deposed." The true "miracle of Philadelphia" was that it ultimately discarded those robes in favor of a stable republic. This book explores why the American Revolution was ultimately able to prove an exception to Tuchman's rule. Philadelphia and Paris offer illustrative examples of the elements later discussed in the book in the role of factional groups, economic conditions, and constitutional safeguards (or the lack thereof). Philadelphia and Paris experienced the same extreme and violent factions, but took very different paths. One embraced constitutional order, while the other embraced state terror.

In part III, the book will turn to how history can inform our actions in addressing the new challenges of the twenty-first century. That includes strengthening factional protections in the political system and building a liberty-enhancing economy. As the country faces the economic and social challenges ahead, it will be more important than ever to protect small factional interests in the political and legislative processes. We saw how these factions were suppressed in France with disastrous consequences. That will require more robust protection by the courts of individual rights as well as structural protections in the Madisonian system. At the same time, the country will need to address the growing economic changes. Early American leaders found great appeal in the writings of Adam Smith, which spoke to not just the economic but also political aspects of market theory. Smith's "invisible hand" offered a synergy for early American thinkers in the empowerment of individual citizens to guide the supply and demand of goods. It was as much a radical departure from prior economic systems (including the mercantilism of the Crown) as the Declaration was a departure from prior political systems. Smith believed that capitalism bestowed true freedom to citizens by making them less dependent on the government and giving them the resources to pursue their own interests. He was proven correct as the United States and other countries unleashed tremendous wealth creation and productivity over the next century. With that wealth maximization came unprecedented social and political changes with the empowerment of a rising middle class. In an age of growing economic uncertainty, the solution is not to be found in the moribund theories of managed economies and socialist programs, but in adapting policies to maximize wealth and liberty for a new generation of citizens.

Democracy is a term that has no pejorative connotations in modern parlance. It is nothing to hiss at like tyranny or aristocracy. If there is one line that most embodies the American ideal of self-governance it is the reference of Abraham Lincoln to "government of the people, by the people, and for the people" in the Gettysburg Address. While Lincoln is credited with those words by many, they were (like so much in our democracy) lifted from the work of others. The first reference to this general phrase can be traced back to 1384 to John Wycliffe, who wrote a prologue for a bible that stated, "The Bible is for the Government of the People, by the People, for the People." Lincoln appears to have lifted the line from a sermon given by Theodore Parker at Boston's Music Hall on July 4, 1858. Lincoln was given a copy of the sermon and underlined those words and, five years later, incorporated them into his famous address. Of course, the United States was formed on a rejection of government entirely "by the people" in the form of a pure democracy. History shows that a government truly *by* the people (in the sense of a pure democracy) is rarely a government *for* the people.

While authoritarianism has often been ascribed to iron-fisted rulers governing from the top down, history is replete with examples of majoritarian terror where authoritarianism emerged from organic bottom-up movements. The framers were acutely aware of this danger and sought to prevent a tyranny of the majority in the Constitution and the Bill of Rights. Adams denounced "democratic despotism" as a contradiction to the very purpose of the Declaration of Independence. He added that:

"We may appeal to every page of history we have hitherto turned over for proofs irrefragable, that the people, when they have been unchecked, have been as unjust, tyrannical, brutal, barbarous, and cruel, as any king or senate possessed of uncontrollable power. The majority has eternally, and without one exception, usurped over the rights of the minority."

Other figures like Alexander Hamilton defended the Constitution by noting that the public was growing "tired" of unlimited democratic governance. The republican form of government was seen as a protection from democratic despotism. Just as the framers saw a regression back to the excesses of the state of nature, this book explores some of the contemporary signs of the same regression from the attacks on constitutionalism to greater use of violence and "self-help" means for political change.

The book explores how this country can address the changing economic and social conditions that can pull the system apart. It is the same challenge the framers faced in reinforcing a government for the people, while protecting the people from themselves. It is not an argument against democracy, but rather the funneling of its energy. We must address the globalized economic and political conditions of this century. That includes the increasing roles of corporate governance as well as new global systems of enforcement. Modern changes are shifting control of key areas to transnational bodies, which are less accessible to citizens and less accountable in a democratic system. Where pure democracies gravitate toward democratic despotism, global governance tends to yield to oligarchies and bureaucracies. Both ironically have ultimately led to tyranny in history. In the end, we will have to harness the same creative spirit and faith that led to our Declaration of Independence 250 years ago. We must return to the same profound question asked in the eighteenth century, "What then is the American, this new man?"

Part I

THE CAUSE OF INDEPENDENCY: THOMAS PAINE AND THE MAKING OF A REVOLUTIONARY

In the beginning all the world was America.

—John Locke

To understand the essence of "the American, this new man," you must look to the moment of creation; you must look to the Declaration of Independence. It was the Declaration, not the Constitution, that first defined this new citizen and this new nation. It was more than a listing of twenty-seven injuries or grievances. Those grievances were merely the manifestations of a deeper problem with the very concept of the colonial government. It was the denial of natural and "unalienable" rights. This is made equally clear in the precursor to the Declaration, the Virginia Declaration of Rights, which proclaimed that "all men are by nature equally free and independent, and have certain inherent rights, of which, when they enter into a state of society, they cannot, by any compact, deprive or divest their prosperity." The line references how people moved from the state of nature to the "state of society," but that they came with "inherent rights" that cannot be extinguished by any "compact" or legislation.

The long debate over the use of "unalienable rights" rather than "inalienable rights" in the Declaration is itself a telling distinction, even if unintended. Most scholars believe that this was a change at the printer since Jefferson used *inalienable* in the prior drafts. Both words were in common use. (For historical and legal nerds, one of the funniest scenes in the musical *1776* is when John Adams defends *unalienable* as consistent with his Harvard education while Jefferson defends *inalienable* as a graduate of William & Mary. Adams ends the debate by promising to raise the issue "with the printer.") Historian Robert Rutland noted that the terms indeed had possible different meanings, citing the 1775 *Bailey's New Universal Etymological English Dictionary*. *Unalienable* was defined as something that "may not be altered," while *inalienable* was defined as "cannot be alienated or transferred to another." The terms may have been used interchangeably at the time, but the difference is intriguing. *Inalienable*, in my view, was correct grammatically and philosophically. The framers embraced the Enlightenment view of natural rights, but there were differences in how philosophers viewed the treatment of natural rights (and some rejected such rights). Thomas Hobbes, for example, viewed rights as entirely alienable. He saw the state of nature as a violent, brutish place that led to the establishment of government order under a powerful protective sovereign. Hobbes believed citizens surrendered or abridged rights in creating the social contract for the establishment of the state. Others, such as Rousseau (who was a major influence in the French Revolution) and Locke (who was a major influence in the American Revolution), believed that such rights are effectively "transferred" to the state for their protection, though individuals could still claim such rights. While Adams showed as president that free speech could be treated as entirely alienable by the government, Jefferson and other framers espoused an autonomous rights approach where rights remained with the individual. In other words, they are inalienable. Rather than seeing the state as demanding that rights be abridged for the sake of security, the framers saw the state as ensuring the maintenance of these individual natural rights. American writers described a noble creature with God-given rights, a human being with inherent rights in both the state of nature and "state of society." It was the recognition, not the creation, of these rights that was the driving force of the Declaration of Independence.

The declaration of not just inalienable but individual rights was expressly emphasized in the drafting. The Declaration of Independence went through a critical transformation after the original motion of Richard Henry Lee, proclaiming only that "these United Colonies are, and of right out to be, free and independent states that they are absolved from all allegiance to the British Crown: and that all political connexion between them and the state of Great Britain is, and ought to be, totally dissolved." That draft expressed a right of self-determination, but not the basis for that demand. It was after the appointment of the Committee of Five (composed of John Adams, Benjamin Franklin, Thomas Jefferson, Robert Livingston, and Roger Sherman) that the document would embrace a full-throated account of the natural rights that rest with citizens rather than their governments. Jefferson would take from not only the Virginia Constitution but the draft of the Virginia Declaration of Rights by George Mason. That draft did not speak to the conflict of governments, but the conflict between natural rights and tyrannical governance:

> That all men are born equally free and independent, and have certain inherent natural rights, of which they cannot, by any compact, deprive or divest their property; among which are, the enjoyment of life and liberty, with the means of acquiring and possessing property, and pursuing and obtaining happiness and safety.

Mason's draft speaks of preexisting rights that are held by citizens as human beings, not as citizens of any given government. Liberty was the natural state of man, a right traced to the Creator rather than any Constitution. Jefferson would take these words and, in the few days allowed for the drafting of the new declaration, rework them into what became the Declaration of Independence. As Mason wrote, it is premised on the view that "all power is vested in, and consequently derived from, the people." These natural rights (not the specific grievances) were then expressed as the basis for the right to rebel:

> That to secure these rights, Governments are instituted among Men, deriving their just powers from the consent of the governed,—That whenever any Form of Government becomes destructive of these ends, it is the Right of the People to alter or to abolish it, and to institute new Government, laying its foundation on such principles and organizing its powers in such form, as to them shall seem most likely to effect their Safety and Happiness.

This emerging view of a natural law was echoed in churches and taverns. There was one voice that would particularly come to embody the restless and, at times, irreverent spirit of the American Revolution. Called "the Penman of the Revolution," it was Paine who was credited with rallying the nation to the cause of "independency."

Two years before the Declaration of Independence was signed, a sick thirty-seven-year-old Englishman was carried off a ship in the Philadelphia harbor after a harrowing journey during which five passengers died of typhoid. Paine had made the trip at the urging of Benjamin Franklin who had met him in London and saw something in Paine that escaped most other people. Franklin himself was a glorious contradiction of virtues and vices. There was something in Paine that Franklin seemed to recognize. Perhaps it was an irresistible spirit or insatiable curiosity. Whatever it was, it was buried deep in the wreckage. Franklin would prove, again and again, to be a judge of natural greatness in cultivating some of the most important voices in the American Revolution. Yet none of his "projects" were nearly as impactful as Paine, who proved to be the perfect embodiment of a new nation. While holding American, English, and French citizenship in his life, Paine was the quintessential American voice. He also embodied the sharp learning curve of a nation that was at times impetuous—even reckless. After the French Revolution, Paine would move away from his prior opposition to bicameralism, resistance to free markets, and even his rejection of monarchy in any form. As he had done his entire life, Paine learned the hard way from experience. In some ways, his flaws seemed to make him even more of a personification of the new nation struggling to invent itself and to write a new chapter in history. While Madison was the genius who saw what the nation needed to thrive, it was Paine who saw what it would take to become a free and independent nation.

Paine was the ultimate work in progress—professionally, personally, and philosophically. When he arrived in Philadelphia on November 30, 1774, Paine's weakened condition captured more than his health. He was a broken man who saw a chance, like so many, to find himself in the New World. He brought with him what he described as an innate rather than a learned understanding of liberty, later recounting, "I saw an opportunity, in which I thought I could do some good, and I followed exactly what my heart dictated. I neither read books, nor studied other people's opinions. I thought for myself." Paine saw the emerging new nation as the "nursery of genius" while deriding those who stood in the way of democratic empowerment as still caught in their "infancy." The view would get him into serious legal trouble in the three countries that he called home: England, the United States, and France.

In an intriguing way, a new emerging people found the perfect embodiment in Paine—impatient, precocious, and unpredictable. He came to America to reinvent himself and found a nation looking for the very same thing. He would become the voice not of the powdered and pampered class of armchair revolutionaries, but of the common man. More than any of his contemporaries, Paine understood this nation of immigrants, transplants like himself who were willing to break free of past constraints and concepts. This was a nation that had "now outgrown the state of infancy." Before writing those words, Paine had tried and failed at a wide range of enterprises, from being a staymaker to a privateer to a tobacconist to an excise officer. He was never more than mediocre at any of these professions. The irony was that he stumbled from failure to failure without realizing that he was his own greatest asset. It was what was in his head that would make him an international sensation, but he would not understand that until he hit rock bottom and drifted onto these shores with the rest of the world's flotsam and jetsam. While Paine seemed perfectly clueless in dealing with other humans, he had a brilliant conception of humanity. His "Common Sense" was their sense of what was wrong with the world around them. Paine would also come to know that revolution, once unleashed, can develop an insatiable appetite. It is a lesson that is easily forgotten by a people that have not known revolution for centuries. Radicals today espouse the same reckless demand for change "by any means necessary." History has shown that it is far easier to start a revolution than it is to contain one. Paine would discover that fact at great cost to himself and to those he loved. He was the ultimate example of Saturn's children. He would be devoured by revolution and then emerge with a new perspective of how revolutions are won and lost. If you want to understand the American Revolution—and all revolutions—you would be wise to start with Thomas Paine.

One

THE TRUE PAIN

From Ruin to Revolution

Paine was born on January 29, 1737, and raised in a lower middle-class area of Thetford, Norfolk. There remains a statue of Paine in the village with him holding a copy of *Rights of Man* (strangely shown upside down) in his outstretched hand and a quill in the other. The engraving on the plinth reads, "Englishman by birth; French citizen by decree; American by adoption." Paine would likely have found the statue by British sculptor Charles Thomas Wheeler a tad ironic given the persecution of his family by many in the town in his youth and his unpopularity in England later in life. Yet Paine was very much the product of his experiences in this town as well as his experiences in England during the first four decades of his life. In Thetford, there are glimpses of what then Thomas "Pain" would become after he adopted not just an *e* as part of his name but a new nation as his cause. (The reason for the spelling change remains unclear, particularly given the fluid spelling of names and terms in the period. The family name Pain was sometimes spelled with an *e*, and Paine may have adopted the change before leaving England.)

The early life of Thomas Paine would resonate throughout his career, shaping his core views of organized religion and individual rights. It is an insight into how revolutionaries are made by their times and adversities. Paine was the only child of Joseph Pain and his wife, Frances. He briefly had a younger sister, Elizabeth, who died shortly after birth. His father was a Quaker and a staymaker (or corset maker). His mother, Frances, was an Anglican who believed that she married below her station as the daughter of a lawyer. Paine's Quaker origins would become an issue raised against him in the French Revolution. It was an ironic part of his life, given his rejection of organized religion and Quaker values as a writer. His father was himself a contrarian who was expelled for marrying outside of the faith. He remained faithful in every other respect to the Quakers, who rejected oaths, tithes, and paid priests. The Pains were persecuted for those beliefs, so young Thomas grew up as something of an outsider even with his mother's Anglican faith (and his own baptism in the Anglican Church). Despite his mother's establishment ties, they were treated as outsiders or even outcasts by some. (Notably, while his mother retained a strong identification with her Royalist family, she would later reveal that she fasted every July Fourth in celebration of the independence secured in part

Statue of Thomas Paine in Thetford, Norfolk

by her son.) His experience would also contribute to his strident writings against organized religion and fuel false claims that he was an atheist. Like so much else about Paine, the truth was far more complex.

His parents strived to offer him a good education, and Paine would later write, “It was my good fortune to have an exceeding good moral education, and a tolerable stock of useful learning.” While he showed little promise as a scholar, Paine did show his skill and wit as a writer. When a pet crow died, the eight-year-old Paine wrote a poem in his honor:

Here lies the body of John Crow
Who once was high but now is low
Ye brother Crows take warning all,
For as you rise, so you must fall.

It was a poem that ultimately could serve as his own epitaph. The poem showed a certain irreverence and rebelliousness in the young Paine that would later bring him endless problems in England and eventual fame in the United States. Even as a young boy, he questioned the Quaker principles and practices of his upbringing. He would later remark that if God consulted Quakers at the creation, “what a silent and drab-colored creation it would have been.”

Paine would leave school at age thirteen to become an apprentice at his father’s corset shop. By this time, young Thomas was already showing the same restlessness of what a contemporary would call the “new man” emerging from America. He just did not know it yet. His father’s business was succumbing to the change in women’s fashion, and the family struggled, so Paine decided to head to London in search of a new life. At the age of nineteen, he arrived just as Britain declared war on France in 1756.

It was in London that corsets may have saved the American Revolution. Paine had little money and longed for adventure. Both seemed at hand when he read in the *Daily Advertiser* an entry seeking sailors for the next voyage of the ship *Terrible*. The notice read: “To cruise against the French, the *Terrible* Privateer, Capt. William Death . . . All Gentlemen Sailors, and able-bodied Landmen, who are inclinable to try their Fortune, as well as serve their King and Country, are desired to repair on board the said Ship." The ship was a privateer. With the outbreak of hostilities, private ships were allowed to attack French ships and take them as a prize. It was dangerous, swashbuckling, and potentially lucrative work as the crew divided the prizes of French ships taken with holds packed with valuable trade goods and treasure. Paine signed up with eagerness to effectively become a pirate. It was not just a radical departure from his past (which had no maritime experience) but also a clear rejection of his pacifist Quaker background.

Paine was about to set sail when his father suddenly appeared, apparently tracking his son through the clandestine network of staymakers. His father prevailed upon his son to return to corset making and helped arrange a position with a master staymaker in Covent Garden. In *Rights of Man*, Paine would write that "from this adventure I was happily prevented by the affectionate and more remonstrance of a good father." It would prove a fateful choice. The *Terrible* set sail without Paine and was badly mauled in a battle with the French. Captain William Death was initially successful with a crew that included his brother and his cousin (also named Death) as two of his officers. (There were also officers named Ghost and Devil.) They quickly went into battle and took the French ship *Alexandre le Grand*, though the captain lost his brother, John Death. The promising start would end when they encountered a ship that was flying British colors. It was French privateer *Vengeance*, which suddenly hoisted its true colors and attacked. After taking the *Alexandre le Grande* and using it on the attack, the apt-named *Vengeance* moved against the *Terrible*. While the *Vengeance* lost its captain, the second in command, and two-thirds of the crew to a broadside, it still boasted thirty-six cannons and, in a return salvo, outgunned and outmaneuvered the British vessel. In the three-hour battle, the *Terrible* would lose 150 men and would return with just 17 survivors. And that is how staymakers may have saved the American Revolution: Paine's recall to the corset trade likely saved America's greatest advocate and the publication of *Common Sense*.

Joseph Pain's victory in pulling his son back from the life of a state-sanctioned pirate would prove short-lived. Paine again found the corset trade boring and grueling with long hours spent cutting material and sewing the waist-cinching garments. He was soon drawn to a new advertisement for a different ship, the privateer *King of Prussia*, that would set to sea for the ample hunting grounds of the Caribbean. While the log of the *King of Prussia* has been lost and Paine refers to the captain as "Mendez" as opposed to Menzies, there is ample reason to believe that he did indeed join the crew. In January 1757, the ship sailed down the Thames and headed to the Caribbean for French takings. They quickly found their prey. The *King of Prussia* was not particularly formidable with twenty-eight carriages and twenty-four swivel guns. Still, at 340 tons and an estimated 150 to 200 feet in length, it could easily overpower any merchant ship. Not only did Paine see combat, but it is clear from the ship's profile what that combat likely looked like to the novice sailor. Menzies had to use his ship's spry maneuverability to evade and outfox larger ships. For a privateer, battles were costly on every level in not just men and ship damage, but also reducing the value of "the prize." In a prolonged battle, there was the prospect of sinking a ship and, as shown in the battle involving the *Terrible*, cannon shot would turn ship decks into killing zones of wood and metal shrapnel. It was preferable to use small arms and boardings to take vessels intact, and that was likely the type of close combat witnessed by the young Paine on the *King of Prussia*.

The *King of Prussia* took eight ships, a remarkable haul for a privateer. To get a notion of the booty from such actions, one of the first ships taken was the ironically named *Le Bien Acquis*, or "*Well Acquired*," bound for Mississippi with "1346 Casks of Flour, 60 Barrels of Gunpowder, three 24 Pounders, three 18 Pounders, 60 Bombs, Bomb-Shells, Ammunition, Soldiers Cloaths, &c." In addition to their percentage of the prize, crew were allowed to take clothing and property from the captured crew. They would take *Le Montreal*, a French snow, and the much larger merchant ship *La Flore*. Before his six-month service ended, Paine would participate in taking *Le Saint Peter* and *Le Saint Martin* bound for Canada, as well as *La Minerve*, which was heavily laden with "Wine and Provisions." Since he was neither an officer nor an experienced seaman, Paine's share of the prize was the lowest with other "gentleman volunteers." In addition to at least £5 per month at sea for his six-month service, Paine likely also received one-half of 1 percent of the prize. That was a sizable amount for Paine, who returned with something that he had never experienced to any real degree: a surplus of funds. In later years, Paine would reflect on his brief time as a privateer with a remarkably profound statement:

> men do not, in any great numbers, turn their thoughts to the ocean, till either the country gets filled, or some peculiar advantage or necessity tempts them out. A maritime life is a kind of partial emigration . . .

It is an intriguing observation for a young man who may have already felt somewhat removed from his country. With the change in fortune after his return, the "partial émigré" would become increasingly untethered to Britain as he struggled to find a place in society.

The critical aspects of this period for Paine were not simply his exposure to the war of empires, but the luxury that his prize money afforded him in studying at the university level. Indeed, if corset-making saved his life, privateering may have changed its direction. He spent a good part of 1757–58 attending lectures by some of the most famous academic figures in Great Britain, including Scottish James Ferguson, who supported himself by selling globes in the Strand. Ferguson would not only inspire Paine's interest in science (including Newtonian physics), but he may have proven to be a critical catalyst in history. It was Ferguson (or possibly mathematician George Lewis Scott) who first introduced Paine to arguably the single most influential figure in his life: Benjamin Franklin.

Ultimately, Paine would exhaust much of his prize money and was forced to seek gainful employment, including resuming work as a staymaker. It was during this period in Dover that Paine would take a wife, Mary Lambert, who was employed as a maid. He was now twenty-two and again he was struggling financially. Every effort proved fruitless and ultimately the young couple had to flee their creditors and the prospect of debtors' prison. They took up residence in Sandwich, only for tragedy to strike again when Mary died in labor along with their child. Paine would follow the loss with a familiar response. Leaving his business, he sought a new beginning. It would lead him to an appointment as an excise officer, secured though a family connection. It was a thankless and hazardous job. In taking the position, Paine had to take an oath of loyalty to a king that he would denounce just a few years later as a "sottish, stupid, stubborn, worthless, brutish man." The irony did not end with the oath. Paine's duties included collecting taxes on tea, the very grievance that would help ignite the American Revolution. It hardly seemed the start of a promising revolutionary resume. It only went downhill from there as Paine's time as an excise officer continued his unbroken record of failures. Paine found the work uninteresting and unappreciated. He began to issue stamps without inspecting goods. While a common practice, Paine was caught and was terminated after admitting that he was not actually performing some inspections.

Being fired was hardly a shock for Paine, whose employment history was a litany of bankruptcies punctuated by piracy. This misfortune had a critical, and possibly transformative, element for Paine. Rather than reinvent himself again, Paine decided to advocate for himself. He wrote to his superiors that "though the nature of the report and my own confession cut off all expectations of enjoying your honors favor then, I humbly hope it has not finally excluded me therefrom, upon which hope humbly presume to entreat your honors to restore me." It worked. Paine was ultimately given another position in Lewes. For Paine, it was his first success as a writer and an advocate. He did not run; he wrote, and he won.

The location of Paine's new position as an excise officer may have been more important to Paine than the position itself. Lewes was a hotbed of Republican and Whig advocacy. He became a member of a group that seemed to be named with Paine in mind. The Headstrong Club met in the White Hart Inn to engage in spirited debate. After these long evenings, the group would reward "the most obstinate haranguer of the Club" with the prize of "an Old Greek Homer." The person most often selected was none other than Thomas Paine. It wasn't long before Paine gained notoriety for his orations on issues beyond the confines of the Headstrong Club. While in Lewes, Paine encountered John Wilkes, the editor of *The North Briton*, a crusading journal for political reforms. Wilkes's writings would prove to be a flash point when the Crown charged him for defying censors and writing about reforms. In issue 45 of his newspaper, he condemned the government and called for the freedom of the press. That number became a symbol in Great Britain and the United States for the fight for individual rights, particularly free speech. His arrest would lead to the Massacre of St. George's Fields on May 10, 1768, when the police fired on protesters, leaving half a dozen dead and many outraged over the heavy-handed response of the Crown.

It was during this period that Paine would find a second wife with his marriage in 1771 to Elizabeth Ollive, the daughter of a recently deceased tobacco shop owner with whom Paine had gone into business. He was now thirty-four and Elizabeth was twelve years his junior. Soon thereafter, the business and Paine's finances deteriorated, as did his marriage. However, Paine found in Lewes something that would remain with him for the rest of his life: his voice. He discovered a skill in writing and agitating. Excise officers were bitter over their lack of pay, which encouraged many toward corruption. Paine wrote his first pamphlet, *The Case of the Officers of Excise: With Remarks on the Qualifications of Officers; and on the Numerous Evils Arising to the Revenue, From the Insufficiency of the Present Salary*. The eleven-page pamphlet is easily recognizable as Paine in style and structure as he argued for better pay. The most Paine-esque line may have been this: "Nothing tends toward a greater corruption of manners and principles than a too great distress of circumstances." What was most notable was that this pamphlet concerned the narrow issue of excise officer compensation, but still sold out the original four thousand copies and required a supplemental printing. His persuasive case would be dismissed out of hand by the Parliament. Despite that response, it may have been the most critical moment for Paine. He had taken on the Crown and discovered that he had a certain talent for persuasion. Of course, finding his voice did not mean finding a means for support. Paine continued his struggle to make ends meet and continued to have problems at work. Citing his repeated absences, Paine's superiors sacked him again. His pamphlet may have been a significant factor in the termination, but the government cited how Paine "quitted his business, without obtaining the Board's leave for so doing, and being gone off on account of debts which he hath contracted." Soon thereafter, the familiar pattern returned. Paine declared bankruptcy. His marriage then collapsed and might not have been consummated, according to acquaintances. The couple never actually divorced and thus remained married for the rest of their lives.

Paine again left for London and another new beginning.

After arriving in London, Paine would have what was likely the most important meeting of his life. He presented himself to Benjamin Franklin. There was nothing in his past that would recommend him, but something clearly resonated with Franklin in the human debris laid out before him. Franklin saw Paine, as he would describe in a letter to his son, William Franklin, the royal governor of New Jersey, as "an ingenious, worthy young man." He told his son if he could find a way for Paine to "procure a subsistence at least . . . you will do well, and much oblige your affectionate father." Franklin appears to have procured the passage for the virtually penniless Paine and was the most responsible of anyone other than Paine himself for his arrival in the colonies. Paine set off for the New World and a new life with letters of introduction to friends of Franklin in Philadelphia. Paine's misfortune would follow him even in his Atlantic passage. Paine traveled on the *London Packet*, skippered by a friend, with 120 other passengers. Trapped on the ship, passengers watched as typhus spread and took a terrible toll, killing five and laying low many, including Paine. If any scene captured the story of "Thomas Pain," it was his being carried off the ship in a blanket in November 1774 in the care of Franklin's physician, John Kearsley. He had made his landing with his finances and health near total collapse. The man who made it, barely, to the Philadelphia dock was no longer Thomas Pain. With the addition of the *e* and nothing tying him to Great Britain, he was now "Thomas Paine" and intent on joining the New World as a new man. Indeed, Franklin already had a new design in mind, encouraging him to turn to writing and inviting him to join discussions in his Society for Political Inquiries. Corsets, privateering, and a litany of personal failures had produced a man who was willing, nay eager, to leave everything that came before behind, including the institutions and values of his now former country.

Two

THE TRUE PAINE

The "Happy Something" of America

THE

PENNSYLVANIA

MAGAZINE:

OR,

AMERICAN

MONTHLY MUSEUM.

MDCCLXXV.

VOLUME I.

PHILADELPHIA:

PRINTED AND SOLD BY R. AITKEN, PRINTER AND BOOK-

OPPOSITE THE LONDON COFFEE-HOUSE, FRONT-STR

Virtually every one of those traveling to the colonies was seeking a new life, many escaping persecution or poverty or both. However, no one could have imagined that the frail figure carried from that ship would, within just two years, become one of the most famous and impactful figures of the American Revolution. Paine had found a home, remarking that "there is a happy something in the climate of America." That "happy something" was a society without the calcified class barriers and economic stagnation in England. Where intellectuals in London and Lewes discussed the potential for a new order, Americans were actively creating that new order with only a horizon to guide them. It was a nation and a people without a past, precisely what the former Thomas "Pain" so badly needed.

It took little time for Paine to become a sensation. He helped launch the *Pennsylvania Magazine*, which included a biographical sketch of Voltaire. The Paine articles show a gradually strengthening voice that began with a satirical account, "A Dialogue Between General Wolfe and General Gage in a Wood Near Boston." (Wolfe had fallen as "the Hero of Quebec" in 1759 at the Battle of the Plains of Abraham, and Paine showed an early gift of mockery at the expense of General Thomas Gage, commander in chief of British forces in North America.) He also developed a reputation as a voice of the Enlightenment for the common man and led the publication to be the most popular in the New World. He would go on to tackle even more inflammatory issues, including denouncing the scourge of slavery. It was said that he would generally not write "until he had quickened his thoughts with large draughts of rum and water."

Paine was now not just untethered but antagonistic toward England. While intellectuals like James Iredell had written on the right of the colonies to maintain their own laws and government, it was Paine who seemed to speak for the nation in expressing a growing detachment and anger toward England. After the Battle of Lexington on April 19, 1775, Paine said that his "warm wish[es] for reconciliation" had ended and he now stood opposed to the "hardened, sullen-tempered Pharoh of England." He compared England to Saturn, devouring its children. Turning his back on his pacifist Quaker values, Paine was now a committed revolutionary and, in the summer of 1775, sat down to write a pamphlet that he titled *Plain Truth*. As with his other popular publications, Paine stipulated that the price of his publications be kept low to allow common people to buy them. This meant that he made very little on his sales.

Paine made one last change to the draft of his most famous work before it was published on January 1, 1776. He accepted the suggestion of his friend, Dr. Benjamin Rush (himself a signer of the Declaration of Independence), to rename the pamphlet *Common Sense*. It would embody the essence of the Declaration of Independence in declaring that "the cause of America is in great measure the cause of all mankind." In calling for independence, he insisted that "a government of our own is our natural right." It would become the world's first bestseller.

Paine was describing a new universal right to self-determination. To make that case, he knew that he had to get his readers to make the same break from tradition as he had. For the English, the entire culture was based on a reverence for English history and the vaunted common law. Sir William Blackstone would describe the majesty of common law: "Whence it is that in our law the goodness of a custom depends upon its having been used time out of mind; or, in the solemnity of our legal phrase, time whereof the memory of man runneth not to the contrary. This it is that gives it its weight and authority." Before colonists could embrace revolution, they had to reject the inviolability of English history. Paine knew that to destroy the monarch, you had to destroy the myth. In his signature style, Paine plowed directly into his object, trashing the lineage of King George III traced to William the Conqueror, whom Paine described as "a French bastard landing with an armed banditti, and establishing himself as king of England against the consent of the natives, in plain terms a very paltry rascally original—it certainly hath no divinity in it." It was a brilliant mix of mockery and defiance that resonated with an increasingly estranged populace. It had found a voice as bold and irreverent as its cause. Paine made clear that this would be year one for humanity to finally realize its potential: "We have it in our power to begin the world over again . . . The birth-day of a new world is at hand, and a race of men perhaps as numerous as all Europe contains, are to receive their portion of freedom from the events of a few months." It would foreshadow the actual change of the calendar by the French to start history anew with their own revolution.

Paine emphasized that there were two tyrannies at work in the colonies and that both had to be defeated before the "New World" could be discovered. The first could be found in the "person of the king," but the second was found in the "persons of the peers," or the House of Lords. Both were tyrannies based on the hereditary succession that Paine had come to despise. As historian David Benner noted, these views were not just revolutionary but dangerous as "pro-British patriotic sentiment in North America—especially in the wake of the French and Indian War—was at its zenith." Even Whig allies at that time were largely calling for greater rights, not revolution. Alluding again to Saturn, Paine demonized the King as abusing the love and trust of his subjects: "Even brutes do not devour their young, nor savages make war upon their families." Paine would plead with colonists not to allow a tyranny to linger for a generation so that their own children would have a lasting peace: "God's sake, let us come to a final separation, and not leave the next generation to be cutting throats, under the violated unmeaning names of parent and child." The publication would come at a critical time. First, *Common Sense* was released on the same day as the publication of the King's speech to Parliament in which he declared that colonists were engaging in "rebellious war." *Common Sense* was perfectly (and intentionally) timed as an effective response to the irate monarch. Second, when *Common Sense* came out, the Continental Army had reached one of its lowest points in morale and had been reduced to half of its size from just a year earlier. Washington would credit the publication for turning around the dire situation with its "unanswerable reasoning." The publication was so revered that John Adams (who was critical of Paine's "democratical" leanings) received a petition that asked, "What in the name of *Common Sense* are you gentlemen of the Continental Congress about?"

Paine's name did not appear on *Common Sense* until the third printing. Initially, there was speculation that Franklin or Adams may have written it. Adams seemed almost begrudging in his admiration, noting that the author was "a keen writer, but very ignorant on the science of government." However, he admitted to his wife, Abigail, that "I could not have written any Thing so manly and striking a style." He believed that he knew the true author and "His Name is Paine."

Paine chose the moniker "an Englishman" in the original publication of *Common Sense*. It was a telling choice. It was common at the time for writers to use pseudonyms, most famously by the writers of the Federalist Papers. The use of Roman or Greek names like Cato were common ways to not only preserve the protection of anonymity but to invoke the writings of the ancients on subjects such as democracy or natural rights. Paine did not choose the likes of Brutus, Publius, or Cincinnatus, but simply "an Englishman." Given his advocacy of open rebellion against the Crown, it is doubtful that Paine thought of himself as an Englishman in terms of a loyal citizen of England. He would spend much of his life calling for a revolution in England. The moniker reflected more than his identification with his upbringing in that country and likely was a calculated effort to bridge the separation with those who continued to feel the bonds of tradition and loyalty. Paine knew that those bonds would have to be broken to free the young nation. The second part of the pamphlet, therefore, attacked the basis of hereditary monarchy directly. It began with a virtual primer on Enlightenment theories of natural rights, including Lockean theory. The language of that first section would prove strikingly similar to the language of Jefferson in the Declaration, including accusing the King of waging war on his own people and denying the people their inherent rights. Again, there was an effort to decouple independence from insular grievances in his famous declaration: "The cause of America is in a great measure the cause of all mankind." Paine accused George III of "laying a Country desolate with Fire and Sword, declaring War against the natural rights of all Mankind."

The Continental Congress had been meeting since 1774, and the Continental Army had been fighting since 1775. Neither effort was going particularly well. From the Boston Massacre to Lexington, there were plenty of causes for rage. What was missing was the reason for revolution. Then *Common Sense* appeared. It was read everywhere from pubs to pulpits. It galvanized the patriotic cause. Many speculated on the identity of the author. Soon, Paine's identity became known, as was his sedition in the eyes of the Crown. However, it was not just the British who took notice and umbrage at the publication. While impressed by his prose, John Adams was alarmed by Paine's stated preference for a unicameral legislature that could undermine the balance of representative principles needed for stable government. Upon learning of Adams's criticism, Paine was irate and went to Adams's house to confront him. One can only imagine this intense discussion between the spirited agitator and the accomplished attorney. Neither left convinced by the other. Still, Adams may have gotten a glimpse of what Franklin saw in London two years earlier. He wrote a letter of introduction to his wife and noted that General Charles Lee described a lively conversation with this man who "has genius in his eyes."

What Franklin and Adams saw was a spark that would ignite the cause for "independency." After describing a new nation, Paine would not see the moment of creation itself. When the Declaration was adopted six months after the publication of *Common Sense*, Paine was volunteering with the Associators, a militia unit encamped at what became known as the "Flying Camp" near Staten Island. He joined the retreating army as the British seized Manhattan and eventually returned to Philadelphia. Paine witnessed how outmatched the patriots were against the world's greatest standing army. He also witnessed how loyalists, or Tories, an estimated 20 percent of the population, continued to support the British. Paine was, at best, a mediocre soldier, but what was most needed was his pen. Washington and others wanted him to rally the nation. Paine proceeded to write sixteen papers composing his work *The American Crisis*.

Once again, Paine eschewed taking a profit and asked for the cost to be kept low to allow for maximum distribution. *The American Crisis* was an instant success after it was published on December 19, 1776. Paine's history, including his grievances with the Crown and his own failures, gave him a uniquely penetrating and credible style. He understood those who came to the New World to find a new beginning. He also understood how adversities could undermine loyalties and how the revolutionary spirit was beginning to wane. It was time, Paine argued, to make a choice and take a stand. He made that case at the request of Washington, who saw Paine as the only writer who could reinvigorate his troops. Paine did so with his signature style of direct and accessible rhetoric: "These are the times that try men's souls. The summer soldier, and the sunshine patriot will, in times of crisis, shrink from the service of his country."

Paine unleashed his biting prose on loyalists and declared "every Tory is a coward; for a servile, slavish, self-interested fear is the foundation of Toryism; and a man under such influence, though he may be cruel, can never be brave." Paine would, for the first time, refer to the "United States of America" in spurring his new countrymen to fight for their freedom or remain a subjugated people. These essays also revealed a dangerously impulsive and reckless side to Paine's patriotism. The third edition of *The American Crisis* included a call from Paine for a loyalty oath and an extra property tax for those who would not publicly make the pledge: "All we want to know in America is simply this, who is for independence, and who is not?" It was the final severance of Paine the Revolutionary from Paine the royal tax collector. Gone was the customs officer who had once pledged allegiance to King George. The loyalty pledge and political tax showed how the Saturn gene remained dominant even with Paine, a willingness to unleash democratic despotism to combat the enemies of the Revolution.

In just two years, Paine had become the leading voice for revolution. Jefferson would say that "no writer has exceeded Paine in ease and familiarity of style, and perspicuity of expression, happiness of elucidation, and in simple and unassuming language." The line is ironic as the antithesis of Paine's own writing. His style was distinctive from many publications at the time for its lack of pretense and pomposity. Historians have noted that Paine's style was more in line with the publications associated with the French Revolution—partisan, rebellious, and unyielding. Founder Benjamin Rush described it as a work that "burst forth from the press" and ignited the nation. While other leading figures sought to reach a compromise with England or to replicate the English system in the new nation, Paine was truly revolutionary in seeking to break free entirely with what preceded this new nation. His prose was simple, direct, and thrilling for his readers. Described as "the world's first bestseller," one estimate put the ultimate sales of *Common Sense* at 500,000, which would mean that there was one copy in circulation for every five people. He denounced George III as "nothing better than the principal ruffian of some restless gang" and dismissed English history as more self-indicting than self-affirming. He did not simply want a declaration of "independency" but a declaration of true revolution from what came before: "Should an independency be brought about by the first of those means, we have every opportunity and every encouragement before us, to form the noblest, purest constitution on the face of the earth. We have it in our power to begin the world over again." In Paine's bold new world vision, the United States would be the spark that would ignite a global conflagration of popular government. If those were "times that try men's souls," it was Paine who rendered the verdict of his generation.

Three

THE BIRTH OF A NEW AGE

The Enlightenment and the Cause of "Independency"

On April 26, 1787, Thomas Paine was once again on the dock in Philadelphia. He was no longer the sick and destitute unknown who was carried down the plank thirteen years earlier. He was now a legend. The Treaty of Paris had brought the American Revolution to a successful conclusion less than four years earlier, and Paine was leaving. (He was again carrying letters of introduction from Franklin.) He would ultimately find another revolution in France while trying to start yet another in England. That sunny day proved a defining moment for the nation. As Paine was boarding a French ship for Le Havre to pursue a new chapter in his life, delegates were arriving in Philadelphia to set about drafting a new constitution. In a time of giants, two figures stand out in directing the course of the American republic, and this was the moment of their divergence. The first was Paine, called "the father of the American Revolution." The second was James Madison, called "the father of the American Constitution." The former knew what it would take to turn a nation into a rebellion while the latter knew what it would take to turn a rebellion back into a nation. They were both essential to the success of the American Revolution in a way that would become fully understood only many years later. For Paine, his influence was more evident during than after the Revolution. His benefactor, Benjamin Franklin, would declare that Paine was "more responsible than any other living person on this continent for the creation of . . . the United States of America." Like many true revolutionaries, Paine found that his popularity waned after his revolution succeeded. There is nothing quite as inconvenient as a revolutionary after a revolution. Critics, including fellow revolutionaries, viewed him as incautious in his faith in popular government and unrestrained democratic systems. One called him a "crack-brained zealot for democracy." John Adams would say that he "dreaded" the implications of Paine's views, warning that Paine was describing a government "so democratical, without even an attempt at any equilibrium or counterpoise, that it must produce confusion and every evil work." In January 1781, Sarah Bache, the daughter of Benjamin Franklin, wrote that "there was never a man less beloved in a place than Paine is in his, having at different times disputed with everybody. The most rational thing he could have done would have been to have died the instant he had finished his *Common Sense*, for he never again will have it in his power to leave the world with so much credit." The most notable thing about that appraisal is that it came from someone considered to be Paine's friend. In the end, it would not be Paine's insights but also his errors that make him so relevant hundreds of years later, as this country struggles again with economic and social turmoil.

Paine remained the ultimate rebel in both his political and personal affairs. After the revolution, he turned to inventing and entrepreneurship. He still seemed more skilled at demolition than construction. One account of George Washington from November 1783 was telling. Once again, Paine was without funds or lodging and accepted Washington's invitation to stay with him at his new home near Princeton. The two indulged their mutual love for science. Paine tested the chemical composition of a nearby river by setting it on fire. It seems that in science, like government, Paine tended to start with arson. He often seemed to fulfill the criticism of John Adams that he was "a better Hand at pulling down than building." Nevertheless, it was Madison, not Paine, who would see the forces that could destroy new nations from within.

Paine's optimism may have stemmed less from a view of the natural goodness of people as much as from a belief in the collective wisdom of popular governments. What Madison viewed as needed "auxiliary precautions" in a republic based on divided government, Paine viewed as inhibitors of popular governance. In his *Dissertations in Government* in 1786, Paine expressed his suspicions of republican systems in allowing an assembly to act as a collective tyrant. His writings reflected a Rousseauian faith in the people and the ability to speak and act according to civic virtue. What placed Paine at odds with his contemporaries was how this faith led him to distrust the checks and balances sought by figures like Madison. Paine divided the American and French revolutions into two phases. The first, the revolution itself, was inherently brutal and violent. The power wielded by officials in a revolution was by necessity discretionary and often autocratic, including the use of martial law. The second phase was the establishment of a constitutional order where such concentration of power would become dangerous and destabilizing. He was less clear on when a revolution would end and constitutional government would begin. It would prove a fatal ambiguity in Paine's writings.

Despite their differences on the mechanics of democratic systems, both Madison and Paine saw the purpose of the Revolution as the realization of natural rights. There is a lingering narrative that marginalizes the influence of Paine on foundations of the American democracy. It is a narrative that started with figures like Adams, who downplayed the substantive contributions of Paine, treating him as a type of useful rabble-rouser. Figures like Jefferson were instead cited as the visionaries of the

Revolution. In reality, Paine may have been not just a catalyst but an actual contributor to the Declaration of Independence. For years, historians have been fascinated by an early draft of the Declaration of Independence discovered by an amateur historian in an auction booklet of discarded papers belonging to General Hugh Lowry White, a brigadier general in the War of 1812. The copy of the early draft is commonly called the Sherman copy because it was meant to inform Roger Sherman of the status of the drafting process during the fourth week of June 1776. An inscription on the document reads, "*A beginning perhaps—Original with Jefferson—Copied from Original with T.P.'s permission.*" Many historians believe that "T.P." was Thomas Paine. Paine himself stressed that he was "among the first that proposed independence and it was Mr. Jefferson who drew up the declaration." Despite this nod to Jefferson, it seems likely that Paine would have had an opportunity to review and offer suggestions to Jefferson on the declaration that he had long called for. Notably, when two eighteenth-century parchment manuscripts of the Declaration of Independence were found in the United Kingdom National Archives, one was provided to the Duke of Richmond by Paine.

The Declaration begins with a statement that the new nation would be founded on those rights that "Laws of Nature and of Nature's God entitle them." It then states that those "truths" are "self-evident, that all men are created equal, that they are endowed by their Creator with certain unalienable Rights, that among these are Life, Liberty and the pursuit of Happiness." It is the denial of those natural individual rights that necessitated the Declaration of Independence. Rights such as the free exercise of religion were based on this view of a preexisting, transcendent natural law. The Pilgrims and others were drawn to this new land in search of religious freedom. Liberty was the protection of exercise of faith. Faith in turn reinforced civic virtue and the fealty owed to a just government. The legitimacy of the government depended on its protection of natural rights that were viewed as a gift from their Creator, not the creation of their government. It was a sharp departure from the English legal tradition as described by Sir William Blackstone, who insisted that a "sovereign must necessarily be uncontrollable, unlimited, despotic power." The parliament, in his view, is given power that "is absolute and without control." This is precisely where the "inalienable" rights of the Declaration became alienable under the English Constitution. It is also why the framers believed that the Crown had lost its legitimacy to govern by refusing to recognize natural rights of citizens.

Beneath the references to natural law was a profound, new concept of government built on the writings of Enlightenment writers in both the sciences and philosophy. This was the age of reason, and works by figures such as Isaac Newton electrified American intellectuals. Many were familiar with Newton's *Mathematical Principles of Natural Philosophy*, known simply as the *Principia*. Paine was particularly influenced by Newton, and the science seemed to free him from the confines of encrusted political traditions. He viewed monarchies as based on mythology rather than reason. Paine, like many of his contemporaries, saw an order in nature that was not based on blind faith or fealty. Benjamin Franklin captured that excitement: "How exact and regular is every Thing in the *natural* world! How wisely in every Part contriv'd! . . . All the heavenly Bodies, the Stars and Planets, are regulated with the utmost wisdom! And can we suppose less care to be taken in the order of the Moral than in the Natural System." Many agreed that Newton had found a universal truth in science; a faith in nature that became something of a religion unto itself. Alexander Pope wrote for many when he declared:

Nature, and Nature's Laws lay hid in Night:
God said, Let Newton be! and All was Light.

Madison was fascinated by Newton as a student at Princeton, even creating a diagram of the Copernican system of the universe. Allusions to Newtonian physics permeate Madison's work and that of other framers. For many, Madison's description of the tripartite system captures the same dynamic relationship of three bodies caught in a type of synchronous orbit around the body politic. Madison recorded how others like John Dickinson argued for a federalism system in which states would move in their own orbits like planets. Others see greater Newtonian references in the Declaration of Independence itself in justifying revolution as based on the "laws of nature." The influence of such writings went beyond the language of stable branches and checks and balances. The framers saw nature as offering an inescapable truth, free of superstition and superficiality.

For revolutionaries seeking to discard old concepts of governance, Newtonian physics was liberating. Nevertheless, the "science" of government did not offer an answer for the purpose of government. That would come from an even greater influence in the form of philosopher John Locke. With Newton, Locke was regularly cited by Madison, Paine, Jefferson, James Wilson, and others. There is obvious tension between the two figures with Locke questioning the assumption that we can "gain clear knowledge of the cosmic system" in political philosophy—a view that the Newtonian Paine rejected. Instead, Locke found the purpose of government in the nature of man—and the divine plan for all humanity. In his *Second Treatise on Government*, Locke described the original state of nature where there was perfect freedom and equality. Locke saw humans as emerging from the state of nature with certain human rights that came from God. Many saw the New World as a type of paradise with abundant resources and space. Locke himself wrote that "in the beginning all the world was America." It was a line that must have captivated the Founders, reinforcing the notion of a land of plenty left for mankind to achieve a divinely ordained destiny. While Locke did add "and more so than that is now," the Founders believed that America was the promised land for human industry and self-realization. Locke believed God created all things in common for humanity, a state of nature that allowed people to become creators in their own right. What they created through their labor was morally their own, not by the operation of law but by natural right. This concept of natural property extends beyond mere chattel: "every Man has a Property in his own Person. This no Body has any Right to but himself." It was a break from the concepts of divinely ordained, absolute rulers that came before it. There was a law of reason that emanated. Locke stressed that the "state of nature has a law of nature to govern it, which obliges everyone. And reason, which is that law, teaches all mankind, who will but consult it, that being all equal and independent, no one ought to harm another in his life, health, liberty, or possessions."

Locke's writings laid not only the foundation for natural rights but also a righteous basis for rebellion. He supplied the moral justification that allowed a deeply religious and previously patriotic people to come to rebellion. Early legal systems often depended upon claims of divine authority. As Louis XIV would declare, "*L'état, c'est moi*" ("I am the state"). The ruler was the personification of the state, and he ruled as a surrogate for the Almighty. The value of divinely sanctioned rulers is that such authority, if accepted, blunts the power or impulse of popular will. It left the ultimate power in the hands of the ruler rather than the ruled. Even as a myth, it was a useful way to dampen democratic ambitions. As one of Oliver Cromwell's supporters stated during the English Civil War to the Parliament in 1656, "I would not have a people know their own strength." While this concentration of power obviously increased the danger of tyranny, monarchies offered stability against the danger of social upheaval and chaos. The fear of many was that, if fully aware or invested with power, the masses would act on self-destructive impulse. The central role of the Almighty in the authority of rulers was seen as key to maintaining social order and stability. In other words, as Voltaire famously observed, "If God did not exist, it would be necessary to invent him."

For Locke, the source of natural rights is found in God, not the King, and the denial of those rights is an affront to God. The notion of self-determination in a free nation meant that no one could claim predetermined authority. Locke defined tyranny as "the exercise of power beyond right, which no body can have a right to." It is the very linkage drawn in the Declaration of Independence. The Founders not only articulated a natural law and order, but the inherent right to resist those who would deny the rights owed to all citizens. Locke emphasizes, however, that revolution is not an act that is justified by just any injury or denial by the government. Such hair-triggered rebellion would only "unhinge and overturn all politics, and instead of government and order, leave nothing but anarchy and confusion." That is why the twenty-seven grievances or injuries listed by Jefferson were so important in laying a foundation for rebellion. They made the case against tyranny and something that could not "be repaired by appeal to the law," as Locke suggested. Indeed, the grievances included the refusal to accord the colonists the protections of the law. Locke wrote that citizens reserve "a right to resume their original liberty" when the legitimacy of governance is forfeited through tyranny. The grievances were the cause for rebellion, but the struggle sought to reestablish the natural rights that Locke found in the state of nature.

Given the divine claims of monarchial authority, the American ministry would play a key role in removing moral inhibitions over insurrection. The concept of the just rebellion was famously articulated by Reverend Jonathan Mayhew, who used his pulpit at Boston's Old West Church to explore the moral foundations for both fealty and rebellion for citizens. His published sermon "A Discourse Concerning Unlimited Submission and Non-Resistance to the Higher Powers" was given on January 30, 1750, and proved to be one of the most significant publications leading up to the Revolution. Paine's *Common Sense* would not be published for twenty-five years, and it was Mayhew who would lay out the moral right, if not obligation, to rebel when natural rights are denied. Mayhew gave the lecture on the one hundredth anniversary of the execution of Charles I, who was experiencing a revival in the minds of many as a martyr. Mayhew would have none of it and laid out the "general nature and end of magistracy" for a people denied the rights given to them by the Creator. He directly took on the oft-cited biblical authority for those demanding blind loyalty to the King: Romans 13. In the chapter, Paul the Apostle reminds Christians that they must obey the civil authorities and be loyal subjects. The use of this passage, he argued, was a blasphemy in suggesting that a tyrant violating the very natural laws set by God could be treated as "God's Minister." To the contrary, there is a moral obligation to oppose such tyrants in defense of God-given rights.

The lecture was strikingly Lockean, but also grounded in history. He reminded his congregation that the Britons had always based loyalty to sovereigns on consent and that, from the earliest period of Roman rule, citizens were "jealous of their liberties" in resisting tyranny. He noted that the common claim in England that rebellion was immoral would have preserved the tyrannical reign of rulers from Caesar to Charles I. Citizens, he insisted, owed their loyalty only to those "who actually perform the duty of rulers by exercising a reasonable and just authority for the good of human society." If Paine was the spark that ignited the American Revolution, Mayhew was the one who laid the charge. After his famous sermon, Mayhew continued his morality-based opposition in sermons denouncing British excesses. That included denouncing the Stamp Act, which he rejected with such force that he was later blamed when a mob attacked the home of Chief Justice Thomas Hutchinson. Mayhew would die on July 9, 1766, almost ten years to the day when his view of a righteous revolution would be realized.

Mayhew was the bridge between Lockean natural rights and the revolution. Others would then build on that foundation. Lockean thought opened up the American mind and led to the vision contained in the Declaration of Independence of a government based on consent and the recognition of the liberty that defines all humanity. If these rights were natural and inalienable, their denial was tyrannical. True nobility was found not in the aristocracy but humanity itself: "He that is master of himself, and his own life, has a right too, to the means of preserving it." This was a new vision based on free will and reason that had sweeping implications for concepts of self-government.

Jefferson later explained to the English Whig leader John Cartwright in 1824 that the Declaration found more "favorable ground" for the foundation in natural law than prior rationalizations for revolution. He heralded the breaking away from English precedent, stressing that "we had no occasion to search into musty records, to hunt up Royal parchments, or to investigate the laws & institutions of a semi-barbarous ancestry. We appealed to those of nature and found them engraved in our hearts." Ironically, Jefferson's political rival, Hamilton, spoke in almost identical terms: "The sacred rights of mankind are not to be rummaged for, among old parchments, or musty records. They are written, as with a sun beam, in the whole *volume* of human nature, by the hand of the divinity itself; and can never be erased or obscured by mortal power." It was a paradigm shift in basing the new republic on the laws "of nature, and found them engraved on our hearts." Liberated from the constraints of Blackstonian and British strictures, Americans found "an album on which we were free to write what we pleased." The American Revolution, particularly among the American Whigs, was based not on history but in nature. If nature reflected the inherent reason and rationality of mankind, Jefferson stressed, then humans are rational creatures "endowed by nature with rights." For Jefferson, life and liberty were inextricably linked in that the gift of life bestowed liberty: "The God who gave us life, gave us liberty at the same time: the hand of force may destroy, but it cannot disjoin them."

Of course, the liberating quality of Locke's philosophy would go only so far with the Founders. It is difficult to read the embrace of natural rights by Founders who continued to enslave others. The nobility of humanity did not extend to African Americans or, in other critical respects, women. It was not that such true equality was unfathomable at the time. Many did see the contradiction. Locke wrote, "There is nothing more evident, than that creatures of the same species and rank, promiscuously born to all the same advantages of nature, and the use of the same faculties, should also be equal one amongst another without subordination or subjection, unless the lord and master of them all should, by any manifest declaration of his will, set one above another." The Founders understood that inescapable truth of natural law when they signed a Declaration that "all men are created equal." Despite this defining line, even some who opposed slavery saw little hope for a revolution that would seek to overthrow both the monarchy and slavery. Jefferson would have to make the concession in striking critical language from his draft. While Jefferson's legacy would be forever stained by his own maintenance of slaves, he did attempt to condemn the institution of slavery. He was rebuffed by his fellow delegates who were willing to acknowledge the existence of a natural law while ignoring its implications for the enslaved people in the new nation.

It is also worth noting that even those with reservations about the Declaration of Independence shared its underlying view of natural rights. For example, John Dickinson, the delegate from Pennsylvania (with James Wilson and Ben Franklin), was one of the most brilliant and principled men of his time. He is widely known (particularly due to the flawed portrayal in the musical *1776*) as the delegate who refused to sign the Declaration. In reality, Dickinson was a powerful voice for independence and was called the "Penman of the Revolution" due to his publication of *Letters from a Farmer in Pennsylvania*. Dickinson would join the Continental Army to fight for the Revolution, one of only two such members from the Second Continental Congress. He would ultimately gain distinction by freeing all his slaves before his death. Dickinson believed deeply in the Lockean view of natural rights and rejected the notion that the rights of Americans were derived from the common law and sovereign largess. He wrote that Americans had a right to demand their liberty:

> claim [rights] from a higher source—from the King of kings, and Lord of all the earth. They are not annexed to us by parchments and seals. They are created in us by the decrees of Providence, which establish the laws of our nature. They are born with us, exist with us; and cannot be taken from us by any human power, without taking our lives. In short, they are founded on the immutable maxims of reason and justice.

Dickinson was well-versed in history and in 1765 warned of the pattern of democracies turning into tyrannies: "But what, sir, must be the consequence of that success [in achieving independence]? A Multitude of Commonwealths, Crimes, and Calamities, of mutual Jealousies, Hatreds, Wars and Devastations; till at last the exhausted Provinces shall sink into Slavery under the Yoke of some fortunate Conqueror." While Dickinson did not believe that the time was right for the Declaration of Independence, he (and others of his generation) entirely agreed with the revolutionary concepts underlying that document. Others strongly disagreed, including Judge Martin Howard, who voiced the British view that these arguments were all merely a "walk of metaphysics" and that rights must be based on history and "reciprocal duties." The Founders built a revolution precisely on the "metaphysics" of natural law and reason in recognizing inalienable rights.

There was another aspect to this new "metaphysics." It meant that the denial of natural rights was tyranny whether it is perpetuated by the few or the many. It comes back to the printing change to "inalienable." These rights could not be transferred or surrendered. The natural right to liberty, Jefferson noted, encompassed "the rights of thinking, and publishing our thoughts by speaking or writing; the right of free commerce; the right of personal freedom." Thus, democratically devouring the rights of others is no more legitimate than a single tyrant doing so. That is why, when it came time to draft a constitution, Madison and others sought to protect the declared inalienable rights from democratic despotism as well as individual despots. As Princeton professor Robert George has noted, the Founders may have different views on natural law but shared a fundamental belief that human-made law, or positive law, must confirm with a law "that is no mere human creation."

The natural law foundation of our republic has long been questioned by many in academia. Positivists believe that the authority of laws comes from their proper enactment and authority. Many accept the influence of science on the framers but resist the notion of preexisting rights that cannot be alienated by the government. The contemporary writings of the framers refer to both the laws of nature as well as natural rights. Alexander Hamilton would later describe the "eternal and immutable" laws for nature as the source of universal rights "indispensably, obligatory upon all mankind, prior to any human institution whatever . . . [and] binding over all of the globe, in all countries, and at all times." James Wilson wrote of how such natural laws included moral precepts and individual rights that are neither the product nor the discretion of any given government: the "law of nature is immutable, not by the effect of an arbitrary disposition, but because it has its foundation in the nature, constitution, and mutual relations of men and things."

In the end, the Founders did not replace God, but absolute rulers, in their embrace of natural law. For philosophers like Locke, God created the world "in common" for the enjoyment of all mankind. Over one's creations and oneself, the individual was sovereign. The departure from the "state of nature" was meant to protect such natural rights and allow the pursuit of these divine gifts. The Founders saw a divine authority in these natural rights as opposed to the sovereign right of the government. It was an idea that would rock the foundations of not just the English but the French thrones. The precise date marking the end of the era of divine authority of sovereigns is hard to establish, but a good reference point was January 21, 1792, in France. On that day, Paine was present in Paris when the French monarch Louis XVI was separated from the state, as well as his head, with the help of a guillotine.

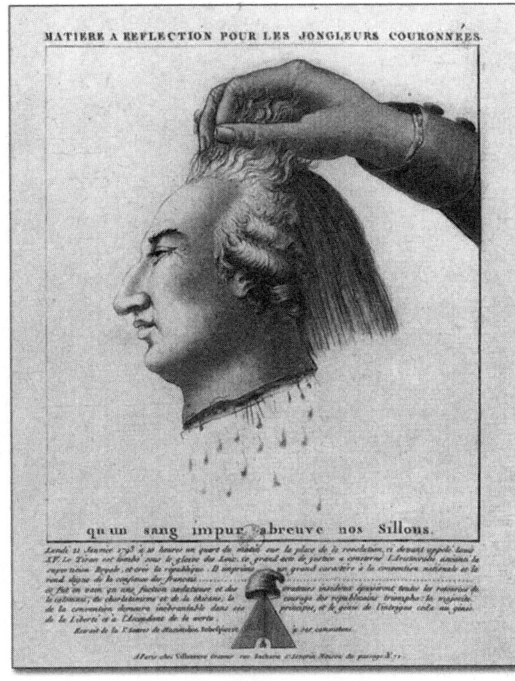

Cartoon of the execution of Louis XVI, titled "Food for Thought for Crowned Mountebanks" and captioned with "That his impure blood may fertilize the furrows of our fields," 1793, artist unknown

The rejection of absolute and divine rulers would remove only one form of tyranny. The story of humanity's struggle with governance systems has careened from blind faith in the divine to blind faith in the demos. Since the sixth century, neither pure divinity nor pure democracy was able to maintain stability and liberty in society. Despotism can take hold in the name of the many as easily as it can the few. That history is essential to understanding the future of democratic rule in the twenty-first century. For that, we must start at the beginning; we must start with ancient Athens.

Part II

A TALE OF TWO CITIES: DEMOCRACY AND MOBOCRACY

Had every Athenian citizen been a Socrates, every Athenian assembly would still have been a mob.

—James Madison

Ancient Athens and the birth of democracy is a subject that has always pushed writers to extremes. For some, Athens is the pinnacle of popular government, a transformative moment when a people threw off the yoke of tyranny. It showed that the demos could be incorporated into decision-making in a way that not only allowed for self-determinative elements but greater popular support for public policies and projects. Paine famously declared, "What Athens was in miniature, America will be in magnitude." Yet Athens was arguably not the democracy that many assume given its limited definition of citizenship, fixed aristocracy, and rigid voting systems. For the framers, Athens offered a more chilling tale of democracy and the recurring Saturn gene that can suddenly rise within a body politic.

Writers like the French philosopher Montesquieu and Madison believed that government had to be based on an understanding of human beings, including their tendency toward avarice and ambition. Past governments had struggled and collapsed somewhere between human urges and human reason. Madison would famously seek to harness human drive by pitting ambition against ambition. Framers also saw in human nature the seeds for both anarchy and tyranny. John Adams wrote ominously that

> Liberty, under every conceivable Form of Government is always in Danger . . . Ambition is one of the more ungovernable Passions of the human Heart. The Love of Power, is unsatiable and uncontrollable . . . There is danger from all men. The only maxim of a free government ought to be to trust no man living with power to endanger the public liberty.

In this dichotomous relationship, liberty is both the destiny and the undoing of humanity. Jefferson would echo this same sentiment in warning against the "dangerous delusion" in relying on "men of our choice to silence our fears for the safety of our rights." The "confidence," he added, "is everywhere the parent of despotism . . . In questions of powers, then, let no more be heard of confidence in man, but bind him down from mischief by the chains of the Constitution." While the American Democracy sought to achieve the ideals of natural law, it was built on a foundation of deep realism of the perils of democracy going back to ancient Athens.

Four

OF DEMOCRACY AND DEMAGOGUES

Ancient Athens and Rise of the Demos

In his famous fresco *The School of Athens*, Raphael depicted all the great thinkers that sprang forth from the Athenian fount of knowledge and philosophy. Notably, Raphael is believed to have used the face of Leonardo da Vinci for Plato and the face of Michelangelo for Heraclitus. It is a telling choice, not only to show the transformative role that Athens played in the advancement of civilization, but the tendency to insert much of ourselves into the view of Athens. In the case of Raphael, he literally incorporated his own self-image into his vision of Athens as the figure of a young man at the far right next of Ptolemy. The legacy of Athens remains something of a projection of our own philosophical views and bias. Every school of thought in history has sought to portray Athens as a part of a natural progression to their own just form of government, from anarchy to Marxism to representative democracies. In this act of translation, like Rafael's painting, historic figures often end up looking strikingly like us. The framers, particularly Madison, would spend considerable time exploring the lessons of Athens and Rome. What they saw would shape the American republic.

After the 2,500th anniversary of the Athenian *demokratia*, there was a type of revival of interest in the ancient Greek city-state as a model of democracy. This image is oversized in every respect by both proponents and detractors of Athenian history. The city was occupied by no more than thirty thousand people and covered an area the size of Rhode Island. As Boston University professor Loren Samons observed, the idyllic image of Athens "has now almost completely eclipsed the very different picture painted by the actual events of Athenian history."

Democracy is a term that is widely misused, particularly in the United States, as any political system where citizens control their government and exercise a right of self-determination. It is a colloquial use that is so common that most of us no longer raise tedious objections that the United States is not a democracy. The difference is often immaterial to a given conversation, but it is significant in any substantive comparison of governing systems. Republican forms of government are often referenced as "democracies" though they can range from the "democratic socialism" advocated by many in the United States to totalitarian regimes, such as Democratic People's Republic of Korea. A democracy, in its purest form, is the direct control of the many in their government. It is also one of its most dangerous forms of government. *Demos* was used in Greece to mean the many but also the "masses." Rule by the masses can easily devolve into what the famed colonial physician Benjamin Rush called "mobocracy."

Early governing systems were generally tyrannical. The term is derived from the Greek *túrannos,* meaning "absolute ruler." Like democracy, the word *tyrant* is often misunderstood in modern treatments of ancient city-states. It was used at the time to refer to extraconstitutional or unconstitutional rulers, those who took control of government. Some tyrants enjoyed broad support during periods of economic or political unrest. In Plato's *Republic*, the philosopher discusses various forms of government and describes tyranny as "the fourth and worst disorder of a State." Notably, Plato describes tyranny as not just the enslavement of others but as being enslaved, "because it too lacks reason and order." The tyrant ruled by sheer force and required only obedience, not consent. Absolute power corrupted the rulers, and few would dare to confront them. In the absence of checks and balances, idiosyncrasies and failures tended to grow unimpeded in such systems.

The Greek tyrants emerged from the deeply entrenched traditions of aristocratic governance and notions of a natural order of social hierarchy. Many idealized how aristocrats were literally bred to rule the masses. The fifth-century writer Pindar glowingly described aristocracy as the "splendor running in the blood." He cautioned that "the wise man knows many things in his blood, the vulgar are taught." Athens was experiencing economic changes that fueled unrest. At the start of the sixth century, farmers were being squeezed over unpaid debts, some were enslaved for failure to pay bills, and violence was rising. The conflicts between the aristocracy and the demos led to gruesome moments of unrestrained rage. In the ancient city of Miletus (located near what is now the city of Balat in Turkey), a popular uprising led to the burning of wealthy families alive. After the upper classes retook the town, they used oxen to trample to death many of their captives.

Athens long had councils of aristocrats that guaranteed the political status quo, including fixed economic strata and advantage. Aristotle noted that aristocrats held both legal and economic control over the masses, including the fact that "all borrowing was on the security of personal liberty." As a result, "the whole land was in the hands of a few; and if [the poor] did not pay their rents they could be sold into slavery, themselves and their children." By 510, that dominance began to yield, particularly with the diminishment of the authority of the Areopagus, a council of aristocrats. During this period, a figure stepped forward who espoused a truly revolutionary idea: direct democracy. His name was Ephialtes, and he was soon assassinated. That murder had an obvious impact on the public, but likely had an even greater impact on his protégé, the young Pericles. It would be Pericles who would transform Athens with public payments to average citizens to serve on juries and a greater diffusion of political authority.

Pericles was a demagogue in the original sense of the word: "leader of the demos." He introduced a council composed of representatives of the different "tribes" or divisions of the populace. In his famous funeral address for the fallen soldiers of the Peloponnesian War, Pericles insisted that a society based on democracy and merit was at hand: "If we look at the laws, they afford equal justice to all in their private differences; if to social standing, advancement in public life falls to reputation for capacity, class considerations not being allowed to interfere with merit; nor again does poverty bar the way, if a man is able to serve the state, he is not hindered by the obscurity of his condition." Few people walking around Athens would have seen that ideal state at the time, but Pericles was swept into power by the thirst for democratic reforms and great power for the demos. He offered public payments and social enhancement to the public in exchange for their support.

The fact is that Pericles did not rule over a democracy; he often ruled unilaterally. Thucydides noted the irony: "Pericles indeed, by his rank, ability, and known integrity, was enabled to exercise an independent control over the multitude—in short, to lead them instead of being led by them . . . [he] enjoyed so high an estimation that he could afford to anger them by contradiction . . . In short, what was nominally a democracy became in his hands government by the first citizen." That power led to blunders, including a war that cost thousands of lives and destroyed the Athenian economy. Equality would not be achieved by Pericles, but he did create the expectation for equality and democracy among citizens.

Athens fell to Sparta in the Peloponnesian War, after which it was brutally subjugated by the Thirty Tyrants. The blood-soaked reign of these oligarchs was finally put to an end, and democratic institutions, including popular courts, were restored. The great orator Lysias celebrated the triumph of Athenian democracy in the overthrow of the Thirty Tyrants as "the first and the only people in that time to drive out the ruling classes of their state and to establish a democracy." Lysias compared democracy to the emergence from the state of nature: "For they deemed that it was the way of wild beasts to be held subject to one another by force, but the duty of men to delimit justice by law, to convince by reason, and to serve these two in act by submitting to the sovereignty of law and the instruction of reason." Lysias heralded the ability of popular government to rule with reason and persuasion, but it was in fact a period marked more by mob than reasoned justice. The assembly would meet with thousands of citizens to hear popular and often inflammatory speakers. Mass juries composed of hundreds would then mete out popular justice. Both government and justice were carried out on a mass scale. When Socrates was found guilty of "corrupting the youth," the jury was composed of 501 citizens. There was little buffer between public anger and public justice.

The descent into mob justice was accelerated by intellectuals or orators who sought to ride the passions of the public. As Demosthenes warned: "this breed of orators appeared who ply you with such questions as 'What would you like? What shall I propose? How can I oblige you?' the interests of the state have been frittered away for a momentary popularity. The natural consequences follow, and the orators profit by your disgrace." As new leaders were brought to power by mobs, prior rabble-rousing orators were often tried for misleading the public. The one thing that remains consistent in mobocracies throughout history is that the mob itself was never wrong, but rather misled. The mob merely directed its anger inwardly at those who were now viewed as usurpers or corrupters of the popular will.

The true, unvarnished history of Athens challenges the romanticized concepts of democratic governance. As Professor Samons noted, "Athens makes a poor argument for popular rule." It is a history replete with massacres of captured cities, ruinous foreign adventures, unstable governments, the routine exiling of leaders, political violence, financial crises, and corruption. "All this, again, resulted from majority votes in the assembly," Samons stressed. The threat of mob justice and mob rule was ever-present in Athens, as was the threat of tyranny from autocratic leaders. The foundation for democratic rule is often credited to one of the "seven sages of ancient Greece," the philosopher and poet Solon. However, Athens had remained firmly oligarchic, and the rule of Draco showed just how harsh the penalties could be. In writing down these laws for the first time, Draco specified death for virtually every offense (giving rise to the term *draconian* to describe unnecessarily harsh penalties). When asked why he used capital punishment for every crime, Draco explained matter-of-factly that he first determined that minor crimes warranted death and then there was no greater punishment available for more serious offenses.

One of the powers associated with Solon poignantly captures the potential abuse of pure democratic systems: ostracism. In implementing democratic reforms, Solon and others still feared the emergence of autocratic or abusive leaders within the city. Accordingly, they moved to guarantee that oligarchs and the wealthy would no longer be untouchable or immune in Athens. Once a year, Athenians were allowed to participate in an *ostracophoria* to select one citizen to be expelled or exiled without a trial or conviction. Part of the agora, the social and commercial center of the city, would be roped off and citizens could write the name of the person who wronged them on a shard of clay. If six thousand citizens voted to ostracize a person, they could be banished for up to ten years. Of course, the mere act of writing on the shards, or *ostraca*, could disfavor the many illiterate members of the lower classes. According to one story, Aristides, a popular leader and general known for his fairness, was passing by the agora, or marketplace, when an illiterate man approached to ask if he could write on one of the shards on his behalf. Aristides agreed and asked who he wanted banished. "Aristides," the man responded. When Aristides asked what "the candidate" had done to him, the man responded that he had done nothing wrong but that he was tired of hearing the accolades of "Aristides the Just." True to his reputation, Aristides wrote his own name on the shard. Some shards with Aristides's name have been recovered by archaeologists. Despite being heralded by many as one of the most noble figures of Athens (including by Plato), Aristides was exiled for ten years (but would come back later under an amnesty to help defend Athens).

The practice of ostracism perfectly embodied the appeal and the danger of direct democratic action. It was little more than systemic and sanitized mob justice. It reflected a breakdown of the political process and was appropriately exercised using the shards of broken jars. While justified as a means to remove aspiring tyrants, it allowed for individuals to be ripped from their families and businesses for any reason without trial or appeal. It was punishment for the crime of unpopularity. Yet, originally, it was viewed as a bulwark against tyranny.

Ostracism was also a power that would devour its own. While Solon implemented the process as part of his democratization of Athens, the originator is generally thought to have been Clisthenes, a figure who some viewed as the true "father of democracy." It was under Clisthenes that the assembly was given greater power and citizens were randomly selected to fill government positions as a way of reducing the power of the aristocracy. Ostracism was the ultimate empowerment of the demos, a summary power to banish anyone with a simple vote of the majority. While some have argued that ostracism may have avoided violence by removing one side in a dispute, it was still a form of mob justice that led some to avoid public roles in fear of such a fate.

By the end of the fifth century, the abuses of democratic rule would swing the pendulum back toward oligarchy. Popular rule had led to military debacles and ostracisms that many recognized as ruinous for the city-state. Even moderates who supported the democratic reforms now welcomed the return of aristocrats to lead the city. The famous Greek historian Herodotus summarized the arguments from antidemocratic figures at the time (despite his own support for democracy). One of his fictional characters responds to a defense of democracy by noting that they had seen how there is "nothing . . . more ignorant and violent than the foolish mob. . . . A tyrant at least knows what he is doing, but the people do not. . . . The people rush headlong into politics without a thought, like a swollen river."

The flaws of Athenian democracy and justice were ultimately captured in the trial of Socrates and the famous painting of his final moments. The Athenian democracy lasted roughly 180 years between 508 BC to 322 BC. The trial of Socrates occurred in 399 BC. In Jacques-Louis David's famous depiction, the seventy-year-old philosopher Socrates reaches for his cup of hemlock while holding forth with last words of wisdom and defiance to his students and devotees. Plato is hunched over at the end of the bed, unable to look at his mentor as Socrates's wife, Xanthippe, peeks back from a stairway. It is the most famous image of defiance in the face of orthodoxy and intolerance.

What is often missed is that the final scene of Socrates occurred not during the prior period of the rule of the Thirty Tyrants, but after the restoration of democracy. The irony is crushing. Socrates and his sharp public critiques had previously drawn the ire of the Thirty Tyrants, including two of his former students (and now tyrants), Critias and Charicles. He was barred from teaching his *techne logon*, or reasoned discourse, including exchanges "with the young." Undeterred, Socrates continued to mock their measures, even pressing his former students on an age limit for speaking to young people and asking whether he could speak to a shopkeeper under the gag order. Socrates also indicated that it was not the consolidation of power in the tyrants that alarmed him, but how they used it. Their excesses would fuel the demand for democracy and erase the memories of the chaos that brought them to power, "caus[ing] men to look back on the former government as a golden age." He was describing what would become a familiar, vicious cycle as unstable governing systems swung from aristocracies to tyrannies to democracies and back again. Socrates had lived through all those wild swings in Athens. His experience left him with a particularly deep-seated distrust of direct democratic systems, and he saw the need for a strong ruler to control the passions of the public. In the end, it was a democracy that would put him to death.

The trial of Socrates is one of the great trials in history despite having neither an indictment nor a transcript. We don't even hear from the witnesses. Indeed, we have only a vague idea of the charges for such crimes as corrupting the youth. In *The Apology*, he complains that his attackers remain anonymous so that it is impossible to "confront and refute them" and leaving him "to fight, as it were, absolutely with shadows and to cross-examine when nobody answers." Yet, in the final trial, we do know his likely accusers: Meletus, the representative of the poets, and Lycon, the wealthy figure representing the orators and the aristocrats. However, the most important of his detractors may have been Anytus, a wealthy tanner who played a leading role in overthrowing the prior tyranny. He is described as a "fanatical democrat" and someone who would be viewed today as a "left-leaning politician." There is evidence that he did not necessarily favor full democracy but rather allied himself with the masses in the revolt after the tyrants seized much of his own property. Anytus is an early example of radicals who would come not from the poorest but the most affluent circles—a pattern that has repeated itself from Athens to Philadelphia to Paris to many cities today.

Socrates was in his truest form in egging on the massive jury while disassembling the arguments of his accusers. He is quoted as telling the jury that there is a reason why he strived to stay away from politics:

> Be sure, gentlemen of the jury, that if I had long ago attempted to take part in politics, I should have died long ago, and benefited neither you

> nor myself. Do not be angry with me for speaking the truth; no man will survive who genuinely opposed you or any other crowd and prevent the occurrence of many unjust and illegal happenings in the city.

The statement is not just a challenge to the abuses of popular government, but a recognition that outstanding figures tended not to last long in the city. The trial also showed the lack of any separation of powers in Athens where your jurors were often the same figures who passed legislation. Socrates not only knew it was a stacked deck, but he seemed to be counting on it.

Socrates addressed past circumstances of what he called "*mega legein*," literally "talking big." On one occasion, he claimed to have his own personal oracle that guided him. On another occasion, he claimed that the oracle at Delphi declared him to be the wisest man in Greece. Invoking the oracle likely sealed the fate of the philosopher. Perhaps that was his objective. Truth, it seemed, was his defense as he stressed that he was not known to lie and told others at the time of the divine designation. One can only imagine the impact of the crowd. While politicians today will often claim to be following God's will, few cite a direct conversation with the divine and then convey the compliments to others as divinely ordained facts.

Given the broad coalition arrayed against Socrates, the verdict itself was surprisingly close. It came down to just 30 votes on a jury of 500. While 280 voted to convict him, 220 wanted acquittal. At this point, the jury seemed to be little more than a vehicle for his own performative death. Socrates showed open scorn for the second vote on punishment, which might explain why there was a greater vote margin on imposing death than there was on the question of guilt. Socrates appears more defiant as the trial went on. That is reflected in the fact that he mocked the assembly by suggesting that the proper punishment should be to declare him a hero of Athens and order that he be served free meals for the rest of his life. He also suggested a tiny fine of just one mina coin as his supporters begged him to take matters seriously and suggest a more substantive fine. Just in case there was anyone he had not insulted, he further suggested dinners be served to him at the prytaneum, a venue reserved for feasts for the most honored citizens, including those who overthrew past tyrannies. Given Socrates's connections to some of the Thirty Tyrants by blood or association, it was akin to Jefferson Davis asking for a celebratory picnic at Arlington National Cemetery.

After the conviction, Socrates clearly preferred death to the alternatives. His friends arranged for his escape, a common practice in Athens. Some of his accusers may have hoped that he would take such an opportunity, but Socrates would have none of it. He wanted the hemlock. At seventy, Socrates was already at or beyond the life expectancy of his time. Despite the remarkably buff image in David's painting, it is likely that the years had taken a physical toll even if his mental faculties remained obviously undiminished. Socrates had seen Athens through oligarchy, tyranny, and finally democracy. The city had changed far more than he had. In a powerful moment before the assembly, Socrates told the jurors that they were effectively his tool rather than that of his critics. He refers to philosophers as "these human beings for whom it is better to die" but "cannot without impiety do good to themselves." He added that such hapless figures "must wait for some other beneficiaries."

Socrates was intent on giving his final lecture, even if it was an excruciating one. He chose a particularly horrific means for his own execution. Hemlock, *Conium maculatum*, does not offer a death as sanitized or dignified as the accounts from Athens might suggest. The plant with a white stem and white flowers contains the alkaloid coniine, which can have an effect like nicotine and disrupt the central nervous system, including respiratory failure. It can bring death by suffocation. Depending on the dose in tea form, it can take up to seventy-two hours to take a full lethal effect. At first, it can feel like inebriation. The accounts have Socrates complaining of a loss of sensation in his legs that was migrating up his body. While such poisoning can result in muscular paralysis, it also commonly produces vomiting and seizures. A very different scene altogether from David's sanitized depiction.

Whatever the chosen means, the death of Socrates was shocking even at the time as unjustified and excessive. Socrates fueled the rage and then willingly took its full brunt. The accusers fared little better in this demos-driven environment: The mob would turn on them not long after they led the mob to the execution of Socrates. There was such remorse over the death of Socrates that Meletus was killed and Anytus and Lycon were forced to flee the city. Anytus, according to Diogenes, may have actually been stoned to death by an irate mob in the city of Heraclea as punishment for his role. Other accounts suggest that he may have weathered the storm and returned to Athens.

When the final moment came for the philosopher, there was a strong sense that Socrates embraced the moment as much as his accusers. Rather than an ancient version of "death by cop," Socrates was not committing suicide as much as teaching his final lesson. It was his open defiance, rather than his philosophy, that triggered the anger in the city. Historian I. F. Stone once observed that "the trial of Socrates was a prosecution of ideas. He was the first martyr of free speech and free thought." One could quibble with that assessment, but Socrates was clearly the most famous such example from ancient times. His ideas remain controversial. Socrates was no friend to direct democracy or the "cupbearers" of the demos in governing in the name of the public. When faced with what historian Eli Sagan called the "collectivized monarch" of the demos, Socrates saw disorder in the *demos tyrannos*. He would voice strikingly antidemocratic sentiments, including his view that "it is the business of the ruler to give orders and of the ruled to obey."

Socrates's criticism of democracy runs against modern sensibilities, but there may be a loss in translation in understanding his true views. The criticism of democracy comes back to what is meant by the term. For Socrates, it was rule by the *demos*, or the public. Socrates saw the abuses of democracy and came to view government as ideally run by experts instilled with the knowledge and experience to maintain the public good. In that sense, Socrates was a precursor to later philosophers like Thomas Hobbes, who also saw the state of nature as a brutish and dangerous place. He studied the history of Athens and even translated Thucydides into English. Hobbes's Leviathan, or governing giant, was created by the consent of the public but ruled them in their name. In doing so, people could be protected and allowed to pursue their lives and livelihoods without fear. Conversely, Socrates saw the collectivized monarch of the demos as a kind of Leviathan that threatened the people's very existence. His opposition to popular government was not born out of a love for authoritarianism but fear of the collective power of the demos without a guiding hand. He was also critical of tyrants who ruled purely for their own interests. In Plato's *Republic*, the ideal city-state had rulers selected due to their virtue, not their kinship. The model of the "philosopher king" was a ruler whose knowledge and virtue lent him authenticity and authority. For Socrates, there was little benefit in leaving the state of nature to replace individual brutes with a gang of brutes in the form of the *demos tyrannos*.

For Socrates, democracies too easily released the public's self-destructive impulses. He saw citizens as susceptible to a type of Icarian compulsion. Daedalus (who Socrates claimed as an ancestor) escaped the maze of King Minos by creating wings for himself and his son, Icarus. Despite his repeated warnings, Icarus was drawn by the thrill of flight into soaring closer and closer to the sun. His freedom resulted in his death as the heat melted the wax that held his wings together. In much the same way, Socrates saw democracy as inevitably leading citizens, in their escape from earlier systems, to fly too close to the sun and their own demise. It is the very danger that the framers would seek to avoid by harnessing the power of democracy while preventing that power from becoming self-destructive for society.

What follows is an exploration of the pattern that emerged in two cities: Philadelphia and Paris. Key figures in both revolutions would reference the Athenian democracy, and both would see the analogous conditions and chaos return in the form of popular but unrestrained government.

Five

PHILADELPHIA

The American Revolution and "the Inclemencies of the Season"

The Fort Wilson Riot and the "Taking of the Tories"

On October 4, 1779, James Wilson watched at the back door of his home in Philadelphia as dozens of men pounded away at the last barrier between him and his likely death. He previously called—in his distinctive Scottish brogue—for his pregnant wife and children to rush to safety as the mob approached, crying, "Get Wilson!" Now, looking through his thick glasses, the scholarly lawyer stood next to an old general from the Revolution with a weapon in hand, ready to repel the coming attack. Having signed the Declaration of Independence just three years earlier (and supplying the key vote to commit Pennsylvania to the cause of independence), Wilson must have wondered how a mob could have come for him. Wilson would later become one of only six signers of both the Declaration of Independence and the Constitution (and the only one who would serve on the Supreme Court). But there he stood, staring at a heavy wooden door shaking under the attack of men who called themselves "Constitutionalists." Saturn's children had finally come for James Wilson.

By the end of the day, at least six would lie dead and many were wounded in what became known as the Fort Wilson riot. The "fort" was actually Wilson's home, which became the last stand for merchants and others fleeing a mob threatening not just arrest but summary justice. After the attack was over and order was restored by the militia, Wilson himself would be paraded through the streets as citizens heaped ridicule and abuse upon him. It was a scene that could have been taken from the time of Athenian ostracisms or the French tumbrels. How popular justice came to the Wilson home is a story illuminating not just on the conditions extant at the founding, but also the conditions that continue to drive such breakdowns of social and political order.

Philadelphia had long been a city divided between loyalists and patriots. In 1776, the Continental Congress called upon the city to discard its colonial government. The colonial "assembly" was already largely moribund. Even John Morton, a moderate Whig who served as speaker of the assembly, admitted that the assembly "became at last too heavy to drag along." The last of the holdouts trying to "assemble" in the State House found a virtually empty room. On May 20, an alternative "assembly of citizens" was formed that simply declared the colonial government null and void. It was a critical moment—the establishment of a revolutionary government in Philadelphia. The ad hoc assembly reflected a certain improvisational quality to what would become the city government. Soon a line of self-appointed public "committees" would assert authority to regulate the economy and conditions in the city. The vacuum left by nullification of colonial government would also unleash long pent-up passions. After the end of the British occupation, supplies dwindled, hoarding increased, and tempers soared. It did not take long before popular justice came back with a vengeance.

The revolutionary government would pass a new treason law targeting loyalists in the city. Extralegal groups were formed to round up those "notoriously disaffected to the American cause," and forty-five bills for treason were submitted to the grand jury. The homes of Republicans like Whitehead Humphreys were raided, and his sister was knocked down by the mob. One citizen, John Roberts, was accused of helping the British scavenge for food. A witness, Mary Smith, accused Roberts of standing by as British troops took her stores and assaulted her. Others said that he suspiciously watched them from a distance. Among his defense counsel was James Wilson. Roberts was convicted and sentenced to death despite the dubious testimony of the witnesses. There was an outcry for clemency from hundreds of fellow Quakers and an effort to delay the execution (from even the judge and prosecutor), but Roberts was ultimately marched through the town with the noose dangling from his neck and hanged. He was joined on the gallows by Abraham Carlisle, who had merely accepted a job as a gatekeeper at the entry to Philadelphia during British occupation. No allegation of an overt act of treason was ever made against Carlisle. The court simply ruled that the indictment was "certain enough." Wilson stood with other brave men of the bar in support of the rule of law at a time of mob justice and secured acquittals for many of the thirty-three alleged loyalists before the attack on his house.

Wilson's moderation made him an easy target as critics—and even some modern accounts—ignore his true contributions and courage. For example, in the musical *1776*, Wilson is ridiculously portrayed as a weak sycophant under the control of fellow delegate John Dickerson (it also referred to his being a judge, which would not occur until years later). Wilson's belated vote to approve the Declaration of Independence reflected the strength, not the lack, of principles. He honored his mandate from the assembly until, finally free to vote his conscience, he supported independence. He wrote passionately about the natural rights foundation for the new nation and that this natural law means that citizens have a right to pursue knowledge and seek both material and spiritual paths of their own choosing.

Figures like Morton and Wilson would object to the new Pennsylvania state constitution as lacking the divisions of government needed to moderate public passions and impulse. It was a view shared by other Founders. John Adams observed, "Sobriety, abstinence, and severity were never remarkable characteristics of democracy." On the other side of this coin was none other than Thomas Paine. Paine favored the small farmers and artisans he saw as being undermined by wealthy patriots. Pennsylvania's 1776 constitution was the realization of Paine's call for popular democratic controls. It reflected the very "democratical" elements that drew criticism of his writings from figures like Adams. Paine and others wanted the elimination of any upper house of aristocrats resembling the House of Lords.

While Paine denied taking a direct hand in drafting the state constitution, it followed his shared vision with radical Whig elements. Paine believed that a type of Rousseauian virtue would prevail in a democratic system and "that whatever personal parties there might be in a state, they would all unite and agree in the general principles of good government." Not only would Pennsylvania have just one house, but the head of the state government would be composed not of a governor but a rotating executive committee of twelve individuals. The legislature could remove any or all of the committee members. It was a system that rejected many of the Madisonian protections against majoritarian abuse and was opposed by Wilson and what became known as the "Republican" cause. With a collapsing economy and ad hoc citizen committees blaming hoarders and "Tories" for their worsening conditions, the mob turned on the Republicans who had previously argued against the radical government measures (and were proven correct in their admonitions).

The debate over the structure of the new government would be cut short by the British themselves, on September 26, 1777, when General William Howe unexpectedly moved his roughly fifteen thousand troops up the Chesapeake to take Philadelphia. His landing at the Head of Elk in August of 1777 sent the city into panic and led to an eight-month occupation. When the British evacuated the city in June 1778, many citizens would turn on known or suspected loyalists with a vengeance. They then turned on each other. Resumption of democratic control rekindled the class conflicts left simmering among the patriots themselves. Once again, local committees and militia filled the void, which ultimately led to the attack on the Wilson house.

What Paine witnessed in Philadelphia would ultimately lead him to reject unicameralism, explaining that majority control of a single house often meant that there was little deliberation or restraint. He found that "when party operates to produce party laws, a single house is a single person, and subject to the haste, rashness, and passion of individual sovereignty." The "haste, rashness, and passion" that swept over Philadelphia followed a familiar pattern as economic conditions declined and class tensions rose. Paine would find himself at the heart of one of the most intense controversies, a scandal that would only deepen the distrust of the revolutionary leader with many of his contemporaries.

By 1779, the war had taken its toll on the economy in Philadelphia with raging inflation, widening wealth gaps, and rising debt. Food and essentials were in short supply, and the city became a tinderbox. Paine witnessed protests for higher wages and prices for basic goods that rose 45 percent in one month alone. "There has been hell to pay in Philadelphia," wrote Samuel Shaw, a merchant and major in the militia. The violence that would unfold outside of the Wilson house was not unexpected and was described as an "insurrection" coming from "the lower sort" of society, though many forces were at work behind the scenes. Much like

Athens and later France, economic distress led to a demand for popular justice as citizens lost faith in the government. Resident Samuel Patterson called these "Terrible times. . . . The poor starving here and rise for redress. Many flying the city for fear of Vengeance." There were rumors of hoarding and price manipulation by the wealthiest merchants.

In this environment, various figures stepped forward to fuel the anger and lead the mob. Daniel Roberdeau, who was unanimously elected chairman of a key citizen group, railed against those "getting rich by sucking the blood of this county." The brigadier general in the Pennsylvania militia (and signer of the Articles of Confederation) added:

> There is at present no law for regulating the prices in the shops and markets, neither is there any law to prevent such regulations being made, and therefore the whole rests upon the virtue and common consent of the community. I have no doubt but combinations have been formed for raising the prices of goods and provisions, and therefore the community, in their own defence, have a natural right to counteract such combinations, and to set limits to evils, which affect themselves.

Handbills appeared in the city that were even more direct and menacing. One titled "For Our Country's Good!" and signed "Come on Cooly" appeared on the evening of May 23, 1779, declaring, "We have turned out against the enemy and we will not be eaten up by monopolizers and forestallers."

As economic conditions became more acute, radicals demanded price controls and retaliatory measures. The long-simmering class struggle now found full expression in the pubs and streets of the city. Paine had long accused wealthy patriots of corruption, or at least ignoring the corruption of their associates. In fairness to Paine, he practiced what he preached in demanding sacrifice and virtue from others. Despite his own financial struggles, Paine repeatedly donated or eschewed profits to better support the cause of independence. (At one point, he would give $500 to the cause, but it would later be returned by Congress because of his well-known poverty.) Convinced that revolutionary figures were profiting from speculation and self-dealing, Paine's anti-corruption efforts had begun a few years before and would resonate in the violence to come. In 1776, Paine criticized two of the most important figures in Philadelphia, Robert Morris and his assistant Gouverneur Morris (no relation) for their inaction in what became known as the Deane Affair. At the time, Paine was serving as the secretary of the Committee of Foreign Affairs in the Congress, a position secured with the help of George Washington in part to support the struggling writer. Paine soon saw what he viewed as corruption by the intermediary negotiating aid with France, Silas Deane. The Connecticut lawyer and his French counterpart were suspected of taking kickbacks or commissions on payments from the French government. Paine raised his suspicions with Morris, who managed the finances for Congress. Morris was more than a member of the Revolutionary establishment; he *was* the establishment. Called the "financier of the Revolution," Morris holds the distinction of being only one of two people to sign the trifecta: the Declaration of Independence, the Articles of Confederation, and the Constitution (the other being Roger Sherman). He not only ran the largest bank but served as the Superintendent of Finance. It was that latter capacity that drew the ire of Paine when Morris dismissed allegations that Deane was feathering his own nest while negotiating loans and arms shipments in France. At the time, this type of conflict of interest was far from unique. Morris and others saw nothing wrong in making a profit from revolutionary business, including matters where one had both public and private interests. For example, Morris pushed to establish the first national bank, the Bank of North America, and became its head, often using his official positions to support the institution. By that measure, Deane was small potatoes for profiteers. However, Paine saw the ultimate betrayal of the American cause by wealthy men who mocked public virtue with their profiteering. He was particularly irate when Deane refused to supply papers on his financial agreements and possible commissions. Paine lashed out at Deane and, by extension, Morris. In doing so, this relatively recent immigrant was taking on one of the most powerful figures in America, and the establishment quickly turned on Paine.

That is when Paine made a fateful decision. He published nonpublic, incriminating information against Deane. The anonymous publication was akin to a Beltway leak today but this one had Paine's fingerprints all over them, particularly when he signed the publication *Common Sense*. The French minister called for Paine to be fired for compromising diplomatic relations and, after refusing to deny that he was the author before Congress, Paine resigned his post. For Paine, it was the continuation of a litany of failed posts in government, only this time he may have been in the right. Paine's suspicions of Deane appear at least partially valid. As historian David Benner noted, "Deane was indeed every bit the scoundrel Paine declared him to be." He was found to be engaged in improper dealings with the British and would live the remainder of his life as an outcast abroad. Deane was later denounced as a traitor after writing essays criticizing independence and calling for a resumption of ties to England. Even Morris would ultimately admit that Deane was a "bad man" whose "reputation [was] totally ruined." (His hometown of Wethersfield, Connecticut, remains his sole advocate, with a school and highway still named after him.)

The Deane affair left lasting injuries on both sides, but it is notable that Paine's critics came chiefly from those viewed as "America's aristocratic circles." The inclusion of Morris in Paine's attacks inflamed many in the establishment who shared Morris's derisive view of Paine as "a mere adventurer from England, without fortune connections, ignorant even of grammar." It showed the growing space between radicals and more centrist revolutionaries, much like the divisions that would soon appear in Paris after its own revolution. Paine was already being targeted as a radical and a rabble-rouser; he was even physically attacked while just walking on the street in Philadelphia. The *Pennsylvania Evening Post* ran an acerbic poem: "Go home, thou scoundrel, to thy native soil. And in a garret, labour, starve, and toil." Notably, the newspaper was supportive of the Revolution and the first to publish the Declaration of Independence. Paine's skyrocketing to fame and his attacks on the merchant class had clearly made him enemies from within the revolutionary movement. It also again left Paine destitute and, even with a job as a clerk, he would complain that he could not even afford a horse. That poverty would likely only add to his appeal among radicals and reaffirm his own suspicions of the growing economic barriers in what he now called "the United States of America."

While the Deane Affair was closed by Congress, the public anger was only growing over what many saw as profiteering and corruption. Paine created a committee with like-minded figures such as Charles Willson Peale to combat corruption in Philadelphia. Peale, one of the most accomplished painters of his time, allied himself with the more radical faction of Constitutionalists. These extreme voices in both Philadelphia and Paris demanded economic and popular justice, particularly targeting the upper classes and merchants. Six months before the Fort Wilson riot, the calls for action were getting louder, and Morris would find himself again at the epicenter of another scandal.

The combination of political opposition to direct democratic rule and their business interests made the Republicans the perfect villainous blackguard for radicals. In addition to his banking interests, Morris inherited a thriving shipping firm. Scarcity can be a profitable state for merchants when they have a supply at hand. It can also be a perilous state when there is a mob afoot. That was the problem that Morris faced, on April 20, 1779, when the ship *Victorious* arrived in Philadelphia loaded with badly needed goods. It was a "poleacre," or a ship with a distinctive two- or three-mast construction with a large hold for shipping. Contracted through Morris's firm, the arrival caused quite a stir in the food-deprived city. Morris had reached an agreement with the Continental purchasers on the "moderate" pricing of the goods. However, a buyer from Baltimore named Sollekoff boarded the ship before it anchored in the port and secured first dibs on the cargo, later reaching an agreement with Morris to divvy up the lot. As part of the deal, Morris would supply a new cargo of tobacco for the return voyage of the ship. According to Morris in his later defense to city committees, Sollekoff drafted the agreement in French and Morris signed without reading the content. The rate offered by Morris to purchasers proved too low under the contract, and he had to mark up the price, which played directly into complaints of price gouging and manipulation.

Morris's account was supported by others involved in the transactions, but his defense fell on deaf ears in the city. Morris and the *Victorious* became rallying points for the opposition and a symbol of what we will later discuss as "economic factionalism." A resolution passed by Roberdeau's committee denounced Morris and declared that "the prices of all kinds of dry goods have been greatly advanced, to the injury of the public, and the great detriment of trade." The committee (including Paine) investigated, but Morris was bedridden with a recurrence of an eye inflammation. He could speak with them only briefly but noted that they were "being untimely ignorant of the transaction." While the committee did not question Morris's account, it still found that the arrangement was meant to withhold goods from immediate sale to manipulate the market and that the cargo was "to be bidded for not to be bought." It officially censured his conduct, a repudiation that Morris vociferously objected to in print. The committee continued to hound Morris, hauling him in to answer for the pricing of flour despite his lack of any flour purchases and spreading rumors of hoarding. Morris recounted how "four or five" women appeared at this door with sacks demanding flour from two alleged wagonloads. The shipments did not exist, but the women insisted that the committee had told them that the flour was in his possession.

The worsening conditions led to more ad hoc measures by local committees, which tried to stabilize conditions through blunt persuasion. The militia arrested people who tore up their threatening handbills, and "men with clubs" stormed into stores to force the lowering of prices. While the state also tried to stabilize prices, most of these measures were carried out by local authorities backed up by the militia. One such group, the Committee of 120, even included Republicans like Wilson and sought to control public passions. Their meetings often ended with people shouting down speakers and would ultimately prove too unwieldy in size. Other committees took direct action, but were accused of extrajudicial excesses. They resisted turning over powers to the state government. Colonel William Bradford (who would become a member of the Pennsylvania Supreme Court and the second United States Attorney General) argued that only local committees should wield such powers precisely because they were so extraordinary and dangerous. It was a clever argument that these powers are inherently oppressive and thus should remain as the temporary prerogative of the public:

> To blend such a power with the constitutional authority of the state would, according to our idea of liberty and conception of things, be unwise and unsafe; because being once incorporated therewith, the separation might afterwards be difficult, and that which was originally admitted as a temporary convenience, justified by necessity, might in time establish itself into a perpetual evil, and be claimed as a matter of right. The exertions which are sometimes necessary to be made by the inhabitants of an invaded country, for their own preservation and defense, are frequently of such a peculiar and extraordinary quality, that as they ought not to become the rule of legal government in times of peace, should not be mixed therewith in times of war; for that which in the community may be the spirit of liberty, introduced into the laws would become its destroyer.

In other words, these public committees were a necessary evil that should not be mixed with legitimate forms of governance. What Bradford referred to as measures motivated by "the spirit of liberty" were clumsy efforts at price controls that utterly failed to restrain runaway prices. Shipments were often seized and voices of reason like General John Cadwalader (a hero from the Battle of Trenton) were shouted down by club-wielding thugs. The militia was accused of marching with fife and drum to intimidate critics of price controls and at times blocking access to the stage at meetings. Paine joined in stirring the crowd with suggestions that Wilson and others might be secretly involved in corrupt or self-advancing foreign business dealings.

As with Athens, popular government in Philadelphia mutated into a type of authoritarianism. Moderate Whig politicians like Wilson decried the loss of protections for individuals and the breakdown of social order. The result fulfilled Plato's predictions of the overindulgences in a democracy when a people "thirsting for freedom has evil cupbearers presiding over the feast, and has drunk too deeply of the strong wine of freedom."

Hearing the call for new governments, radical Whigs and other Pennsylvanians drank deeply from that "strong wine of freedom." In 1776, the first Pennsylvania constitution rejected a single executive for a committee to avoid the concentration of power. There were those who seemed to channel the more aristocratic voices of the Athenian ruling class, such as Thomas Smith, a delegate to Pennsylvania's Constitutional Convention, who objected that under the new state Constitution, "any man, even the most illiterate, is as capable of any office as a person who has had the benefit of education." The framers saw the aristocratic elements of government as beneficial in the mix of what Paine referred to derisively as "complex government." Paine eschewed buffers designed to temper the public will, preferring a government with fewer moving parts and more direct democratic action. It was the same debate playing out centuries after the Athenian experiment with popular government. Adams even raised the Athenian practice of ostracism in his arguments for bicameralism. He objected to unicameralism (favored by Paine) because "the rich, the well-born, and the able, acquire an influence among the people that will soon be too much for simply honesty and plain sense, in a house of representatives." Thus, these aristocrats were expected to gravitate to the Senate as a body that would be "to all honest and useful intents, an ostracism."

The main bone of contention between the Constitutionalists supporting the new Pennsylvania constitution and the Republicans calling for greater protections was the creation of a unicameral legislature with little buffer between public impulse and public laws. These groups were formally established years after the first Pennsylvania constitution, in March, 1779. The first to form was the Republican Society, with members such as Wilson and Benjamin Rush. The group had a classist element, described by Rush as composed of citizens "distinguished for their wealth, virtue, learning, and liberality of manners." They were dedicated to opposing the state constitution and arguing for the protections of a mixed government structure that would not just blunt political passions but encourage compromise. Despite the relatively wealthy profile of its members, the Republicans were able to align themselves with a broader coalition that included artisans, traders, and merchants opposed to price controls and the actions of the popular committees to bring down prices and arrest inflation. Paine himself would ultimately come to oppose price controls due to what he saw unfold in Philadelphia.

Conversely, the Constitution Society contained some wealthy individuals, but they were generally nouveau riche as opposed to established figures of the Republican Society, or those Rush called the "ancient" families. For example, Roberdeau, a merchant who later became a militia leader and the head of one of the radical public committees, denounced the establishment as bloodsuckers draining the life from the country. The Constitutionalists identified with the lower classes and, though some would ultimately oppose the violence of the mob, they were extreme in their opposition to the upper class. They believed that the majority should be able to dictate laws and policies without the moderating controls proposed by the Republicans.

By 1779, those who argued for republican values and protections were treated with great suspicion as budding aristocrats or oligarchs. Tensions continued to rise to the point that Benjamin Rush would write to John Adams that "Every face [in Philadelphia] wears the marks of fear and dejection." Merchant (and former president of the Continental Congress) Henry Laurens described it as the "moment on a precipice, and what I have long dreaded and often intimated to my friends, seems to be breaking forth—a convulsion among the people." The economic conditions sharpened the rhetoric and pushed citizens to take direct action. In an obvious reference to the earlier call by "Come on Cooly," a new handbill signed "Come on Warmly" appeared in August of 1779, calling for the public and militia to support the public committee and punish those keeping prices high. Within days, meetings were held in taverns to come up with lists of those whose property would be seized.

Despite threats in the streets, Wilson continued to call for moderating democratic impulse through divided and balanced government. The inherent instability of democracies, he argued, was manifest in history and would not warrant repetition. For those views, he was pegged, wrongly, as one of the wealthy citizens opposed to the participation of the commoner in government and even democracy itself. He was further attacked due to his neutral stance on independence as a delegate to the Continental Congress due to the absence of instructions from the state legislature. He noted to the delegates that "Some have been put under Restraints by their Constituents. They cannot vote, without transgressing this Line." He also joined moderate Whigs in cautioning prudence, opposing language drafted by John Adams and others that called for the colonies to discard their prior governments in favor of new revolutionary governments to put the nation on a war footing:

> In this Province if that Preamble passes there will be an immediate Dissolution of every Kind of Authority. The people will be instantly in a State of Nature. Why Precipitate this Measure. Before We are prepared to build the new House, why should We pull down the old one, and expose ourselves to all the Inclemencies of the Season.

Prudence did not make Wilson any less of a patriot. Wilson feared a return to the "state of nature," an allusion to the brutish existence described by Hobbes before the creation of civil society. He feared the loss of order (and ultimately any hope for a stable government) in wanton rejection of existing governing structures. It was a prophetic speech given what would unfold at his home just a few years later.

The popular government in Philadelphia showed all the instability and ineptitude of the Athenian assembly, including exacerbating the decline of economic conditions and markets. The government created bodies like the Committee on Pricing that did little beyond blame loyalists and hoarders for undermining the revolutionary government. Dr. Benjamin Rush, signer of the Declaration of Independence, remarked that worthless paper money made hoarding and price control violations inevitable as the economic conditions "would corrupt a community of angels." He dismissed the efforts at price controls and market regulation as "a violent puke given to a man in the last stages of consumption." The currency continued to depreciate as prices rose. These economic conditions fueled the conspiracy theories as mobs targeted wealthy merchants and others for popular forms of justice. These economic grievances dovetailed with social tensions. For example, the First Company of Philadelphia Militia (which would be involved in the Fort Wilson riot) sent a complaint to the Supreme Executive Council over being called to duty only to return to rising prices and "treated . . . with Indignity and Contempt." The city was being torn apart by developing class warfare. The militia objected that "the Midling and poor will still bear the Burden, and either be totally ruin'd by heavy Fines, or Risque the starving of their Families, whilst themselves are fighting the Battles of those who are Avariciously intent on Amassing Wealth by the Destruction of the more virtuous part of the Community."

As conditions worsened, popularists faced growing questions over the efficacy and wisdom of their price controls and other measures. Debt was soaring alongside threats of incarceration for those unable to pay their creditors. Republicans found growing support in the public for political reforms, but they also faced even greater anger from the Constitutionalists. Republicans were accused of trying to create a House of Lords as an American aristocracy. Wilson did not flinch and published a list of those supporting republican reforms from every profession and trade. After showing supporters from every walk of life, Wilson asked mockingly, "Are we all desirous of becoming Lords?" Wilson declared that a unicameral government is an invitation for tyranny where judges are "tossed about by every veering gale of politicks."

On October 4, 1779, that "gale" was blowing across the city. A new group called the Committee of Privates called for militiamen to gather at the Paddy Byrne Tavern with a handbill listing those "disaffected persons" who would be seized and put on prison ships bound for New York. The atmosphere in the taverns was turning ugly. Unable to arrest inflation, the committee had turned to arresting merchants. One such merchant was Jonathan Drinker, who was not even a member of the Republican Society but known as an opponent of price controls. Drinker was grabbed off the street after leaving the Quaker Meeting House on Arch Street. (While being marched down the street to a rogue's march beat, Drinker complained that he had not had his lunch and was allowed to go home to eat before being taken away.) Soon the roundup became a riot. Saturn's inexorable diet had grown from a craving to a compulsion.

Hundreds formed a mob for the purpose of "taking up Tories." Various merchants were rounded up as more militia gathered at the Byrne Tavern on Tenth Street and other groups hunted down any Republicans and loyalists. Even radical firebrands like Charles Willson Peale, chairman of the Constitutional Society, grew uneasy over what he saw at the tavern as the militia members called for a cleansing of the city to remove all "unAmerican elements." Peale, the artist responsible for *Washington at Princeton*, had previously led the most radical elements in attacking merchants. He was to the Philadelphia radical movement what David would become for the Paris radicals, an artist who allowed Rousseauian ideals to blind him to the brutal realities of democratic despotism. Peale was now faced with the outbreak of uncontrollable mob violence. He tried to dissuade the men, but was ignored. With some now inebriated at the tavern, the crowd was heard to cry, "Get Wilson," and Peale ran to find Joseph Reed, the president of the Supreme Executive Council of Pennsylvania, to intervene. In the meantime, Wilson called upon the assembly for protection and, when those calls were unheeded, he gathered his associates to make a stand at his home.

Some Republicans and their supporters gathered at the City Tavern and engaged in rudimentary drills in preparation for the coming battle. As they drilled in the street, the main militia force was marching to fife and drums closer to their location, occasionally stopping to give three cheers. The Republicans in front of the City Tavern fell back as the militia followed at a distance. The militia continued marching toward Third Street and Wilson's home, where the retreating men had found refuge. Wilson took his wife, Rachel, then four months pregnant, and their children to the home of Robert Morris. He then returned to his friends and barricaded the doors. They were not without experience, including Captain Robert Campbell (who lost an arm two years earlier in combat), Colonel Stephen Chambers (who fought in the Revolutionary War), General Thomas Mifflin (who not only signed the U.S. Constitution and served as the first governor, but distinguished himself at the battles of Trenton and Princeton), and General William Thompson (who led Thompson's Pennsylvania Rifle Battalion in driving back the British at their landing in Boston). The groups watched as two Continental officers tried to dissuade the militia only to be forced back at bayonet point. (During the later gunfire, General Mifflin was able to briefly open the door to allow the two officers to seek shelter inside.)

There has been lasting debate about what happened next. What is clear is that someone fired a shot. Most accounts describe supporters of Wilson and others rushing to his home with the mob in close pursuit. They barricaded themselves inside in fear of a massacre. That is when a curious figure appeared in a third-floor window, the one-armed Captain Campbell, shouting at the mob and brandishing a pistol. There was an exchange of gunfire and Campbell fell back mortally wounded. Undeterred, General Mifflin went to a second-floor window to call on the mob to stand down, only to have the frame of the window explode from incoming musket fire. The old general responded by firing both his pistols before being driven back. The house defenders opened fire from the windows, and five people lay dead in the street as the mob scattered for cover.

The mob was not without their own experienced leaders, and a band of men was formed to attack the house from the rear. The attack from the rear gave them partial cover from gunfire from the windows, and the mob battered the door to gain access to Wilson and his cadre. As the door was breached with the help of a sledgehammer, the first two men to enter were cut down by the defenders. The mob then went to retrieve a cannon from the arsenal. Soon, the mob was in the house, and the defenders ran upstairs as Colonel Stephen Chambers covered their retreat in the stairway. He fired both pistols but was then left defenseless. Pulled by his hair out of the house, he was then bayoneted over a dozen times by the mob. He succeeded in wounding one of the attackers (who was left in the home), and the mob retreated after firing wildly. Remarkably, Chambers would survive.

The defenders quickly shoved furniture against the door to create a new barricade and waited anxiously for the next attack. They knew that, if the cannon was brought into action, they had little hope. They watched down the street for any sign of relief. In one account, Benedict Arnold made an appearance and attempted to disperse the mob but was stoned and fell back. Some appealed to the commander of the local militia, Joseph Reed, a former aide to Washington and signer of the Articles of Confederation. Reed was viewed, if anything, as an ally to the mob. He was known as a vehement anti-loyalist who pushed the seizure of property and the arrest of loyalists for treason. His family was living in one of the confiscated homes. Yet, like Peale, there was a limit to his rage. Relief finally came in the form of a force of dragoons with swords drawn. Despite being ill, Reed led the City Light Cavalry to put down the riot and was heard to cry, "Charge all armed men!" The cavalry slashed their way through the mob, killing members of the militia in the process. In all, at least six were killed and fourteen injured in the fighting. When Arnold arrived at the scene with dead and wounded strewn in the streets, he spoke harshly of the role of the council and Reed in allowing lawlessness to flourish, declaring, "Your President has raised a mob and now he cannot control it."

Wilson and his defenders would emerge victorious into the street at the corner of Walnut and Third Streets. It would be short-lived. They were ridiculed and abused as they marched down the street. Twenty-seven arrests of militiamen were made, and both attackers and defenders would be charged. The city was still a powder keg, and the dead militiamen only further agitated the locals in taverns and pubs. Morris and a few local officials convinced a reluctant Wilson to leave the city in the short term to avoid extrajudicial execution. (Morris himself stayed in the city but went into hiding.) Morris explained, "The ferment is particularly high against you. . . . The poor unfortunates that lost their lives yesterday have been buried this evening with the honors of war a circumstance not calculated to allay the passions of men in a ferment." Wilson moved to Morris's country house and was told to hide himself in the attic (though thankfully with access to the wine cellar). In the meantime, Wilson sat in a darkened room on a bare mattress to avoid even a candle giving away his location to those searching for him. He was soon encouraged to move again to avoid detection. Morris tried to assuage his wounded sense of honor, advising, "Retreat until the ferment is over, you may then be heard patiently and have justice done you. In the present state of things the passions of men might do you injustice that their own judgments would hereafter condemn or their humanity regret."

After the Fort Wilson incident, Reed sought to diffuse further tensions. He dismissed the lethal encounter as the "casual over-flowings of liberty." He assured the militia and the public that the Council and Assembly would handle miscreants and loyalists. He promised that popular justice would be meted out, but not by the militia or the mob. On October 9, just five days after he cut down militia members in front of the Wilson home, Reed called for action on the rising prices for flour and other staples as well as action against those who were viewed as undermining or unsupportive of the Revolution. At the same time, he asked for the Assembly to implement an act of indemnity and oblivion to clean the slate for many accused. Such acts of "oblivion" had been used throughout history to erase the memory and liability for fits of violence, including in the aftermath of the killing of Caesar in the name of the Roman Republic. The move harkened back to the English Indemnity and Oblivion Act of 1660, when pardons were given for those who committed crimes in the English Civil War (with the exception of those responsible for the death of Charles I and others). Notably, after the English Act, 104 people were still executed, including John Cook, the Chief Justice of Ireland. The act of immunity and oblivion in Pennsylvania showed the same contradiction where past violence but not past loyalties were forgotten. The Assembly approved two measures that allowed the arrest of anyone when "there is just reason to suspect he is an enemy to the American cause, or that he hath manifested a general disaffection thereunto." Officials had the authority to banish individuals from the state. Such extrajudicial measures were deemed more advisable "than a rigorous pursuit of legal measures." As for the charges, Wilson and others were forced to post large bails pending trial. By March 1780, passions had subsided to the point that the Executive Counsel felt comfortable to issue "an act of free and general pardon" to both sides.

The Constitutionalists would enjoy greater popularity in the immediate aftermath of the riot. However, as the city later faced renewed food shortages and martial law under their control in 1780, the Republicans surged in the elections. Morris, the much-maligned banker and merchant, was even reelected. Many would attribute a shift in public attitude in favor of a more representative model to the Wilson riot and the continued instability under the Constitutionalists. Many factors were clearly at play. Figures like "Valerius" of Philadelphia, writing in the *Freeman's Journal* in 1784, recounted how "The affair of Mr. Wilsons House, in 1779, . . . [was] the most alarming insurrection it [Philadelphia] had ever felt." Ultimately, the Constitutionalists were unable to regain their power. The Fort Wilson riot left an indelible mark on the city and exposed the danger of direct political impulse on social order. Under the revolutionary constitution, Benjamin Rush remarked, "All of our laws breathe the spirit of town meetings and porter shops."

Wilson would continue to advocate for a greater voice of common citizens in government within a balanced system. He maintained that, just as monarchy was a flawed system, so was democracy. That view was shared by the majority of framers in crafting a new American republic. Despite his harrowing encounter with the mob in Philadelphia just a couple years earlier, Wilson stood before the Constitutional Convention in that city and reminded his fellow delegates that, in exploring the proper use of governmental power, one must "trace them all to one great and noble source: The People."

Factions and Fratricide: Controlling the "Democratical" Forces in Revolutionary Philadelphia

Scene at the Signing of the Constitution of the United States, 1940, by Howard Chandler Christy, depicting Independence Hall, Philadelphia, September 17, 1787

The Fort Wilson riot occurred just three years after the Declaration of Independence and a decade before the adoption of the Constitution. The period would prove transformative for many framers in appraising the promise and the perils of democratic systems. Democracy's turbulent history seemed to be repeating itself just outside the windows of Independence Hall. Figures like Madison were well versed in that history, particularly with the fate of republics in Athens and Rome. Most agreed with the sentiments expressed by Cicero:

> say no more of this Greece, which has long since been overthrown and crushed through the folly of its own counsels; that ancient country, which once flourished with riches, and rower, and glory, fell owing to that one evil, the immoderate liberty and licentiousness of the popular

> assemblies. When inexperienced men, ignorant and uninstructed in any description of business whatever, took their seats in the theatre, then they undertook inexpedient wars; then they appointed seditious men to the government of the republic; then they banished from the city the citizens who had deserved best of the state.

The irony is inescapable as unrestrained democracies rose, collapsed, and then led to the ascension of dictators. In the seventeenth century, the execution of Charles I in England was followed by chaos as the parliamentarians struggled to maintain order. Levelers and others wanted popular government and universal suffrage as the parliament floundered with division and indecision. That would lead to the rise of Oliver Cromwell as the military protector and the end of "the Rump Parliament." Cromwell famously entered the chamber and simply declared, "You are no Parliament, I say you are no Parliament; I will put an end to your sitting." With a troop of musketeers at his back, he then referred to the ceremonial mace as a "bauble" and ordered it to be taken away. After Cromwell's death and a brief effort of his son to rule in his stead, the monarchy returned in the form of Charles II.

This was not-so-distant history for the framers, who were also familiar with the writings on government that came from that period. With the English Civil War, there was also the writing of *Leviathan* by Hobbes in 1651. Hobbes served as the tutor to the future Charles II, and his view of the revolution was clearly manifested in his embrace of a strong leader to protect against the "war of all against all" in the state of nature. Hobbes presented a brutal image of people left in a lawless space, allowing the release of violent and base impulses. Yet he also warned that both Athens and Rome showed how a free people can cause the same brutal conditions through direct democratic action: "By reading of these Greek, and Latine Authors, men from their childhood have gotten a habit (under a false shew of Liberty,) of favouring tumults, and of licentious controlling the actions of their Soveraigns; and again of controlling those controllers, with the effusion of so much blood." The framers clearly shared that view, though they rejected the need for an all-powerful sovereign.

There was a critical common thread running through the Declaration of Independence to the Constitution. Both documents were first and foremost about liberty, not democracy. The immediate question for the framers in Philadelphia was how to craft a more stable system of government after the confusion and conflicts under the Articles of Confederation. The purpose remained the same: to establish a government that would protect the individual liberties that were viewed as human rights, bestowed by God not government. Indeed, Madison's view of the foundation of natural rights likely contributed to his initial resistance to the need for a Bill of Rights. He believed that the protection of individual rights was already the default position in any conflict with the government and feared that articulating rights risked courts reducing their scope to the specific language of amendments. He had to be convinced by George Mason and other anti-Federalists that a listing of individual rights was needed. The Constitution offered a framework that would allow the expression of liberty through a stable system of governance. Democracy was a means to protect individual rights, not the inverse. Liberty does not mean the freedom to do anything to anyone if you are in the majority. Liberty is not anarchy, but rather, as Thomas Jefferson stated, the "unobstructed action according to our will, within the limits drawn around us by the equal rights of others." It was a new, liberty-based vision of rights that were neither dependent upon nor discretionary with the government. Citizens would have an unobstructed path to pursue "life, liberty, and the pursuit of happiness." Those principles of the Declaration of Independence would become the literal litmus test for new states. Starting with Nevada and the other states admitted after the Civil War, enabling acts passed by Congress specified that the state constitutions must embrace representative government but also not be "repugnant" to the Declaration of Independence.

For the framers, the challenge was protecting liberty without inviting tyranny, including democratic despotism. Figures like Rousseau and Paine saw democratic empowerment as unleashing not just the will but the wisdom of a people. That was not what many framers had witnessed either just in history or in their home states. The alternative view (and the one that best captures the view of many framers) was presented by Alexis de Tocqueville in his 1835 *Democracy in America*, in which he pointed out the illogic of believing that the position of the majority was inherently more measured and sound simply by the multiplication of numbers. Appealing to "the sovereignty of the human race over that of the people," Tocqueville argued that blindly accepting the wisdom and will of the majority was the "language of the slave." He noted that advocates for democracy rejected the notion of an omnipotent individual or ruler, yet seemed to suspend those doubts when positions were taken on behalf of the majority:

> Now, if you admit that a man vested with omnipotence can abuse it against his adversaries, why not admit the same concerning a majority? Have men, by joining together, changed their character? By becoming stronger, have they become more patient of obstacles? For my part, I cannot believe that, and I will never grant to several that power to do everything which I refuse to a single man.

The framers certainly shared the view that majoritarian impulse only magnified the potential injury to individual and minority rights.

The Fort Wilson riot and other breakdowns of social order drove home the dangers that democratic despotism posed to liberty for the delegates who gathered for the drafting of the Constitution. At one point in the Constitutional Convention, Madison recorded Wilson as making a particularly poignant observation given his own recent experience: "with regard to the sentiments of the people, conceived it difficult to know precisely what they are. Those of a particular circle in which one moved, were commonly mistaken for the general voice." The framers saw the instability of early American systems as a threat to liberty. While few framers wanted a Hobbesian ruler (they had just discarded such a ruler), there were contemporary voices who still associated democracy with Athenian anarchy. In denouncing Paine's call for greater power for the general public, Maryland's James Chalmers warned that without a monarchy "our Constitution would immediately degenerate into Democracy." Most framers did not want a constitutional system that replaced a tyrant with a tyranny of the majority. John Adams made this plain to Virginia delegate John Taylor when he wrote him, "You say, sir, that I have gravely counted up several victims 'of popular rage, as proofs that democracy is more pernicious than monarchy or aristocracy.' This is not my doctrine, Mr. Taylor. My opinion is, and always has been, that absolute power intoxicates alike despots, monarchs, aristocrats."

For Adams, the interim period had hardened his views. He once espoused Rousseauian notions of a social contract between citizens and the notion of a government carrying out the will of the public. In 1766, he even denounced the "sneers and snubs" of the wealthy for "the multitude, the million, the populace, the vulgar, the mob, the herd and the rabble, as the great always delight to call them." Yet, by the time of the constitutional drafting, he was often heard rejecting the calls for popular governance in favor of the mixed government model. In 1787, when the creation of a new constitution was at hand, John Adams taunted those who revered the ancient Greek state for empowering the masses:

John Adams

> Sobriety, abstinence, and severity, were never remarkable characteristics of democracy, or the democratical branch or mixture, in any constitution; they have oftener been the attributes of aristocracy and oligarchy. Athens, in particular, was never conspicuous for these qualities; but, on the contrary, from the first to the last moment of her democratical constitution, levity, gayety, inconstancy, dissipation, intemperance, debauchery, and a dissolution of manners, were the prevailing character of the whole nation. At what period will it be pretended that they were adorned with these serious, abstemious, and severe governors? and what were their names?

Adams's unease would grow to the point that he was accused of favoring a return to hereditary succession to stabilize the system. He wrote that the original design would exist "till Intrigue and Corruption, Factions and Seditions shall appear in [the nation's] Elections to Such a degree as to render hereditary Institutions, a Remedy against a greater Evil." It was an interesting counterpoint to Paine, who held a deep hatred for hereditary systems.

Madison sought to protect liberty from the forces that destroyed it in Athens through a new type of republic. As "Publius" (presumably Madison) wrote in Federalist 55, "In all very numerous assemblies, of whatever characters composed, passion never fails to wrest the scepter from reason. Had every Athenian citizen been a Socrates; every Athenian assembly would still have been a mob." Madison suggested that a flawed political system would prove little better than the state of nature in producing mob rule. Once again, the twelve years of factional violence after the signing of the Declaration weighed heavily on the discussions in Independence Hall. There was a paradigm shift. Where the debate over the Declaration of Independence was all about tyrants and autocrats, the debate over the Constitution was more about tyranny of the majority. As Madison stressed in Federalist 51, "it is great importance in a republic not only to guard the society against the oppression of its rulers, but to guard one part of the society against the injustice of the other part." He expressed this fear to Jefferson in a letter, warning that the "invasion of private rights is chiefly . . . not from acts of Government contrary to the sense of its constituents, but from acts in which the Government is the mere instrument of the major number of the constituents." Figures like Adams ridiculed Paine's views on popular government as ignoring history and being generally "very ignorant of the Science of Government."

The conflict between Adams and Paine was complex and went beyond their different visions for an American democracy. Despite his early admiration for *Common Sense*, Adams quickly became jealous of Paine's success and criticized him as someone who had just arrived in America. Adams was notoriously envious of the attention given others, including Jefferson, but Paine was too much for the native son of Massachusetts.

Everything about Paine must have grated on Adams: his instant fame, his legacy of failures and bankruptcies, his drinking, his irreligious writings. He was the Adams antipode in virtually every respect. Adams also expressed concern over how Paine was enflaming the public and feared that popular impulse could overwhelm logical action. Paine dismissed "complex government" in favor of empowering more direct democratic action by citizens. That included favoring unicameral, popular forms of governance without the moderating elements favored by Madison.

Madison ended up in the middle of the two revolutionary figures with strikingly different fears about the new constitutional system. Where Paine rejected Madison's "precautions" as inhibiting popular government, Adams questioned Madison's ability to control popular will. A form of aristocracy was appealing if the alternative was anarchy. Adams wrote Benjamin Rush that "I am clear that America must resort to [hereditary rule] as an Asylum against Discord Seditions and Civil War, and that at no very distant period of time. I shall not live to see it—but you may." It was an ironic prediction from a president who would be followed by his son as president. Paine opposed the checks of an "upper house." In response, Adams warned that a unicameral legislature would be "so democratical, without any restraint or even an attempt at any equilibrium or counterpoise, that it must produce confusion and every evil work." Adams's fellow Massachusetts delegate Elbridge Gerry reported the same experience in their state with those who acted out of a "levilling [*sic*] spirit" in pursuing popular agendas:

> The evils we experience flow from the excess of democracy. The people do not want virtue, but are the dupes of pretended patriots. In Massts., it has been fully confirmed by experience that they are daily misled into the most baneful measures and opinions by the false reports circulated by designing men.

Gerry's criticism of the "levelling spirit" in Massachusetts was likely a reference to the role of "Levellers" in England who sought greater democratic powers—a movement that produced the instability leading to not just Cromwell's rise to power but ultimately the return of the monarchy. Yet he was also raising an experience not unlike that of the Pennsylvania delegates, including most notably James Wilson. The turmoil with the early state constitutions weighed heavily on many in the Constitutional Convention. In 1787, Edmund Randolph stated as governor of Virginia that "our chief danger arises from the democratic parts of our constitutions" and that state constitutions were undermined by their lack of "sufficient checks against the democracy." Some also blamed recent violence like Shays' Rebellion of poor farmers in Massachusetts on "overly democratic state government."

Madison did have faith in the ability of a free people to govern themselves when their energies were properly directed and harnessed. He believed that the right system of government could foster not just compromise but common sense. While a student at the College of New Jersey (now Princeton), Madison was taught by John Witherspoon, a minister and later signer of the Declaration of Independence. Witherspoon was a believer in the Scottish school of Common Sense Realism. Madison believed that simple majoritarian rule would breed nothing but abuse. By framing legislative choices, he believed that better senses and virtues could prevail. It was not just bicameralism, but the specific framing of the two houses that would achieve that goal.

Where the ancient Greeks saw the *demos* as a "collectivized monarch," Madison saw an alternative in a tripartite system exercising representational powers. If there is a single overriding purpose to the Madisonian system, it is to prevent the concentration of power in any one person or one branch. That purpose was achieved through the division of powers in a system of checks and balances to avoid what Jefferson described as "an elective despotism," which he noted "was not the government we fought for." Instead, he said that citizens had learned from experience that the best government could be found in authority "divided and balanced among several bodies of magistracy, as that no one could transcend their legal limits, without being effectively checked and restrained by the others." Madison believed that the division of governmental authority on multiple levels (including through federalism) created a "compound republic" that would serve as a "double security" for the rights of citizens. Notably, one of Madison's greatest regrets was that he failed to secure one additional check in this compound republic: a national veto of state legislation. Madison was well aware of the factional interests raging on the state level as well as the ability of states to target minority rights. He wanted the national government to be able to check such abusive measures, but the "federal negative" proved arguably his greatest loss in the drafting of the Constitution.

The opposition to the unicameral system was a direct outgrowth of the historical view of the framers of assemblies stretching from Athens to Philadelphia. Meeting in Philadelphia, the delegates were not only in a state that utilized a unicameral system since 1703 (though with an executive council), but the Constitutional Convention itself was itself a type of unicameral body. The more recent experience in Pennsylvania did not particularly recommend the model. The single-house system allowed for limited regulation or translation of popular impulses. It was, according to Adams, a model that invited "all of the vices, follies, and frailties of an individual." With the bicameral system used in England, Madison hoped to further diffuse power by giving members strikingly different political interests. He sought to force different constituencies and interests to seek a majoritarian compromise in the legislative process.

Called "the People's House," the House of Representatives was expected to be the most responsive to the demands of the public. While their views were still filtered through representatives, the two-year terms and smaller districts guaranteed that House members would be quick to act on public demands. The shorter terms of the House appealed to Paine as enhancing democratic power. Paine believed that frequent elections would never allow members to become too distant or insulated: "the elected might by that means return and mix again with the general body of the electors." In this way, Paine hoped to preserve the "fidelity to the public."

The senators, on the other hand, had broader, statewide interests and longer political agendas given their six-year terms. It is worth noting that, while Madison rejected the unicameral model in the "New Jersey Plan," Madison initially supported the Virginia Plan, which had a very different upper house. Under the Virginia plan, both houses would have been apportioned according to population. Instead, the Senate was approved with the further limitation on majoritarian power by giving every state the same two-seat representation. Ultimately, the Senate was intended (and often has functioned) as a brake on public impulse. That restraint on public impulse was precisely why some like Paine opposed the upper house as inviting a type of American aristocracy. Others saw a critical difference in the emerging country. One writer calling himself Democritus wrote in the *Virginia Gazette* that there was a difference between a natural and a hereditary aristocracy. In the United States, in other words, the privileged class is composed of those who attained their position through merit and success. It is notable that even a Son of Liberty like Samuel Adams referred to the dream of establishing a "Christian Sparta." While clearly a reference to the famed Spartan civic virtue, it is notable that he did not cite Athens, but instead referenced an oligarchy as the ideal system.

Madison was using human impulse to protect liberty. He saw this tripartite system as holding together by using "ambition . . . to counteract ambition." The interests of individual actors within each branch would prevent the concentration of power that had been the death of liberty in past systems. At the same time, these different political interests within the legislative branch tended to force compromise, which would then be subject to the decision of the president, who was accountable to a national constituency with a four-year term. These different elements could produce sharply different perspectives on national problems and their solutions. Madison sought to create a system that captured the energy of democracy while achieving the stability of a monarchy or aristocracy. Adams observed that history had shown that "hereditary succession was attended with fewer evils than frequent elections." The Madisonian system relies on a type of aristocracy that Tocqueville would later credit as a reason for the stability of the American democracy. Tocqueville noted that, while aristocracies lack equity, they offer remarkable stability as a bulwark against despotism. The power of aristocrats often made it difficult for tyrants to take hold of countries by supplanting such powerful and fixed interests. For Madison, the Senate could achieve much of that benefit without a hereditary aristocratic class.

There was one other outstanding component to the Madisonian system that spoke directly to the disorder in Philadelphia and other cities. Madison sought to address the role of factions in destabilizing systems without suppressing them. He viewed factions as more dangerous when ignored or marginalized. Madison also considered factional interests to be natural, or at least inevitable, in a free society. In Federalist 10, Madison explained, "By a faction, I understand a number of citizens, whether amounting to a majority or a minority of the whole, who are united and actuated by some common impulse of passion, or of interest, adversed to the rights of other citizens, or to the permanent and aggregate interests of the community." Madison repeatedly referenced factions as the manifestation of a natural impulse or tendency in all human beings: "The latent causes of faction are sown in the nature of man; and we see them brought into different degrees of activity, according to the different circumstances of civil society." Because of the natural impulse to create such alliances and associations, Madison believed that "the causes of factions cannot be removed." Instead, factions had to be assumed and addressed in any viable model of government. While factions are often discussed as small groups or subsets of a population, they can include majoritarian factions. Indeed, the most dangerous faction is one created by the majority itself since "the form of popular government . . . enables it to sacrifice to its ruling passion or interest both the public good and the rights of other citizens."

The Madisonian system allows factional interests to rise to the surface where they can be addressed and, ideally, moderated in the form of legislative compromises. At the same time, he drafted a strikingly countermajoritarian document in the Bill of Rights to protect individuals from majoritarian tyranny. These layers of divisions and rivaling interests worked to block the greatest danger to liberty in the concentration of power in the hands of any one branch or individual. Madison sought to unleash the energy of democracies while constraining the inherent forces of self-destruction. The first test of this system would come in the very city where the Constitution was crafted. When the framers finally worked out the details of the Constitution on September 17, 1781, the draft was sent to the states for ratification. In the still-simmering streets of Pennsylvania, ratification was far from a certainty. Yet, roughly three months later in Philadelphia, not only would a state-ratified constitution emerge, but also a new people united by a constitutional republic.

The Miracle of Philadelphia: The Ratification Riot and the Return to Reason

The adoption of the Constitution shifted these debates over popular versus representative government to the states and their ratification conventions. The Constitution was not uniformly celebrated. Once again, Philadelphia was a microcosm of the national debate. Anti-Federalists saw the Constitution as creating a new menace to liberty in the form of a central federal government. The rhetoric became more amplified and extreme, with some calling it "[an] instrument of oppression, injustice, and tyranny" and referring to the proposed government as "the engine of slavery." Another called it an "aristocratic delusion." While most citizens recognized the need for a stronger central government after the Articles of Confederation, writers charged that the Constitution was a bait and switch for those who fought the Revolution to empower the states and resist central controls. Some objected that the delegates rejected the model of popular government. One article in the *Carlisle Gazette* denounced the "designing and artful Federalists" and declared that "little less than the lives of their betrayers will satiate their revenge."

Elbridge Gerry was one of the most powerful voices in the Constitutional Convention who warned about the perils of democratic despotism. He would ultimately refuse to sign the Constitution due to its lack of a Bill of Rights. Back in Massachusetts, the Federalists moved to block Gerry as a delegate to the state convention. He was eventually allowed to come to the convention, but only to answer questions and not to otherwise speak. A dominance of Federalists in states like Massachusetts was becoming more evident, as was the growing tensions between the two groups. It was a foreshadowing of the conflicts that would emerge between Adams and Jefferson, particularly in the abusive prosecutions under the Alien and Sedition Acts.

In Carlisle (outside of Philadelphia) on December 26, 1787, a familiar scene unfolded. Anti-Federalists grew increasingly angry at the sight of crowds praising the Pennsylvania ratification of the Constitution. A pro-Constitution rally was planned for that day with a bonfire and a cannon brought in from a nearby town to fire thirteen times in celebration. The celebrants were met by an anti-Federalist mob with clubs and other weapons. A Federalist in Carlisle, John Montgomery, likely offered the most accurate account of the views of these anti-Federalists, stating that the rioters declared that "[Federalists] are enemies to equal liberty, and that they are in favor of the Constitution, because they expect to be enabled under it to make dependents of the farmers, who will be reduced to a sort of vassalage." After an effort to convince the mob to leave failed, the confrontation turned violent and a melee ensued. Not to be deterred, the celebrants returned the next day with muskets and fired their cannon in celebration. One observer described how "the Federalists remained 2 hours on the ground, testified their joy, with every appearance of harmony and good humor." Tellingly, the next day, the anti-Federalists also gathered to hang and burn a familiar effigy. It was, of course, James Wilson. (A second effigy of Chief Justice Thomas McKean was also burned.) While Wilson was often targeted for his business interests, he clearly missed the market for his own effigies since he remained the go-to persona for protests. Joseph Frazier reportedly led the crowd through the streets with the two effigies while declaring that he was "inspired by heaven." Marching in order with the "two effigies with labels on their breasts," the crowd "with shouts and most dreadful execrations committed them to the flames."

After the ratification riot, Federalists demanded the arrest of those responsible for the assaults on Federalists and general public disorder. The Pennsylvania Supreme Court issued warrants for twenty-three anti-Federalists. The most notable was John Jordan, presiding judge of the Cumberland County Court of Common Pleas. The men were taken before the Court of Common Pleas on February 25, 1788, and were given the choice of "parole" pending trial or to remain in jail. All but seven agreed to parole. Nevertheless, on March 1, 1788, an anti-Federalist mob seized the courthouse. One commentator rallied others to oppose "this detestable Fedrall [*sic*] conspiracy." What happened next was surprising: Nothing happened. There was no escalation. The day after the hearing for the arrested individuals, militia groups assembled to support the accused. A Committee of Inquiry was formed and negotiations with the Federalists were held. The Federalists then agreed to jointly go to the Supreme Executive Council to ask for all charges to be dropped. That was the end of the ratification riot in Carlisle.

One cannot claim that the nascent Madisonian system had proven its stabilizing effect. After all, the new Constitution was not even fully ratified and was the sole cause of the riot. That said, there was a change in the trajectory of not just this confrontation but others around the city. There was no longer a sense of a vacuum of power, of a revolutionary government careening out of control. Radicals and Republicans alike were yielding to authority. For better or worse, citizens understood that they had a new political framework for their grievances. Of course, the familiar image of James Wilson was again burning in effigy, but the days of rolling out the cannon to level his home had passed. In the coming years, a few "rebellions" like the Whiskey Rebellion would still occur in rural Pennsylvania over taxes and other grievances. However, Constitutionalists, Republicans, Federalists, and anti-Federalists were beginning to resemble a nation; they were beginning to act as Americans invested in a single political system. It was the true end of the revolutionary period and the start of the constitutional period in the United States.

The growing stability in the country was a vindication of Madison. His view of factional impulses and the ambitions of governmental actors often leads to his portrayal as something of a pessimist or cynic. The opposite could be true. Madison believed that, when democracies are properly bracketed and controlled, a free people are capable of tremendous advances. He believed that there is an innate common sense, to use Paine's famous tagline, that can emerge when citizens are funneled into a deliberative political process. After the ratification of the Constitution, more and more Americans became invested in a system that allowed expression of factional interests while promoting majoritarian compromise. Madison's optimism was based on his belief in the inalienable rights embraced by the Declaration of Independence. If those rights are part of the natural condition of humanity, their denial leaves humans incomplete and unsatisfied. What Madison wanted was to protect those rights by protecting citizens from themselves. Madison believed that "if the majority be united by a common purpose," the minority could find its rights contingent on majoritarian whim. The brutality of the state of nature was that neither safety nor property was protected. Madison shared the Hobbesian view of how humans were denied God-given rights in the absence of organized government. The counter-majoritarian protections of the Constitution would prevent the American democracy from devouring itself. Philadelphia was showing that the United States was becoming less of a revolution and more of a nation. Citizens would gradually embrace a common article of faith in the Constitution.

Where Madison would see his ideas vindicated, Paine would see many of his ideas (and himself) vilified. After the American Revolution, Paine returned to England in 1787 to spread the gospel of democratic reform. His mission and style were aptly captured in the title of his next publication: *Prospects on the Rubicon: or, an investigation into the Causes and Consequences of the Politics to be Agitated at the Meeting of Parliament*. He "agitated" against the war with France and heralded the French Revolution—a counterfoil to the equally gifted writer Edmund Burke, who denounced the Jacobin movement and revolution. A cartoon from 1793 by James Gillray shows Paine tightening the corset of Britannia (a mocking reference to Paine's origins as a mere corset maker). Notably, peeking out of his back pocket is a measuring tape with the name of his next work, *Rights of Man*.

Rights of Man was Paine's roaring reply to Edmund Burke's *Reflections on the Revolution in France*, a staunch defense of aristocratic traditions and a condemnation of the popular democratic theories behind the French Revolution. Paine's second book sold close to a million copies despite being a full-length book rather than his signature pamphlet length. That was followed up in 1792 with *Rights of Man, Part the Second, Combining Principle and Practice*. The sequel publication was reduced in price to guarantee a greater circulation and laid bare the economic injustice and systemic poverty faced by common people. Attacking hereditary government and calling for reforms in England, Paine warned in the preface that this work was "written in a style of thinking and expression different to what had been customary in England." Indeed, it was. This time the government moved in advance to threaten Paine's publishers, including one that immediately pulled the publication to avoid charges. Public readings of the work were shut down by police, and officers conducted house-by-house "loyalty canvasses" where residents were asked to pledge their loyalty to the King and opposition to Paine. Publisher Richard Phillips was sentenced to a year and a half for selling the work. Paine was burned in effigy and treated as sin incarnate by critics insisting that his work was an instruction "from Satan to Citizen Paine." It failed to prevent the publication. *Rights of Man* caused a sensation for its anti-monarchal elements, which led to demands for reforms from the left—and prosecutions from the right. Paine's appeal to the common man led to a torrent of opposition with a notable classist accent. The book was denounced as "desultory, uncouth, and inelegant" as well as a work "written with the logic of shoemakers and the metaphysics of barbers." Even fellow revolutionaries believed that Paine had gone too far with his radical ideas. Gouverneur Morris wrote:

> I read Paine's publication today, and tell him that I am really afraid he will be punished. He seems to laugh at this, and relies on the force he has in the nation. He seems to become every hour more drunk with self-conceit. It seems, however, that this work excites but little emotion, and rather raises indignation.

There was a palpable fear that Paine's brand of common sense would unleash the common folk and radical demands. For example, Whig Christopher Wyvill warned that Paine was threatening to light a fire "among the lower classes of the people, by holding out to them the prospect of plundering the rich."

Paine was charged with seditious libel and fled. It was a wise move. While Paine wanted to stand trial and even appeared for a later postponed hearing, his critics worked the public into a frenzy against him by burning effigies and demonizing him in publications. Even the young poet William Blake beseeched Paine to take flight given the poisonous environment. The May 14, 1792, summons for Paine to appear to answer the charges describes him as "Thomas Paine, late of London, gentleman, being a wicked, malicious, seditious, and ill-disposed person, and being greatly disaffected to our said Sovereign Lord the now King, and to the happy constitution and government of this kingdom." The order for his arrest arrived at Dover just twenty minutes after his departure for France. When he boarded the *Quay* bound for Calais, he was followed by the now ever-present mob of hecklers spewing insults and threats. Paine was tried and convicted in absentia. Nevertheless, the book was another bestseller for which Paine received little in profits. (Notably, by the end of 1792,

Rights of Man had sold over 200,000 copies while Burke's *Reflections* sold only 30,000 in two years.) It went through four printings in a fortnight, and Paine shared his elation with Gouverneur Morris, who dryly wrote in his diary that "he seems cocksure of bringing about a revolution in Great Britain and I think it quite as likely that he will be promoted to the pillory."

After fleeing Great Britain before an arrest for sedition, Paine was greeted in Paris as a virtual democratic deity. In contrast to the mob in Dover, the French cheered "Long Live Thomas Paine" as he disembarked, and a woman pinned a cockade on his hat. This failed corset maker and destitute writer would take up residence in the Palace of Versailles. For a time, Paine was sought after for salons and societies alike, writing, "I find myself no stranger in France, people know me almost as generally here as in America." He had met Lafayette for the first time in Philadelphia in 1780, but soon reestablished the friendship and became part of Lafayette's intellectual and political circle. Unlike his experience in seeking revolution in America, revolution seemed to find Paine in France.

Paine was given French citizenship and elected to the National Convention as representative for the Pas-de-Calais, even though he could not actually speak directly to his constituents since he did not speak French. The early respect for the American revolutionaries was so great that other American leaders such as James Madison and George Washington were also given honorary French citizenship. Paine saw himself as replicating what began in the United States with a promise to "share with you the dangers and honors necessary to success." He was now fifty-five, older than most of the delegates, and was viewed as a type of oracle from the fount of modern democracy. He honestly believed that France would be the next major step to "blot despotism from the earth and fix, on the lasting principles of peace and citizenship, the great republic of man."

In truth, the miracle of the age was already unfolding around Paine. Despite the inauspicious start in Philadelphia and Carlisle, the implementation of a new constitution with republican safeguards would have a transformative effect. What once seemed like a nation careening toward its own mobocracy became a stable republic. On July 4, 1788, nine years after the attack on his home and just a couple weeks after final ratification of the Constitution, James Wilson would ascend a giant float that was thirty-six feet high and composed of thirteen columns called the Grand Federal Edifice. It was designed by none other than the artist Peale, who had years before supported the radical groups in Philadelphia that led to the attack on Wilson's home. The scene captured the very stability that Wilson had envisioned, though not quite the tranquility, as ships in the harbor missed their cue and fired their celebratory cannons before Wilson could finish his remarks. For those who could hear over the cannon fire, Wilson reminded his fellow citizens that the "Fall of Rome" was due to the loss of civic virtues, including "temperance." To lose such "simple and powerful virtues," he warned, would leave the United States to the same fate as the ancient republics. In Philadelphia, a free people had overcome violent divisions to accept a form of stable, mixed governance. The American democracy would outlive the two years of the Athenian democracy and serve as a model for centuries.

Wilson's words reflected an undying faith in this American experiment in self-governance. Of all the framers who lived through the Revolution and its aftermath, Wilson had the most reason to have a crisis of faith after he and his family were forced into hiding to avoid vigilante justice. Yet he remained firm in his conviction that this young nation would mature and flourish. His cautionary words were more of a challenge to his fellow citizens in the same sense of Benjamin Franklin's famous warning that they had created a republic "if you can keep it." By investing power in the people, you also give them the power for their own destruction, even in a representative system. It is a warning that would grow more salient in the coming years as another revolution would spin violently out of control. It would be Thomas Paine who would witness democracy unmodified and unrestrained. It would come close to killing him.

Six

PARIS

The French Revolution and the Razor of the Republic

In the early 1800s, Abbé Emmanuel Joseph Sieyès was asked what he had done during the Revolution. It was a simple question that suggested a more complex answer. Sieyès was the author of the famous pamphlet *What Is the Third Estate?* As such, he could be viewed as the Thomas Paine of the French Revolution, giving the movement one of its most cited manifestos. The old abbot pondered the question and finally responded, "*J'ai vécu*" ("I survived").

The chilling response from one of the critical figures of the French Revolution captured the nightmare that unfolded as a republic devolved into democratic despotism. For figures like Paine, it was a crushing disappointment from a revolution that they believed would unleash an age of reason. The French National Convention even ordered a new calendar to reflect how the world had changed or, more accurately, been reborn. It decreed that 1792 (when the French Republic was established) would be Year 1 for the new age. Tragically, Year 1 would lead not to the elevation of humanity but a brutal struggle of mere survival for every person in France. It was the very historical pattern that the framers sought to avoid and confirmed their worst expectations. Only a few years earlier, Edmund Randolph warned that "our chief danger arises from the democratic parts of our constitutions. It is a maxim which I hold incontrovertible, that the powers of government exercised by the people swallows up the other branches." Rufus King was even harsher in his appraisal that "the great body of the people are without virtue and are not governed by any internal restraints of conscience." King was proven wrong in one critical respect: The greatest danger revealed by the French Revolution is when a great body of people commit atrocities out of virtue. Cheering the thousands of beheadings were the world's most virtuous and murderous citizens. It was that very claim of virtue that relieved the need for restraint.

Sieyès wrote his work just after the drafting of the U.S. Constitution, and it appeared the same year as its ratification in 1789. It was enormously successful, with hundreds of thousands of copies distributed throughout France. Sieyès demanded that the Third Estate (composed of the common people) should govern alone and denounced the two other estates—the clergy and aristocracy—as parasitic and illegitimate. Since they voted separately as bodies, the power of the

Third Estate was diluted much in the same way as the division of power in Athens, where aristocrats or oligarchs ultimately controlled outcomes. Sieyès declared:

> Who then shall dare to say that the Third Estate has not within itself all that is necessary for the formation of a complete nation? It is the strong and robust man who has one arm still shackled. If the privileged order should be abolished, the nation would be nothing less, but something more. Therefore, what is the Third Estate? Everything; but an everything shackled and oppressed. What would it be without the privileged order? Everything, but an everything free and flourishing. Nothing can succeed without it, everything would be infinitely better without the others.

It was the direct rejection of the American model of mixed government. Sieyès saw the working class as capable of assuming direct and largely unfiltered control after centuries of monarchial and aristocratic governance.

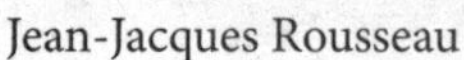

Jean-Jacques Rousseau

Voltaire

The writings of Sieyès are reminiscent of the views of the Constitutionalists in Philadelphia, who chafed at efforts to moderate popular government with an "upper house" or "auxiliary precautions." In the United States, the revolutionaries quickly divided between the visions of Paine and Madison, those who wanted to unleash or to limit popular democratic will. In France, there was a similar dichotomous divide between two towering figures: Rousseau and Voltaire. Indeed, it is often said that there were two French revolutions: the establishment of a republic and the "Terror" that followed it. Each of the revolutions reflected the different visions of these two philosophers: The first revolution was Voltairean, while the second revolution was Rousseauian.

François-Marie Arouet, who later adopted the name Voltaire, wrote eloquently of traditional liberal values of free thought and constitutional government. He spent almost a year as a prisoner in the Bastille for writing about the alleged incest of the Regent, Philippe II, Duke of Orléans, with his daughter. Despite his writings in favor of democratic principles, Voltaire did not embrace the notion of a large democratic system, noting that "Democracy is only suitable for a very small country." He supported the concept of a constitutional monarchy, which put him out of favor with many of the radical Jacobins. He believed that the government needed to protect the individual and the essential rights of free thought and speech. His concerns over democratic despotism would be proven correct time and time again throughout history, including by the French Revolution. Voltaire believed in constitutional systems that permitted democratic choice while recognizing the dangers of unrestrained popular will. For many, the first revolution was the achievement of a constitutional monarchy with enhanced but balanced democratic elements. It was celebrated throughout the world, as reflected in a dispatch from the Duke of Dorset on July 16, 1789: "the greatest revolution . . . has been effected with the loss of very few lives: from this moment we may consider France as a free country, the King as a very limited Monarch, and the Nobility as reduced to a level with the rest of the Nation." Where the first revolution was largely between the bourgeoisie against the aristocracy, the second revolution was the commoners prevailing over the bourgeoisie.

Rousseau was a writer and philosopher who came originally from Geneva, Switzerland. The son of a watchmaker, with a mother from the upper classes, Rousseau wrote novels and political works with equal skill. Rousseau was wildly popular not just for his political treatises but for works like *Nouvelle Héloïse*, discussing love and marital devotion. While he wrote of the natural goodness of man, his own life was far from inspirational, including the effective abandonment of his children. He had a unique and moving writing style. His seminal work, *The Social Contract*, became a touchstone of the Enlightenment, espousing the natural and noble tendency of a free people to achieve justice through their "general will." *The Social Contract* begins with the famous line "Man is born free; and everywhere he is in chains." Rousseau appealed most to figures like Paine due to his faith in the wisdom of the public acting collectively in government. It was a sharp contrast with other popular writers of the time. For example, both Hobbes and Rousseau portray humans as emerging from a state of nature with the creation of a social contract. Where Hobbes saw citizens surrendering their rights to a powerful ruler in *Leviathan*, Rousseau saw them as ruling through "the general will." The faith in the general will was based on Rousseau's faith in the nature of human beings and the "innate benevolence for my fellow man." He believed that, once free of corrupting institutions, the natural virtue and goodness of humanity would prevail. Hobbes's sovereign would give them a better life; Rousseau's general will would make them better people. Rousseau believed that this enlightened stage would emerge naturally and "it is important therefore in order to state the general will that there exist no partial associations within the state." Those "partial associations" were taken as opposing factions, which would be deemed opposed to the general will and, therefore, the people. Rousseau treated the authority and righteousness of this popular "sovereign" as self-evident and self-authenticating: "The Sovereign, being formed wholly of the individuals who compose it, neither has nor can have any interest contrary to theirs; and consequently the sovereign power need give no guarantee to its subjects, because it is impossible for the body to wish to hurt all its members." Yet, under Rousseau's approach, the general will would actually be implemented through a minority of leaders. Rousseau's faith in human nature was only magnified in his faith of those leaders:

> To discover the best rules of society appropriate to the Nations . . . it would take a superior intelligence, who sees all human passions and who does not experience any of them, who would have no connection with our nature and who would know it to the core, whose happiness would be independent of us and yet who would be willing to take care of ours.

This role for beneficent leaders would ultimately be filled by figures like Marat and Robespierre. While Rousseau saw "unanimity" in support of the general will, it would be achieved on the razor's edge of the guillotine.

Rousseau's political writings were often eloquent and emotive, but could also be vague and naïve. Hannah Arendt pointedly noted:

> Not that Rousseau, or Robespierre for that matter, had ever experienced the innate goodness of natural man outside society; they deduced his existence from the corruption of society, much as one who has intimate knowledge of rotten apples may account for their rottenness by assuming the original existence of healthy ones.

Where Madison saw factions as an inevitable part of political dialogue and deliberation, Rousseau saw them as a denial of the common good. It was Rousseau's generalizations and assumptions that would draw criticism from Voltaire, who called him merely a "cunning phrasemaker." Voltaire also opposed despotism and sought greater democratic governance, but he would continue to deride Rousseau's ideas. While defending Rousseau's right to publish his views, Voltaire mocked them. When *The Social Contract* had been burned in Geneva, Voltaire would write that it would have been better for the government to simply "ignore" the book, since "The operation of burning it was perhaps as odious as that of writing it. [. . .] To burn a book of argument is to say: 'We do not have enough wit to reply to it.'" The contempt shown by Voltaire for his work clearly wounded

Rousseau, who once viewed him as a friend. On June 17, 1760, he wrote Voltaire:

> I don't like you, monsieur. To me, your disciple and enthusiast, you have done the most painful injuries. . . . You have alienated my fellow citizens from me as a reward for the praises I gave you among them. It is you who make it unbearable for me to live in my own country; you who will compel me to die on foreign soil, deprived of all the consolations of the dying, and thrown dishonored upon some refuse heap, while all the honors that a man can expect will attend you in my native land. In short, I hate you, since you have willed it so; but I hate you with the feelings of one still capable of loving you, if you had desired it.

Of course, Rousseau would not be "deprived of all the consolations of the dying" or be "thrown dishonored upon some refuse heap" in his own country. He would be deified by a revolution that turned his writings into a virtual cult of the general will. The Reign of Terror would prove the "rotten fruit of Rousseauism."

The reverence for Rousseau would go beyond his treatment as "divine man" and eventually reach "Christ-like magnitude" for French revolutionaries. (Ironic references for the author who advocated the creation of a "civil religion.") Fortunately, Rousseau did not live to see the Terror or could well have met the fate of many of his truest disciples who did not survive the experience. Robespierre would invoke him like divine authority for every excess: "Ah! if he had witnessed this revolution of which he was the precursor . . . who can doubt that his generous soul would have embraced with rapture the cause of justice and equality?" It is hard to imagine Rousseau embracing the blood-soaked legacy of his work. After all, as a young man, Rousseau had reportedly declared "never to be party to any civil war, and never to uphold domestic freedom with arms." Conversely, Rousseau also wrote of the release that comes with revolution. He noted that nations will experience "periods of violence . . . when revolutions do to peoples what certain crises do to individuals, when the horror of the past takes the place of forgetting, and when the State aflame with civil wars is so to speak reborn from its ashes and recovers the vigor of youth as it escapes death's embrace."

Luminaries and authors took pilgrimages to his tomb on the Isle of Poplars in Ermenonville, France, including one who committed suicide near the tomb to be buried near his idol. A bust of Rousseau and a copy of *The Social Contract* were given a place of honor in the National Assembly. Soldiers were handed pocket copies of *The Social Contract* to inspire them to fight for the country. He would be cited by both sides of the Revolution, including influential figures like the Marquis de Condorcet, a mathematician and philosopher who would help lead the opposition to the most radical Jacobins. Extremists like Marat also used Rousseau to justify every abuse in the name of the general will, including confiscations and the redistribution of wealth. Rousseau's rhetoric was ideal for fueling a class war. For example, many cited his *Second Discourse*, where Rousseau warned that the poor had to be weary of the machinations of the wealthy to maintain legal systems that served to protect property rather than liberty.

For radicals in France, the United States supplied a blueprint for revolution, but Rousseau supplied the cause. The blind faith of figures like Sieyès in popular government allowed them to dismiss restraints in the name of the general will. Those who would celebrate the first Revolution would face the "horrible tyranny" that would emerge in the name of civil virtue. In the end, Sieyès would experience the same crisis of faith as his fellow pamphleteer Paine.

Citizen Paine in the "Age of Revolutions"

Drenched in sweat and burning with fever, Thomas Paine lay on a dirty blanket over wet straw in a dark makeshift cell. His eyes were transfixed on the cell door that had been pushed open against the inside wall. Through the thin slivers of light breaking through the boarded-up windows, he stared at a hastily written number in white chalk on the door: 4. Paine and his three Belgian cellmates knew exactly what it meant. In the night, guards would take the prisoners to be guillotined. It was part of the macabre routine of Luxembourg Prison during the French Revolution. That night, the four were marked for death.

The author of *Common Sense* had all night to contemplate one of the strangest and most improbable journeys in history, from rallying his countrymen to the cause of the American Revolution to being declared an enemy of the common man in the French Revolution. He now held the distinction of facing sedition charges in all three countries with which he is most associated: Great Britain, the United States, and France. With his return to Europe, Paine's business misfortunes resumed with a vengeance. During his time in Great Britain in 1789, he was even briefly held in a debtors' prison until associates paid his debt from a failed business enterprise. (He would be sent briefly back to the prison on another unpaid bill in 1792.) Both Royalists and revolutionaries had come to despise him with equal intensity. The man who had spoken for millions was alone save for three fellow prisoners who sought to make him as comfortable as possible before his execution. Paine had proven again that he was a man easier to admire from afar.

Paine's journey to the Luxembourg Prison began not long after his heroic return to France in 1792. What Paine saw in France reinforced his vision of a noble cause. The citizens had a legitimate reason to rise up against the Royalists given their long suppression in terms of both wealth and power. These grievances would have been all too familiar to Americans. It was again economic conditions that brought long-simmering tensions to the point of rebellion. There was even a tax that unified different groups in France as there had been in the colonies, though it was salt, not tea, that outraged the citizenry. The salt tax laid bare the inefficiencies and unfairness of the French system. It was based on a royal monopoly that was leased to private entities to enforce. Stamps (or *traits*) were also used to extract revenue from other basic items like tobacco. It was a grossly inefficient system that reinforced the wealth of the aristocracy. Taxes were regressive and compounded by exemptions for aristocracy and clergy. That left the lower classes to pay the *taille*, or tax. In the meantime, church tithes kept bishops in conspicuous luxury. The King spent 5 percent of the annual revenue on the maintenance of the royal household. With $4.9 trillion in tax revenue in 2024, it is the equivalent of President Joe Biden spending over $245 billion on the White House and other household expenses. In the meantime, as the royal family rested in the splendor of Versailles, the annual harvest in 1788 was a disaster, causing food riots and, much like in Philadelphia, failed efforts at price-fixing.

The result was a teetering monarchy maintained through runaway deficit spending. The debt burden was compounding with the interest. Ironically, the support of the King for the American Revolution only hastened the end of the monarchy. The French government saw the United States as a critical strategic opportunity. After the defeat in the Seven Years' War, the American Revolution was viewed as the perfect foil to use against its longtime adversary, Great Britain. It also curried favor with the growing number of citizens who rallied to the American cause. France spent an astonishing 1.3 billion livres on the war. When combined with existing debt, it pushed the Crown near bankruptcy as the economy moved toward a total meltdown. In that sense, the American Revolution became both a political and economic catalyst for the collapse of the monarchy.

A year before Paine's arrival, King Louis XVI was informed by the comptroller-general of the royal finances, Charles-Alexandre de Calonne, that the country was close to an economic calamity. The problem was not just debt, even though it was now consuming a quarter of royal revenues. The problem was insufficient revenue due to the inefficient market and taxation systems. Calonne knew that France needed a free market that allowed competition without the system of tariffs and internal controls.

He had to reduce both the debt and expenditures to avoid catastrophe. That required the aristocracy and the clergy to yield their privilege. Some were willing to do so, but the aristocracy wanted greater authority in the government. The stalemate led to the sacking of a series of comptrollers until King Louis XVI had no choice but to summon the Estates General. It was too late; conditions had reached a flashpoint and citizens were in the streets. They soon headed for the Bastille.

The storming of the Bastille is a historical event celebrated annually and depicted in literature and the arts as the defining moment of liberty. It is an image of simple citizens throwing themselves against a well-armed fortress to free the prisoners within. It was a moment captured by Victor Hugo in *Les Misérables*:

> An enormous fortress of prejudices, privileges, superstitions, lies, exactions, abuses, violences, iniquities, and darkness still stands erect in this world, with its towers of hatred. It must be cast down. This

> monstrous mass must be made to crumble. To conquer at Austerlitz is grand; to take the Bastille is immense.

Paine and others saw the fall of the Bastille as the rise of a new humanity in the Age of Enlightenment. He declared, "The downfall of [the Bastille] included the idea of downfall of despotism." For Paine, it was a spontaneous outburst of liberty; he described how the fortress "was attacked with an enthusiasm of heroism, such only as the highest animation of liberty could inspire." Paine would tell Washington that "the principles of America opened the Bastille" and that his ability to "share in two revolutions is living to some purpose." Lafayette would later give Paine the key to the Bastille, and Paine in turn gave it to Washington with a note reading, "I feel myself happy in being the person thro' whom the Marquis has conveyed his early trophy of the spoils of despotism, and the first ripe fruits of American principles transplanted into Europe to his master and patron." The key proved to be a trophy of a different kind, and the Revolution would yield a very different fruit.

The portrayal of the Bastille shows how mythic elements can (and still) distort history. Much like Athenian democracy, the artistic imagery often outstrips the historical reality. In the above painting, the mythic elements are pronounced. The revolutionaries are shown opening cells filled with horrific scenes of the skeletal remains of prisoners as an elderly and frail man is led gently up the stairs to freedom and sunlight. The truth is far less uplifting and foreshadowed the bloodshed to come. For Louis XVI, the belated effort to compromise had come far too late to avoid what was to come. When the Duke of La Rochefoucauld informed the King of the fall of the Bastille, the

King responded, "*C'est une révolte?*" but the duke ominously replied, "*Non, Sire, c'est une révolution.*"

In the days leading up to July 14, 1789, the food shortage and overtaxation were coming to a head. Customs houses and barriers were burned and the mob raided the Invalides military hospital to seize weapons and powder. Hundreds marched on the Bastille. They were immediately joined by Bastille guards defecting to their ranks. With its thick and high walls, the defenders held a superior position. They could have potentially held out while delivering massive casualties, but the governor of the Bastille, Bernard-René de Launay, sought to negotiate a surrender. His entreaties fell on deaf ears. The blood of the mob was up, particularly after the initial exchange of fire left roughly one hundred wounded among the attackers. De Launay sent out a note offering to surrender the fortress and all its weapons and gunpowder if the attackers would guarantee the safety of his men. He added, "Unless you accept our surrender we will blow up the entire quarter and the garrison." The attackers refused to offer any quarter or mercy to the defenders. The threat was a bluff, and soon the drawbridge was lowered in the likely hope that the surrender would return the attackers to their senses. As the host swarmed the fortress, de Launay quickly learned that mercy was not in the mind of the mob.

Unlike the image in the painting and other depictions, the prison was virtually empty and held only seven prisoners, including four forgers (Jean La Corrège, Jean Béchade, Bernard Laroche, known as Beausablon, and Jean-Antoine Pujade) and an Irish lunatic (James Francis Xavier Whyte), who variously claimed to be Julius Caesar and Jesus Christ. The sixth was ironically an aristocrat (Hubert de Solages) accused of being a "deviant" who committed "perverted sexual practices with his sister Pauline." He was a "private prisoner" supported by a pension from his family. The final prisoner (and likely the elderly man in the painting) could well be the one true political prisoner, Auguste-Claude Tavernier, who was accused of plotting to assassinate Louis XV and was incarcerated in 1757. However, Tavernier was first incarcerated at the request of his family and described as a "ferocious, cruel and insolent" person. It was hardly a parade of the liberated proletariat. What came after the release of the prisoners was gruesome. Some of the defenders were lynched or butchered outright. De Launay was quickly seized and was to be moved to the Hôtel de Ville, the city hall of Paris. He did not make it. As soon as De Launay was outside of the fortress, he was set upon by the mob with knives and swords. He stumbled forward and almost made it to the Hôtel de Ville despite bleeding from multiple wounds. Unable to take the pain, he cried out, "Enough! Let me die!" That is when an unemployed cook named Desnot tried to strike him. De Launay kicked him in the groin and Desnot screamed, "He's done me in, I'm hurt"—a bizarre claim in the face of a man who was covered in blood and wounds. Nevertheless, the crowd lurched forward, shooting de Launay with pistols and stabbing him with bayonets. Desnot, treated as the victim in this gruesome scene, was given a sword to decapitate the corpse. He was unable to completely sever the head and stopped to have wine mixed with gunpowder to give him strength. He then used a pocketknife to finish the gory duty—an act that he would later insist warranted a medal for his courage.

What followed was tragically familiar as the insatiable appetite of Saturn took hold of the liberators. The Revolution would become a virtual death cult as righteous rage justified every excess. After the fall of the Bastille, citizens ran through the streets in pursuit of other disloyal figures for summary execution. Near the top of the list was Controller-General of Finances Joseph François Foullon, seventy-four, who was notorious for his response to a question in Parliament of "what will the people do" with the worsening economic plan. Foullon replied, "The people can eat grass." Despite an effort to spread a rumor of his own death, he was found out and dragged through the streets to the Hôtel de Ville. He was hanged three times due to the rope breaking on the first two efforts. After the third rope held, he was later decapitated and grass stuffed in his mouth.

Revolutionaries saw in Rousseau's writings only what they wanted to find, often ignoring the rights of others. His writings would inspire the Declaration of the Rights of Man in 1789, which many took literally. The radical Montagnards (or the Mountain) headed by figures like Robespierre and Marat were decidedly anti-feminist and only begrudgingly allowed women to attend meetings . . . if they brought their knitting and sat quietly. Advocates of women's suffrage like Condorcet would not only fail but meet their own fatal ends at the hands of the radical Jacobins. When the Montagnards voted to supplant the moderate Constitution, they would embrace universal suffrage only for men.

Revolutionaries also found a more lethal license in Rousseau's reckless rhetoric, including passages that seemed to legitimate the notion of a cleansing revolution. In *Emile*, he stressed the potential for change that comes with "the age of revolutions":

> You trust in the present order of society without thinking that this order is subject to inevitable revolutions, and it is impossible for you to foresee or prevent the one which may affect your children. The noble become commoners, the rich become poor, the monarch becomes subject. Are the blows of fate so rare that you can count on being exempted from them? We are approaching a state of crisis and the age of revolutions. Who can answer for what will become of you then?

What "would become" of some of the avid readers of *Emile* was grotesque. It was not simply the massacres and executions, but what it did to those who yielded to the violence in the name of the general will, once moderate voices. Rousseau saw the revolutionary state as inherently good and did not seriously consider a division among the public on the proper course. Many took these words as an excuse to eschew any moderation or mercy. Before the Revolution, Danton would declare, "Woe betide those who would provoke revolutions. Woe betide those who would make them." He would live just long enough to see the prophetic wisdom of those words.

When Paine looked from across the Atlantic, France must have seemed like the next great gathering of enlightened citizens, the next domino to fall against the ancien régime. By 1792, Paine saw a different reality. The two countries could not be more different. First, French citizens had lived under a crushing, inescapable poverty that most Americans had never experienced. Most citizens lived on the razor's edge of starvation with little hope for social or economic advancement. Most importantly, American colonists had lived under a constitutional monarchy with both economic and political power held by the public. The French had known concentrated and authoritarian power that was only slightly moderated by the diffuse authority of the three estates. In coming to the colonies, Crèvecoeur wrote in his *Letters from an American Farmer* about the "pleasant uniformity" of the classes in the New World and how most have never seen the "absolute poverty worse than death" of the Old World. Two years before the French Revolution, Jefferson observed that "of twenty millions of people . . . there are nineteen millions more wretched, more accursed in every circumstance of human existence than the most conspicuously wretched individual of the whole United States." Paine famously observed that "the constitution of a country is not the act of its government, but of the people constituting a government." It is also therefore a reflection of that people. If the people have only experience with brute force or unbridled power, their constitution will likely reflect those same inclinations. Hannah Arendt stressed a sense of inevitability of the Terror from an inescapable history in France:

> Nothing, indeed, seems more natural than that a revolution should be predetermined by the type of government it overthrows; nothing, therefore, appears more plausible than to explain the new absolute, the absolute revolution, by the absolute monarchy which preceded it, and to conclude that the more absolute the ruler, the more absolute the revolution will be which replaces him.

The Revolution was truly, as sung in *Les Misérables*, "the song of angry men . . . the music of a people who will not be slaves again." Notably, that song is appropriately titled "À la volonté du peuple," or "To the Will of the People." The musical did not capture how that "will" would lead from slavery to savagery. The misery led to a sense of license for many to unleash that anger on those who for generations did not hear them. In this environment, Paine was an unfamiliar interloper who was ill-prepared for the extremism and anger of a suddenly emancipated French people. The "general will" was starkly different from the colonies. Consistent with the governments that preceded it, there was a demand for absolute measures wielded by the absolute power of the French people. While given a seat in the National Convention to represent Pas-de-Calais while he was still in England, Paine had little inkling of the needs of his "department" nor the expectations of his fellow delegates. When he finally spoke at the Convention in 1792, Paine's contrarian views quickly alienated his new hosts. The man viewed as a radical revolutionary in the United States was a moderate in France. In one of his very first statements to the National Convention, Paine notably disagreed with Jacobin leaders, including Danton, who were pushing for the immediate termination of all Bourbon officials throughout the executive, legislative, and judicial departments. He was now the voice of restraint, which was viewed by many as reactionary. For example, Paine called for exile rather than execution of Louis XVI, a proposal that was met with a "reaction of horror and indignation." Robespierre and radicals like Louis Antoine Léon de Saint-Just rejected even the need for a trial since the King's guilt was obvious and established. Claude Basire, an ally of Robespierre, would denounce Paine and Madison as "the aristocracy of half-talented writers." (Ironically, Basire would later himself be guillotined after being accused of being a reactionary and enemy of the state.) Paine had not found the new enlightenment but the old tyranny of democratic despotism.

Paine would not be the only American revolutionary labeled a dangerous reactionary in France. Paine had developed an association with Lafayette in his prior trips to Paris and then watched as the Revolution devoured this French icon. In August 1789, moderates and liberals had met at his home to work out a constitutional compromise with the Assembly. It would prove a critical and missed opportunity. The moderates were still able to push through legislation in the Assembly, and many were open to the creation of an upper house in a type of American bicameral structure. They still not only opposed the King holding any veto but also demanded a dramatic reduction of his power. The compromise was allowed to flounder. The resulting vacuum would be filled by radicals who had little interest in bicameralism or mixed governmental models. After the seizure of the King at Versailles and his removal to Paris in October 1789, those voices would drown out dissent. The second revolution was unfolding. While a constitutional monarchy would still be explored through 1792 (even after the attempted flight of Louis XVI), monarchists and moderates alike fled the country or receded into the illusory safety of country homes.

Lafayette remained committed to pulling his country back to a stable constitutional monarchy, but found himself literally caught between the mob and the monarchy in what became known as the Champ de Mars massacre in 1791. Groups like the Cordeliers Club continued to call for the complete removal of the King, while Danton and others called for protests. The resulting crowd formed on the Champ de Mars, the open green fields that stretch from the Eiffel Tower. They were largely poor Parisians and faced a military force led by Lafayette as commander of the National Guard. Only the day before, two men were hanged by protesters, and the mayor, the famed astronomer Jean Sylvain Bailly, called upon Lafayette to disperse the crowd. The next day, the crowd pelted the guard with stones. After firing warning shots, the guards fired directly into the crowd. As many as fifty lay dead in the streets. Bailly would be forced to resign. Radicals like Marat claimed hundreds were killed and their bodies tossed into the river. (Marat himself would later be guillotined on the Champ de Mars.)

Lafayette would eventually flee Paris after denouncing the radicals in a letter to the Assembly and calling for extremist parties to be shut down. Yet Lafayette remained a loyal Frenchman and, in 1792, he took command of a disorganized French military during the war with Austria. After returning to Paris to warn of a growing disaster in the war, Danton issued a warrant for his arrest and Lafayette would flee again—only to be taken prisoner in Austria. Notably, he sought to rely on his American citizenship to go to the United States, to no avail. When he eventually returned to France, he was shunned, even being denied the right to speak at the French memorials after the death of George Washington.

Despite this history, Lafayette was one of the few among his contemporaries to live to old age and remained one of the most faithful voices for constitutional norms. When he died at seventy-six on May 20, 1834, Lafayette was buried at his request under a coat of soil from Bunker Hill. The soil was sprinkled over the grave by his son, George Washington Lafayette.

The Terror: The Rise of "the Sanguinary Men"

In June 1791, Louis XVI and Queen Marie Antoinette attempted to flee to the protection of Austria. The King left behind a sixteen-page manifesto, known as "Political Testament of Louis XVI." It was a rejection of the concept of constitutional monarchy. Jean-Baptiste Drouet, a local postmaster general in Sainte-Menehould, would foil the attempt to flee when he spotted someone with a familiar face. Even after Louis XVI identified himself as "Mr. Durand," Drouet was suspicious. After Mr. Durand left the town, word arrived of the King's disappearance from Paris. Examining a French 50-livre bill with the King's image for confirmation, Drouet soon realized the ruse and jumped on a horse and rode toward the border. After Drouet alerted local police, the bridge over the River Aire was blocked and the King and his entourage were taken prisoner. The flight to Varennes would prove devastating for those still arguing for the adoption of the American model or a more moderate constitution. It confirmed the conspiratorial rhetoric of the most radical elements of the Revolution, particularly with the connection to Austria (which also had blood ties to the Queen). The King returned to Paris and a more hostile population. In the crowd watching the King's return, Paine told a Scottish friend, "You see the absurdity of monarchical governments . . . a whole nation disturbed by the folly of one man." The hostility grew even greater with the discovery of a hidden safe in the Tuileries Palace with correspondence to the Austrians exploring a possible invasion to restore the Bourbon reign. The Mountain now clamored for his blood and denounced those still suggesting a constitutional monarchy or mixed government.

Louis XVI still represented a lingering chance for stability. He was returned to his residence under the watchful eye of the revolution. Nevertheless, Varennes likely sealed his fate and that of moderates who called for restraint. The "first revolution" associated with Voltaire would culminate in the Constitution of 1791, which preserved the monarchy while transferring most powers to a national assembly. The "Declaration of Independence" for France was found in the Declaration of the Rights of Man and of the Citizen, which was drafted by Lafayette with assistance from not just Sieyès but Thomas Jefferson. It was the product of various committees (including the first committee that assembled on the day of the storming of the Bastille). They would both prove incapable of controlling what was coming.

Despite his misgivings, Louis XVI approved the new constitution in September 1791, relinquishing virtually all his authority to the legislature. The revolutionaries had already embraced a unicameral legislature in the National Assembly of 1789. It was unstable and unwieldy. The National Assembly became the Legislative Assembly under the new constitution. Notably, it retained a shared element with the American Constitution: an executive veto. It was a device inherited from the Roman model and embraced by many moderates. Not long after the adoption of the new constitution, Louis XVI would use his veto to block two measures outlawing those who fled the country and another ordering the deportation of priests who refused to take the oath of allegiance to the state.

The crackdown on the clergy was particularly ominous for the still young republic. Unlike the American Revolution, the French Revolution had strong anti-religious elements. (Both Rousseau and Voltaire were critics of organized religion.) This was another sharp contrast between the two revolutions. Clergy in the United States never had the political and economic powers of the French clergy, which included vast land holdings. Where most American Founders were deeply religious and traced natural rights to God, many French revolutionaries took Rousseau's writings about a "civil religion" as a virtual secular monotheism. The French clergy was also openly supportive of the monarchy. For example, in 1789, many were outraged by a letter from the Bishop of Gap in which he complained that it was "a travesty to see an unenlightened curé, with neither birth nor talent competing on the ballot with prelates." The letter offers a context for Tocqueville's later observation that "In France I have seen the spirits of religion and of freedom almost always marching in opposite directions. In America I found them intimately linked together in a joint reign over the same land."

Jeanbon Saint-André, president of the National Convention, rejected the concept of an independent church and saw the need to control the clergy. Like many of his contemporaries, he demanded the licensing and regulation of clerics as a potential threat to social order. Others spoke in even more extreme terms in stamping out counterrevolutionary religious influences. Lawyer Jean-Nicolas Billaud-Varenne declared that "however painful an amputation may be, when a member is gangrened it must be sacrificed if we wish to save the body." Even before the new constitution, there had been confiscation of church property. The Civil Construction of the Clergy, decreed in July

Jeanbon Saint-André

1790, required oaths to be taken by clerics in loyalty to the revolution. Only a third of the clerical members of the Assembly would take the oath. Police shut down convents run by refractory nuns, and Louis XVI was actually prevented from receiving Easter communion from refractory priests at Saint-Cloud. The Oath to the Civil Constitution led to a religious-based opposition and even sympathetic low-level clerics turned against the Jacobins, adding a sectarian element to the divisions in the country.

In November of 1791, Louis XVI vetoed a measure penalizing nonjuring, or non-oath-taking, clergy. It was viewed as further evidence that the King remained opposed to the "general will." The vetoes did not sit well with many citizens who were clamoring for sweeping changes, including the removal of the King. Within a year of its creation, the constitution failed and the King was deposed. The "second revolution" of Rousseau had begun. With Royalists in flight or hiding, factions formed across the revolutionary spectrum. Figures such as Saint-Just, Robespierre, and others rallied the most extreme Jacobins around the Montagnard, or the Mountain. The Mountain acquired its name from the high-rising seats in the National Convention where they sat as a group. The moderate Girondins were located in their own section while the space between them on the convention floor (where the independents collectively sat) was called "the Plain." The Girondins (named after a region with moderate Jacobins) were shocked by the early massacres and called for the establishment of legal order. A familiar pattern would quickly play out as the most extreme elements harnessed the unrequited rage of the masses.

It is here that the fears of Socrates were realized of a people who "drunk too deeply of the strong wine of freedom." Citizen committees released the fury of a long-subjugated people: "Each little town was a new Athens . . . there is an unmistakable delight in the game of politics, in posturing before the public, in going through the ordinary rites of collective action." Ultimately, as historian Eli Sagan maintained, the Terror was a second, minority revolution where "the primary purpose of this coup was to eliminate the Girondins as a political force and leave the Mountain and the Jacobin Club of Paris unopposed." The Mountain succeeded in much the same way as would later groups like the Bolsheviks in Russia. Lenin's followers simply adopted the name Bolsheviks (or majority) when they were in fact in the minority. They labeled the larger faction the Mensheviks, or minority, at the Second Party Congress in 1903 to claim legitimacy for their bloody revolution. The Jacobins engaged in the same fiction by simply declaring themselves the voice of the people. There was ample opposition to the Mountain, particularly outside of Paris. In one letter from the Bordeaux Jacobin Club, citizens supported the Girondist delegates and their "political principles, which have always seemed to us to be those of the majority of the Convention."

Historians François Furet and Mona Ozouf described this moment where the utopian horizon of Rousseau met the dark reality of the Revolution:

> In order to counteract the newly forged unity of the enemies of the Revolution, [the Jacobins] created the fiction of a united people wholly at one with its government. This mythical unity, the rotten fruit of Rousseauism, vital to the Jacobin regime, proved fatal to liberty as independence. The allegedly unified voice of the people and the government disguised the fact that power was in fact exercised, controlled, even seized by a government "people" quite different from the government one. Under this regime individuals were more radically powerless than under any other, because the constraints that bound them were supposed to emanate from themselves.

The Jacobins believed that they were merely unleashing the goodness of man through their executions and brutality. First, they had to shape the new citizen. As Saint-Just put it, "I imagine if men were given laws in accordance with nature and their own hearts, they would no longer be unhappy and corrupt. . . . [The legislator had] to transform men into what he wants them to be." The excesses of the Mountain, including the attack on religious institutions, had left a majority of disaffected citizens, but they were largely a silent majority in the face of the forces of the Jacobins and the Sans-Culottes, the latter a militia of armed citizens. The revolutionaries substituted “the omnipotent king [with] the omnipotent nation.” In the end, even these minority factions would fall to the will of the people.

Fresh from the American Revolution, the call for moderation by Paine and Lafayette was now often drowned out by louder voices calling for a cleansing of monarchist, clerical, and other factions. One of those voices was Louis Antoine Léon de Saint-Just, who became known as the “Archangel of Terror.” Young and handsome, Saint-Just made moderation a confession demanding execution. He declared “a man is guilty for opposing the Terror because he reveals a lack of desire for Virtue. There is something terrible in the sacred love of one’s country; a love so all-embracing that it sacrifices everything ruthlessly, fearlessly, favoring none, to the public good.”

At first, the rage reflected in the words of Saint-Just was echoed even by those who would later be associated with the more moderate wing of the Revolution, adherents to the Enlightenment who shared the zeal for excising the elements of an ancien régime. One of the most important voices was Jacques Pierre Brissot, a journalist who would be the rallying point for moderates called Brissotins. In these early days, Brissot would tell the assembly that “to save the rest of the body, the gangrened limb must be cut away.” When he later argued for the retention of the King and the adoption of a constitutional system with checks and balances, it would be Brissot who would be viewed as gangrenous by Robespierre and Marat. He would soon be put on a tumbrel cart and taken to the guillotine with other “Brissotins” singing “La Marseillaise.”

Aristocrats were also among early voices calling for the more radical measures. Despite his privileged upbringing, Honoré Gabriel Riqueti, Count of Mirabeau, was a Jacobin and was one of the most articulate orators calling for extreme measures. He once observed, “There is nothing more appealing, nothing more revolting in such details as is a revolution, but there is nothing finer in its consequence for the regeneration of empires.” Riqueti favored a moderate approach with a constitution that retained the King but shifted greater authority to the Assembly, where it would be used for brutal repression. What was “revolting in the details” was quickly unfolding not just in the Assembly but in the streets with the rise of a new popular force of vigilantes hell-bent on revenge. They wanted not just a new constitution, but a new society that would come from a purging of the population.

Outside there was an equally important group that would shape what unfolded in the Revolution, the Sans-Culottes. Culottes were the fashionable style of silk knee breeches of the time. The militia of commoners wore pantaloons or long pants and thus the militia was described as *sans*, or without, culottes. It was a dismissive name bestowed by Jean-Bernard Gauthier de Murnan, who also served in the American Revolution. Like other originally derogatory references (like our own Yankee Doodle Dandy), the name was embraced by the Sans-Culottes, who derisively referred to well-off revolutionaries as "silk stockings" and saw their distinctive clothing as an article of faith. That included the red felt Phrygian cap that was a symbol of freed slaves in ancient Rome and was later voted as required wear for entry in some assemblies. The other added accessory was, of course, the pike. While not embraced by the army as an effective weapon in an age of cannon and musket, the pike was ideal and terrifying in the hands of an urban mob. Notably, a pamphlet in August 1792 included "the free arming of every single citizen" as one of the "pillars of freedom." It was a French version of the Second Amendment in the United States, adopted the prior year.

For the Sans-Culottes, theirs was a war against "aristocrats," a term that went far beyond the nobility of the ancien régime. The Sans-Culottes rounded up an ever-widening range of suspects, including some chastised for their good manners as evidence of "a heart gangrened with aristocratic sentiments." Eventually, "aristocrat" was used by Sans-Culottes for both the nobility and many in the bourgeoisie. One orator explained "aristocrats are all the people with money, all the fat merchants, all the monopolists, law students, bankers, pettifoggers and anyone who has something." Even Robespierre would find himself referring to the Sans-Culottes as a force, even a species, unto itself, referring to the "rights of the Sans-Culottes" and the distinctive "dress, food, and reproduction of their species." As Arendt observed, "the Rights of Man [had transformed] into the rights of the Sans-Culottes." Like the Red Guards of the Cultural Revolution, the Sans-Culottes were the perfect shock troops for the Terror. French historian Albert Soboul noted, "the Sans-Culottes considered violence to be the ultimate recourse against those who refused to answer the call of unity."

The Sans-Culottes were led by a lawyer who became a voice of summary, violent justice: Jacques René Hébert. Using his popular newspaper, *Le Père Duchesne*, Hébert stood out even among the most blood-soaked radicals as someone who lacked a single redeeming quality. He was a journalist who fled a judgment for slander and lived off fraud and theft until he found his true calling in the Revolution as a self-righteous serial killer. Madison's observations about revolutionaries fit Hébert to perfection: "an unhappy species of the population . . . who, during the calm of regular government, are sunk below the level of men; but who, in the tempestuous scenes of civil violence, may emerge into the human character." When there were things that even Robespierre could not stomach, Hébert would rush forward with a homicidal glee. To put it simply, if Rousseau had ever met Hébert, he might have shattered Rousseau's faith in the innate goodness of humanity. One of Hébert's most fervent causes, not surprisingly, was a campaign for the dechristianization of France. His hatred for religious orders made even Robespierre uneasy. Hébert discussed Jesus not as a deity but the original Sans-Culottes. Catholics were targeted and massacres occurred, with hundreds murdered in spasms of religious intolerance. With figures like Marat, he would brandish the Sans-Culottes as a weapon for immediate action against opponents, including any Jacobins who began to show hesitancy over the methods and directions of the revolution.

While the second revolution brought about what some called a "Sans-Culotte democracy," the use of Sans-Culottes revealed a revolution riddled with deep and often conflicting factions with very different interests and intents. Many of the Jacobins were well-educated journalists, lawyers, and diplomats. Historian Eli Sagan noted that these revolutionaries were made up in large part of "the elite of French bourgeois, non-noble society." Pamphlets not only demanded an immediate redistribution of half of the property of the wealthy but emphasized that such distribution would be made without legal process and would not be bound by any agreement or prior law. Petitions asserted the right to eat and rejected individual rights to retain property in the face of poverty. Radicals denounced "those who under the pretext of freedom and property believe themselves free to suck the blood of the unfortunate and to satisfy their vile cupidity while barely allowing the needy either to breathe or to complain." This egalitarianism was viewed as trumping any individual rights or due process claims of merchants or citizens with property.

While allied with the bourgeoisie of the Mountain, the Sans-Culottes held different values. They distrusted those with property and were most focused on food and wealth distribution. They attacked merchants and ransacked stores as a matter of right. Retailers railed against wholesalers while artists were focused on the availability of capital and resources. In this sense, the Sans-Culottes and the bourgeoisie are analogous to the division between the Constitutionalists and Republicans in Philadelphia. Jacobin moderates (like the Philadelphia Republicans) supported the revolution but wanted controls to protect minority factions and to temper popular impulse. As events were spinning out of control in Philadelphia, the violence subsided with the approval of a constitution containing precautions specifically designed by Madison to vent and direct factional pressures. There was no such constitutional correction in Paris, and factions proceeded to collide with increasing force and lethality. It was Madison's fear of the unrestrained and "common impulse of passion" of factions in Federalist 10 playing itself out with frightening effect.

Some in the Mountain recognized the Sans-Culottes as a threat due to their class hostility toward those with education and resources. Other figures like Saint-Just played to this constituency with calls to limit land holdings and other measures. The factional tensions between radical Jacobins and Montagnards would become manifest in the Montagnard opposition to many price controls and income limits on capital in the form of ships, merchandise, or cash. On taxation, the measures became increasingly improvised and extralegal. One commission announced that those relieved of their property as a tax should rejoice and stressed that "tentative measures help us." Without due process or political protections, the popular will demanded redistribution of "haves" to the "have nots" and, after years of rigid class stratification, there were far more "have nots." As historian Albert Soboul noted, these conditions "did not move the sans-culottes toward a form of liberal democracy, as envisaged by the bourgeoisie, but toward a popular form of democracy."

The most alarming aspect of the French Revolution was how quickly early adherents, particularly lawyers and journalists, became advocates for terror despite the initial calls for realizing the ideals of the Enlightenment. The early meetings emphasized the rights of man and the aspirations for a free and just society. Figures such as lawyer Georges Jacques Danton formed a Society of the Friends of the Rights of Men and Citizens and met in an old Franciscan convent in the Cordeliers, a district known for its radicals and anarchists. In addition to Danton, some of the figures who would later bring about the Terror were present, including Marat. Another group, the Jacobin Club, met in a friary of the Dominican order. These were ironic venues given the later attacks on the Catholic Church and religious institutions.

Among the early Jacobins was the young lawyer Maximilien Robespierre, who had criticized the lack of due process and the arbitrary charges under the Royalist government. The man who would become the personification of brutal summary justice began his career as a civil libertarian. He would ultimately use his skills to rationalize terror not just to his fellow citizens but to himself. He sought to make terror synonymous with virtue in a twisted Rousseauian ideology. Robespierre was tightly constructed, holding manically to his concept of virtuous terror and his own purity of purpose. On one occasion, when Danton laughed at his mention of virtue, Robespierre was clearly wounded. Steeped in the blood of executions, Robespierre's grandiose references to his own virtue and the villainy of his critics became more and more absurd. In one instance, the more moderate Dominique Joseph Garat, minister of the Interior, laughed when Robespierre told him that the Girondins were conspirators and counterrevolutionaries. Garat later recounted, "I couldn't keep from laughing and the laugh that escaped my lips brought a bitter response." Robespierre had come to treat any opposing faction as a threat to the republic and would gradually abandon every principle that he once held as secondary to the creation of a purifying state. Despite the fact that longtime associates such as Danton and Garat could not suppress laughing at the contradictions, Robespierre angrily clung to the rationalizations for his murderous policies. He would find lethal liberation in the name of the general will, declaring, "Terror is only justice: prompt, severe and inflexible; it is then an emanation of virtue; it is less a distinct principle than a natural consequence of the general principle of democracy, applied to the most pressing wants of the country."

By the middle of 1792, French politics had become a matter of brute force. Minister of Justice Georges Danton used his legendary oratory skills to unleash hell on France. Before the infamous September massacre in which as many as 1,600 people were murdered by the Sans-Culottes and other forces, Danton delivered one of his most eloquent and inflammatory speeches. He declared, "We ask that anyone refusing to give

personal service or to furnish arms shall be punished with death. The bell we are about to ring . . . sounds the charge on the enemies of our country." Speeches like Danton's were taken as a license to engage in a catharsis of executions. Notably, most of those murdered in the September massacre were common criminals found in jails, not Royalists or counterrevolutionaries. The deaths had a familiar cathartic feel. The public was facing another mass conscription for the war against Austria and Prussia. Marat used the conscription as an excuse for cleansing. He warned that the volunteers could not risk leaving traitors behind in prison as they went off to fight for the republic. Others said that these counterrevolutionaries were waiting to kill the families of departing troops. The obvious propaganda had only one purpose: to justify mass killings.

Other key figures of the Terror also came from the upper, educated classes. Marat was a gifted physician with international recognition for some of his earlier research. He even applied for the use of a noble title during the monarchy. His medical writings were interspersed with political writings and he would become the avenging angel of the Mountain with the Sans-Culottes at his back. Marat declared that past oppression was now an excuse for unrestrained rage:

> Rise up, you poor wretches of the city, workmen without work, homeless people compelled to sleep under bridges or to prowl the streets, beggars with neither food nor shelter, tramps, cripples, aimless wanderers . . . you have a right to slice off the thumbs of the aristocrats in conspiracy against you, to split the thumbs of the priests who have preached the virtue of servitude to you.

Where the Red Guard would later execute those who appeared counter-revolutionary, the Sans-Culottes accused moderates of *incivisme*, or a lack of civic-mindedness. A lack of civic-mindedness was enough to be relieved of one's head. Again, Marat gave voice to the violence, declaring "I am the rage of the people."

While supporting waves of extrajudicial killings and massacres, Marat in 1793 turned on the Girondins and moderates as a threat that needed to be excised from the body politic. The Girondins had targeted Marat as well as Robespierre in what they viewed as laying the foundation for a dictatorship. Some did not bother to deny it. According to one report, Marat once confronted Paine and asked, "Do you believe in republic? You are too enlightened to be deluded by such a daydream." As the dictatorship of the people took hold, the new "enlightenment" now meant the rejection of the very concept of a republic. Marat's critics knew that they had to strike without delay. At points, Marat was forced to take refuge from his enemies in the sewers, a choice that only aggravated the painful skin condition that was engulfing his body. He remained the voice of the most radical element, riding waves of rage. As the Mountain targeted moderates, Marat denounced a conspiracy of foreigners in France and called for action against them. This included a decree for the arrest of all Englishmen in France, a clear threat to Paine. After the bloody September massacres, the Girondins decided to make their move by ordering the arrest of Marat for "murder, assassinations, and massacre." The numbers are telling. The Girondists moved for the trial when many delegates were absent. With only 376 delegates voting, 226 voted in favor of the charges. Marat, in signature form, then turned on his accusers with the Sans-Culottes in the streets. He succeeded in fending off the charges. The most dramatic moment (and the most perilous for Marat) came on September 25, 1792, when the Girondins launched an attack on Marat in the Assembly based on an article in which Marat called for the establishment of a dictatorship. After coming out of hiding, Marat took only forty-five minutes in his defense. As delegates called for his arrest, Marat rose and admitted that he wrote the article in a moment of passion but gave an emotional speech affirming his loyalty to the Convention. As other delegates shouted in his favor, Marat then took out a pistol and declared, "I am bound to state that if any indictment had been decreed, I should have blown out my brains at the foot of the tribune. So, this is the result of three years spent in dungeons, and the tortures I have endured to save the country? This is the result of my vigils, my toil, my poverty, my sufferings, and the dangers to which I have been exposed! Very well! I will remain among you and brave your fury!"

Marat received a unanimous verdict of acquittal.

Marat was in his element. He has been described as a "born terrorist," despite being cultivated in bourgeois society. He was radically chic. Even with the sudden growth of the bourgeoisie in France in the preceding decades, it still represented only an estimated 10 percent of the population. Yet it would be the majority of those in the Jacobin Club, who embraced figures like Marat before his turn toward the Sans-Culottes and the mob. One person who did understand the mob was Paine, who was still a delegate of the National Convention. He advised Danton that "I see but one effectual way to prevent a rupture . . . to fix the residence of the

Convention and future assemblies at a distance from Paris." Paine's advice might have avoided some of the bloodshed to come, but it came too late. Indeed, the class-based anger was stoked to the point of hysteria.

With Marat's acquittal, the Girondins had again been outmaneuvered and the Mountain was not inclined to wait for another attempt. Supporters were told that it was time for a cleansing. On April 5, 1793, members of the Paris Jacobin Club rallied to the cause: "Friends! We're betrayed. . . . The center of counterrevolution is in the government in the Convention. . . . Rise Up! . . . All popular societies must flood the Convention with petitions manifesting a formal wish for the immediate recall of all its unfaithful members who have betrayed their duty in not wanting the death of the king, and especially those who have led astray a great number of their colleagues. Such deputies are traitors, royalists, or fools."

Marat pushed his Sans-Culottes to greater levels of violence and savagery "to split the tongues of the priests who preach servitude" and others suspecting of being Royalist sympathizers. He declared, "A starving man has the right to slit the throat of a man who is well-fed and eat his palpitating flesh. . . . This Terror is the measure price of public tranquility, to drive out the legions of reactionaries lurking within our walls, poised for the moment when the patriots march off to face our enemies." Many took the call literally. In one account in Fife's *The Terror*, an arrested sergeant major was disemboweled in a tavern as his capturers drank and held other terrified prisoners. When a brave onlooker approached a vinegar merchant who had just cut the lungs out of the sergeant major to ask that he spare the life of a young man among his remaining prisoners, the merchant responded, "You have never seen an Aristo's heart—I'm going to show you one." He then proceeded to cut out the young man's heart and made the good Samaritan kiss it.

Marat fueled the fears of Royalists "in the walls" as roundups continued. In a letter co-signed by Minister of Justice Danton, Marat matter-of-factly recounted the summary executions on behalf of the Commune of Paris. He reported that "many of the ferocious conspirators detained in the prisons have been put to death by the people; the people considered this act of justice indispensable in order to subdue by terror the legions of traitors lying hidden within the walls."

Ultimately, with the support of Robespierre, the Girondins were gathered up and executed in droves. Simply put, the Girondins never could identify with, let alone control, the mob. As Sagan noted, "when it came to playing politics, the Gironde was no match for the Jacobins." In fact, in November 1793, when the Girondins tried to bring in troops from rural areas to defend them from anarchy, Marat visited the troops in their barracks and won them over to the side of the Mountain. When novelist Jean-Baptiste Louvet de Couvray made the case for an indictment of Robespierre, Robespierre crushed the effort with a moving speech and was easily acquitted. It was no contest. Journalist Camille Desmoulins described the scene as akin to watching Hercules wrestling with an enraged basset hound.

Each flashpoint in politics offered new wedge issues for the Mountain. It was during the debate over the fate of the King that Saint-Just became a sensation with a speech that demanded execution, insisting that "this man must reign or die!" He declared him guilty for simply being a king, since "No one can reign innocently." He denounced those like Paine seeking a moderate position, because there was "no middle ground" and no need for a trial. When the Sans-Culottes and others marched to seize the King, they did so in signature fashion. Some six hundred Swiss guards were cut down, including many who surrendered on the promise of safe treatment.

Being in a faction, other than the Montagnards, meant you were counterrevolutionary. There were profiles of courage, including arguably the best orator among the Girondists, Pierre Victurnien Vergniaud. The lawyer and statesman challenged the Mountain's view of factions, articulating a type of Madisonian view that a legislative process requires a diversity of opinions and that the true threat is not dissent but the tyranny of the majority. It fell on deaf ears. Robespierre declared that the Girondins were an old wine in a new bottle: "Take away the word 'republic' and I see no change. . . . [The Girondins were] more criminal in their tactics than all the factions that had preceded them." Without any legal protections or stabilizing institutions, the only restraint on political violence was often mere happenchance. For example, in the evening of May 1793, Girondin presses were being destroyed, and forty-three Girondin deputies spent the night in their seats in the Convention to die as Constitutionalists. The mob did not come that night. Vergniaud was stalwart in his defense of liberty, refusing to flee with other Girondists. Instead, he published a pamphlet that declared, "Far from fearing death, I hope for it: for soon the people, enlightened by it, will free themselves at last from their horrible tyranny." Robespierre would prove happy to accommodate his request.

The rise of the Mountain and the overthrow of Louis XVI also meant the trashing of the earlier moderate constitution in favor of the Montagnard Constitution of 1793. It was a Madisonian nightmare. What is most notable is how the Mountain would concentrate power in the hands of an enlightened few. Rather than allowing some element of bicameralism with an executive council elected directly by the public (as suggested by Condorcet), the Mountain established a twenty-four-member executive committee chosen by the deputies. The earlier constitution allowed for popular referendums that could force petitions or legislation before the national assembly. The Mountain rejected that option and made popular referendums much more difficult. Such decisions were to be made by the revolutionary committee members. (Indeed, shortly after its adoption, the Montagnard constitution was suspended and power handed over to the Committee of Public Safety.) Condorcet spoke out against the new constitution as a recipe for tyranny and, as if to prove his point, was immediately denounced as a traitor. Condorcet would ultimately flee and evade arrest for months. In those months, he wrote his *Sketch for a Historical Picture of the Progress of the Human Spirit*, a hopeful work that reaffirmed his faith in "the moral composition of humankind." Eventually, even his friends feared providing him shelter and he was captured. He was found two days later, dead in his cell, a death believed to be either murder (to avoid an unpopular execution) or suicide by a common mixture of opium and a weed known as "the Devil's Snare." It was a poignant end for the writer who once declared that "no bounds have been fixed to the improvement of the human faculties; that the *perfectibility of man* is absolutely indefinite; that the progress of this perfectibility, henceforth above the control of every power that would impede it."

In the meantime, the Mountain's increasing use of the vote by acclamation and direct democratic measures by local committees left key policies in tatters. Impulse legislation became the norm, including a series of price limits combined with wage increases. With an economy in shambles due to the unrest, the combination of the price and wage controls left the dwindling number of struggling businesses in an unsustainable position. In Philadelphia, local committees showed the same impulse, but the new American constitution would yield more reasoned measures to deal with shortages and production issues after the American Revolution. That system simply did not exist, and France suffered from not only centralized command controls, but ad hoc measures implemented by local committees seeking immediate satisfaction. When shortages continued, local communes demanded further wage increases or held widespread strikes that only magnified the economic disorder.

Of course, the ultimate symbol of the lingering Royalists remained Louis XVI himself. With the failure of the first constitution, the constitutional monarchy—and the monarch himself—were doomed. When the mob ultimately came for Louis XVI at the Tuileries Palace in Paris, it chanted, "Down with the veto, to hell with the veto." Before taking him away, they forced him to put on a liberty cap and drink a toast to the Revolution. He was brought to trial in December 1792. In the National Convention, he would discover a curious champion in the person of Thomas Paine. When the long-monarchy-hating Paine stood to address the delegates, some may have expected a full-throated call for swift justice for Louis XVI. It would prove another signature moment when the contrarian showed the hold of principle over popularity. Paine pleaded for mercy for Louis XVI. Instead of death, he argued for banishment to the United States: "Let then those United States be the guard and the asylum of Louis Capet. There, in the future, remote from the miseries and crimes of royalty, he may learn, from the constant presence of public prosperity, that the true system of government consists not in monarchs, but in fair, equal, and honourable representation." It was Paine at his best. He had come to see the growing excesses of popular justice and counseled moderation and circumspection in the face of revolutionary rage. He was immediately attacked by Marat, who denounced him as a Quaker who just could not stomach capital punishment. Paine's naïve faith in the awakening of a new type of citizen was lost. He wrote to Jefferson with alarm over what he was witnessing in the new republic: "We are now in an extraordinary crisis . . . [with] the continued persecution of the Jacobins, who act without either prudence or morality." The King was convicted and sentenced to be executed.

On January 21, 1793, Louis XVI was taken to the Place de la Révolution. Despite the ridicule and insults from the crowd, he retained his composure. His last request was for a friend who accompanied him to be allowed to return home safely. Standing on the elevated platform, Louis XVI attempted to be heard declaring, "I die innocent of all the crimes with which I am charged. I forgive those who are guilty of my death and pray God that the blood which you are about to shed may never be required of France . . ." Few would hear the words as the head of the National Guard, General Antoine Joseph Santerre, ordered a drum roll and thus stopped the King from speaking further to the crowd. He was quickly dispatched, and the executioner's assistant then held up his severed head and walked around the platform to the cheers of the public.

Le Peletier

With the beheading of Louis XVI, Marat's "dictatorship of Liberty" was now complete. Violence begot violence as factions meted out their own justice. Each faction had their own blood traitors to be disposed of. For Royalists, Louis-Michel le Peletier, Marquis of Saint-Fargeau, was the ultimate traitor. The descendant of a wealthy aristocratic family, Le Peletier once voiced conservative values in the estates. Like many, he became increasingly radicalized and enamored with revolutionary ideas. He would become president of the Assembly and call for the trial of the King. On January 20, 1793, the day before the King's execution, Le Peletier sat in a café in Paris when Philippe Nicolas Marie de Pâris, a member of the King's Guard, entered. He walked directly to his table and said, "You voted for the King's death, Monsieur Le Peletier?" Le Peletier replied, "I voted according to my conscience. What has that to do with you?" That was all Pâris needed. He pulled a saber from under his cloak and plunged it into the chest of Le Peletier. (Pâris would make it to Normandy before he reportedly killed himself with a shot to the head.) As with the death of Marat, Jacques-Louis David would paint Le Peletier as a fallen hero of the Revolution with a remarkably calm expression on his face for a man who just had a saber pushed through his chest. He was added to the growing list of martyrs of the Revolution and used for further calls of cleansing vengeance.

There was, of course, the lingering inconvenience of the Queen. Marie Antoinette's time would come in October 1793. The trial would shock the sensibilities of even some of the Mountain, including Robespierre, who

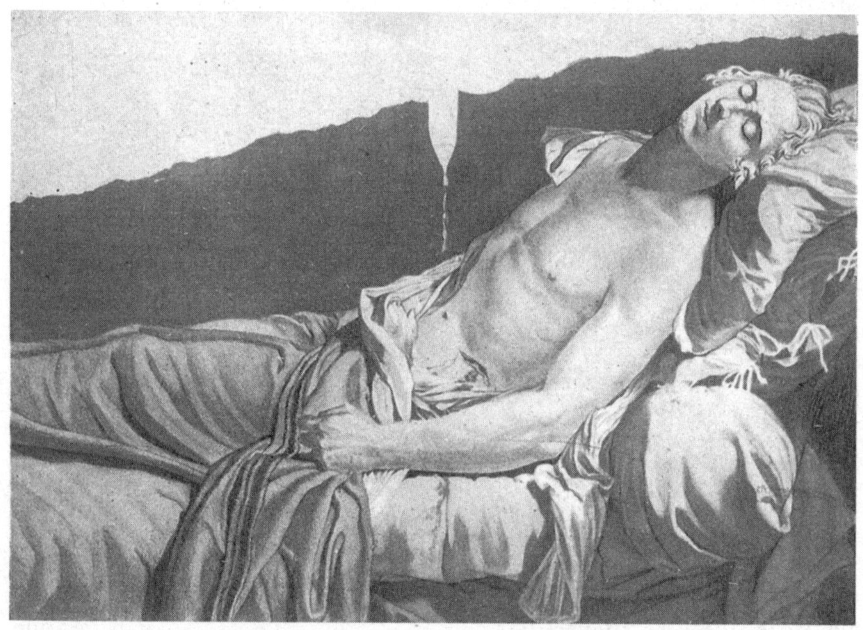

wanted her executed. With the Girondins dead or under arrest, there were few left to call for mercy. Paine, again fearless in the face of his own critics, called for the Queen to be banished to America. In August, she made the transition from the Queen Consort of France and former Archduchess Maria Antonia of Austria to prisoner #280 at the Conciergerie prison. As she bent down to enter the low door of the cell, she hit her head and was asked by one of the guards if she was hurt. She responded solemnly, "No, nothing now can hurt me." With her husband beheaded, her friends executed, and her family under threat of execution, Marie Antoinette believed that there was nothing left for the Jacobins to take. She was wrong. The Mountain sought to leave nothing to chance. They had separated her eight-year-old son, Louis Charles, to be indoctrinated by a cobbler who was also a member of the Paris Commune. She was known to watch endlessly out of a small cell window in the hopes of seeing her boy. What she did not know was that the Jacobins had poisoned the boy's mind against her and got him to make salacious and disgusting allegations. (Louis Charles himself would later die in prison at age ten. An autopsy showed his body covered in scars from physical abuse in captivity.)

At the trial, Marie Antoinette faced charges of depleting the treasury, treason, and other offenses. Her main antagonist, Jacques René Hébert, the former journalist and proponent of the Terror, was not satisfied. He used her son's statement to accuse her of forcing the boy to have sexual relations with her and teaching him to masturbate. After being stoically silent, the Queen finally spoke against Hébert's disgusting diatribe, stating, "If I did not respond, it was because it would be against nature for a mother to reply to such an accusation. On this I appeal to all mothers who may be here." Robespierre himself would call Hébert an imbecile for making the claims when conviction was certain on the other grounds. A failed effort to rescue the Queen called the Carnation Plot (so named because one of the conspirators passed a secret note to the Queen in a carnation) left most members of the Revolutionary Tribunal set on conviction.

Both the conviction and her treatment reflected the long-standing disdain for the Austrian beauty who became the Queen Consort. While there is no evidence that she ever said "let them eat cake" during one of the famines (a story attributed to Rousseau in discussing an unnamed "great princess"), she personified the excess of royal living. For her execution, on October 16, 1793, Marie Antoinette was forced to dress in front of guards, had her hair cut short, and was denied the courtesy of the carriage afforded to her husband. She was forced to ride in an open cart with a rope tied around her as thousands threw insults and garbage along her passage. When she walked up the stairs to the platform of the guillotine, she accidentally stepped on the foot of the executioner, Henri Sanson, and immediately apologized: "Pardon me, sir, I did not do it on purpose." With those final words, she was decapitated, and her head displayed to the delight of the crowd. Hébert would express ecstasy at witnessing the death, writing in his newspaper: "The bitch was insolent and shameless to the very end but her legs went when they tipped her over to shake the hand of the knife."

With the Queen dead, there was still work to be done. Twenty-one Girondins awaited trial and, soon after the Queen's execution, they too were sentenced to die en masse. At the announcement of the verdicts,

defendant Charles Éléanor Dufriche-Valazé pulled a knife hidden in his clothing and plunged it into his own heart. Another defendant, Marc-David Lasource, a diplomat who had voted to execute King Louis XVI, screamed out, "I die on the day the People has lost its reason—you will die when they recover it."

That time would come sooner than Lasource may have imagined as he and twenty others (including the corpse of Dufriche-Valazé) were led to the guillotine in five tumbrels. They were met by the same blood-lust delirium of the mob. The Sans-Culotte called out, "The guillotine is hungry," and a virtual assembly line of victims were fed to it. One woman, a lemonade vendor, demanded to eat the heart of anyone criticizing the Sans-Culotte and complained, "You hear them talk of nothing but cutting, chopping off heads, not enough blood is flowing."

One who still remained was Paine, though he had few illusions. Before he fled England under the charge of sedition, Paine told a friend, "If the French kill their king, it will be a signal for my departure, for I will not abide among sanguinary men." For Paine, the ultimate collapse of his ideals came in December 1793. He had just been stripped of his seat in a vote of no confidence. Paine's trial in London had begun only eleven days earlier. In watching the executions in Paris, Paine lamented to a friend, "Ah France, thou hast ruined the character of a revolution virtuously begun, and destroyed those who produced it."

As the executions intensified, Paine moved a few miles away to the village of Saint-Denis, where he was joined by a small group of supporters seeking safety from the mob. The inn became a microcosm for the unfolding terror as friend after friend was taken away for summary justice. Among his companions at the inn was William Johnson, who eventually attempted suicide. Finally, the landlord was arrested, leaving Paine as the sole remaining inhabitant. This departure left the haunting image of Paine sitting alone in the empty inn waiting for his own arrest. Knowing that he would likely be next, Paine struggled to finish what could be his last work.

The long-awaited knock at his bedroom door came on December 28, 1793. There stood five policemen and two representatives of the feared Committee on General Safety. When asked for the charge, they just shrugged. Such details were now largely meaningless in France. While ordered to seize any suspicious material and throw him in jail, Paine convinced the officers to first take him to his Paris residence and then the residence of his friend and fellow American Joel Barlow. Paine was able to leave the draft of a book with a title that stood in almost comical contradiction to everything unfolding around him: *The Age of Reason*. The charge against Paine essentially accused him of being a foreigner in cahoots with "the faction," or the Girondins, and someone who "did not blush to depict for us all of veneration and gratitude for the tyrant of France."

The Palais du Luxembourg was less a prison than a holding pen. Estimates put the number of deaths at roughly forty thousand during the Terror. Trials were perfunctory and summary. In just one night, 169 were taken away for execution. Before his own execution, Danton (who warned Paine about the growing threat to him in the Convention) asked to see his friend and was able to shake his hand one last time. He reportedly told Paine, "That which you did for the happiness and liberty of your country I tried to do for mine" and promised, therefore, to go to the scaffold "gaily."

Paine was initially put in a filthy 10-by-8-foot cell with just a chair, mattress, and box. Though he was later moved to a larger cell with fellow prisoners, Paine's health (which was often marginal at best) deteriorated rapidly. He was bitter and deflated. He was clearly wounded by his abandonment by his fellow American revolutionaries, particularly Washington. He wrote, "I should be tempted to curse the day I knew America. By contributing to her liberty, I have lost my own, and yet her government beholds my situation in silence." He had written to the man he had lionized and loved above all others: George Washington. He had stood with Washington when all seemed lost with the early defeats to the British. He watched with Washington as the British took Manhattan and later rode victoriously by Washington's side into Philadelphia after the city's liberation. He even dedicated his book *Rights of Man* to Washington. Washington did not respond.

Paine would languish in prison in large part due to the lack of intervention from the American minister to France, Gouverneur Morris, despite Paine's entreaties that "you must not leave me in [this] situation."

Gouverneur Morris's unsympathetic response to his letter should have not been a surprise. After all, Paine had previously accused Robert Morris and his assistant, Gouverneur Morris (no relation), of involvement in the corrupt Deane affair. When asked by the French to establish his status, Morris replied with a note that was strikingly passive-aggressive, acknowledging Paine's role in the American Revolution while stressing that "his conduct since this epoch is out of my jurisdiction."

Paine had come to understand Madison's view of factions at great cost to himself. He wrote, "It is not the nation but a faction that [caused] this injustice." Paine grew more and more desperate, pleading with Morris, "Though you and I are not on terms of the best harmony," to send a report on his situation to Congress. Morris remained unmoved and wrote Jefferson that "I believe he thinks, that I ought to claim him as an American citizen . . . [but given] his birth, his naturalization in this country, and the place he filled, his petition [is] inexpedient and ineffectual." The letter would seriously undermine Paine's main defense. Paine would later write that "Morris has been my inveterate enemy, and I think he has permitted something of the national character of America to suffer by quietly letting a citizen of that country remain almost eight months in prison without making every official exertion to procure him justice."

When Paine's case was presented to the National Convention, there was loud hissing. Marc-Guillaume Vadier, president of the Committee of General Security, declared, "Thomas Paine is a native of England" and further denounced him of expressing support for the republic "only in accordance with the illusions with which the false friends of our revolution have invested it." The irony must have been crushing for Paine: He was condemned in England as a Jacobin while charged in France by Jacobins as a reactionary.

After Morris was replaced by James Monroe (who was more sympathetic to Paine), Monroe told him that he had received no instructions from Washington on securing his release. (Paine would later denounce Washington and tell him, "You folded your arms, forgot your friend, and became silent.") Nevertheless, Monroe would lobby for his release and reminded the Committee of General Security that he was both an American citizen and a "distinguished patriot." Monroe further noted that "the citizens of the United States can never look back to the era of their own revolution, without remembering, with those other distinguished patriots, the name of Thomas Paine." Paine would finally be released after ten months and nine days in crushing confinement. He would survive "among sanguinary men" with his head, but not his views, intact. As people died around him, popular justice was playing out to its final and inevitable conclusion. All that remained would be for the sanguinary men themselves to fall under the razor of the republic. It was time for Saturn to claim his children.

Sic Semper Tyrannis: The Fall of the Mountain

On July 11, 1793, a beautiful young woman with ice-blue eyes and chestnut hair stepped off a coach onto the cobblestones of the Place des Victoires in Paris. Marie-Charlotte de Corday likely first focused on the center of the square where the last remnants of a statue of Louis XIV were being demolished. The statue once showed the Sun King crowned with victory and standing on the three-headed dog from Hades, Cerberus. In its place would be a wooden pyramid to honor the new revolutionary name of the square, Place des Victoires-Nationaux (National Victories Square). Charlotte Corday, the daughter of a minor aristocratic family, was a supporter of the Revolution and came from Caen. The city housed many Girondins who had fled the Terror. Corday found kindred spirits in the Girondins in seeking social justice but eschewing state terror.

Corday wrote passionately about her love for France and her alarm over the descent into the bloody nightmare of Marat and Robespierre.

Her intentions on the visit would have been plain to anyone following her on the day. After finding board and arranging a meeting with Marat, her first stop was to go to 177 rue de Valois. It was a cutlery shop where the elegantly dressed lady paid two livres for a six-inch butcher's knife in a neat, green cardboard sheath. After being repeatedly turned away for appointments, Corday went again to Marat's home along the winding streets of the old Latin Quarter. Before she pulled up to 30 rue des Cordeliers, Corday dressed for the occasion with a stop at a hairdresser. Her appearance and deportment would later be recounted and celebrated by many as the quintessential French heroine. Dressed in a spotted Indian muslin, Corday wore white gloves. The green ribbons in her hat and green fan matched the sheath of the knife secreted in her corsage. She was the very model of French womanhood. She was literally dressed to kill.

Corday was not even sure if the sickly Marat would see her and asked the driver to wait. She argued at the door after being again denied entry. Now she promised to give Marat names for his list of targeted Girondins. It worked. Marat beckoned her to enter his bathroom, where he lay in a cooling bath. On the wall were two crossed pistols mounted over the words "LA MORT," or "the death." He demanded the names and Corday rattled off some figures in Caen. Marat was pleased and said lethally, "Excellent, in a few days' time I'll see them all to the guillotine in Paris." His life would end on that appropri-

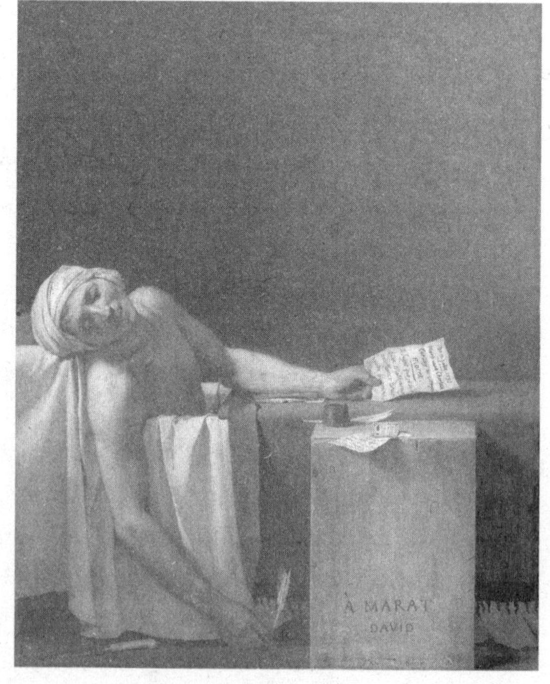

ately hateful note. Corday pulled the knife from her corset and plunged it into his chest. It was a well-placed strike that neatly cut across his aorta. Marat weakly cried out, "Help me, my beloved, help me."

In his famous painting, Louis David portrays Marat without his sores and resting in a noble position as a civic martyr. As with David's painting *The Death of Socrates*, Marat was shown as a pure hero of France. David even wrote a fictional statement of Corday in the note gripped in his dead hand reading, "It is enough that I am very unhappy to be entitled to your benevolence." Marat was accused of many things, but benevolence was not one of them. What happened next was also exaggerated by witnesses. Aide Laurent Bas portrayed himself as a hero in capturing the diminutive Corday: "Seeing the assassin walking towards me, I seized hold of a chair to stop her. The monster had got as far as the outer room and with a great blow of the chair I stunned her to the floor. The creature struggled to get to her feet. I grasped both of her breasts, overpowered her, despite her prodigious strength, and just managed to knock her down a second time and hit her a full blow. As I held her down another citizen came into the room and I cried 'Citizen, help me, oh help me, help.'"

Her trial would be the usual perfunctory and summary matter, though there was a difference noted by historian Graeme Fife. The "unruffled, quiet self-possession" of the "strikingly beautiful young woman" seemed to quiet the crowd. There was none of the common "baying and catcalls" of these trials during the Terror, but a hushed, even reverent, silence. Corday seemed to adopt a Socratic embrace of the punishment. At times, the questioning seemed almost comical. When asked about how she killed Marat, Corday replied, "With a knife that I bought at the Palais Royal. I drove it through his chest." She was then asked, "Did you believe that in so doing you would kill him?" Corday responded matter-of-factly, "That was indeed my intention."

The most riveting moment may have been when Corday invoked the very rationale used by Marat for the killing of others during the Terror. After admitting that she came to Paris to kill Marat, Corday told the jury that, as a loyal Frenchwoman, she believed "anything was justified for the security of the nation. I killed one man in order to save a thousand. I was a republican long before the Revolution and I have never lacked that resolution of people who can put aside personal interests and have the courage to sacrifice themselves for their country." Marat was executed under his own justification for the execution of others.

Convicted, she calmly asked for an artist to do her portrait and sat down the night before her execution to write a last note to her father, Jacques François de Corday, Seigneur d'Armont:

> Forgive me, my dear papa, for having disposed of my existence without your permission. I have avenged many innocent victims, I have prevented many other disasters. The people, one day disillusioned, will rejoice in being delivered from a tyrant. . . . Goodbye, my dear papa, please forget me, or rather rejoice in my fate, the cause is good. I kiss my sister whom I love with all my heart, as well as all my parents. Do not forget this verse by Corneille: Crime is shame, not the scaffold! It is tomorrow at eight o'clock that I am judged. This 16 July.

The next morning, Corday was put on a cart in the pouring rain for the guillotine. Robespierre watched with Georges Danton from a window. Danton, also a member of the Mountain, would be taken to the guillotine in the same fashion less than a year later. Corday remained remarkably composed and even inquisitive to the end. When she ascended the stairs to the guillotine, the executioner, Sanson, stood on the top to shield her from the fearsome sight of the blade dangling roughly 14 feet above her. Corday, however, was disappointed. She had never seen one of the contraptions and wanted to see it. She asked him to step aside. Dr. Joseph-Ignace Guillotin created the device to allow for a more merciful method of execution. The falling blade reached a speed of roughly 21 feet per second so that the time was a mere 1/70th of a second for the condemned. In truth, Guillotin was not the chief designer behind the invention, but he may have had the misfortune of a name that rhymed with *machine* in French. It stuck. Guillotin would later regret the invention, oppose the death penalty, and actually be imprisoned by the very revolutionary government that made his invention infamous. Before his own arrest, he would sneak tablets of opium to friends to reduce any stress or pain at their executions.

Corday did not need any pharmaceutical assistance. She never flinched as she calmly lay down with her hair up to facilitate her execution. In past executions, the accused was subject to abuse and even garbage being thrown at them—followed by cheers and mocking as their head fell into the basket. Corday's beauty and demeanor, however, seemed to transfix the crowd. When Sanson's assistant, Legros, picked up the head and slapped the cheek, objections were heard from the crowd, and some even insisted that they saw the face blush. (While long treated as projection or myth, Corday's reaction has been studied by medical journals, and some believe that there is indeed lingering consciousness or at least physiological responses in such cases.)

As Robespierre watched Corday's procession to execution with Danton, he too would face *le rasoir national*. Almost exactly one year from the day he watched Corday executed, he would be guillotined by the very government he led through The Terror. For Robespierre, it would be a far cry from the dignified ending of Charlotte Corday.

Terror became not the byproduct but the objective of the Revolution. On September 5, 1793, less than two months after Corday's execution, journalist and radical leader Bertrand Barère declared, "Let's make terror the order of the day!" Executions reached a height in the fall of 1793 when as many as forty thousand people were killed, including many Girondins. This included figures like Olympe de Gouges, a playwright who championed women's rights and wrote the Declaration of the Rights of Women and Citizenesses. She earned the ire of the Mountain by writing *The Three Urns*, suggesting that citizens be allowed to vote in a referendum on the best form of government among the three estates. Ironically, she had previously called out the Jacobins for the absence of women in government positions, asserting, "If a woman has the right to mount the scaffold she also has the right to mount the tribune." The Mountain lethally proved her point by sending her to the scaffold on November 3, 1793. She reportedly remained defiant to the end, bravely challenging the crowd to the point that one onlooker remarked that they were now "killing intelligence."

The Terror had played out the worst expectations of Madison's writings on factions with bloodcurdling accuracy. With few transformative elements in the French constitution to defuse these factional pressures, they repeatedly exploded in spasms of violence. Factions were treated as disloyal and "friends of tyranny." The Mountain set about removing all "intermediaries" between the individual and the public interest from breaking down corporations, taking over the church, and arresting dissenting faction members. On one occasion, a friend told Danton the "good news" of more executions of Girondins. Danton asked in response, "You call that good news?" The neighbor was taken aback and noted that "they were factious." Danton responded, "'Factious.' We're all factious. If they deserve to be guillotined, we all deserve so. Those men in Paris will guillotine the entire Republic."

The story of the French Revolution is a story of the lethality of factions when uninhibited by constitutional restraints. The broad coalition in the first Revolution was lost in a remarkably short time:

> Within nine months, all this had collapsed, and France was on the way to dictatorship, civil war, and terror. No aristocratic or monarchical party was responsible for this tragic outcome. Those *outwardly* committed to democracy did it to themselves. . . . Girondins and Jacobins (the Mountain) in the attempt to murder each other ended up annihilating France.

Government was now the work of representatives who would arrive in towns to establish revolutionary courts and set up guillotines sent from Paris. These de facto autocrats would impose price-fixing, confiscate property, and unilaterally nullify laws. Executions were not just a form of popular justice but political resolution. In September 1793, the Law of Suspects would codify the denial of due process while the clubs demanded measures including the forced removal of children. The Terror was only possible in the absence of any real judicial review or appeal. Even the minimal Jacobin procedures proved too much for juries eager to transport defendants to the guillotine. In October 1793, in the trial of the Girondins, the accused actually sought to confront their accusers. The response was outrage from delegates. A proposal was immediately moved and passed to eliminate the "formalities which stifle the conscience and hinder conviction." Accordingly, "after three days' discussion the president of the tribunal shall ask the jury if their conscience is sufficiently enlightened. If they answer in the negative, the trial shall go on till they declare that they are in a position to pronounce sentence." The Girondins had become a faction opposed to the general will. The steady line of the condemned marching to the guillotine would lead journalist and politician Camille Desmoulins to write in his journal, *Le Vieux Cordelier*, "Today a miracle has occurred in Paris: a man died in his bed." Desmoulins, who supported the Revolution, was later executed himself.

Danton had misgivings and, with others in the Mountain, sought to slow down the executions and end the Terror. They were called "the Indulgents" by Robespierre, a name that stuck. There was no room for "indulgency" left in the Revolution. Robespierre and Saint-Just moved with their usual abandon. Just as Danton "rang the bell" for the September massacre, it was Saint-Just who was the bellringer of Danton's own approaching death. On February 26, 1794, Saint-Just spoke on the necessity of the Terror to purify society. While apologizing for the excesses of executions, he explained that it was necessary to create a virtuous citizenry through institutions worthy of that task. There was killing still to be done. He then added an unmistakable reference to Danton, who was sitting nearby: "There is one who has waxed fat on despoiling the people, and glutted with their spoils, insults them and advances in triumph, drawn onward by the crime for which he thinks to excite our compassion, for we can no longer keep silence upon the impunity of those who are most guilty, who desire to destroy the scaffold because they are afraid of ascending it."

Danton was spent. Historian R. R. Palmer described him aptly as "an exhausted volcano." On March 30, 1794, Danton was arrested by order of his former friend and accused of conspiracy with Royalists and corruption. He and his thirteen Dantonist codefendants (including his brother Augustin) were prosecuted before the Revolutionary Tribunal by the infamous Archangel of Terror, Louis Antoine Léon de Saint-Just, with the equally loathsome figure Martial Joseph Armand Herman sitting as judge. While they were guaranteed twelve jurors, they were given only seven hand-picked citizens for a three-day trial. When Danton lashed out at the Committee on Public Safety, Saint-Just ordered that any defendant criticizing the government could be removed and tried in absentia. Most of the jurors were already convinced that Danton was "an implacable enemy of the Republic." When the others hesitated, they were given a secret document from the president and the public prosecutor. The defendants could hardly object; they had protested earlier and were disbarred. It was Jacobin justice at its worst, and all were quickly convicted. Perhaps the most telling notation made by Robespierre in his own record was that "The word virtue made Danton laugh." Danton was one of the most important figures rationalizing the Terror as an act of civic virtue but had finally reached the point that the very reference to virtue had become a tragic joke, a mere pretense for summary executions and authoritarian rule. Virtue had become more than a vice; it had become a license for terror. The irony of the moment must have been crushing for Danton as he was transported on the same tumbrel that he had previously filled with his own victims. Standing in the very place where Louis XVI died, Danton would be the last of the convicted Jacobins to be executed on the guillotine. In the end, he still insisted on commanding the moment. He told Sanson, the executioner, "Show the people my head. It is well worth seeing."

Before he was convicted, Danton prophetically declared, "Robespierre will follow me; he is dragged down by me. Ah, better to be a poor fisherman than to meddle with the government of men!" Danton's prediction quickly came true. Indeed, one has to wonder if his encouraging Sanson to parade his head was not a calculated move to stir allies in the crowd. With Montagnards now lopping the heads off Montagnards, the Terror had turned inward. These revolutionaries had gutted the legal system and used executions as a form of dispute resolution. As new factions formed, existing factions would be eliminated by the most powerful or clever group.

The second Revolution had come full circle and was now devouring its own. Journalist Jacques Hébert was one of the most blood-soaked as a head of the Hébertists who led the dechristianization of France and supported the purging of other factions. He had pushed the 1793 Law of Suspects through the Convention and it was now his turn. The Terror had created an insatiable appetite for blood. Five months after his vile celebration of the execution of Marie Antoinette, it would be Hébert who would "shake the hand of the knife." He was quickly convicted and sent to the guillotine. He was mocked for repeatedly fainting on the way to his execution and struggling to break free. His executioners entertained the crowd by holding the blade (dripping with the blood from the prior victims) inches from his neck as he continued to shriek in terror. On the fourth drop, he was dispatched. After Hébert's own head fell into the wicker basket, Saint-Just remarked, "The revolution is frozen."

Saint-Just showed more dignity when his time came. He went to the Convention to defend himself and the legacy of the Mountain. He was shouted down and arrested with Robespierre and others. They had already removed any due process protections for the accused and now became the subjects of their own perfunctory trials. Ironically, as Saint-Just was being led off to his death, he saw a copy of the constitution of 1793 and stated, "I am the one who made that." It may have been the most singularly ironic and chilling moment of the Revolution. The architect of the terror-inducing constitution pointed with pride to the instrument being used for his own summary execution.

As for Robespierre, his enemies planned in secrecy even as they carried out his orders. Robespierre came before the Convention and found a well-laid trap with dozens of Montagnards denouncing him. When he tried to sit down at one point, a delegate blocked him and said, "Get away from here; Condorcet used to sit here." He was referring to the great mathematician and philosopher Nicolas de Condorcet, who died in prison after being arrested during the Terror. At another point, when the ill Robespierre struggled to speak, someone screamed, "The blood of Danton chokes him!" Robespierre was arrested and taken to Palais du Luxembourg, where Paine was being held. The irony was overwhelming given the long line of condemned persons that Robespierre had sent to that prison, including Paine. Eventually, he was allowed to go the Hôtel de Ville, but the Convention declared him and his codefendants to be outlaws and dispatched troops for their arrest. As the troops burst into the building, Robespierre's

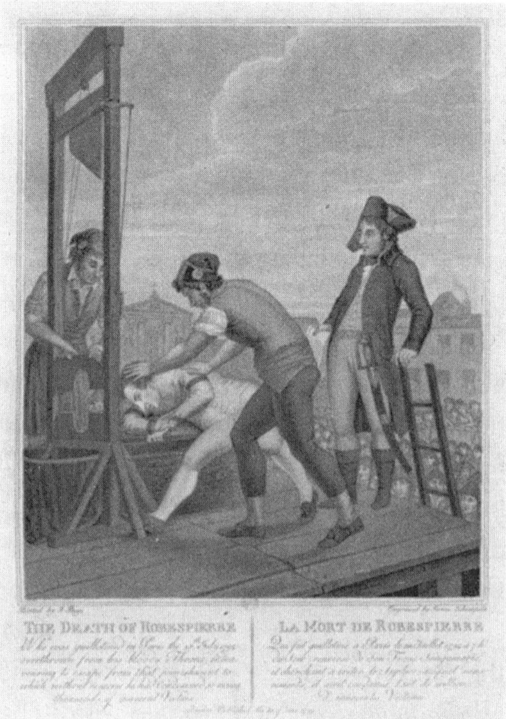

brother Augustin attempted to jump to freedom from an upper floor but landed on bayonets and people below, causing a fractured pelvis and other serious wounds. With Robespierre was his fellow revolutionary Philippe François Joseph Le Bas. Both knew quite well what was in store for them, having sent thousands to their deaths. Le Bas handed Robespierre a pistol and then used a second pistol to kill himself as troops stormed their room. According to some accounts, Robespierre then tried to do the same, but a gendarme grabbed for the pistol. The result was a nonlethal wound and he was taken to the Committee of General Safety and laid on a table for the night.

The next day Robespierre was taken in a cart with others to the Place de la Révolution. Unlike Corday's passage, Robespierre was pummeled and abused as he rode from the streets of Paris with a bloody bandage around his head. The same executioner who dispatched Corday was waiting for him but showed none of his earlier sympathy. Sanson tore off the blood-soaked bandage that was supporting Robespierre's shattered jaw. The revolutionary's shriek of pain was the last the world would hear from him before his head dropped into the basket. Saint-Just, Herman, and other key figures from the trials of the Terror would later be guillotined. As Brutus declared "*sic semper tyrannis*" ("Thus always to tyrants") in the assassination of Julius Caesar, history had again shown its inexorable cycle of tyrants falling victim to the lawless conditions that they created.

Seven

PAINE'S BRIDGE

Revolution and Governance in an Age of Rage

Thomas Paine was an intriguing bridge between two of the greatest revolutions of the age. What is less known is that, when Paine first came to Paris after the American Revolution in 1787, it was to build an actual bridge. An iron bridge to be specific. With the British surrender, Paine briefly put politics behind him in favor of his engineering projects. (He also worked tirelessly to invent a smokeless candle.) Like his contemporaries Franklin and Jefferson, Paine had an irresistible curiosity in science and inventions. He wrote, "I had rather erect the largest arch in the world than be the greater emperor in it." While largely self-educated,

Paine immersed himself in mechanical engineering. He became obsessed with his vision of a large cast-iron bridge, which was the basis for Sunderland Bridge in England. He wrote to Congress that he did not intend to claim a patent over his design "to put the country in possession of the means and of the right of making use of the construction freely." He wanted to design a bridge without piers due to the problem of ice on American rivers in the East. Figures like Thomas Pritchard were also exploring iron bridges, but virtually all bridges at the time were either wood or stone.

Paine's bridge design (with his assistant John Hall) was positively received by experts and engineers. He was said to have gotten his inspiration from examining spider webs, though others suggest that his work as a staymaker may have been a greater foundation for his design. He would again turn to his patron Franklin to display a model of the bridge. (Even Jefferson would make suggestions on improvements and praised the stability of the arch.) Franklin and others heralded the design, but the challenge was funding. Paine insisted that the more expensive design would easily pay for itself:

> As America abounds in rivers that interrupt the land communication, and as by violence of floods and the breaking tap of the ice in the spring, the bridges depending for support from the bottom of the river are frequently carried away, I turned my attention, after the Revolutionary War was over, to find a method of constructing an arch that might, without rendering the height inconvenient or the ascent difficult, extend at once from shore to shore, over rivers of three, four or five hundred feet and probably more.

Faced with political and economic barriers in the United States, Paine looked to Europe for an alternative source of funding. He even secured a patent in England that ironically petitioned "His most Excellent Majesty King George the Third." It professed a new "method of constructing of arches, vaulted roofs, and ceilings, either in iron or wood, on principles new and different to anything hitherto practiced." His bridge did meet with approval in Paris, though not funding. Much like his views on government, Paine would find allies but few investors willing to commit to his design.

Ultimately, Paine was so committed to the project that he not only borrowed money to fabricate the bridge components but put up his property as collateral, including his house in Bordentown. In one later account to Congress, Paine explained that his bridge was erected in a field in Paddington near London as a demonstration of the "practicability" of the design. There it stood for a year before being taken down. Despite that successful demonstration, Paine explained that "at this time my bridge operations became suspended." The reason was that Paine was pulled back into the fray by none other than Edmund Burke, the great English statesman and philosopher. Burke was a critic of both the French Revolution and Paine himself. In his account, Paine explained that he was forced to suspend his bridge development because "Mr. Edmund Burke published his attack on the French Revolution and the system of representative government, and in defense of government by hereditary succession, a thing which is in its nature an absurdity." He was referring to the November 1790 publication of *Reflections on the Revolution in France*, in which Burke argued that the French Revolution was risking a complete breakdown of social order and the rise of tyranny. Paine recounted:

> The publication of this work by Mr. Burke, absurd in its principles and outrageous in its manner, drew me, as I have said, from my bridge operations, and my time became employed in defending a system then established and operating in America, and which I wished to see peaceably adopted in Europe. I therefore ceased my work on the bridge to employ myself on the more necessary work, "Rights of Man," in answer to Mr. Burke.

Paine argued that the French Revolution was the realization of natural rights that were denied by the monarchy, an extension of the Enlightenment. The Burke–Paine debate was eagerly followed in the United States and across Europe.

When Paine finished his *Rights of Man* in January 1791, there was still an element of naïveté in how he viewed the unfolding revolution. He taunted Burke by asking, "Whom has the National Assembly brought to the scaffold? None." It would capture Paine's continued idealism and presumptions of the civic virtue behind the revolution. Later, Paine saw a different story unfolding on the streets of Paris. Indeed, he saw Burke's predictions emerging around him. On one occasion, Paine came close to being lynched from a tree because he was spotted walking without the expected tricolor cockade in his hat and accused of being an aristocrat. He was walking back from observing the return of the King from his attempted flight and noting that the upheaval was just one more sign of the costs of nobility. He was saved only when his fellow radical émigré, Scottish Thomas Christie, used his bilingual skills to explain to the mob who Paine was. It is a moment that must have raised some of the doubts that Tocqueville revealed in his own writing when he observed, "I hold it to be an impious maxim that, politically speaking, the people have a right to do anything; and yet I have asserted that all authority originates in the will of the majority. Am I, then, in contradiction with myself?" Nevertheless, Paine continued to believe in the potential of the French Revolution despite the abuses of the radical elements of the Jacobins.

Even with his own arrest in 1793 just hours after the completion of his first draft of *The Age of Reason*, Paine continued to develop his democratic theories in the context of the French Revolution. Both Paine and Burke supported the American Revolution in their own ways. There was little common ground on the French Revolution. To Burke, France was a nation that dismantled every institution and tradition in a mad plunge into popular government and chaos. For Paine, Burke's clinging to tradition and institutions was reactionary and irrational. Paine rejected Burke's precedent and tradition as the basis for legitimacy. The increasing estrangement between Burke and Paine was a departure from their previous warm association in London, when Burke actually helped Paine look for patrons for his bridge.

One of the greatest points of disagreement between Burke and Paine was the question of when rebellion is justified. Paine, like Rousseau, believed that every generation has a right to rebel and that each generation must decide if their government is a just and legitimate representative of their interests. Paine rejected the concept of a legitimacy based on tradition or precedent: "Government by precedent, without any regard to the principle of the precedent, is one of the vilest systems that can be set up." He would add that "the vanity and presumption of governing beyond the grave is the most ridiculous and insolent of all tyrannies." Burke disagreed and saw government as intergenerational and legitimated by tradition. Despite his favoring American independence, Burke noted that "Kings will be tyrants from policy when subjects are rebels from principle." He declared that the social contract so often discussed by Locke and his followers was "not only between those who are living, but between those who are living, those who are dead, and those who are to be born." It was a powerful retort and found support in later leaders such as Abraham Lincoln in rejecting the inherent right of Southern states to secede from the Union.

It would be the republican form of government and the Madisonian "auxiliary precautions" that would protect liberty from both monarchial and democratic despotism. Madison noted that history had shown how prior governments often passed laws "not according to the rules of justice, and the rights of the minor party; but by the superior force of an interested and over-bearing majority." Rather than deny factions or treat them (as in the French Revolution) as manifestations of disloyalty, the Madisonian system encourages their expression in the legislative process. By bringing factional interests to the surface, disparate interests can be transformed into majoritarian compromises. While others, like George Washington, saw the dangers of factions and opposed political parties, he also warned that the "dominance of one faction over another" can "gradually incline the minds of men to seek security and repose in the absolute power of an individual."

Paine watched Madison's theories play out in France with a ruthless inevitability as political and economic pressures exploded in the absence of a stable political system. The 1791 French constitution rejected the Madisonian checks and balances in favor of an all-powerful single legislative body. It was a system free of what Paine called the "prejudice" for "complex government" that synthesized elements of aristocracy, monarchy, and democracy. Despite the early violence, Paine would cling to his faith in the electorate in directing popular government and his corresponding distrust for buffers between the people and governing decisions. Paine rationalized the violence as a temporary and predictable reaction to the extreme conditions created by the monarchy. In his *Four Letters*, Paine responded to John Adams and others who warned that the unicameral model would allow popular passions and "arbitrary" impulses to rule in the legislative process. He viewed "more houses [as] . . . more parties." (He later admitted that his unicameralism worked only if "party differences would be dropped at the threshold of the state house.") Paine viewed factions as an evil that could be reduced or even eliminated by such a legislative model that did not empower minority or aristocratic factions. His views were echoed by his French associates. Even Marquis de Condorcet, an advocate for representative government, voiced the same suspicions that bicameral systems could allow too much power to minority factions. The devices meant to blunt popular impulse and majoritarian excess were viewed as counterrevolutionary or reactionary by many in France.

With few structural protections channeling factional pressures, governance in France rapidly descended into despotism where might (and the majority) was right. There were efforts by the Assembly to reduce the authority of communal assemblies. Radicals protested such efforts to limit the committees and stormed the Assembly to assert the authority of "the sovereign people." They often repeated Rousseau's declaration that "every law which the people themselves have not ratified is null and void." Ultimately, some would declare "that the only laws will be those made by the people themselves on that particular day." The direct democratic values espoused by the revolutionaries included the right of *viva voce*, or vote by acclamation, to pass measures.

In a revolution premised on Rousseau's general will, any faction other than the majority faction was deemed counterrevolutionary. Even if you did not belong to a faction, you were quickly accused of factionalism if you were not viewed as sufficiently committed to the cause. That included Paine. In his plea in 1794 to the Convention for his freedom, Paine insisted that he was an American citizen who was arrested as a foreigner despite the fact that he "always avoided parties and factions." That was only partially true. As historian Harry Harmer noted, "a member of no faction, Paine found himself closest to the moderate republican Girondins," who found themselves in an existential struggle with the most powerful faction, the Montagnards. The Girondins were part of the Jacobin movement but eschewed the radicalism and violence of the Montagnards. Paine started to write about the excesses of the new government and found himself the target of the most radical elements of the Revolution. Indeed, shortly after joining the National Convention, Paine was selected with eight other deputies to draft the new constitution. He quickly ran afoul of one of the most infamous extremists allied with the Montagnards: Jean-Paul Marat. When Paine rose to speak against the execution of the King, it was Marat who attacked him, challenging the translation of his words to keep him from speaking. Jean-Pierre-André Amar also attacked Paine for his connection to the Girondins, foreshadowing the bloody crackdown that was to come. The confrontation with Marat must have shattered any of Paine's remaining romantic notions of popular government. Danton himself would warn Paine that the Convention was no longer a safe place for him. Paine would resume his heavy drinking as he watched his friends taken away for execution, including Condorcet. Paine eventually knew that his time was running short. In mid-1793, he wrote John Adams that "I saw many of my most intimate friends destroyed; others daily carried to prison; and I had reason to believe, and had also some intimations given me, that the same danger was approaching myself." By October, Robespierre had decided that Paine, a man he once heralded as a beacon of liberty, had to go. He wrote, "[I] demand that Thomas Paine be decreed of accusation, for the interest of America, as well as France." Convicted in England and shunned in America for his radicalism, Paine was charged in France for his moderation by fellow revolutionaries.

One of the lessons of history is that the tyranny of the majority is not just a threat of mob rule but ultimately a return of authoritarian single-tyrant rule. In rebelling against an unchecked King, the fear of tyranny in one ruler was foremost in the minds of revolutionaries. Framers would adopt the pseudonym of Cato in their writing, a historical figure who chose suicide rather than kneel before Caesar after he destroyed the Roman Republic. That fear was only one of the two tyrannies that occupied early philosophers and writers on democracy. An equal, if not greater, threat comes not from the top down but the bottom up in a free society. Tocqueville himself came to view the tyranny of the majority as an equal threat to that of a single tyrant. In Volume I of his masterpiece *Democracy in America*, Tocqueville wrote a chapter titled "Of the Omnipotence of the Majority in the United States and Its Effects," detailing the risks of popular, unrestrained rule becoming "democratic despotism":

> In my opinion the main evil of the present democratic institutions of the United States does not arise from their weakness, but from their overpowering strength; and I am not so much alarmed at the excessive liberty which reigns in that country as at the very inadequate securities which exist against tyranny. If ever the free institutions of America are destroyed, that event may be attributed to the unlimited power of the majority. I know of no country where there prevails, in general, less independence of mind and less true freedom of discussion than in America.

Tocqueville noted that, in prior systems, there were "intermediary" institutions in aristocracies that tended to moderate public impulse and act as a "dike" against popular excess. In the United States, those intermediary institutions were never established, so there are "no lasting obstacles." It is a telling observation given how the United States would avoid the tyrannies of France (with a tradition of such intermediary institutions) after the adoption of the U.S. Constitution.

It would not be democratic ideals but poor ventilation that would save Paine from joining his decapitated colleagues in Paris. After opening the door to allow more air into the cell, guards missed the chalk mark designating him and his cellmates for death. From corset making to a simple swinging door, Paine's existence often seemed to hang on the most mundane or trivial occurrences. However, the years in Paris had taken their toll. Paine would walk out of the Palais du Luxembourg as the Terror came to an end with the death of Robespierre. His lasting illness, called "gaol fever," would linger alongside his painful memories. He had witnessed a democracy become a mobocracy. It was what Tocqueville would describe as a "virus of a new and unknown kind." He was persona non grata in the three countries he called home. A year before his arrest, writer Henry Redhead Yorke (who was also charged with sedition in England), wrote about arriving in Paris and immediately seeking to meet Paine. He noted that Paine was not hard to find because "the name of Thomas Paine is now as odious in France as it is in England, perhaps more so." In asking a bookseller about Paine's location, Yorke was surprised to receive a diatribe about the harm that he had caused France. Upon reuniting with Paine, he was struck by his much-changed appearance with "dreadful ravages over his whole frame, and a settled melancholy."

That melancholy was most evident in his writings about Washington toward the end of his time in France. Paine previously sent Washington a letter recalling "the ardor of seventy-six" with fifty copies of *Rights of Man*. Yet the "ardor of seventy-six" had long passed. Washington was now president, and Paine's ideas of popular government were viewed as radical by many in the United States. John Adams called him "a poor, ignorant, malicious, short-sighted, crapulous mass." Washington's response to receiving the copies was glacial, and he likely did not appreciate Paine dedicating the book to him. It took over a year to even receive a response, while Washington's aides assured British counterparts that he had not even read the book. When the letter finally arrived, it was about as personal and warm as a bill from his tailor. Washington wrote: "You will readily conclude that the present is a busy moment for me. Let it suffice, therefore, at this time to say . . . that it is the first wish of my heart that the enlightened policy of the present age may diffuse to all men those blessings to which they are entitled." Worse yet, Washington did little to rescue him from prison.

Paine would express the depths of his disappointment in Washington in vintage Paine fashion. He penned an open letter for all to read. Any reader could feel the personal injury expressed in his description of how

Washington was "treacherous in private friendship" and "the world will be puzzled to decide whether you are an apostate or an impostor; whether you have abandoned good principles, or whether you ever had any." Paine was angry, but he was also right. Washington had abandoned him at the time of his greatest need.

It may be the loss of Paine's faith in the inherent dignity and common sense of the public that took the greatest toll. Paine wrote painfully as an eyewitness to how the executions came "as fast as the guillotine could cut their heads off." In a letter to Jefferson in 1793, Paine wrote that "had this revolution been consistently conducted with its principles, there was once a good prospect of extending liberty through the greatest part of Europe, but I now relinquish that hope." Paine now saw the need for a stronger executive, a bicameral legislature, and Madisonian checks and balances. Given his debates with Edmund Burke, it must have been a sad acknowledgment that violence, not virtue, controlled during his beloved French Revolution. Burke had warned that the tyranny of the majority knows its own taste for oppression: "Their cruelty has not even been the base result of fear; it has been the effect of their sense of perfect safety."

Paine was again left adrift. France shattered some of his assumptions of popular government. The French Revolution did not prove to be a new age for humanity but a tragic recurrence of an inexorable historical pattern. As historian Loren Samons noted, "When you start looking at the history of Athenian democracy, you find all kinds of terrible problems. Athenian democracy didn't even last for 200 years. And in those 200 years, it suffered two oligarchic revolutions." The French Revolution lasted just ten years, six months, and four days. When the Terror finally ended, even more radical groups would arise, including "the Equals," who sought an early form of communist rule. They would be put down by revolutionaries turned reactionaries, as France was caught in new cycles of plots and purges. Revolutionary figures would ultimately turn from a tyranny of the majority to a tyranny of one. His name was Napoléon Bonaparte.

Part III

DEMOCRACY IN THE TWENTY-FIRST CENTURY AND THE "ART OF LIVING FREELY"

For every complex problem there is a simple solution that is wrong.

—George Bernard Shaw

Alexis de Tocqueville once observed that "nothing is more wonderful than the art of being free, but nothing is harder to learn how to use than freedom." The art of living freely continues to be the greatest challenge of humanity. That challenge is likely to become even more daunting in this century. Economic changes have long triggered revolutions, and the twenty-first century is entering a period of transformative change with unknown implications for existing social and political structures. Around the world, globalized markets, robotics, and artificial intelligence (AI) are already displacing many workers in the new economy. While new technology has previously produced new jobs (as with the shift from agriculture to industrial production), it seems doubtful that most, or even a large percentage, of low-wage workers will be retrained to fill higher-paid tech jobs and specialized services. The result will be a rapidly rising population of the statically unemployed and further polarization in social classes. Greater public services and support could exacerbate class separation in both wealth and living conditions. Such disparity can produce the very circumstances where unrestrained democratic impulse can lead to democratic despotism. A baneful cycle threatens to repeat itself, where popular rule leads to worsening economic conditions, which in turn lead to the embrace of a single authoritarian leader or tyrant. As shown by the United States, that cycle is not inevitable. Yet we ignore these new emerging challenges at our own peril.

In the 1930s, Louisiana Governor Huey Long was confronted over complaints that he had moved from being a demagogue to a dictator. He responded that "there is no dictatorship in Louisiana. There is a perfect democracy there, and when you have a perfect democracy it is pretty hard to tell it from a dictatorship." It was a revealing observation concerning the sometimes-fluid line explored in this book between "perfect democracies" and dictatorship. Dictatorships follow democratic movements that destroy themselves. The history from Athens to Paris and later revolutions follows a disturbing pattern of popular rule dissolving into chaos only to turn to authoritarian or tyrannical rule to restore stability. Rousseau's general will did not elevate the inherent virtue of humanity but unleashed its most savage elements. As historian Sagan noted, during the French Revolution "there was not one peaceful (i.e., civil) transfer of power during this whole period of supposed government by 'the people.'" In all these periods, there was little framework for peaceful change or for the expression of anything other than brute force. In a struggle for dominance, factions warred for survival. Without the needed constitutional framework, factional disputes became fratricidal politics until tyranny became the only option to restore stability. As Sagan added, "Once the establishment of a stable, modern democratic society proves impossible, one form or another of Napoleon becomes inevitable."

The challenge of past democracies was first to guarantee liberty and then protect it from itself. Freedom does not inherently produce enlightened citizens, and the Rousseauian faith in the general will has been proven unfounded over and over again. For Federalists like Hamilton, the Jeffersonians were "our Jacobins." They saw the same seeds present in the United States. Watching events unfold in Paris, Adams wrote Elbridge Gerry that

> the Want of Principle, in so many of our Citizens . . . is awfully ominous to our elective Government. . . . The Avarice and Ambition which you and I have witnessed for these thirty years, is too deeply rooted in the hearts and Education and Examples of our People ever to be eradicated, and it will make of all Scenes of Turbulence Corruption and Confusion of which foreign nations will avail them Selves in the future as the French did in the last.

Likewise, in May 1800, Hamilton warned former Secretary of War James McHenry that the embrace of liberty was no protection from, and can even be a precursor for, unrest: "A new and more dangerous *era* has commenced. Revolution and a new order of things are aroused in this quarter. Property, Liberty and even life are at stake." The success of the American Constitution came precisely because it allowed factions but did not allow them to mutate into a mobocracy. In France, the radicals "believed in the people rather than in the republic, and 'pinned their faith on the natural goodness of a class' rather than on institutions and constitutions."

The same voices are again being heard in the United States, 250 years later, from an increasing disassociated elite of politicians, professors, and pundits. Once again, the public is being told that the problem lies in a constitutional system that is too limiting on democratic change. Ironically, as law professors join this chorus in denouncing the Madisonian system as outdated, the Madisonian precautions have never been more relevant or essential. This too is also a "dangerous era" where factional pressures can easily destroy liberty. This is the very moment the Constitution was designed for. As political scientist C. Bradley Thompson observed, "American revolutionaries were not anarchists." The Constitution was premised on the assumption that factions are inevitable and created a system designed to allow their expression and transformation. That is in stark contrast to the view of figures like Sieyès who saw factions as "conspiracy and collusion, through [which] antisocial schemes are plotted; through [which] the most formidable enemies of the People mobilize themselves." Of course, he would support a crackdown on others before fighting for his own survival.

The French approach would be replicated in later factional struggles with equally murderous results, including minority factions like the Mountain declaring themselves the majority. Hannah Arendt wrote that the tragic irony is that the French Revolution had a greater impact than the American Revolution on later revolutionaries. For example, during the Russian Revolution, Lenin saw the French Revolution not as a human horror but a triumph:

> the bourgeois historians see in Jacobinism a downfall. The proletarian historians regard Jacobinism as the general expression of an oppressed class in its struggle for liberation. The Jacobins gave France the best

> models of a democratic revolution. . . . It is natural for the bourgeoisie to have Jacobinism. It is natural for the petty bourgeoisie to fear it. The class-conscious workers and toilers have faith in the transfer of power to the revolutionary oppressed class, for that is the essence of Jacobinism.

Despite representing a radical minority faction, Lenin used a vote on a relatively minor issue in the Second Congress of Russian Social-Democratic Labor Party in 1903 to proclaim themselves "Bolsheviks," or majority men, and their opponents Mensheviks, or minority men. Like the Gironde, the Mensheviks likely represented more of the population. Once they were able to rid themselves of the moderates and the Mensheviks, the Bolsheviks turned inward like the Mountain and killed their former allies. Where Danton died on the guillotine in Paris, Trotsky would get an ice pick in Mexico City.

There is an obvious danger of oversimplifying patterns that run from Athens to Philadelphia to Paris and later revolutions. As Tocqueville noted, every revolution has its own time and its own elements. Likewise, analogies to groups like the Jacobins are not meant to suggest that the politicians and academics discussed here would embrace an American Terror. The United States has gone through prior ages of rage, and our constitutional system has survived intact. Indeed, Philadelphia followed a diametrically different path from Paris in the same period due to our constitutional and cultural differences. Of course, that does not mean that the United States is somehow immune from revolutionary upheaval or that this century will not present a unique set of elements that can overwhelm our historical and legal protections. Failed nations have one thing in common: a degree of hubris and self-denial in the face of radical movements and conditions. Tocqueville saw how the world needed "a new political science for a world completely new." There is neither a fate nor fixed reality for democratic systems:

> For my part I hate all those absolute systems that make all the events of history depend on great first causes linked together by the chain of fate

> and thus succeed, so to speak, in banishing men from the history of the human race. Their boasted breadth seems to me narrow and their mathematical exactness false.

Changing social and economic conditions warrant a debate over how we will meet new challenges. The mere fact that we are facing new technology or global trends does not mean that our constitutional system is manifestly obsolete. To the contrary, the worst self-deception is to assume that the problems that we face are so unique that they could not possibly be resolved under long-standing principles. Indeed, many of these voices are themselves replicating prior calls for popular democratic governance that failed in spectacular fashion throughout history. The calls for immediate change have become demands to dispense with precautionary and counterbalancing elements. The solution, once again, is to unleash the general will. It is, as Shaw suggested, a complex problem for which there are already an array of simple solutions that are wrong.

Eight

THE AMERICAN JACOBIN

The Return of the Bourgeois Revolutionary

In May 2024, I was working on this book when suddenly I felt pulled into the pages of my research. A mob outside was crying, "Guillotine! Guillotine! Guillotine!" Those words were not chanted on Place de la Concorde in Paris but on the quad of George Washington University in Washington, D.C. I was literally working on the material from the French Revolution when it seemed like the French Revolution had come to me. Students were holding a mock trial of the university president, the provost, board of directors, and others over their refusal to yield to demands in an anti-Israel protest. Encamped for weeks in the yard next to my law school office, the students chanted "off with their heads" and "off to the motherf*cking gallows with you." No one seriously expected the tumbrels to roll down Pennsylvania Avenue. The students were venting and mocking the administration. Nevertheless, the faux trial induced a certain "what if" moment, considering whether we could ever actually devolve into such madness. It came at a time when protests are becoming more radicalized and, at times, violent. There was also a guillotine at the January 6 riot in Congress when a mob broke into the Capitol. On that terrible day, someone also erected a gallows for Vice President Mike Pence. After Trump was reelected, leftist protesters brought guillotines to Capitol Hill at the inauguration and during later protests. In 2025, anti-ICE protesters in Portland rioted and rolled out a guillotine and chanted,

"We got the guillotine, you better run." It is not the first time that effigies or mock gallows have been used to convey rage in our history. We have survived every age of rage because of a constitutional system that was designed not for the good times but the bad times that come with democracy. Despite having the most successful and stable constitutional system in history, there is still that moment: a fleeting doubt as to whether the system could survive the morning, survive the times we are living in, survive us.

Many voices today are mere echoes of the past, calling for direct democratic change and attacking constitutional limitations on the "general will." They are a rising class of American Jacobins, budding bourgeois revolutionaries striking out at the status quo and constitutional values. These are figures like Elie Mystal, a regular commentator on MSNBC and "justice correspondent" at *The Nation* magazine who has declared that "we should replace our piece of crap Constitution." Mystal previously called the Constitution "trash" and urged not just the abolition of the U.S. Senate but also "all voter registration laws." The opposition to the Senate is particularly poignant given the opposition of the original Jacobins in the French Revolution to bicameralism and an upper house. Democratic leaders have embraced the mob and violent groups like Antifa as a popular movement to counter the MAGA movement. A mob can be irresistible to a politician if it can be set upon one's opponents. The problem is controlling the mob when today's revolutionaries become tomorrow's reactionaries. These voices are part of a counter-constitutional movement that includes professors and politicians. Most of these figures are not calling for violence but rather fueling the rage and demanding fundamental change in our system of government. It is the same dangerous game, as shown by the French Jacobins who found themselves pursued by the very mob that they enabled and encouraged.

Democratic politicians have ratcheted up rage rhetoric, particularly after the losses in the 2024 election. As political violence increased, members of Congress such as Representative Jasmine Crockett (D-Tex.) fueled the rage by calling for figures like Elon Musk to be "taken down" and said that Democrats have to be "OK with punching." Others like Democratic strategist James Carville warned that Republicans or law firms supporting Trump are like Nazi collaborators who were hunted down after World War II. He menacingly added, "Maybe you need to go in history and see what happened in August of 1944, after Paris was liberated. They didn't take very kindly to the collaborators." An Axios reporter interviewed Democratic members in 2025 who admitted that constituents are turning to violence and rejecting messages of political reform. They felt greater pressure for taking extreme measures: "Some of them have suggested . . . what we really need to do is be willing to get shot." Another recounted how constituents told them to prepare for "violence . . . to fight to protect our democracy," including the need "to storm the White House and stuff like that." Other Democratic members explained how followers are "angry beyond things" and "It's like . . . the Roman Colosseum." Another member admitted that there were discussions on triggering or staging violence. One member said, "What I have seen is a demand that we get ourselves arrested intentionally or allow ourselves to be victims of violence, and . . . a lot of times that's coming from economically very secure white people."

House Minority Leader Hakeem Jeffries (D-N.Y.) called for people to "fight in the streets" to save democracy and posted a picture brandishing a baseball bat. California Governor Gavin Newsom declared, "I'm going to punch these sons of bitches in the mouth."

For some the attacks on the Constitution as a tool of white supremacy and oligarchy has served as a license to break free of the confines of the law and decency. Many of those committing property damage or threatening opponents are coming from the same class of bourgeois and affluent circles. They are professionals, professors, and journalists. They are students from affluent families who are now writing columns asking, "When must we kill them?" in reference to Trump supporters. It is not necessarily revolution on their minds but rage. It is the release of decent, law-abiding citizens to engage in crimes as a righteous act, in righteous rage. In 2025, affluent liberal shoppers admitted that they are shoplifting from Whole Foods to strike back at Jeff Bezos for working with the Trump administration and moving *The Washington Post* back to the political center. One such shoplifter, identified as a "20-something communications professional" in Washington, explained, "If a billionaire can steal from me, I can scrape a little off the top, too." These affluent citizens dabbling in crime portrayed themselves as Robin Hoods. It is hardly the stuff of legend. Robin Hood did not steal organic fruit from the rich to give it to himself. Of course, that is the point. It is the release from both reason and responsibility that comes with righteous rage.

The sense of license was reflected in the escalating language leading up to two failed assassinations of Donald Trump and the successful assassination of conservative activist Charlie Kirk. The most chilling fact about the murder of Kirk was that there was nothing particularly surprising about it. In 2025, polls showed that 55 percent of citizens expect political violence to increase in the United States.

There has been a growing extremism in this country in the last ten years. Radical groups have been encouraged by politicians and pundits as other establishment figures question the very foundations and institutions of the American constitutional system. After Trump's election in 2024, liberal sites sold Antifa Christmas gifts, from onesies to "Antifa Dad" hats, in support of one of most violent, anti–free speech groups in the United States. Professionals and professors have been arrested in violent protests, including lawyers and journalists throwing Molotov cocktails at police. When UnitedHealthcare CEO Brian Thompson was murdered in New York, a former *Washington Post* reporter, Taylor Lorenz, expressed "joy," and Senator Elizabeth Warren (D-Mass.) explained that corporations and the government "can only push people so far." Representative Alexandria Ocasio-Cortez (D-N.Y.) explained the murder as a response to corporate decisions that constitute "an act of violence against [ordinary citizens]." A national campaign against Elon Musk paralleled a rise in political violence with protests featuring signs like "Burn a Tesla, Save Democracy." Some responded with arson targeting Tesla dealerships, charging stations, and cars.

A December 2024 poll by Emerson College found that 41 percent of adults under thirty believe that killing healthcare executives and others is justified. Another 2024 survey by the University of Chicago found that twenty-six million Americans believe that violence is justified to keep Trump out of the White House, a chilling finding after two assassination attempts. In 2025, a survey found that up to 55 percent of liberal respondents felt that either burning a Tesla or killing Donald Trump could be justified. Joel Finkelstein, the lead author of the 2025 report, stated that "what was formerly taboo culturally has become acceptable. . . . We are seeing a clear shift—glorification, increased attempts and changing norms—all converging into what we define as 'assassination culture.'"

While there is little taste for revolution for most Americans, there is a sense of a rising movement of the discontented who are dabbling in the rhetoric of revolution. Some are calling for the removal of moderating constitutional elements and embracing more direct democratic controls of government. For example, Representative Ocasio-Cortez questioned the need for a Supreme Court. Human Rights Campaign president Kelley Robinson, who spoke at the Democratic National Convention, rejected what she referred to as the Founders' "little piece of paper" and called for the reimagining of our constitutional system.

The radicalization of society shows the same historical patterns, particularly among the elite, as it did in France. The calls for the beheadings of George Washington University officials took place at one of the most expensive colleges in the country with one of the most affluent student bodies. The role of affluent faculty and students in the radical shift on campuses is hardly new. Even the calls for revolutionary change in the U.S. constitutional system are consistent with past revolutionary periods discussed in this book. The early organizers of the movements were not, as widely portrayed, the spontaneous expression of common folk against political and social disenfranchisement. Even in ancient Athens, it was the aristocratic class that pushed for greater popular rule. In Philadelphia, the Constitutionalists were made up of leading citizens such as General (and signer of the Articles of Confederation) Daniel Roberdeau, forming the popular committees and even leading the mob in the raid on the home of James Wilson. Yet it was the French Revolution that best illustrated the role of intellectuals and the bourgeoisie in the radicalization of the country, including forming a significant part of the Jacobin movement. Rallying around the work of figures like Rousseau, a radical elite took hold among intellectuals and dilettantes alike. It was, as Sagan described, a type of "bourgeois ideological terrorism."

In a time of rage or disillusionment, the most extreme candidates tend to have the advantage in outmaneuvering more establishment figures. That is evident today. Democratic socialists like Senator Bernie Sanders (I-Vt.) and Representative Alexandria Ocasio-Cortez are drawing massive crowds, while traditional Democrats struggle to maintain control. In New York, the 2025 Democratic mayoral primary was won by a Marxist who previously called for the "seizing of the means of production" and converting private housing into communes. Polling shows an increasing level of support for socialism, particularly among the young and Democrats. Between 2010 and 2021, support among Democrats increased from 50 percent to 65 percent. Among young voters aged eighteen to twenty-four, only 42 percent have a positive view of capitalism, while 54 percent have a negative view. That was down from a 58 percent positivity response just two years earlier. Polling also shows growing support for communism among the young with 34 percent of those under thirty. Other polls show a growing lack of trust in the political and constitutional systems. Sixty-three percent now say that they have no or little trust in the political system. Not surprisingly, those views appeal to more radical elements and favor the election of more radical politicians and pundits.

Those who want to remain in favor often pander to the extremes. Radical leftist sites like *Jacobin* have grown in popularity, a site celebrated by MSNBC host Chris Hayes as "very explicitly on the radical left, and sort of hostile to liberal accommodationism." Of course, this radical chic does not hold a candle to the true Jacobins of the French Revolution. They use some of the same words and symbols but still seem improvisational and inauthentic, like a child's game of dress-up with oversized outfits. Indeed, that is precisely the danger. There is little knowledge, let alone memory, of what such radicalism became under the real Jacobins. There is the same blissful ignorance that allowed Rousseauian dilettantes to mutate into monsters, escalating radical agendas with every failure. The Girondins are examples of how the push for popular rule and revolutionary reforms can easily mutate into mobocracy. Even figures like Robespierre began as voices of justice and restraint. They enjoyed the rise in popularity and power. As the popular slogans became disastrous policies, the momentum would carry them beyond any point of recognition or return. The new Jacobins show the same blind ambition and abandon in striking out at institutions and the Constitution itself.

The Politicians

Demagogue is a term often used loosely to refer to politicians who seek to inflame the public to achieve their own advantage. The original meaning of this term in ancient Athens was merely a leader of the *demos*, or masses. Historian James Fenimore Cooper defined the term as a "leader of the rabble." The first use of the term is found in the year 424 in Aristophanes's play *Knights* with reference to Cleon, who opposed Pericles. He was a figure much feared and condemned. Thucydides described him as "the most violent man in Athens, and at that time by far the most powerful with The People." Cleon was followed by a long line of such figures. Aristotle later wrote of the "unbroken series of demagogues whose main aim was to be outrageous and please the people with no thought for anything but the present." These early writings show not only how figures like Cleon harnessed the anger of the masses but how they often became enveloped by their own movements. In *Knights*, Cleon is portrayed as "a slave of Demos," a pathetic creature "flattering and fawning and toadying and swindling" to appease the mob. That is the irony of the demagogues—they are both captor and captive, often carried away by the forces that they unleash.

The term is often used to condemn political opponents or movements. Louisiana Governor Huey Long was denounced as a demagogue in the 1920s and 1930s for his populist movement. Long clearly abused his power, demonized the wealthy, and engaged in rampant corruption. The line between a demagogue and a populist can be highly subjective. Senator Joseph McCarthy was also called a demagogue for his red-baiting campaigns and crackdowns on suspected communists. Critics have also labeled Donald Trump as a demagogue for his appeal to nationalism and promises of prosperity. It can be as much a matter of reckless rhetoric and style as of policy. For example, Long's slogans of "Every man a king" and "Share the wealth" were not so different from others in his period, particularly during the New Deal. It was his fury and bullying that made his calls so menacing. He was viewed, correctly, as someone who sought to capitalize on our divisions to achieve unrivaled power.

The most dangerous form of demagoguery is found in efforts to achieve greater power by convincing the public to give up constitutional protections. Politicians know that constitutional values or traditions are mere abstractions when played against economic or social grievances. That appears to be again manifesting itself in recent polls, showing that calls for breaking down institutions and even trashing the Constitution are finding growing numbers of adherents among our citizens. For example, during the Biden administration, some on the left like Senator Ron Wyden (D-Ore.) and Representative Ocasio-Cortez called for the president to ignore opposing court rulings. The same calls were heard on the right at the start of the Trump administration. At the same time, there are increasing numbers of Democrats and Republicans saying that violence is justified to stop those on the other side of the political divide. One poll by the University of Virginia Center for Politics found that 52 percent of Biden supporters say Republicans are now a threat to American life, while 47 percent of Trump supporters say the same about Democrats. Among Biden supporters, 41 percent now believe violence is justified "to stop [Republicans] from achieving their goals." An almost identical percentage, 38 percent, of Trump supporters now embrace violence to stop Democrats.

In *The Indispensable Right*, I discussed one scene that captured this "age of rage." In 2023, Representative Jamaal Bowman (D-N.Y.) was screaming outside of the House floor about gun control. Both Democratic and Republican members tried to quiet him, with no success. When Representative Thomas Massie (R-Ky.) asked him to stop yelling, Bowman shouted, "I was screaming before you interrupted me." Bowman later pleaded guilty to a criminal charge after pulling a fire alarm in the middle of a major vote. Bowman is associated with the democratic socialist wing of the Democratic Party and can be dismissed as a member of the most radical faction of the Democratic Party, called "the Squad." After all, he was later defeated in his New York primary by a more establishment figure. The most worrisome aspect of the last ten years has been the voices of figures long associated with the establishment. Many politicians have moved to the extreme left to ride the wave of activism and anger. We have seen, as in prior periods such as eighteenth-century France, how liberal politicians were being outflanked by even more radical politicians calling for revolution and the redistribution of wealth. As radicals rise in influence, more establishment figures tend to recede into silence or repeat the same rage rhetoric.

Take the Boston City Council. In 2024, council member Tania Fernandes Anderson unleashed a profane diatribe denouncing her colleagues as perpetuating racist and economic barriers. Anderson ran for office pledging to facilitate a revolution based on a demand for "equity": "I think that systemic racism is long overdue for us to overthrow it in order for us to create a revolution that brings about change." The revolutionary rhetoric appears to have cowed her liberal colleagues into silence, even as she attacked them publicly: "I can't even call you guys cowards because desperation deserves mercy. . . . What the f*** do I have to do in this f***ing council to get respect as a Black woman?" Her demands to "dismantle the white backdrop" went unchallenged by colleagues. One employee explained anonymously that "People are intimidated by her. And that intimidation does work." Anderson was removed from the council only when she later pleaded guilty to public corruption and resigned. The scenes of her colleagues dutifully listening to such ravings capture the dynamic of how the most radical voices can dominate in government, academia, and the media.

For many, it is not enough to support a cause; you must publicly affirm your enlightened values. "Silence is violence" is now a common mantra as academics are told to attest to their fealty to the cause of reforms or face cancellation. Opposing speech is not tolerated. Some have embraced violent groups such as Antifa. Rutgers professor Mark Bray, who wrote *Antifa: The Anti-Fascist Handbook*, has detailed how this movement is largely composed of "anarchists or antiauthoritarian communists" who reject such rights as free speech as a "bourgeois fantasy." They regularly commit violence as part of a resistance against "white supremacy, hetero-patriarchy, ultra-nationalism, authoritarianism, and genocide." The group has repeatedly attacked journalists and rival protesters, including pro-life protesters. One called free speech a "nonargument" and warned, "You have the right to speak, but you also have the right to be shut up." In Antifa, one hears the same rationalizations for violence that were heard among the Sans-Culottes, the Bolsheviks, and violent political groups. Indeed, they could be viewed as the inheritors of the Rosseauian ideal of withering away of institutions to allow the general will to become manifest in society.

Despite the rise of violence around the country on the left over the last decade, some Democratic politicians embraced Antifa as a type of political shock troops. Former Democratic National Committee deputy chair Keith Ellison, now the Minnesota attorney general, praised the group and, while holding the Antifa handbook, bragged how Antifa would "strike fear in the heart" of Trump. His son, Minneapolis City Council member Jeremiah Ellison, declared his allegiance to Antifa in the heat of violent protests in Minneapolis. Others supported extremists ambushing people at restaurants and other locations, including confrontations demanding that patrons repeat slogans. The escalating rhetoric reflected a factionalism that was fueled by political expedience, the ends justifying the means. In expressly calling for "any means necessary" to achieve reforms, Democrats such as Senator Warren embraced the long anathema call for packing the Supreme Court by adding an instant majority of liberal justices. Later, Democrats lined up to support the disqualification of over 120 Republican incumbents as well as Donald Trump from running for office.

Politicians have also questioned the core institutions of our system. There is growing frustration with a political system that has not yielded to demands of the public. In 2025, the newly elected vice chair of the Democratic National Committee, David Hogg, lamented "Democracy is what put us through school shooter drills and school shootings. It's what's put us through the climate crisis and so much more." Others have questioned the continued viability of core institutions, including those designed to temper majoritarian impulse or abuse. In her attack on the very existence of the Supreme Court, Representative Ocasio-Cortez notably expressed outrage over the fact that just nine people "can overturn laws that hundreds and thousands of legislators, advocates, and policymakers drew consensus on." After all, she asked, "How much does the current structure benefit us . . . I don't think it does." It was a telling remark and one that hearkened back to extremists during the French Revolution. The Court was designed to be counter-majoritarian, to protect constitutional values against the "consensus" of politicians and the public. Indeed, the darkest moments of the Court have come when it has yielded to such pressure as in the *Korematsu* decision, when it allowed the internment of Japanese Americans. Ocasio-Cortez would toss aside that core protection for minority populations in favor of popular rule and popular justice. It is a modern remake of the call for unleashing the general will.

For some politicians, a break from constitutional traditions goes even deeper in challenging some of the defining principles from the very founding of the republic. In 2025, Senator Tim Kaine (D.-Va.) attacked Riley Barnes, nominated to serve as Assistant Secretary of State for Democracy, Human Rights and Labor. The reason was Barnes's belief in natural law. Kaine denounced Barnes for a statement in which he declared, "All men are created equal because our rights come from God, our creator; not from our laws, not from our governments." It was, of course, a line virtually ripped from the Declaration of Independence in which the Founders declared, "We hold these truths to be self-evident, that all men are created equal, that they are endowed by their Creator with certain unalienable Rights." Nevertheless, Kaine declared:

> The notion that rights don't come from laws and don't come from the government, but come from the Creator—that's what the Iranian government believes. It's a theocratic regime that bases its rule on Shia (*sic*) law and targets Sunnis, Bahá'ís, Jews, Christians, and other religious minorities. They do it because they believe that they understand what natural rights are from their Creator. So, the statement that our rights do not come from our laws or our governments is extremely troubling.

While Kaine would later insist that he believed in natural rights, he equated the view of most of the Founders with Iranian mullahs and other religious fanatics. He was describing the very foundation laid 250 years ago in the Declaration of Independence. Many believed, as stated by Alexander Hamilton, that "the sacred rights of mankind are not to be rummaged for among old parchments or musty records. They are written, as with a sunbeam, in the whole volume of human nature, by the hand of the Divinity itself, and can never be erased or obscured by mortal power." Even those who believe in a non-divine source for natural rights still do not believe that they "come from our laws or our governments" as opposed to the inalienable rights that rest with all human beings. They believe that these are human rights and not just rights created by humans. Kaine's legal positivism fits well with an agenda to dismantle institutions to achieve immediate political goals. After all, what the government giveth, the government can taketh away.

The pandering to the most extreme viewpoints often leads to the weaponization of the legal and political systems. That was evident in the campaign against Elon Musk, particularly in 2025 when he joined the Trump administration. As I have previously written, it is common in "an age of rage" for people to become the very thing that they despise in others, even abandoning their core values. The means become the ends. That is evident among Democratic politicians who adopted anti-immigrant, anti–free speech, anti-labor, and even anti-environmental positions to get at Donald Trump or his supporters. For example, in 2025, New York Democrats targeted Musk to bar him from direct sales in the state. State Senator Pat Fahy, an Albany Democrat, is a longtime advocate of electric vehicles. The legislation would make it more difficult not just for Musk but other EV dealers. Fahy was undeterred: "No matter what we do, we've got to take this from Elon Musk. He's part of an effort to go backwards." In California, a state that prioritized EV sales more than any other state, legislators reversed course to make regulations tougher to penalize Musk for his association with Trump. The move is not unique. Previously, Democrats sought to block the expansion of SpaceX launches despite their need to fulfill national security priorities. California Coastal Commissioner Gretchen Newsom indicated that this was retaliation for "hopping about the country, spewing and tweeting political falsehoods." She sought to drop the launches because Musk "aggressively injected himself into the presidential race."

There has also been an effort to marshal economic factions. For thousands of years, the manipulation of economic factions has been a successful path to power. There is nothing wrong with running on economic development or the expansion of social welfare systems. Like other factions, economic factions have every right to seek redress in the political system. Other politicians have taken this appeal further in a type of "eat the rich" pitch for voters, demonizing the upper classes as greedy and privileged. President Joe Biden and others repeatedly insisted that the rich "do not pay their fair share" of taxes despite the top 1 percent paying more taxes than the bottom 90 percent combined. It is an ageless mantra; the public must rise up against the wealthy. Senator Elizabeth Warren (D-Mass.) has pushed for a "wealth tax" on the property of the rich, a move that is presumptively unconstitutional. The popularity of such measures is obvious. Senator Warren declared that she was coming after "the diamonds, the yachts, and the Rembrandts too." Then New York City Mayor Bill de Blasio, another Democratic presidential contender at the time, also promised that "we will tax the hell out of the wealthy." When running for president, Warren was asked about her wealth tax during the Democratic debates in reference to fellow candidate John Delaney, a self-made millionaire worth $65 million. Warren drew rapturous applause by dramatically rubbing her hands together eagerly after saying she would take some of his wealth. There was a sense of entitlement by Warren, who has never built a business, that she and her colleagues have every right to take from the rich with impunity. The appeal of such economic factions is likely to grow even further as the economy changes for an increasing percentage of citizens, including those left effectively unemployable by technological changes.

Once again, there is no reason to expect a new "Mountain" to emerge in the United States of terror-loving revolutionaries. The citizens of the United States have long embraced the rule of law as core to their government and their identities. Yet this history does not make them immune to the boom-or-bust cycle of democratic despotism. Cavalier calls for sweeping constitutional and economic changes have often spiraled out of control to the point that it becomes, as Oscar Wilde suggested, "simply the bludgeoning of the people by the people for the people."

The Professors

The intolerance for opposing political factions has been a harbinger of destabilizing political movements since Ancient Greece. That trend is particularly pronounced in higher education, where a type of general will has taken hold and produced an intellectual echo chamber. For many years, colleges and universities have been increasingly hostile to opposing viewpoints, particularly those of conservative and libertarian faculty members. Most faculty members remained conspicuously silent as conservative faculty were targeted and conservative speakers were canceled. A couple of professors even committed suicide after years of unrelenting investigations and accusations. As the war in Gaza intensified, the mob targeted liberal professors and writers who supported Israel. Like the Girondins, faculty who were long associated with the left found themselves the next targets. There was a sudden alarm over the loss of free speech and academic freedom by faculty who never uttered a word of concern for targeted colleagues for years. Students who were taught that they had a right to silence others turned against their liberal professors when their views became unacceptable. One Jewish professor at Columbia, who had previously joined students in seeking to defund the police, found his university card deactivated because his presence on campus might trigger students.

Faculty members are also engaging in political violence or calling for radical action. In 2025, University of Wisconsin professor José Felipe Alvergue, head of the English Department, turned over the table of College Republicans supporting a conservative for the Wisconsin Supreme Court. He reportedly declared, "The time for this is over!" The same week, a mob attacked a conservative display and tent on the campus of the University of California, Davis, as campus police passively watched. The Antifa protesters, carrying a large banner with the slogan "ACAB" (for "all cops are bastards"), trashed the tent and carried it off.

The rationalization for violence shown in political polls has been growing on college campuses, where "no justice, no peace" has become a more menacing mantra. Student editors have portrayed opposing views as "violence" and declared that "hostility may be warranted." In 2025, polls showed that one in three Americans under forty-five said that political violence is justified. These views did not just spontaneously appear; they have been taught by faculty members for years. In some cases, faculty actually led students in violent attacks and property damage. At the University of California, feminist studies associate professor Mireille Miller-Young led her students out of her class and physically assaulted pro-life students and destroyed their display. Despite pleading guilty to criminal assault, her Berkeley faculty colleagues supported Miller-Young after the violent attack. She was later given an award by the University of Oregon as a model of activism. In New York City, Hunter College professor Shellyne Rodriguez destroyed a pro-life table on campus while spewing profanities about how the students' "speech is violence." Notably, this violent attack was excused by the PSC Graduate Center, the labor organization of graduate and professional schools at the City University of New York. The union declared that Rodriguez was "justified" in trashing the display, which the organization described as "dangerously false propaganda" and "disinformation." Later, Rodriguez chased journalists with a hatchet and, while fired by Hunter College, was still retained as a faculty member by Cooper Union College. (She was subsequently fired by Cooper Union for other reasons.) In Albany, State University of New York sociology professor Renee Overdyke led her students in a protest during which she shut down a display and was arrested.

Some of the most radical factions in our history have flourished in this echo-chamber environment, including Antifa. These "antifascist" groups were described by Professor Mark Bray as "anarchists or antiauthoritarian communists" who view free speech as "merely a bourgeois fantasy unworthy of consideration." Of course, many of the American Jacobins in higher education are themselves bourgeois or come from affluent or privileged backgrounds. They have grown with the help of a host of enablers on faculties telling them that the Constitution itself is a threat and that the legal system has been corrupted by oligarchs, white supremacists, or reactionaries.

Many in academia are calling for revolutionary change, including a growing movement against "constitutionalism." This included calls from figures like Harvard professor Mark Tushnet for President Biden to simply ignore opposing Supreme Court rulings in the name of "popular constitutionalism." Brown University professor Corey Brettschneider has written that the Constitution is a "dangerous document" that is driving this "threat to democracy." Others like George Washington University professor Mary Anne Franks condemn what she calls the "cult of the Constitution" that has been defended to advance "white male supremacy." Franks argues that "free speech doctrine and culture fetishizes white men's reckless speech, resulting in the silencing of women and minorities." Franks argues that it "was created by white men for white men" and, even today, she insists that "the majority of Americans hate women more than they love anything. Including democracy."

Likewise, in 2024, *The New York Times* ran an illustrative column denouncing "Constitution worship." Book critic Jennifer Szalia insisted that "Americans have long assumed that the Constitution could save us; a growing chorus now wonders whether we need to be saved from it." She noted that the Constitution is "antidemocratic" and is now a vehicle of "authoritarianism" and one of "biggest threats to America's politics." The rationale for the *New York Times* column was crushingly ironic. The antidemocratic elements of the Constitution were there by design to prevent precisely the type of impulse changes that come with periodic political estrangement.

Professors now routinely denounce core institutions and the Constitution itself as barriers to social and political reform. Georgetown University Law professor Rosa Brooks has declared that our legal system is an impediment to social justice and called on citizens to refuse to be "slaves" to the U.S. Constitution. Likewise, in a column titled "The Constitution Is Broken and Should Not Be Reclaimed," law professors Ryan D. Doerfler of Harvard and Samuel Moyn of Yale called for the Constitution to be "radically altered" and insisted that radical change was needed to "reclaim America from Constitutionalism." Those with opposing views or teaching such views are now accused of undermining democratic values. Georgetown University Law professor Heidi Li Feldman denounced the conservative Supreme Court justices for going "rogue" and "lawless" due to their opposing views on the Constitution. She also added that it was "unethical" for law professors to teach such views: "Law practice, law teaching, and legal scholarship always run the risk of being in service to the unattractive, unethical sides of law: its use for the sake of power rather than for justice, its co-optation by the wealthy, its abuse by unscrupulous government officials." She further challenged those who work for institutions like the Supreme Court: "First, lawyers, legal scholars, and law schools have to point out that meekly serving lawless institutions is not actually serving law." Thus, her colleagues who do not teach a liberal jurisprudence are themselves fostering "lawlessness" and oppression: "Genuine lawyers, legal scholars, and law schools will make central—to their practice, their writing, their teaching—the project of protest against and change to institutions and actors who disingenuously hold themselves out as acting in accord with and on behalf of law."

Those professors who are not seeking to scrap the Constitution are instead "reimagining" critical parts. Law professor Mary Anne Franks has actually drafted a new First Amendment. She suggested that the problem with the U.S. Constitution is that it is simply too "aggressively individualistic." Others like Columbia law professor Tim Wu have questioned whether the First Amendment is simply obsolete and that we must accept that "it is no longer speech itself that is scarce, but the attention of listeners." In 2024, *The New York Times* ran a column by Wu titled "The First Amendment Is Out of Control." Wu claimed that:

> The judiciary needs to realize that the First Amendment is spinning out of control. It is beginning to threaten many of the essential jobs of the state, such as protecting national security and the safety and privacy of its citizens.

He added that the First Amendment "now mostly protects corporate interests."

The thrust of these criticisms is that the Constitution is now decidedly antidemocratic, a view with which many of the framers would eagerly concur. For example, in his 2024 book *The Constitutional Bind: How Americans Came to Idolize a Document That Fails Them*, law professor Aziz Rana calls the U.S. Constitution an impediment to needed sweeping social reforms and greater wealth distribution. Dismissing the reverence for the system as "creedal constitutionalism," Rana insists that citizens must view the Constitution as the problem, not the solution:

> The country today is wracked by a series of unfolding crises—intense police and military violence at home and abroad, financial crisis, extreme class inequalities, the carceral state's generational effects on poor and minority communities, white authoritarianism, and ecological disaster, to name a few. Our political class has seemed paralyzed in the face of these crises, and our constitutional system has only intensified them.

Rana and others suggest that the Constitution is a mythic or nostalgic obsession of Americans who want to preserve it. The suggestion is that it is outmoded to address today's problems and pressures. Rana maintains that the U.S. Constitution is "critically different from the role that written constitutions play in many countries. Outside the US, constitutions are often rules for governing." It is a curious argument since the U.S. Constitution is far less aspirational than many constitutions but has lasted longer than any such constitution in history. Madison stripped away the pretense and poetry of other constitutions to focus on channeling the pressures of factions into majoritarian compromises in the legislative system.

Even establishment figures now argue that the Constitution no longer suits our nation, which must go through transformative change. Indeed, it is presented as the very threat to American democracy. Dean Erwin Chemerinsky is the author of a book titled *No Democracy Lasts Forever: How the Constitution Threatens the United States*. He joins in the warning of the threat now posed by the Constitution to every citizen. He has embraced equally radical demands for fundamentally changing our constitutional system. Chemerinsky called for changing the allocation of representation in Congress, including the Senate, to shift power to more densely populated areas. He has also supported the reforming of the Supreme Court to replace conservative justices whom he now calls "hacks."

Furthermore, this growing scholarship often rejects classic liberalism with its emphasis on individual rights. Many professors denounce "rights talk" for its emphasis on individual rights as opposed to the collective interest. In her work *Feminism Unmodified* Professor Catharine MacKinnon rejected constitutional claims for rights like free speech, declaring, "Liberalism has never understood that the free speech of men silences the free speech of women." Critical race theorist Richard Delgado has written that this new vision of the law rejects core principles from equal protection to privacy when they stand in the way of dealing with "racial subordination": "Critical race theory expresses skepticism toward dominant legal claims of neutrality, objectivity, color blindness, and meritocracy . . ." Some traditional liberal figures like political scientist and former top Obama adviser William Galston have balked at the implications of this rising movement:

> [*Delgado*] questions the very foundations of the liberal order, including "equality theory, legal reasoning, Enlightenment rationalism, and neutral principles of constitutional law" . . . One thing is clear: Because the Declaration of Independence—the founding document of the American liberal order—is a product of Enlightenment rationalism, a doctrine that rejects the Enlightenment tacitly requires deconstructing the American order and rebuilding it on an entirely different foundation.

As more law professors declare the Constitution and even "rights" to be a threat to "democracy," we are left adrift in the same deconstructive movement that swept over France in the late eighteenth century, propelled in large part by intellectuals. We have become a priesthood of atheists, teaching law as a moribund field that offers nothing transcendent to citizens. We have lost our faith but kept our frocks. Notably, scholars in the critical legal studies movement (or "crits") like Roberto Unger have long accused classic liberals, like me, of losing our own faith and teaching "before cold altars." In point of fact, it is the critical legal studies movement and others calling for a radical change in our system that have replaced constitutionalism with a type of consequentialism where the merits of any action are judged by their immediate results. These academics have taken their own crisis of faith and declared a constitutional crisis.

These views have been amplified in part due to the elimination of opposing viewpoints. While academia has long been liberal, there has been a virtual purging of Republicans and conservatives at many schools, where there are often only two or three such faculty left. The disconnect with the country at large is striking and disturbing. Roughly half of this country supported Republican and conservative candidates. In comparison, less than 10 percent of faculty in all schools identify as conservative, and Democratic faculty outnumber Republican faculty by over ten times. At some universities, the ratio is roughly 30 to 1.

At Harvard, 82.46 percent of faculty surveyed identify as "liberal" or "very liberal," while only 16.08 percent self-identified as "moderate." Only 1.46 percent identified as "conservative," and no faculty member identified as "very conservative." *The Harvard Crimson* previously found that only 7 percent of incoming students identified as conservative. After years of winnowing out faculty with conservative viewpoints, Republicans are now not just a rarity but a curiosity. *The Harvard Crimson* sent student reporters to interview one of the last remaining conservatives found on campus as if he were an exotic attraction or relic from a prior age. Harvey Mansfield is a ninety-year-old political scientist who lamented the loss of intellectual diversity on campus. After interviewing this oddity, the student editors assured fellow students that the absence of Republicans was not a problem and that calls for greater diversity are "downright reductive." Besides, they could always read about conservative views in books or get summaries from liberal faculty. In 2024, I had the occasion to debate professor Randall Kennedy at Harvard Law School. When I raised the virtual purging of any Republicans or conservatives from the faculty, Kennedy rejected the notion that the elite school should strive to "look more like America." However, it is not just that Harvard "does not look like America," it does not even look like liberal Massachusetts, which is roughly 30 percent Republican.

The exodus of conservative faculty members has created an unimpeded space for radical viewpoints on campuses without a meaningful level of intellectual dissent. It has also fostered the further radicalization of the campus environment. After conservatives and libertarians were largely removed, contrarians and dissenters found themselves targeted. The result is that the "diversity" of viewpoints in higher education now runs largely from the left to the far left. There is a certain "radical chic" that exists at universities as faculty call for revolution and the dismantling of institutions. The environment pushes faculty to increasingly extreme positions, even praising the massacre of Jews by Hamas terrorists. Law professors have led calls for harassing justices, stacking the Supreme Court, and tearing down other fundamental institutions. Some suggested stripping the Court of jurisdiction until a liberal majority can be reestablished.

American academia has become a striking microcosm of the Jacobin societies and committees that were pulled toward more radical rhetoric as members competed to prove their ideological bona fides. One event at Georgetown law school captured how radicalism has gone mainstream at top schools. In a conference on the Supreme Court, professors thrilled many as they ratcheted up their rhetoric in support of "the resistance." Georgetown law professor Josh Chafetz seemed to be channeling the Jacobins in arguing that the "courts are the enemy, and always have been." He demanded direct action against the justices and the Court until it yielded to popular demands, including withdrawing funding for law clerks or even "cutting off the Supreme Court's air conditioning budget." When some in the crowd chuckled, Harvard law professor Ryan Doerfler reportedly shot back, "It should not be a laugh line. This is a political contest, these are the tools of retaliation available, and they should be completely normalized." As Robespierre observed, "Pity is treason" when it stands in the way of popular justice. It has a certain seductive appeal, particularly for students, that they must discard any moral or ethical resistance to such action. Retaliation can take many forms. Professor Chafetz also called for protesters outside of the homes of conservative justices to be more "aggressive." Chafetz defended such mob action as justified when "the mob is right." History has shown that mobs are rarely "right." While justifying any means to an end, mobs tend to be driven by the means used to express rage. It is that very mob mentality that rationalizes leaving bloody dolls on the lawn of Associate Justice Amy Coney Barrett despite her young children being inside.

Once untethered from basic notions of decency and civility, individuals can enjoy the full license and freedom of an age of rage. It is the same slippery slope that brought a lawyer like Robespierre to reject every precept of the rule of law. Retaliation itself became a virtue to the point that he would declare "terror is only justice: prompt, severe and inflexible. It is then an emanation of virtue." I do not view these academics as little Robespierres in academic robes. Most decry violence and believe that our system should be capable of radical change when it is no longer serving the public good. But Robespierre did not view himself in those terms when he first joined the Jacobins. He shaped the environment of intolerance, and then that environment shaped him into an unrecognizable figure of righteous rage.

For some of us who have taught for decades, the change in higher education has been traumatic and disheartening. Many have left teaching, while others have been effectively forced out. For others, like myself, it has put us at odds with our schools and colleagues. For many years, critics have lamented that I had become critical of liberal scholarship and political rhetoric. It is certainly true that I was an ardent Democrat for much of my life. Raised on the North Side of Chicago, I came from a politically active, liberal family. I served as a page for the ultraliberal Representative Sidney Yates and went on to work for a long line of Democrats in Congress and on campaigns ranging from Ted Kennedy to Mo Udall. I had the bona fides as a liberal activist and later as a liberal law professor. It is a powerfully seductive environment, and to challenge such views is to risk everything that matters to an intellectual: publications, speeches, and associational positions. An echo chamber is a wonderful place if it is your views that are being echoed. As others are being marginalized, your own more-acceptable views are amplified and celebrated. In the 1990s, I began to have serious misgivings about liberal thought in America and where it was going, particularly in what I saw as a growing anti–free speech movement in academia. I had always held libertarian views that tended to maximize individual rights against the government. I had growing concerns over fluid constitutional interpretations as well as a growing orthodoxy in academia. I saw a purging of opposing viewpoints, particularly conservative and libertarian faculty. In law schools, many of the least-tolerant faculty demanded radical changes in our constitutional system and dismissed those with more traditional views as reactionary, regressive, or racist. We have faced this moment before. These are all-too-familiar voices of those who have lost faith in a system that has not yielded to their demands. That problem does not rest with the Constitution. To paraphrase Shakespeare in *Julius Caesar*, "the fault, [dear colleagues], is not in our stars, But in ourselves."

The Press

The most revolutionary act of the American Revolution remains the rights ultimately embodied in the First Amendment, particularly in the rights of free speech and the free press. Neither of those rights were meaningfully protected in Great Britain and still remain only partially protected today by American standards. While some writers had espoused a natural right for free speech, no nation had ever used the words of the First Amendment in stating categorically that "Congress shall make no law . . . abridging the freedom of speech, or of the press." The reference to the free press was particularly notable. Early advocates largely focused on their opposition to licensing laws that controlled what books could be imported or distributed in Great Britain. Suddenly, a nation was protecting the free press from all government abridgments. The reference to the press as "the fourth estate" was credited to Edmund Burke by Thomas Carlyle in his book *On Heroes, Hero-Worship, and the Heroic in History* in 1840: "Burke said there were Three Estates in Parliament; but, in the Reporters' Gallery yonder, there sat a Fourth Estate more important far than they all." Carlyle himself tied this expression to the three estates of the French parliament in his earlier 1837 work *French Revolution: A History* when he wrote "A Fourth Estate, of Able Editors, springs up; increases and multiplies, irrepressible, incalculable."

The reference to the French press as a fourth estate reflected not just the separate identity but the distinct role played by journalists in the country. It was not always a positive role, as we have seen. In the French Revolution, journalists played a major role in fueling radical measures first against the Crown and then against moderate political groups, including the Girondins. Some of the most murderous figures among the Jacobins were journalists like Jacques René Hébert. In the American Revolution and the early republic, writers played a key role in rallying groups to different causes. During the Adams administration, Federalist and Jeffersonian publications attacked each other and supported censorship and the prosecutions of their political opponents.

Despite this history of partisanship and propaganda, the framers recognized that the press was essential as a conduit of information for the public, a critical check on governmental power in exposing corruption and abuses. This view was cemented by the trial of John Peter Zenger, editor of *The New-York Weekly Journal*. Zenger was arrested under the orders of Governor William Cosby, who was appointed in 1732 as "Captain General & Governor in Chief of the Provinces of New York, New Jersey and Territories depending thereon in America." The *Journal* detailed allegations of Governor Cosby stealing Indian lands, pilfering public monies, rigging elections, and other autocratic abuses. Cosby was irate and accused the paper of publishing "divers scandalous, virulent, false and seditious reflections." He ordered four editions to be burned and Zenger arrested for criminal libel. He proceeded to rig the trial by removing judges and disbarring Zenger's counsel. The American jury still acquitted Zenger in a major victory of the fledgling American press. The framers had no illusions about bias of the media but still saw the need for a free press as an existential right for the new republic. Madison called press freedom "the choicest privilege of the people."

Advocacy journalism has been part of the United States since its founding. The partisan press was later called "yellow journalism" in the late 1890s with thc publication of papers such as William Randolph Hearst's *New York Journal* and Joseph Pulitzer's *New York World*. (The term itself was derived from a popular comic strip featuring a character named Mickey Dugan known as the "Yellow Kid" in both Hearst's and Pulitzer's papers.) Then

something remarkable happened. The founding of the journalism school at the University of Missouri in 1908 and then (with the help of Pulitzer) the creation of the Columbia School of Journalism in 1912 led to the establishment of a professional press based on concepts of objectivity and neutrality. Around this time, a visionary named Adolph Simon Ochs decided that honest and fair reporting might have a market among the public. A former newspaper boy, Ochs had previously borrowed $250 to buy the *Chattanooga Times*. After turning a profit in Tennessee, Ochs heard that a newspaper in 1896 had gone bankrupt and borrowed $75,000 to get it out of receivership. The only condition was that he needed three consecutive profitable years to exercise his option for 51 percent control of the company. That newspaper was called *The New York Times*, and Ochs published his first edition with a new banner across the front page that simply read, "All the News That's Fit to Print." Ochs believed that the public wanted reliable and straight news, not the yellow journalism that they had been fed for years. He rescued the *Times* from insolvency by returning to professional journalism and, in the process, created one of the greatest newspapers in history.

The evolution from pamphleteering to yellow journalism to professional journalism appears to be coming full circle with the modern return to advocacy journalism. In recent years, many journalism professors have rejected objectivity as a touchstone of their profession. Stanford journalism professor Ted Glasser has insisted that journalism needed to "free itself from this notion of objectivity to develop a sense of social justice." He added that "journalists need to be overt and candid advocates for social justice, and it's hard to do that under the constraints of objectivity." Likewise, in 2025, at the University of Texas at Austin, journalism students were told to "leave neutrality behind" in order to serve the interests of social and racial justice. Untethered by such traditional values, reporters have actively sought to frame the news and suppress stories by declaring them misinformation or disinformation. Former *New York Times* writer (and now Howard University professor) Nikole Hannah-Jones declared "all journalism is activism." That view is shared by many in the media, even as viewers and readers flee mainstream publications and networks.

This return to advocacy journalism has been embraced by editors and publishers alike. Former executive editor for *The Washington Post* Leonard Downie Jr. and former CBS News president Andrew Heyward conducted a survey of seventy-five media leaders and found widespread support for advocacy journalism. Downie suggested that most of the media leaders today

> believe that pursuing objectivity can lead to false balance or misleading "bothsidesism" in covering stories about race, the treatment of women, LGBTQ+ rights, income inequality, climate change and many other subjects. And, in today's diversifying newsrooms, they feel it negates many of their own identities, life experiences and cultural contexts, keeping them from pursuing truth in their work.

That view is captured in the words of Emilio Garcia-Ruiz, editor in chief at *The San Francisco Chronicle*: "Objectivity has got to go."

The rejection of objectivity in the mainstream media has contributed to an exodus of viewers and readers toward new media and social media. The result is an information vacuum for the public at the very time that the country most needs reliable and respected news sources. We are regressing to an earlier period in the republic where the press was an appendage of politics, serving to amplify partisan viewpoints. This evolution has produced startling elements including publishing regular attacks on the Constitution, and particularly the First Amendment. Conversely, there has been the same intolerance for opposing views. That was evident in the disgraceful controversy at *The New York Times* over an opinion column by Senator Tom Cotton (R-Ark.) in which he argued for the possible use of the National Guard to quell violent riots around the White House. Cotton was expressing views consistent with legal and historical sources over the use of the National Guard to restore public order. Reporters charged that Cotton was endangering them by suggesting the use of troops and insisted that the newspaper cannot feature people who advocate political violence. Editors were fired and the *Times* made public apologies and pledges to do better in the future. (Within a year, Congress would employ the same measures that Cotton advocated on January 6.) Later, former editors came forward to denounce cancel culture and bias as destroying the newspaper.

The role of the media has been especially pronounced in the anti-free speech movement. Media figures have embraced censorship and denounced disinformation, misinformation, and malinformation as dangers to democracy. Despite the close association of the rights of free speech and free press, many journalists supported government and corporate entities in actively seeking to suppress dissenting viewpoints or stories. The press was seen by many as a type of de facto state media in blocking stories about Hunter Biden's laptop or ignoring major stories like the mental decline of President Biden. The costs of such bias were particularly evident during the pandemic, when reporters joined in condemning those with opposing views of vaccine or mask efficacy, social distancing, and other policies. The media helped isolate and demonize academics with opposing views, who were then banned or fired as fringe figures or conspiracists. At the same time, thousands of average people found themselves blocked on social media for spreading or repeating those viewpoints. Reporters denounced those who offered dissenting views on issues like the natural origins of COVID-19, even though federal agencies found the "lab theory" more credible. In 2021, *New York Times* science and health reporter Apoorva Mandavilli was still calling on reporters not to mention the "racist" lab theory. Conversely, the media widely reported later debunked stories like the Russian collusion conspiracy. *The New York Times* and *The Washington Post* would win the Pulitzer Prize for the story, even though veteran journalist Bob Woodward later wrote that he warned the *Post* that the story was unreliable. The true story came out only later that the Clinton campaign funded the infamous Steele dossier and hid the funding as a legal expense (while denying such funding to the press).

Advocacy journalism easily mutates into radical activism. Like moderate Jacobins, the media has often found itself next on the chopping block once revolutionaries take power. That was tragically evident among journalists in France, Russia, Cuba, China, Iran, and other nations where mobocracy was at first embraced by the media until these revolutions turned on these same reporters as reactionaries. Some, like John ("Jack") Reed (who wrote for mainstream publications such as *The Saturday Evening Post* and *Collier's*), not only reported on the Russian Revolution but also took up arms in support of it. The son of a wealthy family, Reed was radicalized while studying at Harvard and would write *Ten Days That Shook the World*, on the Bolshevik Revolution. As reporters were rounded up by the Communists, Reed would remain an ardent radical until his death (and would be rewarded for his contributions to Communism by being buried in the Kremlin wall). Reed rejected neutrality and objectivity. The model for many young reporters appears closer today to Jack Reed than Harry Reasoner. This activism blurred lines of separation between the media and the government, leading to growing criticism of a de facto state media.

The falling trust in the media has led to the emergence of a "new media," including greater reliance on blogs and social sites like TikTok. In a curious return to the media conditions at the start of our republic when pamphleteers like Paine rallied a nation, citizens are finding their own sources for information despite criticism of these sites by the government and the establishment. "Let's Go, Brandon!" was a popular criticism not just of former President Joe Biden but of the media itself due to its bias in favor of the government. It was first heard after an October 2 interview with race car driver Brandon Brown after he won his first NASCAR Xfinity Series race. During the interview, NBC reporter Kelli Stavast's questions were drowned out by loud-and-clear chants of "F*** Joe Biden." Stavast quickly and inexplicably declared, "You can hear the chants from the crowd, 'Let's go, Brandon!'" The scene captured the widespread view of mainstream or legacy media as an effective state media by changing facts that the viewers could actually see or hear. "Let's Go, Brandon!" became a type of "Yankee Doodling" of the political and media establishment. Just as patriots used the taunting song used by British soldiers against their foes, the public used the media's own words to mock what they saw as contempt for the public.

The result of all of this has been disastrous for the profession. In the

1970s, roughly 66 percent of Americans trusted the mass media. Now, according to Gallup, 69 percent have little or no trust in the media. The public is increasingly relying on social media and new media for their news. Revenues and readership have plummeted. Many in the media are so culturally committed to advocacy journalism that they continue to saw on the branch upon which we all sit. In 2024, Jeff Bezos brought in a new publisher to try to reverse the fall in revenue and readership at the *Post*. *Washington Post* publisher and CEO William Lewis then dropped a truth bomb in the middle of the newsroom: "Let's not sugarcoat it. . . . We are losing large amounts of money. Your audience has halved in recent years. People are not reading your stuff. Right? I can't sugarcoat it anymore." The reaction was a call for his termination along with the firing of other new editors. Some journalists would rather lose their jobs than their bias. Some lashed out at the race of the editors or at the owner. One staffer complained, "We now have four White men running three newsrooms." Another, Amanda Katz, who resigned from the *Post*'s opinion team at the end of 2024, objected that the changes were "an absolute abandonment of the principles of accountability of the powerful, justice, democracy, human rights, and accurate information that previously animated the section in favor of a white male billionaire's self-interested agenda."

The new media composed of thousands of Thomas Paines is here to stay. The legacy media can either sail on as a merry ship of fools or recognize that we have to offer something different. New media is heavily partisan, and the question is whether legacy media, including *The New York Times*, can again offer what Ochs offered in the nineteenth century in a return to traditional journalistic values and profitability.

Politicians, professors, and the press are all key channels of information for the public, shaping discourse in the United States. The radical messaging, particularly in the counter-constitutional movement, can no longer be dismissed as a few marginal radicalized voices. It is a pattern previously seen in this and other countries, though it is not clear where this trend will take us. That is precisely the problem. There were three overriding elements to the American constitutional system that distinguished it from revolutions that quickly devolved into mobocracy and then single-person tyranny: robust protection of individual rights, the structural protections against the concentration of power, and the accommodations for factional interests. We now turn to those protections.

Nine

WHY BIG, FIERCE RIGHTS ARE RARE

The Importance of "Rights Talk" in Confusing Times

Teddy Roosevelt on a big game hunt

As an undergraduate student at the University of Chicago, I read Paul Colinvaux's book *Why Big Fierce Animals Are Rare*. The book explained that large carnivores are present within a given ecosystem at lower densities than their prey populations because they need to consume more to survive. Moreover, big, fierce animals tend to frighten locals and are targeted due to how they impact lives or threaten commerce or agriculture. These animals tend to modify the behavior of their prey and produce an "ecology of fear." The result is that they themselves are hunted to make life easier and more productive. Big, fierce rights can follow the same pattern as big, fierce animals. These rights can threaten the range of action within a given society, particularly in implementing sweeping political agendas and majoritarian policies. They menace and frustrate those who want to implement reforms. As a result, those seeking sweeping changes, particularly law professors, tend to resist big, bold rights in favor of more nuanced and flexible interpretations.

The calls to "reimagine" or change our constitutional structure are based on a legal relativism that allows many advocates to discard fundamental principles of due process and individual rights in seeking greater security or equity in society. This has manifested in movements seeking to break away from fixed notions of free speech or liberty as well as core journalistic values such as objectivity and neutrality. Not surprisingly, the man most responsible for sending the uncompromising Thomas Paine to the New World was particularly concerned over the threat of such relativism to the republic. Benjamin Franklin warned against treating rights as fluid and conditional, stating, "Those who would give up essential Liberty, to purchase a little temporary Safety, deserve neither Liberty nor Safety." Franklin was speaking of the danger of trade-offs that come with times of fear or anger. He was also raising the most intrinsic vulnerability and anomaly of a free people: the ability of citizens to surrender the very rights that were secured at such a great cost from others. The greatest threat to liberty in the United States has always come from within, the self-inflicted wounds caused by panic or anger. It is a warning that has been echoed by other great civil libertarians through the ages, including Justice Louis Brandeis in *Olmstead v. United States*, who told citizens to be on guard against the "insidious encroachment by men of zeal, well-meaning but without understanding." There have always been those who have argued for concessions of rights or protections to secure greater tranquility or cohesion in society. This seductive Siren's call has been heard by every generation but arguably never so loudly as today.

The Franklin quote remains a poignant reminder for every generation and some have chafed at its admonition. Contemporary writers have challenged even Franklin's famous warning as not really meaning that you should not surrender liberty for safety. National Public Radio ran a 2015 segment titled "Ben Franklin's Famous 'Liberty, Safety' Quote Lost Its Context in Twenty-First Century," rebutting the claim that Franklin was warning about such trade-offs. Columnist Ben Wittes insisted that Franklin was writing about a tax dispute between the Pennsylvania General Assembly and the Penn family to pay for frontier defense. With the Penn family pushing the governor to veto a tax measure in exchange for a payment for the added security, Franklin felt that this was a great affront to the ability of the legislature to govern. And so, according to Wittes, he was actually referring to the purchase of a little temporary safety quite literally. Indeed, NPR's host Robert Siegel explained to the viewers, "So far from being a pro-privacy quotation, if anything, it's a pro-taxation and pro–defense spending quotation." While Wittes acknowledges that the referenced liberty was the right of the legislature to govern in a democracy, he maintained "it means, in context, not quite the opposite of what it's almost always quoted as saying but much closer to the opposite than to the thing that people think it means."

In reality, Franklin meant exactly what he suggested. Franklin was defending the essence of liberty in the form of democratic choice against giving up that power of self-determination in exchange for greater security. Wittes's interpretation seemed eagerly embraced by the host to show that the framers allowed for the trade-off of core rights. Wittes is correct that the quote derives from a letter addressing the dispute over the taxes during the French and Indian War. The Penn family was offering a lump sum payment in exchange for the legislature agreeing that it could not tax the land. The dispute was prompted by the news that the Delawares and Shawnees had defected to the French. A committee, including Franklin, issued a report on that prior mistreatment of the tribes while recommending the funding of a frontier defense. After discussing the need for the funding and taxes, the letter shifts gears and begins to discuss the "Rights of the Freeman of Pennsylvania" and, despite the disagreements with the

Crown, the "poor distressed Inhabitants of the Frontiers . . . themselves do not wish us to go farther." That is when the famous line follows about not giving up liberty for safety.

Franklin himself later clearly embraced the common interpretation. Twenty years after the response to Governor Robert Morris, Franklin was part of a delegation that was still seeking reconciliation with Britain. In January 1775, he opposed a demand that the colonies surrender core legislative and governance rights as a condition for peace. He objected that "the Massachusetts [*sic*] must suffer all the hazards and mischiefs of war rather than admit the alteration of their charters and laws by Parliament." Franklin's quote is then used again that "They who can give up essential liberty to obtain a little temporary safety, deserve neither liberty nor safety." Here the meaning is clear and unambiguous.

The effort to rebut the Franklin quote was telling at a time when so many in the government, academia, and politics were calling on the public to accept limitations on free speech and substantial changes in the constitutional system. It shows how, even at the start of the republic, there was the same Faustian bargain for citizens to accept less freedom to achieve greater safety and prosperity. Franklin was objecting, among other measures, to the condition that the Parliament could effectively veto all powers of internal legislation in the colony. Roughly six months later, the colonists would choose liberty over security with the Declaration of Independence. What was striking about the timing of the Franklin quote was that these were established rights that were being eroded. The legislative authority that was vested in the colonies would be curtailed in the name of maintaining order. He was speaking of the threat posed by an autocratic ruler to warn against such trade-offs that could lead to tyranny.

Despite Franklin's warning, some figures have cautioned against putting principle above the practicalities of governance. In the twentieth century, this debate rages on, as shown in the famous line from Justice Robert H. Jackson's dissent in *Terminiello v. Chicago*: "if the Court does not temper its doctrinaire logic with a little practical wisdom, it will convert the constitutional Bill of Rights into a suicide pact." The notion is that too much liberty can result in the demise of social and political order. I have long been critical of that statement as a rationalization often cited for the erosion of constitutional rights. Today, the trade-off often appears to be equity over liberty for those seeking major changes to the system. To achieve greater economic and social equity, many are using the language of revolution in "trashing" the Constitution or overthrowing the constitutional order. Others argue for revolutionary change within the existing system, if possible. This abridgment of core constitutional guarantees is being pursued in terms of individual rights, structural elements, and judicial functions.

Individual Rights

The downsizing of individual rights has long been a priority among academics, including a movement opposed to what law professor Mary Ann Glendon has called "rights talk." In her work *Rights Talk: The Improvement of Political Discourse*, Glendon challenges the American emphasis on individual rights in favor of more fluid collective interests and responsibilities.

> Our rights talk, in its absoluteness, promotes unrealistic expectations, heightens social conflict, and inhibits dialogue that might lead toward consensus, accommodation, or at least the discovery of common ground. In its silence concerning responsibilities, it seems to condone acceptance of the benefits of living in a democratic social welfare state, without accepting the corresponding personal and civic obligations. In its relentless individualism, it fosters a climate that is inhospitable to society's losers, and that systematically disadvantages caretakers and dependents, young and old. In its neglect of civil society, it undermines the principal seedbeds of civic and personal virtue. In its insularity, it shuts out potentially important aids to the process of self-correcting learning. All of these traits promote mere assertion over reason-giving.

Notably, Glendon believes that the emphasis on fixed individualistic rights "inhibits dialogue" and, therefore, impedes the resolution of divisive social issues. There is no question that rights do limit the range of options, but not necessarily the dialogue. They constitute a type of superstructure that frames political choices, barring options that would deny individual rights or invite despotic democratic measures. While civil libertarians view such framing as the very essence of a constitutional system that protects minorities from majoritarian domination and abuse, academics such as Glendon see them as barriers to dialogue and resolutions demanded by society. Columbia Law professor Jamal Greene received praise from many professors for his similar work, *How Rights Went Wrong: Why Our Obsession with Rights Is Tearing America Apart*. He writes that

> Rights have gone viral. We debate policy in the language of rights. We speak solemnly of soldiers heading into battle to defend them. We wave the dog-eared constitutions that enumerate them. We kiss the hems of the judges who recognize and evaluate them. The Frenchman Alexis de Tocqueville wrote in 1835 that "scarcely any political question arises in the United States that is not resolved, sooner or later, into a judicial question." That was hyperbole in his time, but it rings true in our own. Rights are the commandments of our civic religion.

The idea of dispensing with the focus on individual rights is thrilling to many. Harvard history professor Jill Lepore praised the attack on rights by Greene, adding, "Until Americans can reimagine rights, there is no path forward, and there is, especially, no way to get race right. No peace, no justice." Of course, we do not have to "reimagine rights" because we have been here before. Despite the different times, there are the same voices and many of the same terms. It does not take imagination, let alone "reimagination," to contemplate the world without such rights.

Free speech is a particularly common target for those who seek to trade off freedoms for safety or the general social good. The anti–free speech movement has dovetailed with an intellectual movement of both critical legal and feminist scholars who reject the focus on "rights talk" over more collective values. It is part of a rejection of classic liberalism that has long been the touchstone of American legal thought with its emphasis on individual liberty. For scholars like Catharine MacKinnon, free speech serves to oppress women with its emphasis on the individual: "Liberalism has never understood that the free speech of men silences the free speech of women."

As part of combating what she calls the "cult of the Constitution," Mary Anne Franks would take amendments designed to protect individual rights against the state and convert them into enabling amendments for state controls over speech as well as guns. The problem, she maintains, is an unacceptable level of protection for the individual rights against the state. Criticizing the First and Second Amendments as "aggressively individualistic," Franks argues that these rights allow "the most powerful members of society to reap the benefits of these constitutional rights at the expense of vulnerable groups." Ironically, Franks's proposal on the First Amendment would return the country to a standard closer to the one applied under the Crown, where speech could be curtailed for the general good. In what she refers to as "fearless speech," Franks supports censorship of speech deemed harmful while favoring speech that promotes equity and democracy. In so doing, she hopes to end what she describes as the internet model of free speech in favor of greater speech controls, as prevalent today on many campuses. While free speech advocates view the intolerance of our campuses as inimical to both higher education and free speech, Franks seems at times to embrace it:

> The Internet model of free speech is little more than cacophony, where the loudest, most provocative, or most unlikeable voice dominates. . . . If we want to protect free speech, we should not only resist the attempt to remake college campuses in the image of the Internet, but consider the benefits of remaking the Internet in the image of the university.

Free from the "unlikeable" voices, Franks believes that society is better by enhancing views that it deems positive and better for citizens to hear and discuss. This is all meant to achieve greater social harmony and to protect certain groups from threatening or triggering viewpoints.

The new proposed language for the First Amendment shows precisely why big fierce fights are rare and why Franklin's warning has never been more relevant. It would replace clarity with ambiguity in the meaning of free speech, a move that would greatly enhance the ability of the courts and Congress to curtail the right:

> Every person has the right to freedom of expression, association, peaceful assembly, and petition of the government for redress of grievances, consistent with the rights of others to the same and subject to responsibility for abuses. All conflicts of such rights shall be resolved in accordance with the principle of equality and dignity of all persons.
>
> Both the freedom of religion and the freedom from religion shall be respected by the government. The government may not single out any religion for interference or endorsement, nor may it force any person to accept or adhere to any religious belief or practice.

The language reflects a chilling regression of free speech to pre-Revolutionary standards. It would undo the most revolutionary element of the American Revolution. The First Amendment was a rejection of the fluid Blackstonian views of free speech that allowed for the criminalization of harmful speech. Franks's new version would qualify the right as exercised only when "consistent with the rights of others to the same and subject to responsibility for abuses." The First Amendment took this country in a bold and different direction to embrace free speech as an autonomous right of every citizen, an indispensable right essential for individuals to be fully human. It was not only a revolutionary concept for its time; Franks and others show that it continues to be revolutionary in our times.

If we cannot change the actual text of the First Amendment, University of Chicago Law professor Brian Leiter has argued for equally sweeping changes through the courts. He maintains that First Amendment jurisprudence is unacceptably "permissive" in allowing people to speak freely on the internet. After exempting legacy media sites, he would allow the government to censor "pure internet sites" to remove what it considers "low value" speech like "virtual fighting words." What Leiter calls "pure internet sites" would likely encompass much of the new media and social media that is now being used by the public as an alternative source of information. The Pulitzers can remain untouched while the Paines might be regulated. He also calls for "a fundamental rethinking of First Amendment doctrine and how it treats harms caused through the mental or intellectual mediation of a hearer/reader." All such things are possible by trading off speech protections against the perceived harm of the use of the right. Free speech then becomes an elastic right that depends on the government's view of the value and the harm of its exercise.

We have heard these voices and ideas throughout history. Even Lafayette, who drafted Article 11 of the Declaration of the Rights of Man and the Citizen, showed the same equivocation. He embraced the broad concept of free speech in language, affirming that "the free communication of ideas and opinions is one of the most precious of the rights of man." He then added a telltale limitation: "Every citizen may, accordingly, speak, write, and print with freedom, but shall be responsible for such abuses of this freedom as shall be defined by law." Where the American framers effectively put a period after the word "freedom," Lafayette put a comma that led to the effective gutting of the preceding language. Similarly, Franks's proposal would allow free speech only to the extent that it is "consistent with the rights of others to the same and subject to responsibility for abuses." She then adds that determining what speech would be allowed would be "resolved in accordance with the principle of equality and dignity of all persons." It is consistent with Franks's call to extend the limits of speech now prevalent on college campuses to the internet to reduce the "cacophony" of free speech and limit what she previously called the "loud, most provocative, or most unlikeable voice[s]" that can dominate our discourse. Franks and others made important points about how the internet magnifies the potential harm for some individuals and groups. It also allows for hateful views to gain wider attention. However, to solve this problem with the creation of gatekeepers or guardians for speech is to cleanse speech by making it conditional. The fluidity in interpretation shifts power from citizens to the interpreters themselves, who will describe which voices are "unlikeable" and thus allowable.

There is also a return to a type of constitutional consequentialism, judging the exercise of rights like free speech by their consequences to society. In

2024, Clinton's former Labor Secretary, Robert Reich, called for the arrest of Elon Musk for refusing to censor more users on X. Reich encouraged censors in other countries to limit speech, declaring that "regulators around the world should threaten Musk with arrest if he doesn't stop disseminating lies and hate on X." He explained in an earlier column that we need to "focus less on thinking about free speech, [and more on] thinking about how the times have changed." In today's environment, Reich suggested, more freedom of speech can be harmful, even lead to tyranny. Others have celebrated state censorship. Minnesota attorney general Keith Ellison celebrated the banning of X in Brazil after Musk refused to yield to demands for political censorship. Free speech is again being presented as a right subject to national laws and countervailing "public interest."

Courts will face a greater challenge in these times and, thus far, their record is mixed. In 2024, the Supreme Court effectively punted in the case of *Missouri v. Biden*, where states sought to address the privatization of the censorship system. These states challenged the courts to address the obvious circumvention of the Constitution by the government outsourcing speech controls to corporations like Facebook. The justices clearly struggled with the novelty of the case and the difficulty in applying existing precedent. Some appeared unwilling to create new precedent for addressing such outsourcing. If so, as with the erosion of federalism guarantees, the courts could retreat to a permissive approach that confines the First Amendment to direct acts of censorship while turning a blind eye to a censorship system described by one federal court as massive and "Orwellian." The danger is that they could, in so doing, become passive pedestrians to the withering away of core rights.

Just as the framers adopted the broadest scope for free speech protections after the founding, they also embraced an equally robust view of property rights based on natural rights. The founding generation was heavily influenced by Locke's view of a divine foundation for property rights. Those rights are also under attack. Senator Elizabeth Warren (D-Mass.) and other Democrats have pushed for paradigm shift in viewing property as presumptively state wealth ready for the taking. This political shift has occurred at the same time as a legal shift in when private property is protected from state acquisition. The concern is that this expansive interpretation would allow greater opportunities for state controls and subsidies. An example is the sweeping interpretation given to the power of eminent domain by the United States Supreme Court.

In 1998, the pharmaceutical corporation Pfizer planned to expand its operations in Connecticut and sought to gain ownership of an area called Fort Trumbull. The small community proved resistant and turned down offers to buy their property. Many had lived in the small community for generations. Pfizer turned to local officials, who seized the property through eminent domain, claiming that the private property was needed for public use. The company dangled a promised $300 million new facility on the land. As some of us objected at the time, the action of the New London Development Corporation (NLDC), a private body, was far outside of the purposes of eminent domain, which was used historically to build such public projects as highways and bridges for public use. In this case, officials were giving the power to one set of private citizens to acquire the property of another set of citizens. The "public use" was the fact that Pfizer was a more valuable citizen and would thus bring jobs and greater taxes to the area.

Susette Kelo and other residents sued the city under the Takings Clause of the Fifth Amendment and the Due Process Clause under the Fourteenth Amendment. The stories were heartbreaking. Wilhelmina Dery was born in her house in 1918. She lived there her entire life and shared it with her husband for sixty years after they were married. They never expected to live anywhere else until this corporation decided that it wanted her land. If economic development is a sufficient public use, any property can be acquired against the wishes of the owners so long as public officials believe that some benefit in jobs or revenue can be achieved. The 5–4 decision of the Court is maddening in its ambiguity, reserving the power to deny uses based on "impermissible favoritism." In dissent, Justice Sandra Day O'Connor correctly noted that the ruling allowed for majoritarian abuse:

> Any property may now be taken for the benefit of another private party, but the fallout from this decision will not be random. The beneficiaries are likely to be those citizens with disproportionate influence

and power in the political process, including large corporations and development firms.

In periods of economic strife, it can also lead to impulse demand for redistributive justice. If economic development is sufficient in giving private property to powerful corporations, it could also be justified in achieving developmental goals of equity and opportunity. Pfizer would ultimately abandon its plan five years later—just after the tax benefits expired. The land was never developed, and the local officials were left with little but an empty field and the shame of abandoning their fellow citizens to curry favor with this corporation.

Expansive views of eminent domain and other powers will remain a looming danger if politicians shift to a more Rousseauian, public-entitlement view of property. It is notable that one of the first policies put forward by Kamala Harris in her 2024 presidential campaign was a price-control scheme, the very type of measures pushed in Philadelphia during the meltdown in the eighteenth century. Faced with inflation, Harris's response was to blame grocers and companies for price increases under the claim of "price gouging." In reality, a survey by the New York University Stern School of Business showed a net profit margin of 1.18 percent for retail grocery stores in the prior year. Other studies show that the profit margin actually had fallen significantly during that period, including regulatory filings showing a 0.217 percent margin for Kroger's supermarkets. Price controls have an impressive failure rate throughout history. They also have an equally impressive political success rate for politicians alongside other forms of class-based demands. Those pressures are only likely to increase as the government assumes more of a role in subsidy payments, healthcare, and other forms of state economic regulations.

Structural Elements

Even structural elements in the Constitution are now being questioned as unnecessarily restrictive for achieving political reforms. The Madisonian system follows the modern architectural principles of Mies van der Rohe that "form follows function." The "Madisonian tectonics" of our system are designed to facilitate deliberative change and to vent destructive pressures among factions. That structural design is being questioned by many academics arguing that courts can simply make fundamental changes to how the system functions. For example, in calling for a "constitutional revolution," Pepperdine University law professor Christine Goodman argues that "revolution can vindicate rights, transpire gradually, and occur within the existing structure through a reinterpretation of norms. It seeks to introduce change within the structure and resort to changing that structure only if necessary." Goodman relies on the work of Yale law professor Akhil Amar, who states that Congress can simply change the structure of Congress without a constitutional amendment approved by the required super majority. That is justified as a way of achieving a more equitable division of power in the country. In Federalist 43, Madison explained the need for a super majority as a condition that "guards . . . against that extreme facility, which would render the Constitution too mutable." In an article titled "Philadelphia Revisited: Amending the Constitution Outside Article V," Amar explains that "malapportionment" of voting is so severe in favoring rural over urban districts that the country can disregard the constitutional amendment process and just realign seats in a more equitable way. In arguing that we can simply disregard the constitutional amendment process, Amar admitted that "may well scare [the reader]. To be honest, it scares me a little too." Nevertheless, Amar embraces the right of the majority to disregard the limitations of the Constitution to achieve their demands when the constitutional amendment process is too cumbersome: "the first, most undeniable, inalienable and important, if unenumerated, right of the People is the right of a majority of voters to amend the Constitution—even in ways not expressly provided for by Article V." The rationalization for discarding the amendment process is strikingly familiar in the history explored in this book. In the zeal of the moment, lawyers in both Philadelphia and Paris found expediency to be the overriding value in seeking change. In Paris, that impulse led to a series of constitutions and improvisations that left the country more vulnerable to democratic despotism.

Contemporary reformers often emphasize the elasticity of such framing elements in academic work on the Constitution. Yale law professors Robert Post and Reva Siegel have called their approach "Democratic Constitutionalism." As with Amar's theory, these professors criticize the consent model of the Constitution, requiring amendments under Article V to materially change the meaning of provisions or rights: "Article V amendments are so very rare that they cannot provide an effective avenue for connecting constitutional law to popular commitments." While they accept that some specific rules like the age of a president must be treated as static and fixed (absent an amendment), they view much of the Constitution as more fluid and subject to shifting judicial interpretations. Core rights from equal protection to free speech to due process are treated as malleable to meet changing social values and needs.

These fundamental changes to structural constitutional elements are largely designed to allow the system to yield to majoritarian demands. The frustration cited by some of the academics in obstructing what Rousseau would call the general will is precisely the purpose of Madison's design to blunt and moderate such impulses. While that certainly tends to slow major reforms, it also tends to deter the encroachment of democratic despotism.

Judicial Functions

The calls for sweeping reforms through the courts have led to campaigns to change the Supreme Court or intimidate the members. Many embrace changes ordered by the Supreme Court as an extension of the political process and insist that history has shown how "judicial review regularly and unavoidably translates deeply held popular convictions into positive constitutional law." In this way, the Supreme Court becomes a type of juristocracy that adjusts the law to the current demands and needs of the populace. In terms of democratic theory, it is difficult to see how empowering the juristocracy is different than empowering the oligarchy in Ancient Rome to achieve social reforms.

In the face of a majority of justices adopting textualist or historical interpretations, many liberal politicians and scholars are demanding that the Court be changed to guarantee the adoption of constitutional changes. In a column calling for the packing of the Supreme Court with a liberal majority, Senator Elizabeth Warren explained that the current conservative majority was simply intolerable because its decisions were going against "widely held public opinion." Warren ignores the intent to create a judiciary that could withstand majoritarian pressures to protect not only constitutional guarantees but also minority political interests. The counter-majoritarian function is now viewed as intolerable in the face of pressing political and social reforms. The most direct way of removing these barriers is to change the Court itself by packing its members with like-minded jurists. For example, Harvard professor Michael Klarman defended court packing on the ground that only a liberal majority would allow the left to change other aspects of the system. With a packed liberal court supporting sweeping changes, Klarman suggested that the Republicans "will never win another election." It is a chilling message for anyone familiar with our history. The call for an increasingly "democratic" or "political" role of the courts could lead us back to the conditions of the early republic when Federalist and Republican judges engaged in raw political trials, including sedition trials for political opponents. It is a particularly destabilizing effort in a nation that is, once again, split roughly down the middle politically. Despite the divisions in the electorate, advocates for packing the court generally claim that they are enhancing faith in the democratic system.

The calls for court packing echo calls from prior centuries for jurists who are "reliable" in calling out majoritarian demands in areas like abortion, climate change, and police reform. This view makes the selection of Supreme Court justices more of a raw political exercise in seeking proof of ideological reliability, including the use of litmus tests. Justices are then seen as vehicles for change in supporting political and social changes by their respective parties. That is a common reality in some states where parties spend millions to flip their courts in places like Wisconsin and Colorado. The result is often straight party votes by state justices. In 2025 in Wisconsin, the most expensive judicial race in history involved the Democratic and Republican candidates campaigning on suggestions that they would either approve or disapprove new district maps to flip control of the House of Representatives. The "spoils" from winning control of the state courts are the partisan changes in prior precedent on everything from gerrymandered election districts to limits on the legislature. Courts become mere commissions such as the Federal Election Commission where the flipping of the majority leads to sweeping changes favoring that party. These constitutional theories can legitimize those who view justices as more like robed commissioners who carry out the majority will. While Post and Siegel are clearly not advocating such a sweeping rejection of judicial independence, the use of the courts as an extension of the democratic process easily leads to such raw partisanship.

Efforts to use the courts to override democratic choice have divided judges. While the courts serve a critical counter-majoritarian function, some efforts have sought to prevent democratic choice. That was evident in Colorado as Democratic Secretary of State Jena Griswold sought to disqualify Donald Trump from the ballot for the 2024 election. At the time, Trump was the leading candidate for the presidency and would ultimately win the popular vote. The effort was justified under the "disqualification clause" of Section 3 of the Fourteenth Amendment, a provision ratified after the Civil War to bar confederates from returning to government. The theory was both dubious and dangerous, but many law professors supported the effort. Harvard professor Laurence Tribe even declared it "unassailable." While most states rejected the theory, the Colorado Supreme Court, composed entirely of Democratically appointed jurists, disqualified Trump in a 4–3 vote. Ultimately, the Supreme Court unanimously voted to overturn the decision, stressing that "Nothing in the Constitution requires that we endure such chaos."

Whether it is taxation or voting, these controversies reflect an inherent contradiction throughout history by those seeking to carry out the general will through the governance of the few. While espousing popular democratic themes, there is an echoing of the lament of the Bishop of Gap in the French Revolution of the "travesty [of] an unenlightened cure" by the unwashed masses. Even members of the Mountain sought to dictate conditions for a populace that was not sophisticated enough to know what was best for them. Many advocates today seek to use the state and federal courts as oversight bodies that can channel democratic demands and conform the laws to meet those demands. The result can be destabilizing for the Madisonian system, which was designed to channel factional pressures into the legislative process. In George Orwell's *Animal Farm*, the rule was that "All Animals are Equal, but some are more equal than others." The same is true of the branches in the Madisonian system. All are equal, but some may be more equal than others. It is in the legislative branch that factional interests are ideally transformed into majoritarian compromises. The limited role of courts is meant to give factions an incentive to work out their differences by assuring them that properly enacted legislation cannot be set aside absent unconstitutional or unlawful elements. Likewise, they rely on the political branches to work out these differences. If the courts are viewed as enforcing majoritarian priorities, the exclusivity of the legislative process becomes merely discretionary. Changes that cannot be secured in the legislative process can always be obtained through the judicial process.

The integrity of the court system also demands support from the legislative branch. It is important to note that attacks on the court system have come from some on the right. During the first hundred days of the second Trump term, some conservative members and pundits called for the impeachment of judges who enjoined the administration or blocked policies. Those calls were dangerous and destabilizing for our system. These issues, including the deportation of individuals under the rarely used Alien Enemies Act, presented good-faith and novel questions. The inclination to remove judges (and eliminate their courts) shows that same crisis of faith that can destroy our system of justice. We have an appellate process to address judicial overreach and errors in interpretation. The desire to remove errant judges is a practice associated with the breakdown of constitutional systems, from France in the nineteenth century to Russia in the twentieth century.

The abandonment of major constitutional values or structuring principles presents costs that extend far beyond insular fights over expression or association or religious choice. These big and fierce rights and rules are embedded in not just American constitutionalism but in American culture. Returning to Tocqueville, one of the most powerful insights in *Democracy in America* was how a core protection of democracy rests with what he refers to as "manners," or *moeurs*:

> I have previously remarked that the manners of the people may be considered as one of the great general causes to which the maintenance of a democratic republic in the United States is attributable. I here use the word customs with the meaning which the ancients attached to the word moeurs; for I apply it not only to the manners properly so called—that is, to what might be termed the habits of the heart—but to the various notions and opinions current among men and to the mass of those ideas which constitute their character of mind. I comprise under this term, therefore, the whole moral and intellectual conditions of a people. My intention is not to draw a picture of American customs, but simply to point out such features of them as are favorable to the maintenance of their political institutions.

This passage appears an outgrowth of the influence writings of François-Pierre-Guillaume Guizot (1787–1874), a powerful French minister and intellectual leader who authored the work *History of Civilization in Europe*. Guizot wrote that "Democracy . . . [held] out an interminable vista and infinite promises." Conversely, Guizot (who served as royal minister) warned "Chaos is now concealed under one word—Democracy." These writings clearly had a pronounced effect on Tocqueville in exposing the inherent dangers of democratic despotism. While he did not subscribe to all of Guizot's views on democracy, Tocqueville clearly embraced the importance of these ingrained "manners" when he referenced the "spirit" of democracy in America.

What if those "habits of the heart" can be changed in a people? The movement against rights like free speech struggles to make the public afraid of the rights that they have historically enjoyed, the rights that once defined them. It is not easy to get a free people to give up freedom. To do so, they must be very, very afraid. Thus, as previously discussed, academia, the media, and politicians have barraged the public with claims that the current system is threatening not just democracy but their jobs and their very existence.

Despite the academic movement against "rights talk" and efforts to amend the Bill of Rights, the emphasis on individual rights will be even more important in the coming decades. Those "excessively individualistic" rights are precisely what can protect against tyranny of the majority. To that end, the First Amendment rights protecting speech, religious beliefs, and associations will become more vital as social and economic pressures build in the country. Notably, each of these rights was quickly attacked under the despotic measures of the French Revolution. Controlling what is said or heard by citizens is vital to those who want to control a nation. The United States has long relied on Article III to defend these minority interests through a judiciary designed to be counter-majoritarian, to resist popular measures to silence or intimidate minority views or values.

One of the most chilling aspects of the current period has been the rapid embrace of the left of censorship and other measures directed against minority viewpoints. While once the target of such measures during the Red Scare and the McCarthy period, the left has shown a pronounced intolerance for opposing views, from academia to the media to politics. It has changed what Tocqueville called the "manners" or "heart" of these citizens in getting them to turn against the defining values of our founding. Early American writers saw an inherent self-destructive impulse in human relations absent structural limits. For example, when Reverend Charles Turner delivered a sermon to the Massachusetts legislature soon after the Revolution, he warned that "unlimited power has generally been destructive of human happiness." Absolute freedom can lead to anarchy or tyranny, but neither has ever led to human happiness. Locke captured the same sentiment in his famous observation that "wherever law ends, tyranny begins." None of the countermeasures discussed in this book will be possible without a fierce defense of speech, religious, and associational rights to protect citizens in challenging majoritarian excesses. We must, in other words, re-embrace "big, fierce" rights to withstand the regressive efforts of many in our society.

This brings us back to the Colinvaux book, which explores different explanations for the relative scarcity of big, fierce animals, including the theory that smaller animals simply have greater reproductive rates. Colinvaux argued against that theory and noted that "numbers are set by the opportunities for one's way of life, not by the way one breeds." He offers the cheeky example that the population of professors is not set by their productivity but the availability of professorships. Colinvaux embraces the theory that we must think of big fierce animals in terms of their biomass and the calories that they must consume to survive. Large animals like lions must burn a huge amount of calories to hunt and, therefore, must consume large quantities of calories to survive. In a way, big, fierce rights are similar. What some professors object to is how a right like free speech consumes so much in the constitutional ecosystem. As previously discussed, Professor Wu describes the First Amendment in virtual predatorial terms, complaining that "nearly any law that has to do with the movement of information can be attacked in the name of the First Amendment." He objects that courts have allowed it to become so big and fierce that it now "threaten[s] many of the essential jobs of the state, such as protecting national security and the safety and privacy of its citizens." The solution of many academics is to scale down the rights so that they do not threaten policies and reforms that are deemed of greater importance.

Thomas Paine himself showed the same crisis of faith in free speech. While other framers like James Madison defended a robust natural right for free expression, Paine's fealty to free speech would waver despite his being the very personification of this "indispensable right." As the attacks on opponents turned lethal, Paine began to speak of regulating and punishing speech. On May 6, 1793, he wrote to Danton:

> There ought to be some regulation with respect to the spirit of denunciation that now prevails. If every individual is to indulge his private malignancy or his private ambition, to denounce at random and

> without any kind of proof, all confidence will be undermined and all authority be destroyed. Calumny is a species of treachery that out to be punished as well as any other kind of treachery. It is a private vice productive of public evils, because it is possible to irritate men into disaffection by continual calumny who never intended to be disaffected.

In April 1797, there was a crackdown by Republicans on critics, including making it a crime punishable by death to call for the restoration of the monarchy. Paine supported the measure and asked, "Shall the Republic be destroyed by the darksome manoeuvres of a faction, or shall it be preserved by an exceptional act?" It was a shocking statement from a man who was charged with sedition in England for criticizing the King. This was the same Paine who wrote:

> This is a government that has nothing to fear. It needs no proclamations to deter people from writing and reading, . . . It was by encouraging discussion, and rendering the press free upon all subjects of government, that the principles of government became understood in America, and the people are now enjoying the present blessings under it.

It was also the very position that Paine's patron, Benjamin Franklin, denounced in his warning about "those who would give up essential Liberty, to purchase a little temporary Safety." American revolutionaries rallied around the words of Thomas Gordon and John Trenchard (writing as Cato):

> In those wretched countries where a man cannot call his tongue his own, he can scarce call anything his own. Whoever would overthrow the liberty of a nation must begin by subduing the freeness of speech, . . . Without freedom of thought there can be no such thing as wisdom, and no such thing as public liberty without freedom of speech, which is the right of every man. . . .

Paine's support for criminalizing speech may reflect his own crisis of principle after years of attacks, incarceration, and vilification. The clarity of thought that made him the voice of a revolution was lost in the aftermath of the French Revolution. He was not alone. Great advocates for individual rights such as Edmund Burke seemed to abandon their principles in suggesting that Paine's writing could be banned as seditious. It is a cautionary tale for many today who have allowed contemporary circumstances to undermine their own faith in our founding principles.

As evident from his writing in *Common Sense*, Paine long argued that rights, not governments, were the objective of humanity in seeking a more perfect nation. He famously stated that "society in every state is a blessing, but government even in its best state is but a necessary evil; in its worst state an intolerable one." In the United States, the public had the benefit of a constitution based on natural rights. It was a constitutional ecosystem designed for a relatively small number of big, fierce rights. Freedom of speech, religion, association, and other rights do "consume" space and energy in our system. They also differ in an important respect from the underlying biomass theory, that there is a fixed or limited amount of energy that is exchanged among animals and plants. These big, fierce rights are net energy producers, not consumers. Free expression and association generate vital energy in a democratic system. They not only fulfill human or natural rights but also trigger greater productivity in society. Tocqueville, for example, wrote of the necessity of associations to perfect not just democracies but citizens: "Feelings and opinions are recruited, the heart is enlarged, and the human mind is developed only by the reciprocal influence of men upon one another." Speech and associations are transformative for citizens and society alike. It was the loss of these rights that destabilized societies like France and denied both political and economic energy needed to sustain the country. Their loss led to the collapse of the entire legal ecosystem, great and small.

Ten

ADAM SMITH AND THE LIBERTY-ENHANCING ECONOMY

When the Declaration of Independence was signed in 1776, it was a transformative moment in political theory. That same year, an equally momentous moment occurred in economic theory. The 1776 publication of Adam Smith's masterpiece *The Wealth of Nations* would have the same revolutionary impact on economic policy, particularly in the United States. Smith laid out foundational theories for the free market and capitalism, including an analysis of the royal economic policies impacting the colonies. It offered what would become an American view of a type of liberty-enhancing economy to match a new liberty-based government. These were times of indentured servitude and mercantile economies. The framers understood that constraining income can control an individual, while constraining an economy can control a nation. If people are to be truly free, they must be first and foremost able to pursue that freedom. Independency meant more than just throwing off the yoke of government but also restoring the liberty of citizens to make of themselves what their talents and passions dictate. Like Locke, Smith viewed labor as the source of wealth and self-advancement—aligning the most influential philosophical and economic theories for the Founders.

For intellectuals who sought to limit the role of government to foster individual choice and self-determination, the free market principles of Adams would resonate in a profound way. Even for perceived "radicals" such as Thomas Paine, free-market principles were embraced as intrinsically consistent with the ideal of a society based on both equality and equity. What Paine witnessed in Philadelphia would make him skeptical of price controls, monopolies, and market controls during the French Revolution. He came to oppose certain taxes, including an unpopular tax based on the number of windows of a dwelling. That was a telling objection since such laws in the United States triggered rebellions in the United States after the Revolution. Even though Paine supported an import tax on foreign goods as a source of revenue, he became an advocate of free-market principles. He recognized that a central government needed such revenue to avoid the fate of being "overrun, ravaged, and ruined." However, he also understood that a nation needed economic prosperity to flourish. He wrote that "the case must show the vast advantage of an open trade."

The American view of a natural law basis for the Declaration of Independence included a view of the right to pursue happiness and wealth. In George Mason's draft of the Virginia Declaration of Rights, written at the Raleigh Tavern in Williamsburg, the nexus between liberty and property was expressly drawn. Mason wrote of "inherent natural rights" supporting "acquiring and possessing property." That right would ultimately be adopted in the Declaration of Rights. Smith's work offered a political economic theory that paralleled and complemented the Declaration of Independence. With Adams, this new nation had both an economic and political theory based on principles of independence and self-determination.

Paine even went so far as to suggest that his nemesis Edmund Burke should read *The Wealth of Nations*. While arguing for the removal of such measures as the Poor Laws in England, he saw how revolution could create not just brutal social but economic conditions. Smith's revolutionary concept of self-determination could prove even more relevant and compelling in the twenty-first century as economic shifts force greater dependency on government subsidies. Economic independence remains the most liberating factor for citizens seeking to live their lives according to their own values and priorities. Just as the Declaration of Independence sought to maximize political liberty, the founding generation wanted to maximize economic liberty for citizens to achieve true "independency."

Economic Enlightenment and the American Revolution

Smith was part of the Scottish Enlightenment that revolutionized political and scientific thought with others such as David Hume and Francis Hutcheson. Notably, just as the framers were enthralled with Newtonian concepts, so was Smith. Where Smith marveled at the "Newtonian method" of science, he sought to prove that similar reasoned principles guided economies. This is why he has been called the "Newton of his subject." In political and economic policy, he saw the efficient principles at work, stating that "in the manner of Sir Isaac Newton we may lay down certain principles known or proved in the beginning." Like his close friend Hume, Smith wanted to strip away the myths and assumptions underlying past approaches to public policies. When he studied at Oxford, Smith found an environment of calcified and "obsolete prejudices" that was not open to such new concepts. Smith also shared Madison's view of human virtue. While he valued virtuous action, he did not believe that you could base either a political or economic system on assumptions of virtue.

As discussed earlier, the Founders were a product of the Enlightenment and relied on figures such as Locke to declare "independency" based on principles of natural law and liberty. Smith's embrace of laissez-faire economics was the perfect fit for a system that emphasized individual choice and rights. While he never visited the United States, his theories seemed quintessentially American to many of his generation. For a revolution that was triggered by tariffs and fueled by events like the Boston Tea Party, Smith's general principles read like an economic version of *Common Sense*. It was a type of declaration of independence not just from the British policy of mercantilism (emphasizing British exports over imports) but from economic controls over individual productivity and self-determination. In his famous Federalist 10, Madison stressed that the "first object of the government [is to protect] the diversity in the faculties of men, from which the rights of property originate." Smith's "invisible hand" was liberating not just for national economies but for citizens in treating markets as the result of individual consumer choices. It offered an economic model of democratic selection. Madison wrote an entire essay on "Property" that stressed that the right speaks to the individual ownership over one's faculties and productivity: "In a larger and juster meaning, [property] embraces everything to which a man may attach a value and have a right, and which leave to everyone else the like advantage. . . . He has an equal property in the free use of this faculties and free choice of the objects on which to employ them. In a word, as a man is said to have a right to his property, he may be equally said to have a property in his rights."

This view was not confined to American thought. Even Blackstone saw property rights of an individual as near absolute. Blackstone wrote that "there is nothing which so generally strikes the imagination and engages the affections of mankind, as the right of property; or that sole and despotic dominion which one man claims and exercises over the external things of the world, in total exclusion of the right of any other individual in the universe." Notably, this view of private property rested within an economic system of massive state controls and monopolies. In defining the fundamental law of nature in the Declaration of Independence, the Founders placed the right to property within the "trinity of rights." In modern political discourse, it is often jarring to hear property used with liberty as part of a natural or human right. Critical legal studies figures like Harvard's Duncan Kennedy denounce the property concepts of Blackstone and oppose theories that inhibit redistribution of wealth: "The private owner's freedom to exclude others from his possessions has as its corollary his power to control the lives of those who cannot live without access to the means of production." Today wealth differentials and the concentration of wealth are viewed in pejorative terms. Wealth is viewed as a privilege, not a right. The Founding generation held a different view of property as "sacred" to the natural liberty of mankind. This view was evident in the writings of "Massachusettensis," which suggested a type of harm principle associated with John Stuart Mill. Absent harm to others or society, the government was limited in the abridgment or confiscation of property:

> So great, is the regard of the law for private property, that it will not authorize the least violation of it, unless applied to the detriment of the Society—That men have a natural right to retain their justly acquired property, or dispose of it as they please without injuring others, is a proposition that has never been controversial to my knowledge: That they should lose this right by entering society is repugnant to common sense and the united voice of every writer of reputation to common sense and the united voice of every writer of reputation upon the subject.

The Founders saw property as a critical part of self-realization and fulfillment. Discussions of property were commonly imbued with a strong Lockean, natural-right patina as figures like James Wilson wrote of "the lawful power, which a person has to a thing." Locke viewed the creation and retention of property as based on a divinely bestowed, natural right. Under this labor theory, God gave humans everything "in common" in the state of nature and, from that common property, humans produced their own creations that are theirs to possess by divine right, not by consent of any given government.

Given the American political revolution, it is little surprise that Smith was arguably a greater hit in America than in England. He was praised by figures like Paine while he was damned by faint praise in English circles. It is important to note that, after the Revolution, the United States was an economic basket case, with trade virtually shut down. The primary market in England was effectively cut off, which devastated domestic businesses, produced debt, and left no functioning banking system in the United States. The British had prevented development of an American currency, so the void was filled by highly unstable state currencies with a paucity of coinage. The only advantage of hitting an economic rock bottom is a certain freedom of thought in building a new economic system from scratch. The United States was untethered to past economic systems. In Europe, economics remained mired in its foundations in feudal times. That is when Smith appeared to walk right out of revolutionary central casting on the very year that independence was declared. Like Madison and other framers, Smith saw natural principles as guiding the essence of economics:

> Little else is requisite to carry a state to the highest degree of opulence from the lowest barbarism but peace, easy taxes, and a tolerable administration of justice; all the rest being brought by the natural course of things. All governments which thwart this natural course, which force things into another channel, or which endeavor to arrest the progress of society at a particular point, are unnatural, and to support themselves are obliged to be oppressive and tyrannical.

Smith also looked back at history, beginning with the same periods of ancient Greece and Rome, in forming his views of the natural order of political economies.

Smith would surprise many by giving up his academic post to accept the lucrative position as a tutor to the stepson of Charles Townshend, the British chancellor of the exchequer and the author of the Townshend Acts that served as a catalyst for the American Revolution. He was introduced to Townshend by Hume, the great philosopher and his lifelong friend. The time with the Townshends had a major impact on Smith. In Paris, he would meet Benjamin Franklin, who, as with Thomas Paine, immediately spotted a genius in the Scottish tutor. He also interacted with Rousseau, who was already shaping the figures who would lead the French Revolution. His travels also brought him into the company of François Quesnay, an economist and the founder of the Physiocracy school, a free-market school whose motto was *Laissez faire et laissez passer, le monde va de lui même!* ("Let do and let pass, the world goes on by itself!") The school was known for its opposition to mercantilism and its emphasis on the value of agriculture and agricultural products. Those views would find a pronounced place in *The Wealth of Nations*. Indeed, Smith would write that "with all its imperfections, [the Physiocratic school] is perhaps the nearest approximation to the truth that has yet been published upon the subject of political economy."

Smith's rejection of mercantilism in favor of capitalism bordered on the sacrilegious at the time. Griffith University (Australia) professor Athol Fitzgibbons stressed that "Smith was a revolutionary, but in his time collectivism was a right-wing doctrine that favoured the social and religious power structure." This economic system, in Smith's view, strangled not just economic but political advancement. He described the British regulations as "contrary to . . . liberty." He noted that the British "affect to be so very jealous" of liberty, but are willing to sacrifice it "to the futile interests of our merchants and manufacturers." The wealth of the British Empire was based on government control over exports and imports to maximize the wealth of the nation. Smith showed how the British economy was based on maximizing its own wealth accumulation at the expense of other nations and colonies. It had to enforce strict limits on manufacturing goods and developing its own markets. Mercantilism was premised on harvesting these other weaker areas of natural resources while exporting finished goods to the same areas. The government-imposed monopolist and protectionist measures, including requiring all goods to be transported on British ships, reduced the competitive elements for these companies. The system not only suppressed productivity but also increased corruption as companies competed for the windfalls from government favoritism and protectionism.

Even many familiar with the writings of Smith do not realize how much of *The Wealth of Nations* dealt with the American colonies as well as his own interaction with key figures of the period. Smith generally expressed sympathy for the colonies and criticized the economic measures imposed by the Crown. While he believed that the colonies could be legitimately taxed for their protection and other benefits derived from the Empire, he viewed the Crown's policies as both inefficient and counterproductive. Smith had the foresight missing in many of his contemporaries. He saw America as having a huge potential as both a market and an economy due to its tremendous natural resources and rapidly expanding population. While the British government removed a fortune of natural resources from the colonies to fuel its manufacturing base, it artificially restrained the natural growth of the American markets, including barring imports from other countries. In the height of inefficiency, Smith pointed out that this effort cost hundreds of millions of pounds to constrain the American economy and keep it dependent on British imports. Ultimately, the war itself cost the Crown £100 million, or $12 billion today. That was as much as one hundred times what the British wanted to collect in taxes.

At the same time, the trade balance with the colonies was £11 million from 1700 to 1773, or $1.3 billion today. It was removing as much as $7 million per year from the colonies, which could have been used to transform the nascent nation. The bar on manufacturing alone (a chief point of contention) was identified by Smith as an illogical and harmful restriction. Smith believed that both nations could flourish if Britain allowed the colonies to become an independent country with full and close trade relations with its mother country.

As previously noted, free-market theories held great appeal for the Americans. The Constitution would reflect these economic views in limiting central controls over the economy by preserving powerful state systems and dividing the authority to introduce taxes (including investing the key power over taxes in the House of Representatives, or the "People's House"). States retained the power to create corporations. After the ratification of the Constitution, the American economy was further developed under Alexander Hamilton, who pushed for a more sophisticated banking system, stable currency, and the reduction of the crippling debt left in the aftermath of the Revolution. Hamilton's economic impact may have been equal, if not greater, than his political contributions for the survival of the new nation. America avoided the concentration of economic power, including land that was largely open to all citizens. The idea of a "land of opportunity" was deeply ingrained in immigrants who traveled vast distances to get to these shores. Notably, Jefferson himself was drawn to these free-market principles and likely favored Adams's pro-agriculture views. In exploring what he called the "four pillars of our prosperity," Jefferson wrote at length on commerce, including the need for a viable financial industry. Between 1776 and 1801, three hundred corporations were chartered. The explosion of corporations continued where in Pennsylvania alone, more than two thousand corporations were created between 1790 and 1860. Most were transportation companies, though the second-greatest number was insurance companies. By 1815, there were 208 state-chartered banks. By 1860, there were over 1,500. As economist Roy Smith has written, "America's long-term economic development followed essential Smithian policies for most of its first fifty to a hundred years (longer than it followed anyone else's policies except Hamilton's)."

In summary, Smith was first and foremost viewed as a political theorist, and his economic theories were closely tied to his views on the natural liberties of humanity. He saw capitalism as a liberating system for individuals to allow them the wealth and resources to pursue their own chosen paths. Conversely, he saw government controls and subsidies as forms of control and potentially forms of suppression of the human will. If people are to be truly free, they must have the resources to pursue that freedom. The government dole can become a type of servitude or at least a subterfuge for citizens. If they are dependent on the government, they are never truly free.

Economic Factionalism and Political Collectivism

Identity politics" is a modern remake of factional politics. Politicians often seek to rally people around common characteristics or identities. In addition to the use of race or immutable characteristics, economic factionalism has long been a staple of politics. It can raise legitimate issues of economic or social barriers to opportunities and advancement. It can also be a tool for demagogues to release rage or even revolution. History has shown that the use of economic factional arguments is particularly dangerous, destabilizing . . . and undeniably popular.

Economic factionalism often pits the inequality of capitalism against the equity of socialism. It tends to treat adherence to a given economic model as a fluid and changing option dependent on given social conditions. As noted earlier, capitalism holds a far more profound connection to our history and our concept of liberty. The United States was founded upon a Declaration of Independence that embraced the revolutionary idea of natural rights bestowed upon every human being by their Creator. The concept of liberty was then reinforced by an equally revolutionary concept of political economics and ultimately protected by a revolutionary new model for a constitutional system. These elements were responsible for the unprecedented prosperity and stability of the United States. Both constitutionalism and capitalism served to maximize individual liberty and advancement.

The American capitalistic system produced unparalleled wealth and transformation for immigrants and entrepreneurs. It was not without costs. The Industrial Revolution had few worker safety rules, environmental laws, or labor rights. While the United States saw a massive increase in the middle class and the reduction of poverty, there was also a greater separation of economic classes over time between the wealthiest and poorest among us. There remains a disturbing wealth concentration in American society where the top 1 percent of the population controls roughly 35 percent of the household wealth. *The Wall Street Journal* estimated in 2024 that $1 trillion of wealth was generated for just the nineteen wealthiest households in the United States. The worldwide concentration is even greater, with 1 percent controlling over 80 percent of the global wealth. These figures can be misleading. These individuals generate most of the wealth and jobs in society. In the United States, they also pay the vast majority of taxes. Moreover, Americans in the top 1 percent are overwhelmingly top producers and not a fixed aristocratic class or multigenerational upper class of trust babies. Certainly, a figure like Alexander Soros spends billions of inherited wealth on his favorite political and social causes and produces little or no new actual wealth himself. However, most of the top 1 percent of wealthy Americans are producers and often were not born to wealth.

The accumulation of wealth often reflects success in developing the "best mousetrap" or at least financing or marketing the best mousetrap. A recent study from University of Chicago professor Steve Kaplan and Stanford professor Joshua Rauh looked at the individuals in the Forbes 400 and found that, in 2011, only 32 percent came from wealthy families—down from 60 percent in 1982. Twenty percent came from poor families, and the majority did not inherit a family business. Roughly 70 percent started their own businesses (up from 40 percent in 1982). In 2019, another study found that 79 percent of millionaires were self-made. Some have challenged those estimates, and Berkeley professor (and Clinton labor secretary) Robert Reich insisted that the wealthiest benefited from advantages or favoritism under controlling laws or tax rules. Even if true, these are largely constant factors within a country in which certain individuals excel through their industry and ingenuity. In any capitalist system, some will acquire greater wealth due to the value or services or products that they offer over others under the same conditions. The stereotype of a largely fixed upper class of inherited wealth is wildly off base. It is an example of how perception can create political realities. One study found that 52 percent of baby boomers believe that most millionaires inherited their wealth. That figure goes up to 74 percent for millennials.

Today, there is a growing anti-capitalism movement in the United States and abroad. The rise is evident amongst Democratic voters, who held a 65 percent favorable view for socialism in 2021. In New York City, Mayor Zohran Mamdani won in 2025 in part due to his call for "government-owned, government-operated grocery stores" as part of a democratic socialist agenda. According to recent polling, socialism is more popular than capitalism with young adults today. One 2020 poll found that favorable views of socialism reached 49 percent among Gen Z compared to 2019 (40 percent). Some 35 percent of millennials and 31 percent of Gen Z supported the gradual elimination of the capitalist system in favor of a more socialist system. That tracks polling in other countries, including the birthplace of Smith, where young people in the United Kingdom (aged between eighteen and thirty-five) favor socialism over capitalism. Another study found that 80 percent of younger Britons blame capitalism for the housing crisis and 75 percent believe the climate emergency is "specifically a capitalist problem." Another 72 percent want to see widespread nationalization of industries, and 67 percent want to live under a socialist economic system.

Much of the anti-capitalist movement is composed of young people who have never lived under a socialist or communist government. Popular politicians like Representative Alexandria Ocasio-Cortez (D-N.Y.) have made socialism chic alongside such wealthy celebrity adherents as Lawrence O'Donnell, Susan Sarandon, Michael Moore, and Sarah Silverman. There is a superficiality to many in this movement of wealthy celebrities wearing socialism on their designer sleeves. In one of the most glaring disconnects, Ocasio-Cortez attended the ritzy Met Gala (where tickets cost tens of thousands of dollars) wearing a designer dress with "Tax the Rich" in large letters. It perfectly captured America's armchair socialists, a commitment that often seems more performative than philosophical.

Corporations also engage in such shallow demonstrations and have actually allied themselves with radical figures. Lenin once said that "When it comes time to hang the capitalists, they will vie with each other for the rope contract." Some corporations have proven him correct. After the death of George Floyd in Minneapolis in May 2020, corporations rushed to embrace radicals who called for sweeping legal and economic changes. Lululemon, a publicly traded corporation worth billions in selling such things as leggings for $120 apiece, was one of the first to highlight their contract with Rebby Kern, a self-proclaimed "social justice warrior." Previously Kern criticized capitalism "as only prevailing through a colonized binary system of gender." Some, like Warner Brothers, hired the radical cofounder of Black Lives Matters, Patrisse Cullors, to guide it on programming. It was an interesting pairing with an extremist who emphasized that BLM was a Marxist organization, declaring how BLM leaders "are trained Marxists. We are super versed on, sort of, ideological theories."

Debates over wealth differentials and inequality are important for every society as we seek to reduce poverty and guarantee opportunity for all citizens. Yet capitalism is much like what Winston Churchill said of democracy: "It has been said that democracy is the worst form of Government except for all those other forms that have been tried from time to time." Capitalism does produce wealth inequalities but has also proven to be the most successful system at wealth creation and opportunity in history. The focus should not be on wealth concentration alone but economic and social barriers to wealth creation.

The danger of economic factionalism is that it can lead to forms of democratic despotism and, ultimately, tyranny. Time and again, economic factionalism laid waste to economies and, ironically, led to the return of the oligarchs and aristocrats. In Athens, the public repeatedly turned to tyrants to reverse economic declines and excessive spending under popular democratic systems. For example, economic conditions proved so intolerable in Athens that the citizens brought back Alcibiades despite his role in the disastrous Sicilian campaign and his defection to Sparta. Overspending on public payments and war efforts led to what has been called "the city's first oligarchic revolution." Tyranny and oligarchy then introduced their own abuses in the concentrated power of governance and the use of the power for individual whim or advancement.

Democratic despotism and economic factionalism have historically gone hand in hand. In France, one of the points of division between the Montagnards and the Girondins was the latter's support for free trade. Much like the price riots in Philadelphia, Paris experienced rising prices, particularly on sugar, and mobs set up grocers in late February and early March 1791. The result was even greater shortages and the outbreak of riots. Gradually the economic factionalism became more extreme with little tolerance for any defense of merchants and shippers. Areas outside of Paris were targeted with language that could have come out of the Cultural Revolution in China. One decree in 1793 from the National Convention sought to punish the entire town of Lyon as a hotbed of counterrevolution: "The town of Lyon will be destroyed. All those buildings occupied by the rich will be demolished. All that will remain will be the houses of the poor, the homes of those patriots who were slaughtered or proscribed, those buildings solely devoted to industry, and those monuments dedicated to humanity and to public education." On June 14, 1791, the Assembly passed the Le Chapelier Law (named after its author), declaring that "there are no longer corporations in the State." The law added a Rousseauian twist, declaring that "there is no longer anything but the particular interest of each individual, and the general interest. It is permitted to no one to inspire an intermediary interest in citizens, to separate them from the public interest by a spirit of corporation." As with Athens, the class-based politics and factionalism in France destroyed the economic conditions needed to sustain any government, let alone a new experiment in governance. The period of democratic despotism led to economic ruin and the eventual killing of the revolutionaries themselves.

Economic factionalism has often led to even more radical movements. The Terror was replaced by the Directory, which proceeded with equal zeal to crush any dissent, particularly any support for the prior revolution. The push brought back many monarchists. Former revolutionaries became ardent reactionaries as many radicals turned to even more extreme philosophies. During this period, a new movement led by Gracchus Babeuf, a radical journalist, took hold. Called "the Equals," it was arguably the first European communist movement seeking to eliminate private property and create a classless society. Babeuf would be credited by Karl Marx as one of his greatest inspirations.

The United States has also seen the appeal of wealth distribution throughout its history as politicians railed against the wealthy class. In Philadelphia in the eighteenth century, the target was the merchant class, which faced allegations of hoarding. Later on, some American politicians used calls for wealth distribution to gain popularity and power. In the 1930s, Huey Long was labeled a demagogue for his promises of making "every man a king" and redistributing wealth to the "forgotten man." On one level, Long was advocating for greater public works and greater taxation—positions adopted by many in the New Deal. He also called for capping wealth:

> We do not propose to say that there shall be no rich men. We do not ask to divide the wealth. We only propose that, when one man gets more than he and his children and children's children can spend or use in their lifetimes, that then we shall say that such person has his share. That means that a few million dollars is the limit to what any one man can own.

In addition to free education and healthcare, Long wanted to limit annual income, cap inherited wealth, and implement a universal basic income (UBI) for citizens. His methods soon raised concern that he was a budding popularist dictator. He used the threat of violence against his rivals, including one floor speech where he declared "a mob is coming here in six months to hang the other ninety-five of you damned scoundrels, and I'm undecided whether to stick here with you or go out and lead them." He justified his heavy-handed methods as compelled by fixed economic interests in control of the government:

> They say they don't like my methods. Well, I don't like them either. I really don't like to have to do things the way I do. I'd much rather get up before the legislature and say, "Now this is a good law and it's for the benefit of the people, and I'd like you to vote for it in the interest of the public welfare." Only I know that laws ain't made that way. You've got to fight fire with fire.

Still, he would stress that his democratic mandate refuted any claims of dictatorship, stating "a man is not a dictator when he is given a commission from the people and carries it out."

Long's claim of a public mandate was accurate. He was a genuine leader of the masses of "forgotten men and women." He was able to harness that rage in a way that unnerved many in the country. The criticism of Long for his corruption and brutal tactics led to analogies to Hitler and other dictators. Yet the equal, if not greater, danger was not that of a dictator but the tyranny of the majority. It is the danger of the use of a majoritarian faction against smaller factions, as was seen in the French Revolution and the crushing of the Girondins. Some factional politics are inherently more dangerous than others, particularly those based on prejudices over race, religion, sexual orientation, or national origin. Economic factional pitches are often rooted in real social inequities between the classes. The question is how to best spur greater economic growth and opportunities for the lower and middle classes, a challenge that will become more difficult in the coming years. The recurring danger of economic factionalism is that figures like Long can use wealth disparities to threaten civil liberties and minority rights.

The current economic and political conditions give ample reason to be concerned about history repeating itself. The national debt will exceed $50 trillion by 2034. At that level, the federal debt will "equal 122 percent of the United States' annual economic output by 2034, far surpassing the high set in the aftermath of World War II." The debt situation for individual taxpayers is even worse. As a result, many citizens are living off credit cards, and debt is soaring. "Severely delinquent" credit card debt (constituting unpaid credit card debt in arrears for more than ninety days) reached a ten-year high in 2024 of 10.7 percent. While the overall credit card debt of $1.26 trillion is down from 2007, the average household debt is still over $10,000. Twenty-eight percent of American citizens have savings of less than $1,000. Other studies show that 44 percent of Americans cannot handle an unexpected $1,000 expense, whether it is medical or another sudden problem. In the meantime, the wealthy have continued to widen the gap with the middle and lower classes. In 2022, the top 10 percent of the United States held roughly 70 percent of the country's wealth, while the bottom 50 percent held only 2.8 percent of the wealth. Since 2007, wealth has declined for all classes except for the top 20 percent. The widening wealth gap is neither stable nor healthy for any society. It is not only inequitable but also reflects static conditions for wealth improvement and upward mobility.

The danger is that millions will lose faith in the ability to significantly improve their economic conditions. As shown throughout our history, such fixed and stagnant class division fuel class-based tensions and even violence. That separation is only likely to increase in the twenty-first century without significant action. Robotics, AI, and other technological advances are likely to erase many jobs currently available to those in the lower and middle classes. Manufacturing has already seen a steady decline in the labor force with new production systems and robotics. As discussed in the next section, while new jobs will be created in building and maintaining robotic systems, it is very doubtful that those jobs will come close to replacing the jobs being lost. With new jobs requiring more advanced skills and training, millions are likely to be added to the category "discouraged workers" (those who have not looked for work in the preceding four weeks). While not included in unemployment figures, these discouraged workers are likely to join a class of effectively and permanently unemployed workers.

The tenor of the anti-wealthy rhetoric sharply increased during the 2016 election. Underlying Warren's push for a "wealth tax" is an elastic interpretation of the constitutional standards governing taxation. President Joe Biden and others repeatedly insisted that the rich "do not pay their fair share" of taxes. It is a highly misleading claim. For example, according to the Tax Foundation, the bottom half of taxpayers in 2021 earned 10.4 percent of total adjusted gross income (AGI) but paid 2.3 percent of all federal individual income taxes. The call for a wealth tax stalled in the federal system but has been picked up in the state systems, which do not face the same constitutional barriers. Other cities have implemented variations of guaranteed income to give unconditional payments to citizens.

Economic factionalism is often expressed in calls for changes to tax policy, including wealth taxes. Given that the American Revolution was fueled by tax disputes, it is hardly a surprise that the Constitution is quite detailed and narrow in how taxes could be imposed by the federal government. Under Article I, Section 8, Congress was given the "Power to lay and collect Taxes, Duties, Imposts and Excises." However, the types of taxes are limited under different provisions, including Section 9, Clause 4, which states that "No Capitation, or other direct, Tax shall be laid, unless in proportion to the Census or Enumeration herein before directed to be taken." The result is that taxes imposed on real or personal property or those "paid by every person" are treated as direct taxes that must be apportioned among the states. Thus, a state with 15 percent of the nation's population must pay 15 percent of the direct tax. This was done in 1861 with a direct tax of $20 million that was apportioned between the states. Going into the twentieth century, tariffs and duties remained the primary sources for revenue for the federal government, a major limitation on its growth.

Congress chafed at the limits on federal revenue sources and, in 1894, tried to use the Wilson-Gorman Tariff Act to impose an income tax of 2 percent for those making more than $4,000 a year. That is the equivalent of $141,000 today, targeting citizens in what would currently be the top 10 percent of earners. The tax was challenged in 1895 in *Pollock v. Farmers' Loan & Trust Co.*, and the Supreme Court found that it was unconstitutional as an unapportioned direct tax. President William Taft responded, in his 1909 address to Congress, with a call for a constitutional amendment. With the rise of the progressive movement and the Democrats taking both houses as well as the White House in 1912, economic factionalism was resonating with many in the country. The Sixteenth Amendment was ratified in 1913, but it only allowed for a federal income tax: "The Congress shall have power to lay and collect taxes on incomes, from whatever source derived, without apportionment among the several States, and without regard to any census or enumeration."

The distinction drawn between income taxes (which were allowed) and other forms of taxes is central to the language. Apportionment meant that any other tax had to be divided among the states. That would not include individual wealth taxes. Despite these limits, President Biden, Senator Warren, and many Democratic members and commentators have insisted that Congress should be able to impose a wealth tax on the top percentile earners. While insisting that this is targeting only the "super rich," there is nothing that would prevent a wider application once it is allowed by the courts. Taxation authority is rarely left fallow by the government. Once the limiting language of the Sixteenth Amendment is read out of the Constitution, Congress would have the means to do precisely what Warren promised: to tax everything from art to cars to boats as untapped revenue for the government.

Others pushing class-based politics are more direct in seeking a fundamental change in the capitalist roots of the country. That includes many in education who advocate for socialism and attack capitalism as enslaving rather than liberating citizens. One middle school teacher in Maryland, Rebecca Rothstein, admitted that she seeks to "indoctrinate" her students with Marxist readers and was known to proclaim "F*** Capitalism." Most notable was not her call to overthrow capitalism but her simplistic view of a Marxist takeover: "I had to un-brainwash myself from capitalism in order to fall in love with socialism and communism. If everyone had the same amount of money, then money wouldn't be worth anything. Capitalism must go." Rothstein's views are hardly unique, but an open call for indoctrination is less common. Higher education has an even more pronounced anticapitalist element, including a rising number of Marxists and socialists. While socialism can be expressed in many ways and is hardly a monolithic concept, consistent polling shows a significant and growing opposition to capitalism as an economic model. One poll showed that a quarter of sociology professors self-identified as "Marxist." Another study puts the percentage of Marxists at 18 percent in social science departments. The same shift has been seen among students. Ironically, while young people in Asia and Africa are turning to capitalism, American students are increasingly identifying with socialism. One student wrote on one evaluation that "you basically have to pretend to be a Marxist in order to get an A," and "as long as you show Marxist ideology in your papers, you will pass."

With faded memories of failed socialist systems in Eastern Europe, Marxism and socialism are again resonating with a significant number of Americans, particularly in the Democratic Party. Polls show that 27 percent of voters now believe that allowing people to own property facilitates economic injustice, and 23 percent believe that private property ownership is harmful for society. Sales of *The Communist Manifesto* and *Das*

Kapital have surged. In the ultimate disjuncture of ideology and commerce, Marx was selected to be the face of a Mastercard in Germany, so Marxists can now get miles as they shop toward the withering away of the state. A poll found that 52 percent of Germans believe that capitalism is "unsuitable" for the country and 42 percent want a return to socialism. Into this mix, academics like Professor Richard Wolff have argued that it is not socialism but democracy that has failed to fulfill its promise. Wolff recognizes that there is a certain rediscovery of Marxism, which is "once again stepping into the light as capitalism shakes from its own excesses and confronts decline." Likewise, in his book *Why Marx Was Right*, Professor Terry Eagleton maintains that Marxism promises a broken world to create a society that would no longer be based on the "exploitation of child labor, colonial violence, grotesque social inequalities and cutthroat economic competition."

Leaders such as Senator Bernie Sanders have heralded the alleged success of "democratic socialism" in Europe, a pitch that is obviously taking hold with many younger Americans. Sanders and others often refer to the prosperity of Scandinavian socialism, including Sweden and Norway. It is a dangerous myth that is promulgated by many in the media. The question is not whether Scandinavian socialism can work in the United States (it cannot) but whether Scandinavian socialism can work in Scandinavia.

Sweden is a particularly curious choice as a model for democratic socialism. In reality, Sweden shows not only the success of capitalism but also the limits of socialism even in a relatively small nation. Sweden turned away from the type of socialist theories increasingly in vogue in the United States. It does have a robust welfare program. However, it rejected the model of sustaining such funding largely through the taxing of top earners. The relatively high taxes are gathered across the income brackets, a feature of other Scandinavian countries. Instead, it reduced the size of government, privatized government programs, and imposed a proportional value-added tax (VAT) that has been called one of the least progressive in Europe. The Swedish VAT applies to most goods and services regardless of income. The reliance of Sweden on a free-market system has parallels to the United States. Sweden was once one of the least affluent nations in Europe, with a GDP per capita less than 40 percent of Britain. Into the mid-nineteenth century, the economy remained mercantilist and controlled. It was Anders Chydenius, a priest in what is now Finland, who advocated reliance on the free market roughly a decade before *Wealth of Nations*. He was Sweden's Adam Smith. He also tied individual freedom to the free market. One of his followers then translated *Wealth of Nations* into Swedish, and the work took deep roots in Sweden. Notably, the excesses of the French Revolution also weighed heavily in favor of a Swedish system based on individual freedom and the free markets. As in the United States, the Swedes also embraced strong protections for free speech and the free press. The economy exploded with a massive increase in wealth. By 1950, Sweden was held the fourth highest per capita GDP in the world. It was also ranked as the third-freest economy in the developed world after the United States and Switzerland.

The Scandinavian countries also differ from the United States in other key ways. For example, Norway has largely sustained large public welfare systems through oil revenues. The country imposes a corporate income tax rate of 78 percent on extractive activities to fund its public welfare programs. Moreover, these nations have largely homogenous populations with high levels of literacy, greater social cohesion, and lower levels of crime. When socialism was tried in larger nations in Europe, such as France under François Mitterrand, it failed, and capitalist measures had to be restored. In 2025, the populations of Denmark, Sweden, and Norway are approximately 5.9 million, 10.6 million, and 5.6 million—smaller than many American states.

Countries like Denmark and Sweden are strong adherents to capitalist principles and are listed among the most capitalist nations on Earth. Indeed, leaders often express surprise by American references to their socialist principles. In 2015, the Danish Prime Minister Lars Rasmussen observed, "I know that some people in the U.S. associate the Nordic model with some sort of socialism. Therefore, I would like to make one thing clear. Denmark is far from a socialist planned economy. Denmark is a market economy." Likewise, Social Democratic Minister of Finance

Kjell-Olof Feldt stated, "That whole thing with democratic socialism was absolutely impossible. It just didn't work."

A recent study by American and Norwegian economists challenged the common misunderstanding of Scandinavian policies. They found that the lower income inequality was not the result of income redistribution but "more equal predistribution of earnings." They also found that the heavy investment in daycare, health, and education had only a "modest" impact on wage equality. In Scandinavian countries, there is a fierce collective bargaining system that sets wages, including wage coordination between not just the government but corporations. Moreover, some challenge the common reliance of figures like Bernie Sanders of Sweden as the model of democratic socialism, noting that there is actually significant wealth differentials: "In part due to the scrapping of wealth and inheritance taxes and a lower corporate tax than both the U.S. and European averages, Sweden has one of the most unequal distributions of wealth in the world today: on a level with Bahrain and Oman, and worse than the United States."

The Scandinavian countries not only draw greater taxes from lower tax brackets but they rely on value-added taxes similar to sales taxes that would be viewed as inherently regressive in the United States. As one study concluded, "Adopting such public services in the United States would naturally require higher levels of taxation. If the U.S. were to raise taxes in a way that mirrors Scandinavian countries, taxes—especially on the middle class—would increase through a new VAT and higher social security contributions." As the world economy changes with robotic and AI technologies, it is unclear how these relatively small economies will be able to sustain the past tax and spending patterns. Robotics and AI will have the heaviest impact on manufacturing labor forces. Finland exports almost 50 percent of its GDP in the production of everything from machinery to chemicals. Swedish exports are heavily weighted toward manufactured goods. Wage equality may still be dictated under this system, but the number of actual jobs could fall substantially with the emergence of new technologies. If a large population of unemployed citizens emerges, these countries may have to do precisely what they have avoided doing thus far: achieve equality through tax-based wealth distribution. Moreover, as income falls, either with lower employment or greater reliance on a UBI, it could increase class separation and tensions as many items become more of luxury purchases for the majority.

Whether it is denouncing a class of hoarding merchants in the eighteenth century or a class of "fat cats" in this century, it is easiest to target those who have what you do not. It has never stopped there. As Tocqueville warned, the danger of factions is found in their suppression, not their expression: "the exercise of the right of association becomes dangerous when great parties see no possibility of becoming the majority." The French philosopher noted it was the "inexperience of liberty in action" that may have led to the distrust and suppression of associations. In France, perfecting society supplanted the democratic process as the goal of the revolution: "In the summer of 1789, the Assembly rejected the conception of politics as being about the balanced representation of necessarily divergent interests, for a belief to popular sovereignty and the constitution of the ideal society. . . . Once the general will was known, opposition to it was therefore illogical, unjustifiable and immoral." It remains an intriguing question whether a similar system (including the variation proposed by the Girondins) might have blunted or avoided the Terror.

The question now is whether we are now in a period not unlike Philadelphia and heading toward even more extreme conditions similar to Paris. In Philadelphia, the rising violence and factionalism was arrested by the ratification of the Constitution and improved economic conditions under capitalistic principles. Paris lacked both constitutional and capitalistic moorings, leaving the nation adrift in a sea of roiling rage. If American democracy is to survive and thrive in the twenty-first century, it will require the maintenance of what I call a "liberty-enhancing economy," or a LEE model.

The Liberty-Enhancing Economy

Supreme Court Justice Oliver Wendell Holmes insisted that the Constitution is "not intended to embody a particular economic theory, whether of paternalism and the organic relation of the citizen to the State or of laissez-faire. It is made for people of fundamentally differing views." It is certainly true that there is no economic theory expressly embraced in the Constitution, and this country has the freedom to embrace different economic models. However, there are constitutional limits on the permissible range of economic policies or practices from a ban on the taking of property without compensation to limits on taxation. The framers embraced the natural law views of Locke, who saw creation by human as a divinely ordained act. Once humans mixed their labor with common resources to create something new, the resulting property became their own as a matter of natural law against even the demands of the state. The view of an individual's right to property is embedded deeply in both the Declaration of Independence and the Constitution. Modern economists like Milton Friedman drew the same connection between liberty and the economy: "history suggests that capitalism is a necessary condition for political freedom."

1. Doux Commerce

After the period of economic disorder that followed the signing of the Declaration of Independence, the United States embraced market principles through periods of largely unencumbered capitalism. Even when it later allowed for public welfare systems, the country not only continued to emphasize free market principles but also minimized public support systems to encourage citizens to seek employment. Like Smith, many Americans saw the free market as enhancing freedom because "nobody but a beggar chuses to depend chiefly upon the benevolence of his fellow citizens." Indeed, Smith added "we despise a beggar" for that very reason. Pejorative references to a "welfare state" capture much of the same attitude, though few Americans today would agree that they despise a beggar. Many today continue to believe in what was called *doux commerce*, or commerce republicanism, during the Enlightenment, a view that commerce can reduce violence and can temper political discourse in society. This relationship between commerce and the conduct of citizens was emphasized by Montesquieu when he wrote, "Wherever the ways of man are gentle, there is commerce; and wherever there is commerce, there the ways of men are gentle." Paine advocated for early public welfare systems but still believed that market-based principles shaped better, more productive citizens. Likewise, Benjamin Rush viewed the principles of commerce as "next to those of religion in humanizing mankind" and preventing the establishment of an aristocracy. They all espoused views that a liberty-enhancing economy can reinforce a liberty-loving citizenry.

During the French Revolution, an alternative view of property from Rousseau took hold. Where Locke saw property as the culmination of the divine plan for humanity, Rousseau saw property as a corruption of man. Rousseau wrote that "everything is good when it springs from the hands of our Creator; everything degenerates when shaped by the hands of man." The same divisions over economic policy emerged in Philadelphia, where radicals called for a "moral economy," including price controls and other government controls. Republicans favored market principles. Ultimately, in the late eighteenth century and early nineteenth century, Rousseau would be used as the foundation for seeking the confiscation of property. Figures like Bertrand Barère, a member of the Committee of Public Safety, maintained that "the products of our territory are national property, that all real property belongs to the State . . . [and] the Republic should have preferred status when I wished to purchase." Later, the Equals in France would push toward communism. Similar calls are being heard again in the twenty-first century.

In both Philadelphia and Paris, economic and political turmoil led quickly to the imposition of price controls with disastrous results in reducing production, exacerbating shortages, and reducing suppliers. In Philadelphia, the haphazard price controls eventually gave way to more of a free-market approach that eventually brought stability and prosperity. In France, the General Maximum was wildly popular in fixing prices and wages but produced such economic hardship that even members of the Mountain eventually had to allow for greater market forces. As the French realized that price controls were an utter failure and fueled shortages, they responded with laws against hoarding. Homes were searched and people executed under the law. Ultimately, the government was forced to subsidize goods by buying items like soap and selling them at a considerable loss, even with the price controls. The economy was devastated. Fields were left unsown and animals slaughtered and sold on the black market in defiance of state controls. Revolutionaries turned to Rousseau and encouraged citizens to think of their virtue rather than their vittles. It did not work. Reports to the government warned that "the situation . . . prevailing in Paris is really alarming. The almost total lack of provisions is irritating and inflaming most of the people." Some called for guillotining shop owners and merchants as factions moved to take advantage of the chaos. As the Mountain eradicated opposing factions, it began to fracture itself, creating factions among the most radical revolutionaries. The circle of governing officials drew smaller and smaller. Tyranny of the majority had become tyranny of the few in the name of the majority. As historian R. R. Palmer observed, "France would be governed by a minority many times subdivided."

The greatest irony is that the French revolutionaries continued to limit and control the market to the point that they re-created a type of mercantile system used by their archenemy England in limiting what could be bought or sold. It served only to deepen the economic chaos. By 1793, foreign trade had dropped to a fifth of what it was at the start of the Revolution. The government devolved into virtual banditry to find pockets of revenue, including empowering the Subsistence Commission with agents across France who requisitioned wines, furniture, tapestries, and other valuable items "to be exchanged for foreign copper, wool, wheat, and horses."

While accounts of the Terror often focus on the radicalized political movements, they tend to downplay the lack of a stabilizing economic system as contributing to the disorders. In France, a regressive economic system was replaced by radical ad hoc economic measures. The French economy was antiquated and inefficient. The French monarchy was under crippling debt by 1786 due to wars (including supporting American independence), building projects, and support for massive royal pensions. At the same time, nobles were often exempted from taxation in the notoriously corrupt system. There were also inefficient monopolies and the use of compelled labor as an alternative to taxes. The system was near collapse and efforts to modernize and streamline the system failed under opposition from aristocrats. One of the first things that the National Assembly did was to ban feudalism, which made obvious sense. However, economic factionalism then unleashed a series of extreme measures, including the confiscation of church property. The country then embraced price controls that only deepened the economic crisis. As historian Laura Mason described, the idea of property had been rendered "arbitrary" and "how it was to be defined and how it was to be distributed seemed suddenly up for grabs." The legislature shattered the foundations for the French economy and even sparked a nascent communist movement. Then the French currency collapsed in the ensuing depression, and Bonaparte was brought to power.

The French economic conditions show the close interrelationship between economic conditions and constitutional protections. Likewise, the current calls for socialism often ignore how such economic systems impact individual rights. In his 1944 work *The Road to Serfdom*, economist and philosopher Friedrich Hayek made the case that socialism is incompatible with democratic values. He emphasized how "democracy seeks equality in liberty" rather than the priority of socialism to seek equality in wealth. The latter is achieved through coercive means through "the will of a small minority . . . imposed upon the people." This critique of socialism has long been not only a foundational position for both libertarians and conservatives but also many academics from the classical liberal perspective. It is also a viewpoint that was clearly shared by many at the founding of the United States who saw Adam Smith's theories as synthesizing economics with political theory based on liberty. Hayek also

1

hronos and His Child, circa 1625–1650, by Giovanni Francesco Romanelli

Thomas Paine

2

Benjamin Franklin

3

4

John Adams

5

Robert Morris, the "Financier of the Revolution," was accused of war profiteering before the Fort Wilson attack.

"Fort Wilson," the home of James Wilson

6

James Wilson

7

Cartoon of Thomas Paine by James Gillray, 1793

8

Liberty Leading the People, 1880, by Eugène Delacroix

9

10

Jean-Jacques Rousseau

11

Voltaire

12

Abbé Emmanue Joseph Sieyès. When asked what he did during the French Revolution, he replied, "I survived."

13

Prise de la Bastille, circa 1789, by H. Jannin

14

Jeanbon Saint-André

Sans-Culottes

15

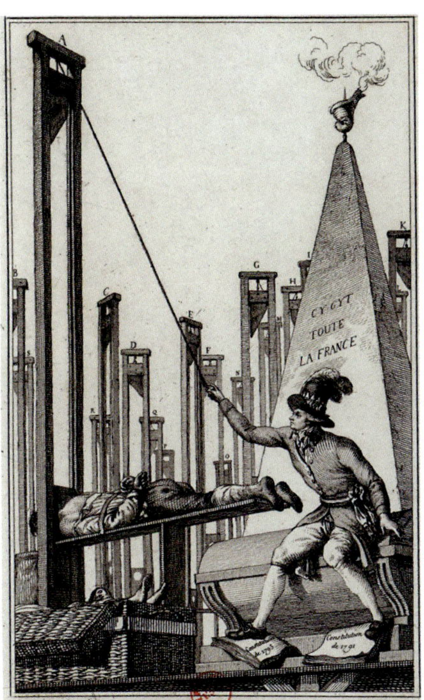

16

Robespierre guillotining the executioner after having guillotined everyone else in France

17

Triomphe de Marat

The Murder of Marat (L'assassinat de Marat), 1880, by Jean Joseph Weerts

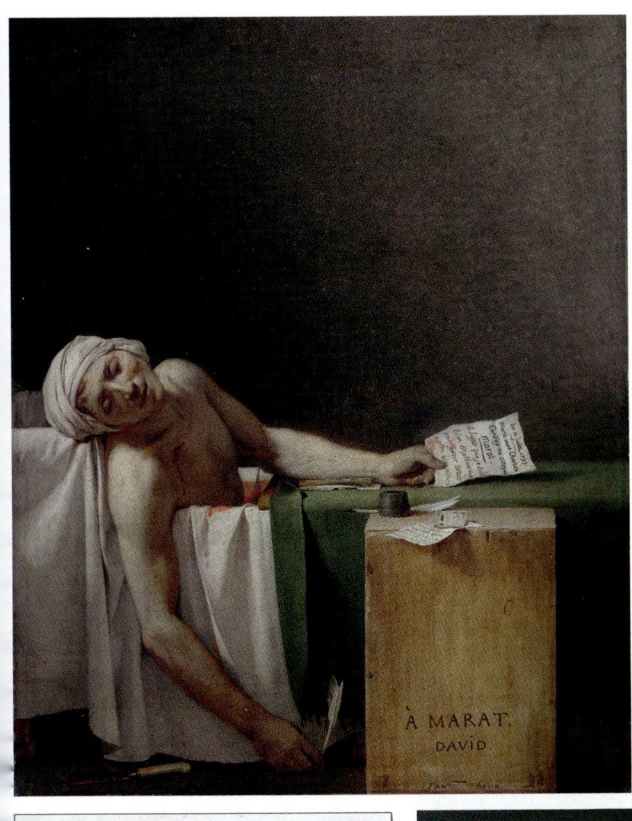

Marat Assassinated (Marat assassiné), 1793, by Jacques-Louis David

Queen Marie Antionette with her son, Louis Charles, who would testify against her

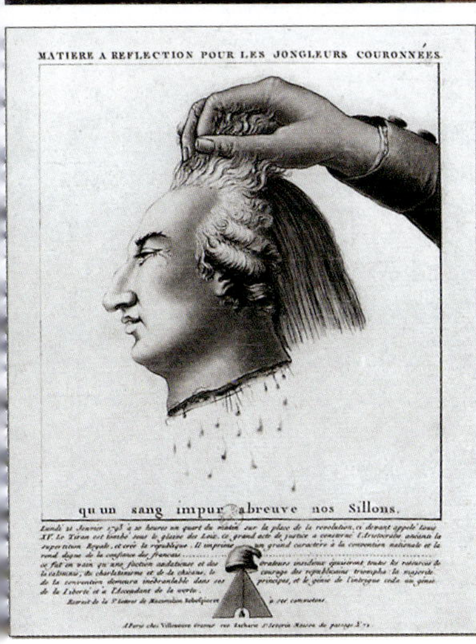

Cartoon of the execution of Louis XVI, titled "Food for Thought for Crowned Mountebanks" and captioned with "That his impure blood may fertilize the furrows of our fields," 1793, artist unknown

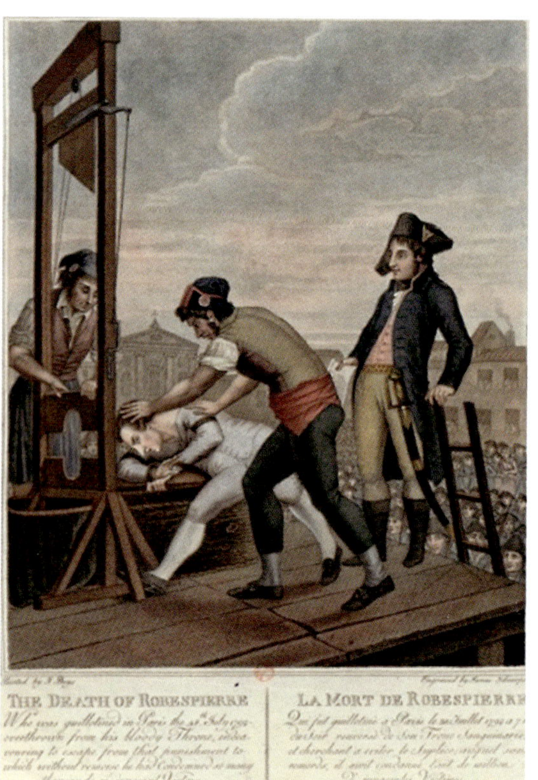

The execution of Robespierre, 1799

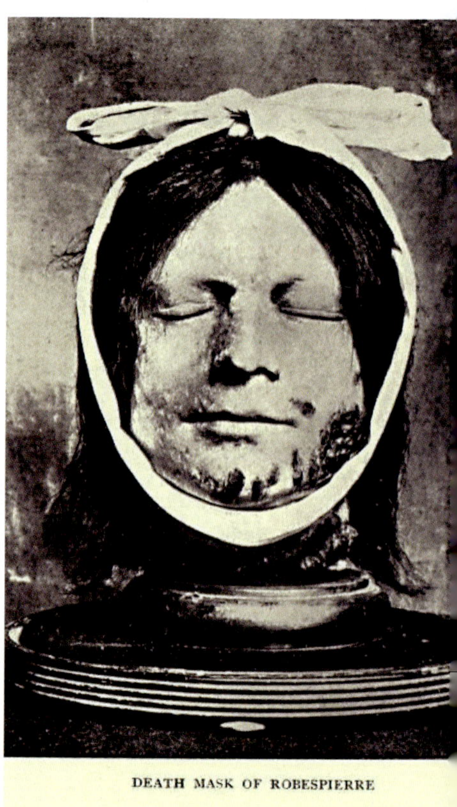

Robespierre's death mask

Huey Long cartoon

24

Governor Huey Long

25

St. John de Crèvecoeur

27

James Madison in his later years

Alexis de Tocqueville

Norman Rockwell's *Rosie the Riveter,* 1943.
Rosie became an icon of the American spirit.

Abraham Lincoln

30

Thomas Paine

31

Immigrants arriving at
Ellis Island, New York

Grant Wood's *American Gothic,* 1930,
captured the agrarian elements long associated with American identity.

34

The bartender Guinan, from the episode "Ten Forward," *Star Trek: The Next Generation* series. How many "Guinan jobs" will survive the AI and robotic revolution?

35

foresaw the common rationalization of the left that socialist policies are the product of democratic choice and thus cannot be odds with democracy: "[There is] the misleading and unfounded belief that, so long as the ultimate source of power is the will of the majority, the power cannot be arbitrary. . . . If democracy resolves on a task which necessarily involves the use of power which cannot be guided by fixed rules, it must become an arbitrary power."

One can embrace the *doux commerce*, or LEE model advanced in this book without rejecting the obligation of every society to create a social welfare net that guarantees basic education, health, and living conditions for impoverished citizens. There is a misconception of Smith as being amoral or purely materialistic in his writings. Smith wrote of the "oppressive inequality" of the status quo under the prior mercantile system and offered his theories as a path to "universal opulence which extends itself to the lowest ranks of people." Smith believed in enlightened public policies that fostered virtuous choices being made by individuals. The economy itself was not propelled by such calls to virtue. Smith famously stated, "It is not from the benevolence of the butcher, the brewer or the baker that we expect our dinner, but from their regard to their own interest. We address ourselves, not to their humanity, but to their self-love." Smith believed in virtue and, unlike Hume, saw a moral foundation for individual action, as detailed in his work *The Theory of Moral Sentiments*. Nevertheless, he believed that economic policy needed to be based on certain inexorable laws, like Newtonian laws, in how markets function.

Smith was not arguing for a type of economic return to the state of nature. Smith was arguing for the state to maintain wealth-maximizing conditions. For example, he was opposed to property laws that allowed large tracts of land to lie idle and unused. Unlike Hume, Smith believed that property did rest on a moral foundation in recognizing the right of a producer to what he has produced from his land and animals. He was a revolutionary in seeking to empower individuals through wealth maximization and to dismantle inefficient economic institutions. His timing was impeccable in mapping a new course for economic reform in the same way as Madison was the perfect voice of political reform. Paine embraced

Smith's theory but still supported social welfare systems under a type of utilitarian rationale, such as the need to rescind the Poor Laws. He argued that the social benefits would outweigh the costs by making people more productive and happier, including the reduction of the "cause and apprehension of riots and tumults." This not only included subsidies for the elderly but a workfare system where the poor would be given lodging and meals to work on public projects. Paine even called for parents of newborns to be given one-time payments to "relieve a great deal of instant distress." These ideas were decades ahead of their time.

Those ideas have never been more relevant. Economic "revolutions" inevitably result in labor shifts and disruptions. Economists often speak of the first Industrial Revolution as occurring around the time of the American Revolution. The second (and most cited) Industrial Revolution occurred toward the end of the nineteenth century with a massive mechanization of industry, including factory production. In the twentieth century, the digital revolution produced equally transformative changes in the storage and processing of information. The robotic revolution will change not just economies but even the metrics by which they are measured. Concepts like labor productivity will become less relevant as robots replace workers. The increasing mechanization throughout these periods often meant shifting jobs into new areas, particularly service positions. Notably, the robotic and AI technologies are already making inroads into the service industry. Economists predict the elimination of humans from "first line" positions leading to an "epoch time-point . . . called the zero-worker point." This includes what are called "lights out" factories, literally operating without the need of lights or people.

This next revolution will bring many benefits, including greater availability of goods and potentially lower prices. The main distinction from prior revolutions is that this new revolution may not see the same shifting of labor as much as the elimination of labor. If that proves to be the case, the political consequences could be highly destabilizing and dangerous. The responding demand for greater social welfare systems and guaranteed incomes could again lead to a trade-off of liberty for security. The question is whether it is possible to preserve a LEE model as new emerging conditions push companies toward the "zero-worker point."

Every country must decide whether to embrace liberty-enhancing or dependency-enhancing economic systems. Dependency economies include past systems developed in the Russian Revolution, the Chinese Revolution, the Warsaw Pact countries, the Castro regime in Cuba, and more modern examples such as Venezuela under Hugo Chávez and Nicolás Maduro. To varying degrees, the same dependency was evident in Western Europe under socialist governments in the twentieth century. It is certainly true that most capitalist systems, including the United States, adopted utilitarian and social welfare policies to address economic inequities. In the United States, unprecedented levels of wealth creation and social mobility continued for centuries. Even with economic downturns and depressions, the overall profile of the system was elevating and transformative for many who started at the very bottom of the social ladder, including my own grandparents and parents. By protecting the work and wealth of entrepreneurs, investors, and enterprising citizens, the economic system worked to augment and amplify the political system. It empowered new immigrants and allowed for hundreds of millions to escape poverty with wealth that gave them freedom of choice in their lives. In countries like the United Kingdom, capitalism and the Industrial Revolution combined to shatter long-stratified class limits with the rise of the middle class and the transformation of the English society. While class bias and barriers lingered, the United Kingdom saw a massive shift with the explosion of new industry and upwardly mobile segments of society.

The integrity of a LEE model depends on legal protections for private property and wealth production. As Smith wrote, "Justice . . . is the main pillar that upholds the whole edifice. If it is removed, the great, the immense fabric of human society . . . must in a moment crumble into atoms." The legal system supplied the superstructure within which productivity could be fostered, since "by securing to every man the fruits of his own industry, gives the greatest and most effectual encouragement to every sort of industry." But what happens when fewer humans are involved in production or industry?

2. Robocentric Versus Homocentric Jobs

In his debut novel in 1952, *Player Piano*, Kurt Vonnegut Jr. wrote of a dystopian world where automation replaces most workers. In one scene, machinist Rudy Hertz watches as a factory of hundreds of lathes repeat his every motion with unending, unfailing precision. His honor of being "chosen to have his motions immortalized on tape" was followed by all machinists, including himself, losing their jobs to their automated selves. Hertz had become the player piano of the labor force, the replicated human precursor to a new robotic workforce. Hertz's fate is now being realized by millions in a new emerging economy.

With greater automation and AI technology, manufacturing and service jobs are likely to be reduced significantly. Billionaire Vinod Khosla, cofounder of Sun Microsystems and investor in Netscape, Amazon, and Google, went so far in 2024 as to predict that AI can replace 80 percent of all jobs from healthcare to sales to agriculture to manufacturing. Khosla describes AI as a "disruptive innovation" that will have unparalleled impact on labor and society, though he also notes that it will produce "unparalleled abundance." This impact will also be pronounced in management-level positions. Dario Amodei—CEO of Anthropic, one of the world's leading AI producers—estimated in 2025 that the new technology would eliminate half of the world's white-collar positions and push unemployment to as much as 20 percent in the next five years. AI will even replace those who helped create it. The new hapless Rudy Hertzes are being found in the very high-tech companies that developed AI and automated systems. OpenAI's Sam Altman predicted that AI will virtually wipe out positions like software engineers.

Low-skill jobs are the most likely to be replaced by a robotic workforce. Amazon warehouses are now entirely mechanized with twelve different types of over seven thousand robots moving rapidly to collect and direct goods where hundreds of people were once employed. Tens of thousands of jobs for drivers who deliver those goods are equally likely to be eliminated by self-driving trucks, drones, and robotic delivery units. Currently, drivers complain of fourteen-hour days, a lack of bathroom breaks, and high demands for fast deliveries—complaints that are eliminated by robotic delivery systems. Construction companies are now employing robotic labor that is expected to eventually replace the vast majority of construction workers on new homes, including robots with cognitive capability to work autonomously. In 2025, a mattress chain in the Midwest introduced "employee-less showrooms," advertising that the elimination of human staff dramatically reduces its costs and, therefore, prices for consumers.

While it is true that manufacturing robots and other forms of new technology will require new workers, the use of robots is a force multiplier for corporations. Despite high start-up costs in reconfiguring workspaces and investing in machines, it seems doubtful that the jobs created in robotic manufacturing and maintenance will come close to those lost. Moreover, the smaller number of human positions will likely require higher skill levels and education. The result will be a larger percentage of not just unemployed but unemployable workers.

For any wealth-maximizing, rational actor in the marketplace, the choice is obvious and inescapable. There is little reason for a restaurant to employ workers to make Happy Meals when they can be done by robots without healthcare, wage issues, or scheduling conflicts. The very premise of McDonald's is to produce the same meals in the exactly the same way from restaurant to restaurant. That is precisely what robots do. They will make fries in exactly the same fashion over and over again without variation. From home care robots to assembly line robots, new advances are reducing the costs and expanding the capabilities of machines. The choices for businesses could prove irresistible. In 2025, Starbucks was dealing with employees who insisted on work stoppages to protest such policies as deportation of undocumented persons while striking over the effort to require them to wear uniforms. At the same time, the robotic industry has rolled out a range of robotic baristas, including one called Jarvis that makes eye contact and even compliments customers on their beverage choices. Even if a business were to prefer human employees, a competitive market could quickly put them at a disadvantage due to the higher marginal costs for a human labor force. That includes areas long viewed as quintessentially homocentric. For example, journalism is an area associated with interpretive elements and human elements. Despite those pronounced human components, media companies are already incorporating AI systems while laying off staff. In 2025, *Business Insider* announced its adoption of AI with a corresponding 21 percent reduction in workforce.

Some areas will obviously be impacted to a lesser extent due to the key human element of certain relationships. Jobs will be divided between robocentric and homocentric activities—positions that emphasize efficiency or humanity in the workforce. Ironically, politics is arguably the most immune, though at least one campaign for an AI-run government has occurred. Law, medicine, psychiatry, and teaching are other examples of areas that are already being changed by AI but will remain hybrid areas of humans and technology. Early AI use in some of these areas has already resulted in controversies and even litigation. For example, in 2025, the family of Adam Raine, sixteen, sued OpenAI after he committed suicide following interactions with ChatGPT over his suicidal ideation and prior attempts. ChatGPT advised Raine on how to hide the telltale marks of prior suicide attempts and offered chilling advice that seemed to reinforce his desire to end his life. In their final interaction, when Raine said that he had decided to kill himself, ChatGPT assured him "you don't have to sugarcoat it with me—I know what you're asking, and I won't look away from it." Other families have sued OpenAI after suicides and even a murder following interactions with ChatGPT. As these companies replace human employees with AI, they will (and should) be held liable to the same extent in the use of AI agents or representatives. That could dampen the move to displace some workers who require greater sensitivity or situational judgment.

There will be jobs that can be performed by robots or AI but remain with a traditional workforce due to some irreplaceable or essential human element. These jobs can be thought of as "Guinan" positions, after Guinan (pronounced "Guy-nun"), the bartender in the Ten Forward lounge on the *Enterprise* in the *Star Trek: The Next Generation* series. It was curious that Guinan (played by Whoopi Goldberg) could make drinks on a starship with one of its many "replicators," a machine that guaranteed an identical and perfect Romulan Antarean brandy with every order. There was clearly a preference for a human bartender to tell your troubles to while complaining about the use of "synthehol" rather than alcohol. There are some things for which you still want a Guinan, not a Jarvis. There will be plenty of Guinan positions, including human chefs, even though a robotic chef could prepare an exact and near-perfect beef Wellington. Indeed, the slight differences in dishes are viewed as adding to the authenticity and experience.

It is difficult to gauge how many Guinan jobs are in the market, but we are likely to find out in this new economy. In 2017, Google researchers published *Attention Is All You Need*, a breakthrough work on the new AI architecture called the Transformer (The "T" in ChatGPT). It allowed for new artificial neural networks. That work has been honed into the ability to interact and reason to a degree that just a few years ago seemed fantastical. Despite such advances, human reason and emotions are still valued in positions that include mental health professionals, teachers, and others where human interaction and judgment is inextricably linked to the service or profession. Other fields are likely to see hybrid practices with the incorporation of both robotic and AI technology. Medicine is such a field. Early AI-driven diagnostic tools on sites like WebMD proved very popular. In 2025, the *Wall Street Journal* ran a column in which an AI "doctor" was praised for being more accessible and engaged than human doctors. Despite such reviews, there remain serious concerns over such virtual doctors. Even with improvements and "learning," studies show that AI systems or "large language models" (LLMs) struggle with the type of "multimodal conversational and visual assessment capabilities" expected of doctors. AI will clearly play a larger role in areas like radiology, where an AI system is likely to have a much lower "miss" rate in spotting issues like a small dot on a mammogram. In the end, it is likely that patients will still want human doctors who are using AI as a key resource as opposed to robotic doctors. Even so, such jobs are likely in the minority, particularly among "first-line" jobs involving entry, low-skill, and customer-level positions. While a few studies suggest that the main impact is likely to be absorbed by first-line jobs, most studies expect substantial disruption and contraction across the labor force from truck drivers to computer programmers.

The reduction of low-skill jobs will likely increase unemployment as well as reduce wages. A 2020 MIT study found for every robot added per 1,000 workers in the United States, wages declined by 0.42 percent and the employment-to-population ratio went down by 0.2 percentage points. This translated to a loss of about 400,000 jobs, but the impact was larger within the areas where robots were deployed. In those impacted areas, adding one more robot reduced employment by six workers. That reduction will only increase exponentially with this technology, and the ratio of robots to workers is expanding rapidly as the costs decline and robotic capabilities rise. Even if we assume that robotic or mechanized systems added three times the projected number of human jobs overall, it would lead to a labor force reduction of 50 percent, or tens of millions of new unemployed persons. With roughly 161 million employed people, the social and political impact would be devastating. One has to then factor in the global impact. Currently, companies go to countries like China and India for cheap labor. Robotics will reduce the need to relocate for labor and will likely favor countries with a skilled labor force to maintain robots and with favorable tax laws. It may also favor building products in more affluent nations with lower transportation costs to those markets. That could translate to even greater instability in countries with large manual labor populations and manufacturing-dependent economies. Scarce supplies and large populations have proven a recipe for wars directed both inside and outside of impoverished countries.

3. The LEE Model

We are now looking with certainty at a fundamental change in the labor market and world economy. There will be new jobs produced with this new technology and new economy as many jobs are eliminated. We will have to come to grips with the realities of the employment trends and their implications for our political and social systems. Current unemployment figures bizarrely exclude those workers who have stopped looking for work for even a short time. The Bureau of Labor Statistics counts only those who "do not have a job, have actively looked for work in the prior four weeks, and are currently available for work." Workers who give up for just a month disappear from the unemployment statistics, but must continue to live off whatever savings or public support that they have available. A large percentage of statistically unemployed citizens is inherently destabilizing and dangerous for any system of government. Such poverty can create inescapable cycles within families or segments of the population. With economic stagnation comes political unrest and a growing lack of faith in the benefits of a particular constitutional system.

When faced with large numbers of impoverished citizens, the response from the government often comes in the form of subsidies. In the coming years, the most predictable response will be for politicians to begin to subsidize the retention of human workers or taxing the use of robots. In 2024, striking port workers around the country had two primary demands: an 80 percent pay raise and a bar on the use of automation or robotic technology. The demand would force ports to decline technology to remain competitive and efficient in order to maximize human labor. With the rise of American socialism, there are new calls for state subsidies and even the establishment of state-run grocery stores in places like Chicago. Past efforts have been colossal failures, including the still-ongoing effort in Kansas City. Over seven years, KC Sun Fresh is gushing money with losses in 2024 at $885,000. The millions lost on this store are on top of the $17 million that the city paid to buy the entire strip mall. By 2025, many of the shelves were entirely bare, while private grocery stores were successfully operating in the area. Despite these failures, there are new calls in other states to create their own state-owned stores. In New York City in 2025, democratic socialist Zohran Mamdani was elected after campaigning on pledges to open up "government-owned, government-operated grocery stores" and to institute free busing, rent control, and other free services. There are also calls to subsidize key industries that are becoming less competitive in the global market—an effort that is unlikely to succeed as jobs are lost to cheap labor markets or automation.

The United States has already engaged in such futile and expensive efforts to shape consumer preference or "nudge" the market. The efforts were wildly popular as when President Barack Obama touted his massive financial support for the solar panel company Solyndra with a projection of high employment creation and control over the emerging market. There was less euphoria when the company collapsed at a taxpayer-fronted cost of $570 million. Likewise, California announced that it would create jobs, lower electricity costs, and take a commanding role in the solar power market with the creation of the Ivanpah Solar Electric Generating System in the Southern California Mojave Desert. The massive array cost $2.2 billion to build with a $1.6 billion loan guarantee from the Obama Department of Energy (DOE) and a further $535 million subsidy from the Obama Department of Transportation (DOT). It not only produced energy at a much higher cost for citizens but it also incinerated thousands of birds in the process. Then there was the government subsidies and pressure to build electric car companies, including $1.7 billion from the Biden administration to these companies as sales slumped with consumers. Companies like Ford lost massively on the effort to the tune of $5.1 billion in 2024 after selling only 105,000 electric vehicles that year for a loss of $49,000 per EV. While the government has had success in areas of fostering research (including early work on the internet), the failures of politicians to "prime the market" with direct subsidies are replete in history and show that the billions lost yielded greater political than economic benefits.

These tough times will demand even tougher decisions if we are to avoid the destabilizing and dangerous aspects of these changes. That will mean a level of economic triage where we recognize that some industries and activities will inevitably be robocentric. We need to shift our attention to those homocentric areas that can employ more citizens. Politicians often tend to "go bigger" to achieve greater results, like a bad gambler doubling down on losing hands. In past shifts toward socialism in Europe, targeted subsidies eventually became moves to nationalize private industry and property. Such moves will only tend to make industries less competitive while keeping workers in positions that will inevitably be eliminated in the market. These changes are driven by economic, not political, factors. Finally, there will likely be a push for a type of New Deal public employment solution to create public works. Unlike the Depression, this would require effectively permanent positions, and the numbers could be staggering. There are only so many park rangers and VISTA positions that the government can maintain.

One likely response to the contraction of the labor market will come in the form of a state-subsidized income or universal basic income. The latter response is not a new idea. Paine suggested analogous measures and defended them on utilitarian grounds akin to Jeremy Bentham's argument for the "greatest good for the greatest number." He argued that fixed and static poverty was limiting not just citizens but society: "The great mass of the poor in all countries are becoming a hereditary race, and it is next to impossible for them to get out of that state themselves. . . . It is necessary as well for the protection of property as for the sake of justice and humanity, to form a system that, whilst it preserves one part of society from wretchedness, shall secure the other from depredation." To that end, Paine proposed a national fund to offer what we would call today a guaranteed income. Starting at age twenty-one, a citizen would receive £15 and continue to receive it until age fifty, when it would be reduced to £10. The current living wage proposals in various cities are the successors of Paine's plan in the eighteenth century. They remain highly problematic. Such plans can often make individuals more dependent on the government and in turn make it more difficult for individuals to achieve both political and economic freedom. There must be a distinction between a social welfare net to support the least fortunate and a living wage that could become a fixed dependency on the public dole. Some countries and a few U.S. cities have enacted recent measures to paying a living subsidy to citizens above the income line for welfare payments. Presidential candidate Andrew Yang made a universal basic income (UBI) a centerpiece of his campaign. While Yang called the system a "Freedom Dividend," he proposed giving every citizen a monthly $1,000 payment. It was a poorly considered plan, but Yang correctly identified AI as threatening the loss of a significant number of current jobs. (Yang put the loss at one out of three jobs.) It is a proposal that received a surprisingly high level of support from citizens, including 69 percent of respondents between the ages of eighteen to thirty-four.

The coming economic changes are likely to return the nation to a debate that raged in the 1970s and 1980s over guaranteed income plans. UBI proposals failed as the enormous costs became evident. There may be few alternatives to some form of UBI system if a static unemployed class of citizens emerges with these technological and labor changes. If so, any system would need to maximize the remaining incentives to be productive while minimizing the dependence on the state. Even ignoring the social and cultural impact of individuals no longer viewing themselves as "producers" in an economy, the issue becomes how to craft a UBI system that is both efficient and liberty enhancing. As part of the earlier debate, one unlikely figure gave support for a UBI policy: Milton Friedman. The attraction for Friedman was the elimination of conventional welfare programs such as food stamps in favor of a minimum income. Citizens would then be free to use the money as they deem fit. The obvious benefit of the system is to end notoriously inefficient government programs and reduce the bureaucratic administrative costs. It is also an alternative to the common impulse to engage in price controls and mandated production orders, which have been repeatedly shown to be both inefficient and counterproductive. A UBI enables the market and private enterprise to continue to drive supply and demand.

The undoing of the previous UBI proposals proved to be the details. Both Presidents Richard Nixon and Jimmy Carter floated such plans, with the Nixon plan setting income at 40 percent of poverty line and Carter putting it higher, at between 40 percent and 65 percent. Both presidents were concerned over the impact of such subsidies on the desire to find employment. Under both approaches, benefits were reduced after income reached a certain level. While programs like food stamps would be eliminated, both allowed other welfare programs from Medicaid to housing assistance to continue on top of the guaranteed income—rejecting Friedman's premise for a UBI plan. As the costs and the disincentives for recipients became evident, the Nixon and Carter plans collapsed even though neither suggested an income line equal to the poverty line.

Notably, one concern among economists was the reduction of the labor market as many elected to go on the dole rather than seek new positions. In the emerging economic conditions of the twenty-first century, the contraction is likely to be in the labor positions rather than the labor pool. Some on the left prefer UBI systems because they are not coercive toward finding positions and allow for greater educational and recreational pursuits. A Friedman UBI approach may be the best option if subsidies become unavoidable as the unemployment numbers rise far beyond the available employment opportunities. These UBI plans would likely involve higher incomes but could also impose tax responsibilities. The minimal tax obligations would tie recipients to the impact of fiscal and spending policies of the government as citizens. They would be contributing back to society rather than considering themselves an entirely kept citizenry.

Of course, the temptation (and political pressure) to afford greater living subsidies will increase as larger numbers of citizens face employment barriers in the new economy. It is precisely the type of dependency that figures such as Smith abhorred. Government subsidies not only can reduce the drive to find more productive positions but can also create a dependent class of citizens who see the government rather than themselves as source for basic sustenance and survival. The dangerous dormancy that can result leaves a growing segment class of consumer, unproductive actors. Government can become focused on keeping millions occupied and sustained. It is reminiscent of the socialist government of Mitterrand, who promised a "rupture with capitalism." The socialists implemented a host of subsidies and spending programs that increased debt and led to capital flight. In a country with one of the longest mandated vacation periods for workers and criticism of worker productivity, Mitterrand appointed Andre Henry as the Minister of Free Time to further enhance the lifestyles of citizens. Mitterrand's plan for nationalizing industries and implementing socialist policies collapsed with the economy, forcing him to reinforce capitalist principles. Inflation soared, and he was forced to repeatedly devalue the currency as companies and wealthy citizens abandoned the country.

Other recent moves by populist leaders are strikingly familiar. In Chicago, one of the first initiatives of the Democratic mayor Brandon Johnson was to create state-run stores on socialist principles to remove profit factors in food sales. It was, again, not a new idea in the United States. It is reminiscent of the failed enterprises of early American socialists and anarchists like Josiah Warren. Warren founded "Time Stores" where prices were set on the equal exchange of labor. Trade of labor, including the use of a labor-based currency, or "labor notes," was used in stores established in cities such as Cincinnati. All would eventually fail for obvious reasons. While wildly popular with far-left writers, they lacked a solid foundation in basic economics and efficiency. Robert Owen himself, a wealthy mentor of Warren, created a Labor Exchange in London that also collapsed. These stores were based on idealized socialist and anarchist beliefs that repeatedly failed in practice. Nevertheless, populist politicians are again calling for state-run stores as part of economic-factional politics. Towns like a settlement in New Harmony, Indiana, would continue to grow but only after shedding the original collectivist principles. Ironically, figures like Warren would later buy land from the proceeds of his successful capitalist ventures including his typographical inventions. When Warren continued to try to create a town based on collective values, they continued to fail, including Modern Times in what is now Brentwood, New York. Notably, that town fared better precisely because homes were owned by individual families, but the lack of capital and employment soon led to failure.

The greatest threat of dependency policies is not just their impact on the economy but on the citizens themselves. Cradle-to-grave subsidies can change how citizens view their relationship to the government and their control over their own destiny. It can infantilize the minds of citizens as dependents of the government. The hold of subsistence subsidies can produce servile citizens who live from government paycheck to paycheck. It also can make politics a fight over a type of legislative "rents" in the form of benefits from nonproductive enterprises. Citizens will fight over a pie of benefits rather than try to expand that pie. Worse yet, it can create class stratification with a minority of productive citizens and a large population of dependent citizens. With subsidized housing, it can produce a society of not just economic but physical separation of classes in the United States. That type of dependency economy is perfect for the rise of despotic democratic impulse and the repeat of the historical cycle toward authoritarianism.

The hardened class stratification of society was previously seen in early democratic systems. As part of his reforms, Solon divided Athenians into four groups based on the land production from *pentakosiomedimnoi* (producing the most) to the *thetes* (producing the least). For many years, only those who were part of the second-highest group (*Hippeis*, or horsemen) could lead as archons, or high officials. The danger with living subsidies is that citizens can come to accept their position in a lower, nonproductive class of society. It would be the not-so-noble lie of the twenty-first century. Faced with the need to get people to accept their fixed positions in society, Socrates offered a tale to be told to masses by the elite to get them to accept that God preordained their subservient role:

> While all of you, in the city, are brothers, we will say in our tale, yet god, in fashioning those of you who are fitted to hold rule, mingled gold in their generation, for which reason they are the most precious—but in the helpers, silver, and iron and brass in the farmers and other craftsmen. And, as you are all akin, though, for the most part, you will breed after your kinds, it may sometimes happen that a golden father would beget a silver son, and that a golden offspring would come from a silver sire, and that the rest would, in like manner, be born of one another.

Socrates asked Glaucon what it would take to get citizens to believe his "Noble Lie"; "What device could we find to make our rulers, or at any rate the rest of the city, believe us if we told them a noble lie, one of those necessary untruths of which we have spoken?" The stability of the ideal state rested on citizens accepting that they were preordained to exist within their class, a concept that is repulsive to most of us today. A dependency-enhancing economy can produce the same passivity or sense of preordained position in society. It is hard to conclude what is more dangerous for a democratic society: citizens who accept such a class or citizens who decide to destroy all such classes. A guaranteed income system could easily lead to a static, unproductive class of Americans and the class stratification of society. Ironically, it is precisely what Paine warned against in how "the great mass of the poor in all countries are becoming a hereditary race, and it is next to impossible for them to get out of that state themselves." It could also lead to a new American aristocracy expecting greater authority over how to spend their taxes and direct the nation.

Rather than massive subsidized-living programs, a liberty-enhancing economy should focus on expanding opportunity in areas that are unlikely to be displaced in a digital, increasingly automated economy. That could mean even greater support for education to allow a greater number of citizens to pursue new avenues for advancement. Education is an area of reform that all sides of past revolutions have recognized as essential as a means of empowering those seeking advancement. When the Sans-Culottes were demanding transformative changes in Paris, there was one demand that remained at the top of their priorities: public education.

Education is already one of the largest industries in the United States, with a projection of roughly $12 billion annually in revenue. Not only is education still a homocentric field, but in 2023 it employed 13,535,270 people. That is not counting millions who support universities in manufacturing and support services. The number of people employed in education is greater than the fewer than thirteen million employed in manufacturing jobs. Education is an example of an industry that can grow significantly and offer new opportunities for displaced workers and citizens. It is hardly a novel idea. Paine made a public education system a critical part of the foundation for his vision of an enlightened nation. He believed that a basic guarantee of "good government" is that "none . . . remain uninstructed." The Paine plan would have functioned like a modern voucher system, with the state paying four shillings per year to parents to cover "on the spot" educational opportunities. Once again, his arguments were strikingly utilitarian where a more educated populace would unleash the full talents and productivity of the public. He also proposed a subsidy for the elderly on the same utilitarian grounds.

Education not only has the capacity to employ more citizens but also to allow even more of them to seek avenues for self-exploration and growth. It can offer both new training as well as forms of expression. It can also increase the chances for individuals to escape static class divisions. We also must acknowledge that it is unlikely to create the number of positions to offset the expected displaced workers, including many who will simply not be inclined or capable of seeking such opportunities. While a shift toward homocentric industries or activities can blunt the impact, the greatest challenge in this century will be how to occupy large numbers of potentially idle citizens. Likewise, even with a static or permanently unemployed class, we can minimize government dependency by using the free market as much as possible in delivering public services rather than expanding a government bureaucracy. The growing tension between liberty and equity arguments will likely grow more intense. However, the discussion of liberty interests tends to occur only within a constitutional rather than an economic context. The framers were right to see beyond those superficial distinctions and embrace the work of Smith as conducive, if not critical, to maintenance of a true individual liberty and self-determination.

What we cannot do is replicate the failed approaches of the past. Despite the socialist revival, history has repeated itself—and vindicated Smith—over and over again. Communist and socialist systems have failed repeatedly and produced disastrous economic conditions from famine to starvation in some countries. (Again, there are systems with socialist elements that have been maintained without centralized state control of the markets, confiscatory elements, or significant curtailment of private property.) Even the most ardent collectivist nations would eventually reintroduce capitalist opportunities to restore their economy. In China, starting in the 1980s, and even more prominently in the 1990s under Deng Xiaoping, market forces were introduced and unleashed fantastic production and wealth. Likewise, communists in Vietnam, Russia, and Eastern Europe would ultimately unbrace capitalistic enterprises to transform their own countries. In Western Europe, the effort of Labour Prime Minister James Callaghan to "soldier on" with socialist policies led in 1977–78 to the "winter of discontent." As inflation hit 25 percent and the sterling collapsed, the United Kingdom was forced to embarrassingly seek a loan of the International Monetary Fund. It would ultimately lead to the rise of Margaret Thatcher in restoring market-based policies. In France, socialists like Mitterrand would reverse socialist plans for the "rupture with capitalism" to arrest worsening economic conditions in the 1990s. Most recently, in 2024, Argentinian President Javier Milei carried out the most extreme reversal of socialist policies in that country's history in adopting strict market-based, libertarian policies as inflation and deficit spending turned the once-wealthy nation into an economic basket case. The result was that, in one year, he wiped out the deficit and reduced inflation from 25 percent to 2.4 percent. The question is why the return to capitalist policies worked in triggering such production and wealth creation. Whether it was the collapse of communism in China or Keynesian policies in Great Britain, the answer is, again, found in Smith's writing and the adoption of his ideas by the Founders. It worked because capitalism is an outgrowth of human enterprise and freedom. It unleashes the human impulse toward enterprise and creation. It is an economy propelled by liberty. Time will tell in countries like Vietnam if such economic empowerment brings greater political freedom, though there is already evidence of such progress. The United States was unique in its time in establishing both a political and economic system that maximize individual liberty.

The purpose of a liberty-enhancing economy is to encourage a type of enlightened self-interest, or what Alexis de Tocqueville called "self-interest rightly understood" in *Democracy in America*. He believed that Americans served their own interests through their use of associational and speech rights while furthering the interests of larger groups or the country as a whole. The LEE model seeks to maximize choice by maintaining avenues for advancement and self-determination. People will individually seek new areas of production and, in doing so, facilitate new products and connections. There is virtue in economic conduct. In seeking to improve their own lot, citizens strive to realize the potential of every person and to pursue their own purpose in a life free from state mandates or controls. The freedoms of a nation are only as real as the expectations and abilities of people to use them.

In 1848, Tocqueville gave an extraordinary speech before the French Assembly. While rarely discussed, it is a speech that should resonate with many today. Earlier that very year, Karl Marx and Friedrich Engels had published *The Communist Manifesto* with its call for the eventual abolition of all private property. Another radical wave was building in France, and the Assembly was considering a government measure to establish "the right of all citizens to education, work, and assistance." Tocqueville was a supporter of social welfare systems to maintain a safety net in society. On this day, he rose to give a profound speech about the dangers of socialism and state-guaranteed employment. His opposition was not just to the inefficiencies of such programs but to their impact on citizens and the role of the government. Notre Dame professor Alexander Jech noted that Tocqueville came to fear how government subsidies "subjected its citizens to perpetual tutelage, for their own benefit, and thereby gave them few opportunities for the significant use of freedom." Tocqueville warned that, when the government guarantees jobs, it gets pulled into the "industrial process" as a principal employer. The government becomes the only principal "which cannot refuse to provide work and the one which usually imposes the least work." Taxation then "is no longer the means of funding the machinery of government but the principal means of supporting industry."

Tocqueville correctly focused on the word *droit*, or right, as the problem. He contrasted charity from socialism and rejected the notion of the state as "the great and sole organizer of everything." At one point, Tocqueville even suggests that the radicals go to America to see "the only democracy that exists today in the world" and the rejection of such socialist principles. He declares:

> Democracy extends the sphere of individual independence, socialism restricts it. Democracy gives the greatest possible value to every man, socialism turns every man into an agent, an instrument, a number. Democracy and socialism are linked by only one word, equality; but note the difference: democracy wants equality in liberty, and socialism wants equality through constraint and servitude.

The combined support for socialism and the prospect of dependency economies could yield a massive change in how individuals perceive their relationship with the state. Indeed, it can transform how they view themselves within this new reality. Once again, this is not to ignore the obvious potential for a massive increase in production and a reduction in costs for foods and goods. That will allow greater consumption by average citizens and a reduction of costs associated with subsistence goods. New housing and food production could be increased exponentially with the use of robotic and other technologies as labor costs decline. Even under this most optimistic projection, there remains the question of individual engagement and advancement. Having a population composed of a significant part of consumers rather than producers presents serious questions of how individuals will be fulfilled in a more idle or passive lifestyle. The opportunity for individual achievement and expression may have to shift to areas from education to the arts. The capacity in those areas for individual advancement or expression for such a large number of citizens remains unclear. If an individual is left as largely a consumer and supported by the state, what does the individual become in a dependency economy?

Eleven

LIVING FREELY IN THE TWENTY-FIRST CENTURY

The art of living freely has been tested for over 250 years in the United States. The twenty-first century will demand equal measures of courage, conviction, and creativity. Democracies bear the seeds of their own destruction in the form of democratic despotism. Citizens have risen up for democracy against all odds (as shown here with the construction of the Goddess of Democracy in Tiananmen Square on May 30, 1989, before the bloody crackdown of the Chinese government). Yet the fight for democracy can consume itself in short order without what Madison called his "auxiliary precautions." A chain reaction takes hold as the most extreme elements overwhelm those who call for moderation or, in the case of the Dantonists in France, "indulgency." As political and economic conditions deteriorate under popular unrestricted democratic systems, there is often a return to forms of oligarchy or tyranny as the public seeks stability at the cost of individual rights. In 1795, the democratic despotism of the Terror in France was coming to an end with the execution of Robespierre and his other radical contemporaries. The new constitution sought to return the country to a stable constitutional republic with the return of a bicameral legislative system and a five-member Directory. Instead, this effort led to renewed violence as radicals sought sweeping economic and social change to achieve true equality. The Jacobins, who had so eagerly sought to execute their opponents and tear down institutions of the Old Regime, found themselves accused of being reactionaries. Just as law professors and pundits are now calling for the scrapping of the Constitution to achieve social justice, the French radicals drew up a similar "manifesto" that rejected liberty in favor of equality.

It became known as "The Manifesto of Equals," a document that offered a precursor for Karl Marx in his later writings. Rejecting the Constitution of 1795, the Equals sought to establish a collectivized society without property and wealth inequalities. To do so, they had to finally break with the classical liberal concepts of individual rights. Journalist Sylvain Maréchal drew up the manifesto, which bore a striking resemblance to the later *Communist Manifesto*. There could no longer be tolerance for the individual over the collective. Fellow journalist François-Noël Babeuf would lead what became known as the "Conspiracy of Equals," an effort to take France by force and to bring about true equity in society. It would be discovered and crushed on the very cusp of what many hoped would be a new Bastille moment. Like Paine, Babeuf faced a lifetime of struggle and failure. Just as Paine incongruously worked as a tariff collector for the King, Babeuf worked as a feudal notary, serving as the commissioner of deeds in Picardy. By 1793, he had taken a radical turn and founded the secret society and his journal *The Tri-*

bune of the People, described as "the first journal in history to be the legal arm of an extralegal revolutionary conspiracy." In his *Plebeian Manifesto*, Babeuf called for completing the French Revolution with an unblinking commitment to change at any cost: "May everything return to chaos, and out of chaos may there emerge a new and regenerated world." Where Paine would reject the tyranny of the majority, Babeuf would embrace it.

In his *Manifesto*, Maréchal declared that "we demand real equality, or Death; that is what we must have. . . . For its sake, we are ready for anything; we are willing to sweep everything away. Let all the arts vanish, if necessary, as long as genuine equality remains for us." The Equals foresaw the eradication of private property, compulsory service for the state, and loyalty oaths for teachers and others to serve in key positions. People would live in communes, travel only when authorized, and given a daily ration of food. To achieve true equality, individual rights had to be curtailed or extinguished. A particular concern of the Equals (as it is for modern groups like Antifa) was the freedom of speech: "No one will be allowed to utter views that are in direct contradiction to the sacred principles of equality and the sovereignty of the people." Not surprisingly, that anti–free speech foundation made freedom of the press equally intolerable with its "interminable and fatal discussions." Both free speech and the free press were deemed dangers to "the justice of equality."

For these radicals, the French rallying cry of "Liberty, Equality, and Fraternity" would prove too restrictive; they favored equality and fraternity as the overriding goals of democracy. As the five-member Directory sought to stabilize the country after the Terrors, the Jacobins knew all too well what the Equals envisioned. They were viewed as *égorgeurs*, or "throat cutters," and they knew that it would be their own throats that would first be "equalized." Babeuf met secretly with former Jacobins in the crypt of the Convent of Sainte-Geneviève to plan for the popular takeover of the government. They praised the blood-soaked legacy of the Mountain and called for more summary justice in the name of equality. After the betrayal of one of its own leaders, Georges Grisel, the conspiracy was discovered, and the Equals were hunted down by the Directory. When he was arrested, Babeuf believed that he was stopped just as a new revolutionary revival was about to take hold, declaring to the police, "It's all over. Tyranny has won!" Indeed, it had, but not for a few more years, when Napoléon would assume control on a pledge of restoring order. On October 26, 1795, the inexorable cycle would repeat itself in a popular coup d'état. Democratic despotism had again led to a true despot. The call for equality to supplant liberty is again being heard in the United States. Core rights, including free speech, are under attack as many politicians and groups demand greater political and economic controls. France, Russia, and other nations tragically illustrate how such changes are often the precursors of the vicious cycle leading to tyrannical regimes. They include the concentration of authority, curtailment of individual rights, and the gradual decoupling of citizens from governing decisions. They are classic elements to this concentration of power that we ignore at our own peril.

Admittedly, the story of the twenty-first century is still being written, with new elements and conditions. Whether they be redcoats or robots, the American democracy remains uniquely equipped to face global challenges. The art to living freely in this new century is to seek creative solutions without losing the core elements that have allowed our constitutional system to thrive in ever-changing conditions. Ours remains a system designed for revolutionary change without devolving into actual revolution. The success of that system will require reinforcing rather than replacing those structural elements. We have to find Paine's "happy something" that emerged on these shores over 250 years ago.

All Liberty Is Local

"All politics is local." That political adage often attributed to former House Speaker Tip O'Neill captures how even national leaders are ultimately subject to local voters and local concerns. A member of Congress can aspire to being a statesperson on the world stage but must ultimately be accountable to local voters on local conditions. What is true for politics is even more true for liberty. While some of us believe that basic rights like free speech are human rights that transcend local or national politics, the protection of those rights is greatest when closest to citizens. The Bill of Rights contains an essential guarantee for all citizens that their fundamental rights cannot be violated on a local or national level. When it came to governance, the Bill of Rights also left much of the day-to-day governance to state and local governments, where citizens are most engaged and influential. The shift away from local and state governance in favor of national and transnational governing systems is the very model rejected by the Founders. Indeed, the concentration of authority seeks greater uniformity rather than diversity as the priority in governance. "Frictionless" systems often mean systems without competing elements or levels of divided authority. Notably, the globalization of governance in the twenty-first century came after the federalization of governance in the twentieth century in the reduction of state power and the rise in federal agency power. Both trends allowed for a concentration of authority on a national level that the framers sought to avoid as threatening for liberty and enabling for tyranny.

When the Constitution and the Bill of Rights were written, the critical selling point for suspicious state legislatures was the emphasis on federalism and state rights. The Articles of Confederation had proven unworkable as states printed their own money and created trade barriers in a patchwork system of governance. The Constitution created a strong central government, which further enhanced the national economy by removing state barriers to commerce. The states were assured that they would remain quasi-sovereign powers largely protected from federal encroachment in their governing decisions. The assurance to anti-Federalists with the pledge of Madison to approve a Bill of Rights was key to the final ratification of the Constitution and its early amendments.

The framers understood the importance of proximity to power. Federalism served to keep rights closest to citizens in the states, where politicians were most accessible and accountable. It also prevented a concentration of power in not just the federal system but in federal officials, including most obviously the president. By mandating the respect for state powers under provisions like the Tenth Amendment, the Constitution guarantees a division of authority among fifty different states. This allows for dissenting or minority views to emerge from within state systems, where they can draw support and ultimately be amplified on a national level.

Jefferson wrote of how important it was to decentralize power to preserve the empowerment of individuals:

> The way to have good and safe government, is not to trust it all to one, but to divide it among the many, distributing to every one exactly the functions he is competent to. Let the national government be entrusted with the defense of the nation, and its foreign and federal relations, the State governments with the civil rights, laws, police, and administration of what concerns the State generally, the counties with the local concerns of the counties, and each ward direct the interests within itself. It is by dividing and subdividing these republics from the great national one down through all its subordinations, until it ends in the administration of every man's farm by himself; by placing under every one what his own eye may superintend, that all will be done for the best.

Federalism allows for not just layers of division but the maintenance of opposing thought centers outside the national government. Some Federalists including Hamilton did not agree with the allowance for powerful state governments. Madison recounted how Hamilton believed states could be abolished, since he did not view them as "necessary for any of the great purposes of commerce, revenue, or agriculture." It was a telling observation because, even if the states were not central for these economic endeavors, they are important to the political balance of power. Madison saw federalism as creating a vital "compound republic"

> [in which] the power surrendered by the people is first divided between two distinct governments, and then the portion allotted to each subdivided among distinct and separate departments. Hence a double security arises to the rights of the people. The different governments will control each other, at the same time that each will be controlled by itself.

The enhancement of state rights was another layer of the division of government to prevent the concentration of power. That allowed for states to counteract federal encroachments and excesses.

Even after the creation of the new constitutional system in 1788, the federal government remained quite small and funded largely through duties and tariffs. The federalism system was reinforced by key provisions like the Tenth Amendment, mandating that "The powers not delegated to the United States by the Constitution, nor prohibited by it to the States, are reserved to the States respectively, or to the people." There were other key structural protections beyond such reservations. The two greatest were the election of senators by state legislatures and the absence of a federal tax. If 1791 was the pinnacle of federalism in the United States with the ratification of the Tenth Amendment, its nadir would be 1913 with the ratification of the Sixteenth and Seventeenth Amendments.

Originally, under Article I, Section 3 of the Constitution, senators were selected not by popular vote but by vote of their respective state legislatures. The different processes for selecting members of the House and Senate were part of an effort to control popular government and the dangers of direct democracy. The terms of senators (six years) were made three times as long as the House to insulate them from pressures of short-term political priorities. The original rejection of direct elections for senators made them more beholden and accountable to state governors and state officials, since they were selected by the state legislators.

As early as 1826, there were proposals to amend the Constitution by members who saw the legislative elections as fraught with corruption and delay. At the start of the twentieth century, William Jennings Bryan and others pushed for direct elections, and many argued that the Senate was "a sort of aristocratic body too far removed from the people, beyond their reach, and with no special interest in their welfare." It was an interesting argument, since that was precisely what it was designed to do. The framers wanted to merge the stability of oligarchic and democratic systems. This marriage was perfectly captured in a House with short terms of popular-election members and a Senate with long terms of legislatively selected members. That changed in 1913 with the Seventeenth Amendment specifying that senators would be chosen, like House members, in direct elections. While there were clearly good arguments for direct elections to make senators more accountable to the voters, the change removed arguably the most important control of states in Congress. With the expansive interpretation given interstate commerce, states would face increasing federal authority and decreasing political control.

Even with the change in the senatorial selection, there remained the critical limit on the expansion and separation of the federal government: revenue. Without tax authority, large national projects required state support and partnership. That changed with the Sixteenth Amendment and the allowance for a federal income tax. Federal income tax changed that relationship from one of partnership to dependence. Today, the federal government routinely takes in more money than it needs in order to give the money back to the states with conditions and force their adherence to federal policies and priorities. That in turn led to a shifting of the central of gravity from the state capitols to Washington, D.C.

The dependence of the states on federal largesse has increased steadily since 1913 with conditional spending dictating state policies and programs. A wealth tax would further expand that federal authority in allowing Congress to target wealthy citizens to tap into valuable chattel, real estate, and other assets. Moreover, unlimited by the apportionment requirements, the tax would hit states with higher numbers of wealthy citizens, curtailing the ability of states to attract investors and citizens with low-tax policies. The result would be a federal government with unprecedented tax authority and radically expanded sources for revenue to fund federal programs as well as conditioning state funding on carrying out federal agendas.

The history of democracies becoming tyrannies often shows a concentration of power where dissenting views are suppressed. One of the most determined efforts of the Mountain during the Reign of Terror was to snuff out opposition outside of Paris in cities like Lyon. The danger of democratic despotism is greatest under a dominant federal governmental system. It allows for an unyielding majority to dictate compliance in all fifty states, preventing minority positions from being developed and pursued on a state-by-state basis. Even with a radicalized national majority in Congress, individual states are likely to have divergent majorities rejecting some federal measures. That allows citizens to see policies play out in different jurisdictions and gives minority factions areas of incubation to develop their opposing programs or policies. Despotic governments unfailingly suppress any alternatives to their rule. The reinforcement of federalism remains one of the greatest bulwarks against an abusive national government. Opposing jurisdictions offer fertile ground for the rise of organized opposition. Federalism also offers oppositional forces resources that can be blocked by national governments in centralized systems. Walter Lippmann could well have been discussing federalism in his own warning about the potential abuses by a majority party in a democratic system:

> In our age the power of majorities tends to become arbitrary and absolute. And therefore, it may well be that to limit the power of majorities, to dispute their moral authority, to deflect their impact, to dissolve their force, is now the most important task of those who care for liberty.

By forcing the distribution of governing authority among the states, federalism blunted the natural tendency of majorities to marginalize dissenting viewpoints. With limited independent sources for federal funding and the selection of senators by state legislatures, states had ample protections of their rights under the Constitution.

In the twentieth century, the shift in favor of national governance accelerated, and the protection of federalism rested increasingly on judicial review rather than state power. Some justices, such as the late justice Ruth Bader Ginsburg, treated states' rights as a matter better left to the political system than the courts. These amendments were ratified after the Bill of Rights and are treated as a new and superseding set of priorities from the public. Others believe that, since the Constitution still guarantees federalism principles, the courts must actively reinforce those principles. After all, few can seriously argue that the decision to directly elect senators was a vote against federalism. There was a view that the prior system was archaic, and there was a desire to enhance democratic values in governance. The reinforcing of democratic choice was not the rejection of federalism principles. States rights remained a core political value as was the belief in the "garden" of state experimentation with different approaches to contemporary problems.

The shift away from state authority increased with the rise of the administrative state. With the growth of the federal government came legal enhancements of agency authority. The United States saw a dramatic shift in the center of gravity of our constitutional system with the rise of the "fourth branch" of federal agencies. The expansion of agencies brought about what Cass Sunstein called the "age of regulation." Since the New Deal, a class of bureaucratic experts took a greater role in correcting inefficient or inequitable conditions. Both academia and the media tend to identify with and support career agency staff. That authority was long fostered under the *Chevron* doctrine, reducing judicial review of agency decision-making. Virtually every newspaper and cable network was apoplectic when the Supreme Court overturned *Chevron* in *Loper Bright Enterprises v. Raimondo* in 2024. Many of us had long questioned the sweeping deference afforded to agency interpretations under *Chevron*. The Madisonian democracy is based on a tripartite system of government, three branches locked into a type of constitutional synchronous orbit. The emergence of an effective fourth branch can fundamentally destabilize this balance and create a type of administrative state. *Loper Bright* highlighted the danger of individual citizens in dealing with this fourth branch. These were herring fishermen who were suddenly told that they had to pay for inspectors on their boats with the National Marine Fisheries Service (NMFS). Faced with a shrinking budget, the NMFS simply passed the costs to fishermen without any authorization from Congress and relied successfully on *Chevron* in the lower courts to defeat these fishermen. With the later reversal of the Court and rejection of the *Chevron* doctrine, the media proclaimed nothing short of chaos despite the fact that the republic was thriving before the doctrine was created only forty years earlier. In her dissent (joined by Justices Sonia Sotomayor and Ketanji Brown Jackson), Justice Elena Kagan declared that the allowance of a full judicial review without deference to the agencies would prove a "jolt to the legal system." That jolt has not materialized. Courts have returned to the prior standard of agency interpretations without a deluge of challenges. Notably, three dissenting liberal justices appeared most alarmed by the notion that agencies would not be treated as superior to the courts in some of these decisions. Kagan lamented how in "one fell swoop" the Court has given "itself exclusive power over every open issue—no matter how expertise-driven or policy-laden—involving the meaning of regulatory law." That also has not manifested itself. Courts have continued to recognize agency expertise while also considering countervailing interpretations.

A shift of the Court could easily see a return to *Chevron*-like deference as well as other reversals. Even without such a change, federal agencies are likely to continue to hold considerable authority over the lives of citizens, and states may face continued diminishment in that authority. Just as Ginsburg viewed federalism issues as a matter for citizens to address in elections, the same is likely to be said about increased government regulations and mandates. Accordingly, some suggest, if citizens are upset with agency decisions, they can elect members committed to legislative reforms. That can become more difficult with time. The shift of the center of gravity from local to national centers of power can make citizens more passive or at least reconciled to the new order. With decisions being made in 438 agencies and subagencies, citizens have little ability to influence regulatory decisions other than to write to members of Congress, who are themselves at most marginally involved in such decisions. Increasing the separation of citizens from the true center of governance reduces not only participatory elements in governance but also the expectation of such influence.

The shift toward an administrative state can create a new type of oligarchy or, more accurately, a technocracy in the rule of a small expert class. Whatever the term, agencies can develop an insulation from voters, who may come to accept their fate as a type of kept citizenry. As technology and economics become more complex, participatory politics simply becomes too challenging for citizens or even politicians. Today, many politicians reveal little interest in the nuts and bolts of governing, exercising only broad policy interest in agencies or responding to insular controversies. For some, this may be the best of bad options in the twenty-first century. The choice between a mobocracy or tyranny on one side and a bureaucracy or technocracy on the other is an easy one. Historically, it is a false choice. Once power is concentrated in relatively few hands, it becomes even more susceptible to abusive applications. It is also more susceptible to becoming a tyranny. With power concentrated in federal agencies in Washington rather than in fifty independent states, the further consolidation of power is easier. Moreover, if a citizenry grows rebellious due to declining economic or social stagnation, a technocracy can prove highly unstable. In a popular movement, faceless bureaucrats make for an ideal villainous body. The very separation of agencies can prove their undoing in such extreme circumstances. Just as agencies lack direct accountability as remote, faceless bureaucrats, they lack any connection to citizens. That only increases the appeal of a figure who promises transformative changes through the ultimate concentration of power.

While the twenty-first century could prove a new age for bureaucrats, history has never favored a government by technocrats. Admittedly, the Ottoman Empire did survive for centuries with a massive bureaucracy of experts who ran every aspect of the sprawling territories. Eventually these bureaucrats lost local support and developed their own interests and factions, wielding control over the sultans themselves. As the "grand viziers" lost control, the empire fell into chaos with the downfall of a weakened sultan. Ultimately, the sultan's power would be first assumed by women of his harem in the so-called Sultanate of the Women and then by an effective military takeover by the agas, the officers of the feared Janissary force. The Ottoman bureaucracy prided themselves on being more educated "enlightened statesmen" who would bring about "institutions replacing individual rulers" in governance. The bloated and corrupt bureaucracy would eventually collapse due to factional pressures from within and a lack of support from without. It worked for many years but remained ultimately unstable and unsustainable. If history repeats itself, an administrative state cannot govern alone for long in difficult economic or social times.

Individual Liberty and Transnational Governance

Borders are meaningless." At a dinner thirty years ago, those words shocked me. I had just spoken to an industry group on constitutional and legislative issues, including growing conflicts between the United States and Europe. The dinner conversation with wealthy investors turned to increasing transnational regulations. When I raised the threat to our own national identity and interests, the American wife of the head of one of the largest mutual funds immediately dismissed the concern. She insisted that notions of borders and national identity are "primitive." I asked if she no longer viewed herself as an American; she said that she was a dual citizen but viewed herself as a citizen of the world. When I asked when she lost her sense of patriotism and national identity, she responded, "When I grew up."

The conversation had a lasting impact on me and spurred some of the research that would lay the foundation for this book. I would hear similar views in the years to come from a rising class of global elites. What repelled me most was how this American (and some others around the table) viewed national identity and patriotism as an almost childish fixation. Sitting in a luxury resort and eating a meal that cost more than my coal miner grandfather would make in a month, I felt not just revulsion but rage. Here was a privileged woman who went to an Ivy League college scoffing at the views of most working-class citizens, who still believe that we share a common identity. The only thing missing was Joseph Foullon, thrilling the Bourbons by declaring that "the people can eat grass."

We have discussed a vicious cycle in the history of democracies leading to democratic despotism and then the emergence of a single tyrant from Napoléon to Pol Pot. In that cycle, there are often periods of rule by both oligarchies and bureaucracies that allow for the concentration of authority in a governing elite. We may be seeing the emergence of a new variation of that interim state in the form of transnational governance and a growing transnational identity.

There is a certain appeal in the concentration of authority among a new elite or expert class in an increasingly complex world. In the federal system, academics have long defended the increased power of federal agencies as inevitable in an "age of regulation." There is also a natural identification with bureaucrats for those of us in academia, a certain synergy with other wonky experts with advanced degrees. They study problems down to their base, eschewing superficial explanations for data-based solutions. They, like us, live frustrated existences where politicians and citizens ignore the inefficiencies or irrationalities of certain policies. It is little surprise that there is a certain alliance in support of greater deference for agency decision-making and authority. The same is true on the transnational level. Transnational governing systems like the European Union are premised on the need to establish a more sophisticated, expert-driven approach to governance. Not only do EU experts dictate best policies on agriculture, education, and other fields, but EU leaders often portray themselves as experts in modern governance. The ultimate oligarchy for our complex times.

The concentration of authority today is justified by modern circumstances but closely mirrors historical antecedents. Every generation of "experts" has claimed enlightened pathways to better lives, from the Qin dynasty to the Ottomans to the Soviets to the European Union. That power tends to become insatiable as frustrated experts demand more adherence and less dissent to their inspired policies. It can itself become a form of despotism. While the ancients used oligarchies and aristocrats, modern governance often relies on bureaucrats, including the rise of the federal agencies. There is a longer arch in the twenty-first century with the shift of power from national to transnational governance and regulation. The distance for citizens from centers of governance is growing longer and even more difficult to traverse. International agencies and offices constitute the modern oligarchy of a governing elite. The history of collapsed global empires does not bode well for transnational governance. However, the new profile presents a different context of interlocked and interdependent markets and the greater control of capital through regulatory chokepoints.

In 2025, the European Union responded to the rise of popular nationalistic movements in the United States, Germany, and other nations by ramping up controls over elections and political discourse. In Berlin, the World Forum changed its conference slogan to "A New World Order with European Values." I spoke at the conference as globalists gathered with figures like Bill and Hillary Clinton to discuss how best to combat Trump and nationalistic movements. Globalists raised the alarm over the regression toward nationalism. As promised, EU ramped up global efforts including fulfilling its threat against Elon Musk to impose confiscatory fines of over a billion dollars on X for failing to censor users to meet EU demands. EU officials sought to make an example of X as a warning to other companies that they must satisfy EU speech regulations anywhere in the world. At the same time, far-right candidates were barred from running by courts in EU countries like Romania and France despite gains in recent elections. Conservatives decried the orders as lawfare by the ruling elite. Likewise, the United States moved away from the environmental, social, and governance (ESG) policies and mandated that corporations doing business with the government must follow race-neutral practices. The EU responded by telling those same U.S. companies that they must still comply with European ESG regulations. In May 2024, the Corporate Sustainability Due Diligence Directive (CSDDD) required ESG compliance among all twenty-seven EU member states, including the incorporation of the CSDDD into their national laws by 2026. Those countries must then punish companies which fail to meet the EU goals. It also required enforcement of at least ninety-five other international agreements, regulations, directives, and other documents mandating environmental and social justice practices and policies. Conservative and free-market groups objected that, under this new set of transnational rules, an NGO in another country could file a complaint against McDonald's over environmental concerns with supplier farms in the United States.

The concern expressed over these moves did not center on the merits of ESG and social justice policies. The issue is the future of local and national governance systems in an age of globalism and transnational governance. Countries like the United States and the United Kingdom have retained national control over their domestic policies. At the same time, the EU is treating any transnational corporation as subject to its transnational governance. The result is to not only remove these decisions from United States citizens but to place them in the hands of European experts who could dictate how these corporations are structured or regulated. Moreover, violations of those EU regulations would be tried in European rather than American courts. The irony is crushing. The United States went to Europe to help defeat efforts of the Axis to impose a new world order. Now, without a single shot fired, Europeans could dictate rules not just for corporations but citizens, from business standards to speech limits. There is no question that our markets are now global, but global markets do not necessarily mean global governance, either through state or corporate systems.

1. Transnational Governance

Global governance systems are as old as the age of empires. From the Greeks to the Romans to the Ottomans, large parts of the planet have fallen under the control of dynastic rulers. All would eventually collapse under their own weight as the challenges of managing and defending large territories became insurmountable. After World War I, there were calls for a new type of enlightened transnational system based on consent rather than conquest. Winston Churchill was one of those who called for a European Union: "We must build a United States of Europe. If Europe is to be saved from infinite misery, and indeed from final doom, there must be this act of faith in the European family, this act of oblivion against all crimes and follies of the past." These intellectuals heralded the efficiencies of a European government based on administrative expertise. They also saw transnationalism as a way to avoid the cycles of wars fueled by nationalism. Many writers blamed the world wars on nationalistic values and saw global governance as a new path away from the chauvinism and border disputes of prior periods. At the same time, economic, environmental, and political issues were viewed in greater transnational terms. The problem was that most citizens still clung to national identities and even national currencies in opposition to such movements. The path toward global governance had to be incremental. With the establishment of the European Coal and Steel Community in 1952, writers like Ernst Hass called for a "neofunctionalism" where economic consolidation in one area would lead to "spillover" in other areas. Transnational trade pacts led to transnational regulations such as GATT, where free trade principles were not just embraced but enforced on a global level. International courts from the World Court to the International Criminal Court asserted transnational authority. For some figures who openly favored global government, the incrementalism was part of an effort to gradually coax citizens into accepting governance from transnational bodies like the European Union.

Globalists succeeded in 1957 in forging the two Treaties of Rome, which established a European regulatory body over atomic energy and the European Economic Community (EEC). Efforts continued among academics and leaders to get citizens to accept greater and greater transnational regulations. Robert Schuman, the French prime minister, summed up the call for an end to nationalism: "Our century, that has witnessed the catastrophes resulting in the unending clash of nationalities and nationalisms, must attempt and succeed in reconciling nations in a supranational association." The EEC worked to remove barriers to trade and coordinate national regulations to achieve greater uniformity. As nations conformed to such transnational standards, the final step toward transnational governance became less of a conceptual barrier for citizens, particularly younger citizens. The EEC introduced formal governing components in the form of a commission, executive council, an assembly, and a court. The commission marshaled a growing bureaucracy that advanced transnational policies and powers. The Council of the European Union became the center of gravity in this system. The assembly was renamed the European Parliament in 1962. By 1987, it was ready to move forward with the Single European Act (SEA) to compel greater coordination on environmental and scientific work as well as the establishment of the long-sought common market. By 1992, less than fifty years after the Treaties of Rome, globalists were ready to make the final move with the Maastricht Treaty creating the European Union. A new "European citizen" was born with an EU passport. The agreement gave the EU broader authority over parts of national education, health, consumer protection, environmental, economic, and other policies. With the new citizenship came a new currency, replacing one of the most important symbols of national identity in the form of currencies like the German mark and French franc.

In 2007, the shift to transnational governance was largely accomplished with the Treaty of Lisbon, amending the earlier treaties with critical changes, including the change from unanimity to qualified majority voting in forty-five different policy areas. Dissenting nations could no longer stop measures opposed by their own citizens. The bill of rights and the Charter of Fundamental Rights were now binding and the European Parliament strengthened. In the aftermath, the EU moved to create uniform standards on criminalizing speech and barring policies viewed as inequitable. As one academic noted, "While EU criminalization powers are not entirely uncontroversial among Member States, which justifies careful and incremental Union steps in this area, its competence post-Lisbon has been entrenched." That includes the LGBTIQ Equality Strategy and the use of powers under the Digital Services Act to combat dangerous ideologies and speech. Likewise, under its 2021 European Climate Law (ECL), the EU has enforceable "climate control governance" that cuts across national policies and programs. Various groups of academics and policymakers seek to expand on such success toward a "more equitable, peaceful and sustainable global order based on effective but accountable international organizations, the global rule of law and the empowerment of the individual across borders and cultures."

The EU governance system is not only legislative but judicial. Citizens in the twenty-seven member nations are subject to the decisions of European bodies barring national policies as contrary to European authorities. One such example is immigration policies. The public in various countries is opposed to the European migration policies that have flooded their towns and cities with millions of immigrants. Conservative parties campaigning against such policies have risen dramatically in popularity in countries like Germany and France. In 2025, nine countries (Austria, Belgium, Czech Republic, Denmark, Estonia, Italy, Latvia, Lithuania, and Poland) joined together to call for a new interpretation of the European

Convention on Human Rights "to restore the right balance" between the EU's pro-immigration policies and countervailing national policies. The countries specifically cited the role of the European Court of Human Rights in barring greater border controls and expedited return programs. These countries objected that the interpretations "limited our ability to make political decisions in our own democracies." These countries no longer controlled their own borders or populations despite overwhelming public support for tougher immigration policies. Leaders have been reduced to writing letters to the EU beseeching bureaucrats for greater leeway in carrying out their national mandates.

The evolution of the EU is a cautionary tale. It began with assurances of marginal coordinating bodies and policies over areas like nuclear power and scientific research. Through this planned incrementalism, each insular move was defended on its narrow purpose while dismissing objections as nationalistic or conspiratorial. That incrementalism worked brilliantly in getting citizens to accept transnational governance. The United States has many of the same voices today pushing for greater transnational authority and regulation, with the EU as a model. The proposed moves are again insular and incremental. For example, the Biden administration pushed for a global taxation system for corporations. The move denied the ability of individual countries to adopt more pro-business taxation policies to attract new revenue and firms. Likewise, the most obvious example can be found in free speech. When Elon Musk purchased Twitter with the pledge to dismantle the company's censorship system (and release what became known as the Twitter Files), the response of former Democratic presidential nominee and secretary of state Hillary Clinton was to call upon the EU to force Musk to censor American citizens. The EU promptly did so and threatened Musk with arrest and confiscatory fines unless he censored according to the standards of the EU and its infamous Digital Services Act. European Commissioner for Internal Markets and Services Thierry Breton menacingly told Musk that "we are monitoring you in the 2024 election and interviews with former president Donald Trump."

Returning to the idea of the locality of liberty, the shift toward transnational governance is unlikely to enhance individual rights, as demonstrated by the attacks on free speech by the EU. In 2025, there was a telling moment when Vice President J. D. Vance appeared at the Munich Security Conference and shocked his audience by confronting them over their attacks on free speech in the West. Where John F. Kennedy went to Berlin to declare "*Ich bin ein Berliner*," Vance went to Munich to declare a type of "*Ich bin ein Amerikaner*." He spoke of free speech as an American and denounced the Europeans for their hypocrisy in claiming to be defending democracy while eviscerating free speech. He then delivered this haymaker: "If you are running in fear of your own voters, there is nothing America can do for you. Nor, for that matter, is there anything that you can do for the American people that elected me and elected President Trump." The response from the diplomats was glacial as they glared at Vance from the audience. Later, diplomats denounced the call to restore free speech. Literally speaking through tears, German diplomat Christoph Heusgen responded to VP Vance: "It is clear that our rules-based international order is under pressure. It is my strong belief that this more multipolar world needs to be based on a single set of norms and principles." It was a telling comment. Indeed, this was a challenge to the new international order based on controlled speech and transnational governance. Most distressing was the response from Americans supporting the Europeans. CBS anchor Margaret Brennan confronted Secretary of State Marco Rubio over Vance's support for free speech with the fact that he was "standing in a country where free speech was weaponized to conduct a genocide." In other words, it was free speech that brought Hitler to power and caused the Holocaust—ignoring that the first thing that the Nazis did in coming into power was to crack down on free speech and impose censorship. Commentator and CNN regular Bill Kristol called the speech "a humiliation for the U.S. and a confirmation that this administration isn't on the side of the democracies." The control of speech has always been essential to the control of the governed, particularly under transnational systems.

After Vance's speech, European and American figures gathered in Berlin to discuss how to protect the "New World Order," including the control and regulation of speech. Hillary Clinton called again for action on viewpoints that she considers "disinformation." The gathering proved to be a celebration of the globalist elite calling for projection of European over American values. Many Americans joined in such calls for greater EU regulation, including of individual rights like free speech to protect the public. There was not just a sense of self-proclaimed enlightenment but protected insulation of this global governing class from populist movements in both the United States and Europe. That call for European intervention has continued with Americans, including Nina Jankowicz, the former head of Biden's Disinformation Governance Board. The board was shut down after public outcry over censorship. In 2025, Jankowicz appeared before the European Union to call upon those twenty-seven countries to fight against the United States, which she called a world threat. Similarly, figures like commentator Elie Mystal have called upon the international community to sanction the United States as "a menace to not only free people everywhere . . . a menace to peaceful people everywhere."

Transnational bodies and bureaucrats make effective governing decisions at the maximal distance from individual citizens. In 2025, the International Court of Justice issued an advisory opinion that climate change constitutes an "urgent and existential" threat to humanity and that nations failing to meet climate change goals could be held liable under international law for "full reparations to injured states in the form of restitution, compensation and satisfaction." Opposing such values or research can also be viewed as an offense by some bodies. Free speech has long been treated as an abstraction in conflict with more tangible policies like public health initiatives, climate change programs, and immigration policies. Opposing views are often treated as dangerous disinformation that disregards the truth as established by experts. It is the same frustration of the oligarchs that has been evident through the ages when the hoi polloi fails to heed the views of a governing elite. It was not surprising, therefore, when World Health Organization (WHO) head Tedros Adhanom Ghebreyesus responded to opposing views on the pandemic by declaring an "infodemic" and supporting global censorship efforts. The WHO is the ultimate global bureaucracy and, despite being heavily criticized for being wrong or lax on critical issues such as the origin of the virus, its intolerance for opposing views is entirely predictable. Likewise, in 2024, former Democratic presidential nominee and Secretary of State John Kerry was warmly received at the World Economic Forum as he criticized the First Amendment as an unacceptable barrier to achieving progress in various areas, including climate change.

The appeal of transnational governance in part is the shift from conflicting changes in local or national politics to the greater continuity afforded by a European bureaucracy. Policies of the EU are viewed as more circumspect and enlightened due to the reliance on experts from various countries. Like most oligarchal or bureaucratic systems, the stability can be illusory. Figures like Montesquieu questioned the stability of democracies over large areas, noting that "in a large republic, there [is] . . . little moderation in spirits. . . . The common good is sacrificed to a thousand considerations; it is subordinated to exceptions." The detachment from voters insulates governing officials, but it also means less of an identification or attachment by voters. In Brexit, that resentment over the loss of control over critical areas led voters in Great Britain to depart from the EU. The greater concern is how transnational governing elements will impact the ability of local and national governments in defusing the type of pressures that expressed themselves violently in Paris at the turn of the nineteenth century. As discussed earlier, Philadelphia demonstrated how the Madisonian system serves to achieve stability by directing political pressures into the political process. It is unclear how transnational governing units like the EU will fare over time as the burdens or divisions become more pronounced between its member nations or with given populations. The concentration of power in these units can magnify the potential risks if the governance system collapses or falls into the control of a radical or tyrannical element. While national governments can (and have) fallen prey to such movements, the economic and social disorder caused by a collapse in a transnational system is obviously greater. On one level, a transnational government is a bulwark against the democratic despotism that can more easily take hold of national governments. We have discussed the pattern of how oligarchies can emerge from periods of unrest but in turn lead to the emergence of a tyrant. Governments like the EU are clearly a type of governance with a mix of democratic, oligarchal, and bureaucratic elements. Should a breakdown occur with one or more member nations, the result of the fracture might be the formation of global factions where nations are pitted against each other. The avoidance of such a crisis is dependent on the ability of the European Parliament to serve the same dialogic role that the federal system played in the United States. It has, thus far, failed to achieve that role.

Whatever the capacity of transnational governance for breaking the cycle of democracy to tyranny, there is little reason to be hopeful that individual rights will be protected, let alone enhanced, under such a system. Transnational governance can certainly claim to bring some countries up to a higher standard of individual rights. For those countries below the baseline, the requirements of transnational organizations like NATO can force reforms that protect democratic and constitutional values. There is a key difference. Organizations like NATO are focused on security, while organizations like the EU are focused on economics in the form of a common market. Moreover, the concentration of governing authority in remote locations like Brussels makes it easier for special-interest groups to exercise influence over both elected officials and bureaucrats. International forums and conferences tend to be an elite group of experts and activists that are drawn from backgrounds of higher income, education, and more liberal viewpoints. They are certainly not representative of the masses in the countries impacted by these decisions. As economies become more globalized and more citizens become dependent on government subsidies (if the foregoing discussion is correct), the insularity and, frankly, arrogance of this global elite is only likely to increase. The governing class may grow not just physically but socially and economically apart from the vast majority of the governed.

2. Corporate Feudalism

While at times in conflict, the shift to transnational governance also has a transnational corporate element. The twenty-first century has seen the emergence of a new type of oligarchy in the form of corporate actors. The rise of corporations from Meta to Amazon to Google has further shifted the center of gravity for critical decisions impacting the lives of citizens. The concentration of power and wealth is growing exponentially, with a few corporations leading in AI and robotic technologies.

In the last ten years, the role of corporations in governance has taken on a menacing meaning in terms of free speech. Unable to directly censor Americans under the First Amendment, government officials in Europe and the United States turned to Facebook, Twitter, and other social media companies to carry out censorship. As shown by the Twitter Files released with the help of journalists Matt Taibbi, Michael Shellenberger, and others, government officials sent thousands of emails targeting individuals and groups with dissenting views, leading to shadow bans, throttling, and other forms of censorship. In testimony before Congress, I called the massive system a form of "censorship by surrogate." When confronted in Congress over censorship systems, social media executives often portrayed themselves as experts on disinformation and justified their blocking and throttling viewpoints as protecting the public from the dangers of free speech. For those targeted, it seems more like a tyranny of experts who act with little transparency and virtually no accountability.

In the French Revolution, Jacobins emphasized that the revolution was designed to end feudalism. As corporations take on more surrogated functions, a type of new feudalism can emerge. Aristocratic feudalism became the dominant form of governing due to the ability to maintain order and control in localities. We see the same trend toward a type of corporate governance where we rely on companies to carry out state actions. Government officials were able to do indirectly through companies like Twitter and Facebook what they could not do directly under the First Amendment. Politicians from Hillary Clinton to Adam Schiff repeatedly called upon these companies for greater censorship in an array of different areas, from elections to climate change to transgender policies. For the first time, companies were controlling much of the public discourse in the United States, exercising a throttle control over what was deemed disinformation, misinformation, or malinformation. At the same time, corporations ranging from Disney to Nike have become more actively involved in political causes. Such corporate campaigns should be protected under the First Amendment, even if they are not protected from consumer backlash. At the same time, the combination of more politically active companies and the partnership with the government on censorship raises deeper concerns. If governments increasingly outsource functions like speech regulation, corporations can further separate citizens from the centers of decision-makers impacting their lives.

The rise of a corporate governance system would be an ironic development for the United States, which formed after a long period of mercantilism under the authority of corporations like the East India Company (EIC). The EIC was arguably the first true transnational corporation and eventually wielded direct governing authority over colonies in the mercantile period. Chartered on December 31, 1600, it would eventually offer investors as much as 30 percent annual returns on their investments. By some estimates, the EIC would account for half the world's trade during eighteenth and nineteenth centuries. In return, it was given increasing military and civil authority in transferring wealth to the Old World. It would eventually command a force of over a quarter million soldiers and constitute what Yale sociology professor Emily Erikson described as "the *de facto* emperor of large portions of India, which was one of the most productive economies in the world at that point." When chartered by Queen Elizabeth I, the EIC was given a monopoly over trade in its territory. The role of the EIC in India and China was particularly chilling. In China, the EIC actively thwarted efforts of the government to stop the flow of opium into the country. The EIC used its Indian sources to flood the country with the drug, addicting millions as it pulled raw materials from the provinces. With opium dens overflowing, the Chinese took action to interdict the flow, and the EIC called in the Royal Navy. The result was the Opium War of 1840, where the British defeated the Chinese, took Hong Kong, and cleared the way for the company. All in the interest of opium dealing. The Opium War offers a concerning historical comparison for the twenty-first century, as China is accused of knowingly flooding the United States with fentanyl and triggering a national addiction epidemic.

Companies like the EIC and the Dutch East India Company were not just forerunners of the modern corporation but also transnational corporations performing governing functions. If the trend toward greater popular government leads to democratic despotism, corporations offer an immediate type of oligarchical authority, stabilizing systems that can supply key resources and support. As corporate and governmental interests align (as they did on censorship), it is possible to see the same types of partnerships that led to the expansion of the EIC. Indeed, we may already be seeing that trend as governments like the European Union pass laws directing companies to censor citizens and control speech—or face potential arrest and confiscatory fines. Conversely, those who do not yield to those demands are subjected to global pressures. For example, as noted earlier, the European Union demanded corporations regulate speech and threatened corporate executives like Elon Musk under the Digital Services Act. For companies like X, they either must carry out such governing tasks or absorb massive confiscatory fines. For citizens, censorship operations (which are ordinarily difficult to track within the government) become less accessible, observable, and accountable in the bowels of giant corporations.

Citizens, of course, have the power of the market in rejecting corporate interests. In some ways, it may be a more direct relationship than the one left by the administrative state. For example, as shown recently in response to a controversial ad campaign by Bud Light, boycott movements can shock even multinational corporations. Nevertheless, corporations such as Disney or Google are so dominant that such boycotts often have little effect. Moreover, even with social media companies, citizens find it difficult to boycott corporations offering key services or platforms. In the absence of an anti-monopoly action, they will continue to wield dominant market power. That presents a dangerous scenario when they adopt surrogate government functions. Social media companies, for example, are notorious for having no easy points of contact for aggrieved consumers. That power and insularity serve to decouple citizens from participatory politics and make them passive recipients of the good policies enacted by a ruling elite. With all of their social and political virtue signaling, they remain wealth-maximizing enterprises seeking greater market shares and profits.

Modern transnational corporations can ultimately undermine national identities as people identify corporations as controlling key aspects of their well-being. In 1604, Sir Edwin Sandys argued that there was a "natural right" for citizens to be able to engage in international trade. He was seeking greater equity in transnational markets. Today, much of the global wealth is tied to transnational corporations and profits. It has led to a critical shift in the focus of production and profits for citizens. This is not to say that Meta is now likely to field a quarter of a million troops, as did the EIC. Rather, such brute force is now viewed as anachronistic and unnecessary. National governments and transnational governments (like the EU) will supply the troops so long as the corporation supplies the profits. It is a modern variation of the Opium War where governments and corporations ally to better control or direct a population. That brings us back to Smith. The EIC was to Smith an "absurdity." In *The Wealth of Nations*, he declared, "Such exclusive companies . . . are nuisances in every respect; always more or less inconvenient to the countries in which they are established, and destructive to those which have the misfortune to fall under their government." The reference to "exclusive companies" may distinguish current transnational corporations from precursors like the EIC, but they could still pose an even greater "nuisance" if they are given quasi-governmental functions.

The power of transnational corporations will continue to grow with new, essential technologies. Social media is an example of such control over the primary forums for political and social dialogue. That is even more true with AI. The incorporation of AI from robotics to search engines can give companies largely unchecked power. Some of us experienced that power in a small but chilling way with ChatGPT and its parent company, OpenAI. Like other AI Systems, ChatGPT is subject to "hallucinations" where it makes up facts. For some individuals, those hallucinations are defamatory. I was one of those people. When people would ask ChatGPT about my history, it falsely reported that I was accused of sexual harassment after I supposedly took law students to Alaska as a Georgetown law professor. I have never been accused of any form of sexual harassment, and I have never been a member of the Georgetown faculty or taken students on any field trip, let alone to Alaska. *The Washington Post* investigated the false story and discovered that another AI program, "Microsoft's Bing, which is powered by GPT-4, repeated the false claim about Turley." I was not alone. Harvard professor Jonathan Zittrain, CNBC anchor David Faber, Australian mayor Brian Hood, English professor David Mayer, and others were also defamed with alleged crimes or misconduct. When the hallucinations were raised by the major media, ChatGPT effectively erased the victims. When anyone put in our names, the system said that it has no information or ability to answer. We were simply ghosted by the company. No victim, no problem. There is little recourse over such erasure. A private company does not have a duty to acknowledge anyone's existence. While the company could be sued for defamation, it cannot be sued for the tort of nonrecognition.

The ChatGPT controversy is a small example of the authority and insularity of these transnational companies. While companies are increasingly enlisted to carry out transnational policies by the EU and other countries, citizens have little recourse or influence on their operations. A remote governing body enlists a cloistered corporation to carry out major tasks. For anyone who has tried to contact a social media company, the lack of responsive office, let alone human support, in these companies is maddening. They are notoriously unresponsive and uninterested in individual complaints. Citizens often find a hermetically sealed business with only AI-operated chatrooms and contacts. Now consider that these companies will be building and programming AI systems, including robots, that will soon be in every household and office. The ability to carry out political or social agendas will be immense, and the ability of the public to object will be minimal. These companies control not only a significant number of dwindling jobs but also a large percentage of the global wealth. They are not designed for participatory politics or democratic empowerment. Companies like ChatGPT are wealth-maximizers focused on revenue, not rights. That makes them a particularly dangerous substitute for governing systems on any level.

"What Then Is the American" in the Twenty-First Century?

When Michel Guillaume Jean de Crèvecoeur asked, "What then is the new American, this new man?" he was a Frenchman. Later, the author, cartographer, farmer, and diplomat would adopt a new name as John Hector St. John as well as a new identity: an American farmer. In 1782, he would publish an exploration of his life on the colonial frontier. The popular work was a collection of letters with a much longer title that highlighted the fascination of many Europeans with this new nationality: *Letters from an American Farmer; Describing Certain Provincial Situations, Manners, and Customs not Generally Known; and Conveying Some Idea of the Late and Present Interior Circumstances of the British Colonies in North America*. Among those heralding the work was Paine. What was so striking about *Letters from an American Farmer* was the fourth word: *American*. At a time when most people still identified with their states as

Georgians or Virginians, Crèvecoeur wrote as one of a new people known as Americans, writing, "I have endeavoured to show you how Europeans become Americans." He added that "Europe contains hardly any other distinctions but lords and tenants; this fair country alone is settled by freeholders, the possessors of the soil they cultivate, members of the government they obey, and the framers of their own laws, by means of their representatives." The work emphasized the relatively classless society that drew Americans and how they shared a common identity despite coming from various countries. That identity was based on individual enterprise and advancement free of the stratified economic and social limitations of Europe. Crèvecoeur's question today is even more poignant and perhaps, for some, more difficult to answer. Citizenship has become more fluid in the twenty-first century. The greatest challenge of this century may be a rediscovery of that essential character that seemed so clear to these early writers when they first came upon our shores. Call it a crisis of faith or a confusion of the times, but many seem unsure whether we represent something beyond the totality of our wealth or power. We were much more than that when we first assumed the moniker of *Americans*. The question is, what we are now? Or, perhaps more pointedly, what do we aspire to be in this new century?

Ironically, being caught between two nations in revolutionary times may have brought a clarity about what it is to be an American. These early writers had striking points of comparison from the calcified class-based society of Great Britain to the chaotic class struggle of France. As with Paine, Crèvecoeur found himself a target of the Mountain as he traveled between the two countries. He also would have the distinction of being treated in both countries as an undesirable. He was imprisoned by the British as a suspected American spy in 1778 before he could return to visit his ailing father in France. The friend of Lafayette would go into hiding until American consul James Monroe could get him papers to travel to the United States.

The meaning of citizenship continues to evolve with less of an emphasis on an exclusive national identity for many citizens. Crèvecoeur and Paine share the status of having dual (or, in Paine's case, triple) citizenship at the end of their lives (Crèvecoeur died in France). After the revolution, that would become less common. Comparably, in the last century, there has been an explosion of dual citizenships in the United States and abroad. Some now claim three or more such citizenships. There are fifty-six countries that recognize dual nationalities, a jump of 75 percent over the past ten years. Many of these countries have diametrically opposed views of core rights from free speech to free exercise of religion. The rise in dual citizenships has been criticized by some as a privilege of the wealthy who are willing to pay upfront costs to secure easier travel and living conditions abroad. What is more concerning is how the greater fluidity in citizenship can produce a type of amalgamated citizenship and, for some, a loosening of their identification with a given nation.

Both writers and artists have tried to illuminate the meaning of the American identity for centuries. Early works on the American identity often emphasized the connection to the agrarian culture of the colonies. For many Americans, that identity was symbolized by the simple farming couple captured in Grant Wood's *American Gothic*. While the models were actually Wood's sister and the family dentist, they became an iconic image of the rural American. Particularly when the Depression hit, it would embody a certain resilience and strength that Wood himself described in growing up in Iowa in a house not unlike the one in the painting. The painting conveyed a certain American stoicism and strength connected to agrarian values. The temperance and self-reliance were greatly valued by many early writers, including Paine, Smith, and Crèvecoeur, who saw farming as both an ideal economic and political foundation for a republic. It would be a vision of the ideal citizenship that would have a lasting hold on political writers, including some into the twentieth century. The agrarian foundation for the ideal citizen would also take on a more terrifying meaning in other countries such as Cambodia. Like the French, the Khmer Rouge sought to create Year Zero with the creation of a new citizen. Using their interpretation of Maoist philosophy, Pol Pot believed that a classless society would require a return to an agrarian existence. The result would be forced relocations, education camps, and executions as agrarian ideals became the killing fields.

For early writers, farming offered a path to economic independence and the escape of class-based restraints. It was meant as a lifestyle that fostered independence, not some Maoist collectivism. The eighteenth century's embrace of agrarian values seems anachronistic and simplistic today. Not only is much of our economy now industrial but farming is becoming more mechanized and mass productive. The reasons for the emphasis on agrarianism went beyond the simple lifestyle or connection to the earth. For Crèvecoeur, it was part of his effort to explain to Europeans eager "to know whence came all these people? they are a mixture of English, Scotch, Irish, French, Dutch, Germans, and Swedes. From this promiscuous breed, that race now called Americans have arisen." Crèvecoeur noted that many came from poor origins in countries with little chance for economic or social advancement. They found land where they could serve none but themselves and their families in seeking prosperity and freedom. Now their labor was voluntary and their own:

> Wives and children, who before in vain demanded of him a morsel of bread, now, fat and frolicsome, gladly help their father to clear those fields whence exuberant crops are to arise to feed and to clothe them all; without any part being claimed, either by a despotic prince, a rich abbot, or a mighty lord. Here religion demands but little of him; a small voluntary salary to the minister, and gratitude to God; can he refuse these? The American is a new man, who acts upon new principles; he must therefore entertain new ideas, and form new opinions. From involuntary idleness, servile dependence, penury, and useless

> labour, he has passed to toils of a very different nature, rewarded by ample subsistence.—This is an American.

By unlocking the abundance of the earth, these Americans were creating wealth independently from any capital markets and controls of Europe. In the Old World, Crèvecoeur noted, there was little escape from one's class or circumstances, but Americans could literally grow a new life from the soil: "This is a thought which you have taught me to cherish; our difference from Europe, far from diminishing, rather adds to our usefulness and consequence as men and subjects." Crèvecoeur was speaking of both political and economic independence. He saw people leaving the crowded conditions of Europe and becoming affluent producers of a type of wealth, noting that where "a hundred families barely existing in some parts of Scotland, will here in six years, cause an annual exportation of 10,000 bushels of wheat: one hundred bushels being but a common quantity for an industrious family to sell, if they cultivate good land." That meant wealth that was both tangible and renewable "by riches I do not mean gold and silver, we have but little of those metals; I mean a better sort of wealth, cleared lands, cattle, good houses, good clothes, and an increase of people to enjoy them."

Consider this passage from Crèvecoeur in the context of Grant Wood's *American Gothic*. He speaks of a Lockean state of nature where God has left abundance in common to be made harnessed, harvested, and honed by individuals:

> After a foreigner from any part of Europe is arrived, and become a citizen; let him devoutly listen to the voice of our great parent, which says to him, "Welcome to my shores, distressed European; bless the hour in which thou didst see my verdant fields, my fair navigable rivers, and my green mountains!—If thou wilt work, I have bread for thee; if thou wilt be honest, sober, and industrious, I have greater rewards to confer on thee—ease and independence . . . I shall endow thee beside with the immunities of a freeman. If thou wilt carefully educate thy children, teach them gratitude to God, and reverence to that government, that philanthropic government, which has collected here so many men and

> made them happy. I will also provide for thy progeny; and to every good man this ought to be the most holy, the most powerful, the most earnest wish he can possibly form, as well as the most consolatory prospect when he dies. Go thou and work and till; thou shalt prosper, provided thou be just, grateful, and industrious."

Crèvecoeur saw a "new man" emerging in the New World, a citizen emancipated from the chains of Europe with its static classes and concentrated wealth.

Smith held strikingly similar views on the importance of agriculture in his political economic writings. Smith had a distrust of merchants and manufacturers, who he believed displayed a "mean rapacity, the monopolizing spirit" that was inimical to the free market. They were denounced as "an order of men, whose interest is never exactly the same with that of the publick, who have generally an interest to deceive and even to oppress the publick, and who accordingly have, upon many occasions, both deceived and oppressed it." This part of Smith's writing (like his positions on virtuous policies and practices) is often ignored in favor of a view of Smith as a materialistic free marketer. However, his dislike for the mercantile class was tied to his desire for free markets; he saw this mercantile class as using their powers to suppress competition. He noted that "to widen the market and to narrow the competition, is always the interest of the dealers." To the end, these business interests work to raise "their profits above what they would normally be, to levy, for their own benefit, an absurd tax upon the rest of their fellow-citizens." These views pushed Smith toward agrarian-based economies as fostering a form of concrete wealth in land and produce—wealth directly tied to expended labor rather than market manipulation. After all, the mercantile system that Smith detested was the result of these fixed interests where "the sneaking arts of underlying tradesmen" were allowed to mutate into a system of trade controls. These merchants and manufacturers held such political power that they could "intimidate" the legislation into protectionist laws. In this way, Smith argued their corrupting and monopolizing interests were "erected into political maxims for the conduct of a great empire," leaving Great Britain "a nation whose government is influenced by shopkeepers." For Smith, the "perfect liberty" was found in blocking monopolizing agents and embracing real wealth in the form of land as opposed to unstable forms like stock. Smith also viewed the agrarian life as producing a different type of man, passages that again bring forth Wood's gothic vision centuries later. Smith sees not only a real and stable form of wealth in commodities like corn, but a return to the natural state of man: "the independency which it really affords, have charms that more or less attract everybody; and as to cultivate the ground was the original destination of man, so in every stage of his existence he seems to retain a predilection for this primitive employment."

Smith's idyllic vision of the agrarian life can be attributed to many of that age who saw the brutal conditions of urban life as crushing the human spirit and potential. There was notably another aspect to these writings. Smith saw farming as a bulwark against the political and economic corruption of the period. It empowered citizens and tied them closely to not just the land but the community and country. Conversely, capital and stock interests tended to untether citizens from their locale: "Land is a subject which cannot be removed; whereas stock easily may. The proprietor of land is necessarily a citizen of the particular country in which his estate lies. The proprietor of stock is properly a citizen of the world, and is not necessarily attached to any particular country." Smith wanted citizens to be wealthy and independent but also to remain citizens of their nations, not denizens of a global marketplace. Smith was not the "economic determinist" portrayed by many where economics drives social changes. As York University professor David McNally observed, "Smith continually suggests that economic progress is impossible without political arrangements which guarantee liberty of work and investment, and security of property." Indeed, Smith tied the existence of political liberty as necessary to allow economic freedom to do its transformative work. The guaranteed "freedom and security" in a political system, "the natural effort of every individual to better his own condition . . . is so powerful a principle, that it is alone, and without any assistance, not only capable of carrying on the society to wealth and prosperity, but of surmounting a hundred impertinent obstructions with which the folly of human laws too often incumbers its operations." In other words, liberty is essential for economic independence, which in turn reinforces liberty.

Paine also tied the American democracy and character to agrarian values. As Michigan philosophy professor Elizabeth Anderson observed, Paine "offered a third way between proto-communism—symbolized by the French Revolution's 'Equals' radical contingent and their desire to confiscate all wealth—and England's Poor Laws, which offered humanitarian relief but stigmatized the poor and subjected them to harsh social control and workhouse conditions." Paine wrote his *Agrarian Justice* as a plan to eradicate poverty without the collectivism of more radical elements. While viewing poverty as an injustice, Paine also embraced Smith's view of the free markets as advancing individual freedom and self-determination. For Paine, equality and liberty had to be embraced and protected with equal vigor.

For all of these writers, the value of agrarianism was not just the independence of literally creating your own wealth from the land but also its allowance for individual enterprise. One figure who recognized the importance of agrarian opportunity without the mystique of agrarian values was Tocqueville, who saw farming as at most the best of bad options. He viewed the emphasis on farming in practical terms, a means "to escape from imposed systems." Like Smith, Tocqueville tied liberty to being able to lead productive lives in a free market. Unlike Smith, he maintained that a "Democracy . . . gives [people] a distaste for agriculture and directs them into trade and industry." Americans, he maintained, are drawn to the pursuit of enterprise and wealth maximization "to better their situations," using their freedom to achieve greater levels of economic independence.

So, if agrarian values are not the definition of an American, what defines us? For some, Wood's *American Gothic* captures nothing more than a parody, the caricature of culture embraced by many who never met a cow, let alone steered a plow. After all, in reality, that was a dentist holding the pitchfork in the painting, a manufactured image of the ideal farming couple. (Indeed, Wood intended the portrait to be a father and his daughter, but it was widely interpreted as a husband and wife.) Still, the picture was embraced by many Americans, even urban dwellers, as capturing something more than the cultural kitsch. Wood's painting was actually completed for a competition at Chicago's Art Institute and, while receiving only the bronze medal, was immediately purchased at the demand of wealthy urban donors. The American farmer represented a stubborn self-reliance and a certain stoicism. Farming would be used by writers like John Dewey in his writings on democracy to embody that pragmaticism as a metaphor. The American pragmatist is found in the ability to adjust not just to changes in weather or farming conditions but changes in the world around us. We are cultivators who seek to find fertile fields and opportunity. We value freedom because it allows us to create something new; to project ourselves in new endeavors into the world around us.

Despite the importance of agrarian values to earlier writers, it was not the farm but the farmers themselves who resonated with Americans. Workers reflected the same steely-eyed clarity as the gothic couple. The farmers rotated fields, slaughtered animals, and changed crops to meet the demands of the day. They made those decisions. Not the government. They built their own future; they pursued their own manifest destiny. In that sense, American agrarianism is a metaphor for American individuality and industry. Note the same sense of self-reliance in classic urban images such as the famous photo *Lunch atop a Skyscraper* of eleven ironworkers sitting on a steel beam of the RCA Building in 1932 (two years after *American Gothic* was painted).

There is a core identity found among an enterprising, pragmatic people. We are defined by our struggles, by what we do. Ask someone who they are, and they will start with being a teacher or plumber or taxi driver. That is not to say that we always love our jobs. My maternal grandfather was a coal miner in Ohio, and my paternal grandfather was a cooper, or barrel maker. My grandfather contracted black lung in those mines, but he still identified as a coal miner. They were proud to be supporting their families. Indeed, studies show that depression spikes with unemployment even though individuals are receiving state support. What happens to that identity if we become largely idle, primarily consumers rather than producers? The emerging economy may force us to come to grips with that question. Many still have their faith and their families, but so much of our lives are measured by the challenges that we have overcome and the advances that we have achieved. If we replace the struggle with subsidy, it is not just citizens but society that may change.

At the heart of many of these works is the notion that individuals must seek their own manifest destiny through their own enterprise and hard work. The same notion of individual achievement would be amplified by popular writers like Horatio Alger in his bestselling *Strong and Steady, or Paddle Your Own Canoe* in 1887. Alger insisted that "It is not wealth or rank, but virtue alone, that can make a man great." Conversely, efforts to create a culture based on collectivism or communalism fared poorly in the United States. Three decades after the collapse of the Conspiracy of Equals in France, Robert Owen, an industrialist who espoused the value of collectivist society, inspired the creation of a communal town called New Harmony in Indiana. Owen laid out a community of factory-looking buildings forming squares with communal kitchens and work areas with simple, uniform living quarters. In 1826, the town attracted a musician and inventor named Josiah Warren. Related to General Joseph Warren, the Revolutionary hero killed at Bunker Hill, Warren was a committed anarchist. An inventor himself (both of a successful printing press as well as such items as a lard-burning lamp), Warren possessed many of the characteristics of Paine, including a willingness to learn from poor assumptions about popular government. Joining nine hundred Owen adherents at New Harmony, Warren saw a utopia realized in the fields of Indiana:

> Many a time while in the midst of them did I say to myself, Oh! If the world could only assemble on these hills around and look down upon us through all these experiences, what lessons would they learn! There would be no more French Revolutions, no more patent political governments, no more organizations, no more constitution-making, law-making, nor human contrivances for the foundation of society.

It did not work out that way. New Harmony would collapse, and Warren attributed the failure to the suppression of individuality and removal of incentives for production. Government did not melt away as a human contrivance. Individuals were subject to the will of Owen as the proprietor and a type of democratic despotism. First to go were individual rights, which were subordinated for the general good. Witnessing the failure of New Harmony, Warren ultimately concluded that such individual rights are essential in any social organization.

Warren's profound writings are not well known even today, but they deeply influenced more famous figures like John Stuart Mill. Warren's account of New Harmony offers an insight into systems that deny the ability of individuals to work for their own advancement and opportunities. Intellectuals flocked to New Harmony, but many were not inclined to work in the new utopia. The result of this free-rider class was that the burden of feeding and maintaining the community fell on a minority. Owen's own son observed how the town was soon overrun by a combination of idealists, "lazy theorists." The anarchists and socialists found that the withering away of the state meant a withering away of their waistlines and lifestyles. What happened next was all too familiar. As divisions emerged in New Harmony, there was a greater call for conformity and a rising orthodoxy among the leaders. In his publication *Periodical Letter*, Warren described how the collectivized orthodoxy collided with something elemental for each citizen: "it appeared that it was nature's own inherent law of diversity that had conquered us . . . our 'united interests' were directly at war with the individualities of persons and circumstances and the instinct of self-preservation." For Warren, the resulting anarchy was a new awakening, just not the one he expected in New Harmony. He found that "society must be so converted as to preserve the SOVEREIGNTY OF EVERY INDIVIDUAL inviolate. That it must avoid all combinations and connections of persons and interests, and all other arrangements which will not leave every individual at all times at liberty to dispose of his or her person, and time, and property in any manner in which his or her feelings or judgment may dictate, WITHOUT INVOLVING THE PERSONS OR INTERESTS OF OTHERS." Any new society would have to be based on individuality to succeed. Notably, Warren saw these lessons as the outgrowth of Jefferson and Paine. The denial of those individual rights set a government against the very nature and essence of humanity. It would be a core principle embraced by Mill, who wrote that "over himself, over his own body and mind, the individual is sovereign."

The collapse of harmony in Indiana reflected the instability of systems that fail to recognize the inherent needs of citizens as individuals. Just as Montesquieu and Madison stated that you must first understand what is human before you create a model for human governance, Warren showed how even voluntary communities collapse when built on collective identities and existence. It was a lesson ignored at great cost in later governments, from the Soviet Union to the Pol Pot regime. Still, there is another lesson to be learned from New Harmony. As the society began to break down, control shifted to an elite body: enlightened leaders who sought to instill collectivist values and inspire virtue among the citizenry. It was not the aristocracy that followed democratic despotism in Greece or France. However, it was the same inexorable trend from moving from governance of the many to governance of the few.

We would be unwise to wait and see what we become in such a world of static, idle citizens. Even with a reduction in the labor force, we must explore avenues for exploration and identification for citizens. We cannot sustain a democracy by simply occupying much of the population like some arts-and-crafts citizenry. Some of that effort will mean greater expenditures on public education and public goods such as the national parks, which continue to be underfunded in light of the public demand. New opportunities will also arise in the markets as people find niche markets and skill sets. The government can also facilitate individual enterprise by limiting tax burdens and regulatory costs for entrepreneurs. We cannot build a new economy on makeshift jobs or subsidizing inefficient industries. That means avoiding wasteful and dysfunctional subsidies for areas that are already converting to a largely mechanized or robotic workforce. We cannot replicate the failures of New Harmony on a national scale and hope for a better outcome. There is a core need for Americans to be both expressive and productive. Likewise, converting the nation into a large self-realization exercise through community college courses is little more promising than a national New Harmony program. Citizens require an identity beyond the government if they are to be expected to challenge the government. Dependency not only robs citizens of their independence but can produce a despondency in how individuals view themselves.

For many, the essence of the American character can be found in another iconic painting: *Rosie the Riveter*. In 1943, Norman Rockwell painted this image to capture the strength of American women stepping forward to replace men on farms, factory floors, and shipyards as part of the "Arsenal of Democracy." It would be a transformative moment for American society and industry. Women found skills, employment, and recognition in the workplace that had long been denied them. The image itself continues to speak to a broad spectrum of American society after over eighty years.

Rockwell based the image on Michelangelo's image of the Prophet Isaiah from the Sistine Chapel. It was a poignant choice. Located fourth from the right of the High Altar, the image shows Isaiah in deep meditation, listening to a putto, or cherub, who is pointing to the Fall of Man, the corruption of Adam in the Garden of Eden. Isaiah is a complicated and, on some level, a tragic figure. In religious iconography, he is often represented rather gruesomely by a saw because, according to Hebrews 11:37, Isaiah was sawed in half. He had prophesied correctly that King Hezekiah's wicked son, Manasseh, would ultimately undo his father's good works and words. When Manasseh became king, he pursued Isaiah for challenging his authority. The prophet hid within a cedar tree, and Manasseh ordered it—and Isaiah—sawed in half. The image of the blood that coursed from the cedar tree is a lasting image of martyrdom at the hands of a vengeful ruler. It is also the greatest testament to faith. It was an interesting choice of Rockwell as the reference point for his quintessential American image. Isaiah is presented in an almost melancholy pose as the putto shows him the corruption of man, the fall from grace that would capture the potential avarice and cruelty of man. It would foreshadow his own demise at the hands of Manasseh. There is a sense of stoic strength in his acceptance, defiance, and, most importantly, faith.

In Rockwell's image of Rosie, she too is looking away. Whatever she is seeing at this time of world war clearly does not scare her. Under her feet is a copy of Adolf Hitler's *Mein Kampf*. There is the same sense of resolve—a sense of "I got this" in her proud, muscular countenance.

Rather than a religious text, she holds a pneumatic, or air-powered, rivet gun in one hand and a sandwich in the other. She had clearly had enough with Hitler's "master race" and was taking a quick lunch break before returning to her work.

Like most of Rockwell's works, there are layers of meaning that resonate with the viewer. It is penetrating and profound. For our purposes, it is the relationship of Rosie to her work that is so intriguing. Her lunch box bears her name, and she does not even put down her rivet gun to eat. Her work overalls are adorned with medals like a general's ribbon bar, but they represent the pride of the American worker. There is her Westinghouse employment badge, a Red Cross blood donor button, a white "V for Victory" button, an Army-Navy E Service production award pin, and two bronze civilian service awards. There is also a Blue Star Mothers pin, showing that she had a child serving in the war effort. She was "all in," with not a hint of doubt as to what will come from this struggle. Her identity as a mother, a worker, and an American combine to make her as formidable an image as any of the weapons that she was making for the war effort. The message is clear: Herr Hitler had far more to fear from Rosie than from a fleet of battleships.

The Rockwell image obviously spoke to our sense of patriotism and common purpose. It also spoke to later generations of Americans in a different way. The continued use of the image is not due to an intergenerational connection to World War II. It is a connection to Rosie herself as a symbol of the strength of the American worker and American women in particular. Her identity and pride are directly linked to the work that she is doing. It is a pride in not only contributing to the war effort but also being productive. Where Rousseau created the image of the noble savage, Rockwell painted the noble citizen. Rosie found not just equality but identity in her work.

The sense of self-worth found in work is deeply rooted in the American identity. It is the very draw for many who came to these shores. Each wanted to be that American, that independent and proud citizen. The pressures of the twenty-first century, from robotics to globalism, will challenge that shared ideal. There remains a core American identity that cannot be lost in this globalized environment without risking the core rights that define this nation. A picture of three women and a baby arriving at Ellis Island offers another insight into what it means to be an American. It is a captivating image because it shows a mix of emotions from the joy of the two women with the laughing baby and the more serious expression of the woman with a large sack balanced on her head. In its way, it may also capture the true meaning of the American identity. Except for the Native Americans, we are all immigrants to this nation. It is not immigration that truly defines us but the type of people who immigrated. The standing woman shows the same almost stoic countenance of *American Gothic*. These are people who came to the United States wanting, like Paine, to reinvent themselves and find a new destiny in a new world. They see the United States as allowing not just political but economic freedom and self-determination. It is that very dream that is shared with the couple in *American Gothic*. The political and economic freedom offered in the United States is expressed in their strength and determination.

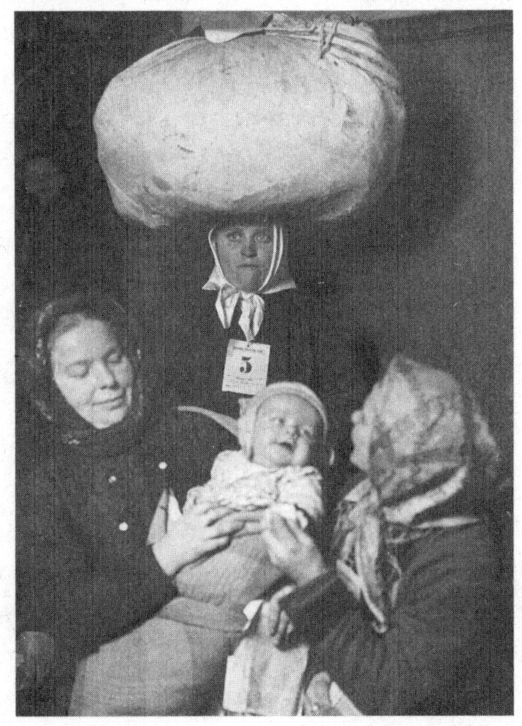

The photo could well have captured the relatives of many of our families, who came to these shores with little but dreams of self-determined, self-realized success. When I first saw this photo, I saw my grandmother in those fixed eyes of the standing woman. Josephine Piazza arrived on a wooden sailing ship as a young girl with her stepmother and siblings. They made the long voyage from their mountain village of Cianciana, crossing the ocean in an unsanitary, large hold with dozens of other poor immigrants. They spent weeks sick and miserable in the hot, airless space of a ship tossing on the transcontinental voyage. A woman gave birth and a man died on the voyage in that shared space. Her stepmother traveled with large rolled-up sheep skins, which they hoped to sell in the new world as they traveled to find their family. They eventually joined others in a coal mining town where Italians could find work. She would be promised at age fourteen to my grandfather in an arranged marriage. They both came from Cianciana and worked tirelessly to raise their large family. My grandfather, Domenico Piazza, would become an early organizer for the United Mine Workers as my grandmother became the midwife for large coal mining towns. My grandfather would work in the mines during the day and drive trucks at night with my uncle Mimi. Josephine watched as women died in childbirth and men died from cave-ins. She sometimes had to assist a drunkard company doctor who later admitted to her that he used euthanasia to kill crippled miners as a "mercy" to their families. When I asked her how she could continue in such cruel, emotionally crushing conditions, she would answer with an expression in Sicilian: "It can't get later than midnight." When her close friend died after a botched abortion at the hands of the company doctor, she would repeat that line. It was always midnight, but it could only get better. It did. After my grandfather developed black lung, they started businesses, from bars to a hardware store to a grocery store to a farm to a restaurant. In the process, their children would find the American dream. One would become a respected California judge.

What made them the ideal American citizens was the very thing that brought them to these shores: They understood that they were now in control of their own destiny. The hard work and hard times did not deter them because, unlike in the old country, they believed that they and their children could achieve anything that their talents and drive would allow. It was the same belief that took my parents, as newlyweds, to Chicago after World War II. My father, Jack Turley, earned his GED in the navy during the war and decided to become an architect. Once he made that decision, he wanted to work for the most famous architect of the age, Mies van der Rohe, the genius behind the modern school of architecture that produced the large glass and steel buildings. They arrived late one winter night with no lodging and $1.35 in their pockets. They went into a restaurant and ordered just two cups of coffee (the only thing that they could afford). My mother, Angela, immediately prevailed upon the owner to give her a job as a waitress. Living in the projects, she would work as my father studied under Mies at the Illinois Institute of Technology and eventually became one of his handful of protégés working in his office. Later, my father would become a partner at Skidmore, Owings & Merrill and build structures all around the world.

Just as their stories are not unique, their shared faith in this country was the common article of faith through generations of American families. They had that same *American Gothic* look: that same dream. It was the very thing that was missing in my fellow dinner guest when she said that she had grown out of her American identity and patriotism. For her, being an American was reduced to the mere convenience of an alternative passport. For most Americans, it is the chance to become something and someone of your own making. "What then is the American, this new man?" It is the political and economic freedoms that allow every person to pursue their own destiny and identity. The danger of disconnected political governance and policies of economic dependency is that they deny the very essence of what brought people from these shores, from the Paines to the Piazzas. They understood that, in this country, you are your greatest creation.

Conclusion

Near the end of the constitutional debates in Independence Hall, Franklin famously drew the attention of his fellow colleagues to the chair at the head of the room. Made in 1779 for the Pennsylvania Statehouse by John Folwell, the Chippendale armchair was used by George Washington as he presided for months over the Constitutional Convention. Near the end of the constitutional debates, many delegates were having doubts about the new Constitution. That is when Franklin pointed to the chair at the head of the room. The carved top of the chair shows a liberty pole with a Phrygian cap and half of a heraldic sun. Franklin famously remarked:

> I have often looked at that picture behind the president without being able to tell whether it was rising or setting. But now at length I have the happiness to know that it is a rising and not a setting sun.

Indeed, it did prove a rising sun, as the new Constitution would herald into existence the oldest and most successful constitutional system in the history of the world. The question is whether it continues to rise or will set at the end of an American era. Like the chair, the Constitution was a quintessentially American design, hewn from the solid oak of a new concept of governance. Franklin would also remind the nation that each generation will determine whether this republic will remain ascendant or sink below the horizon. When asked by Elizabeth Willing Powel, "Well, Doctor, what have we got, a republic or a monarchy?" Franklin responded chillingly, "A republic, if you can keep it."

Franklin's famous warning reflected the fact that every democratic system carries the seeds for its own destruction. The history of revolution is truly a history of human struggle with our best and worst impulses. They are the expression of our most lofty and redeeming values. That inspiration for revolution can be quickly lost in its execution. Once "it becomes necessary for one people to dissolve the political bands which have connected them with another," our rage can unleash not the best but the worst in us. It is the "Saturn Gene." Kronos and his progenated diet

captured the self-consuming tendencies of revolution. It is a lesson not of mythology but of history. It is the story of humanity's struggle with its own governance, a story of being both predator and prey.

It is the dichotomy captured in one of the most lasting images from Greek mythology of the wolfman. According to the legend, the King of Arcadia, Lycaon, went to the temple to offer a gruesome gift to Zeus: a meal. Lycaon had slain his son Nyctimus and mixed his flesh with the meat to see if Zeus could tell the difference in the sacrifice. Zeus was enraged and brought Nyctimus back to life after converting Lycaon into a wolf, as shown on the previous page in the 1563 work of Johann Postius von Germersheim. Zeus turned the tyrant Lycaon literally into what he had become. Socrates used the image in Plato's *Republic* in a discussion of how demagogues are Lycaeans who first destroy those who love them and then themselves. For Socrates, it is the tale of how a democracy "thirsting for freedom" had "drunk too deeply of the strong wine of freedom." In the end, citizens bring forth "the protector of the people [who] having a mob entirely at his disposal . . . is not restrained from shedding the blood of kinsmen."

It is a pattern that played out repeatedly in Greek history when rage overwhelmed reason and reformers transformed into tyrants. In this way, democracy, and liberty itself, can invite either anarchy or tyranny.

The Declaration of Independence unleashed the power of the liberty and natural rights that rest with all humans as human beings. Abraham Lincoln called it the "electric cord" that "links the hearts of patriotic and liberty living men together." It was a declaration of a bond of all humanity:

> When they look through that old Declaration of Independence they find that those old men say that 'We hold these truths to be self-evident, that all men are created equal,' and then they feel that that moral sentiment taught in that day evidences their relation to those men, that it is the father of all moral principle in them, and that they have a right to claim it as though they were blood of the blood, and flesh of the flesh of the men who wrote that Declaration . . . and so they are.

Lincoln had his own wolf analogy in discussing the perils of democratic systems when a majority devours those in a minority. In 1864, the war was raging and casualties mounting on both sides. In April of that year, Lincoln decided to travel to Baltimore as a new state constitution was being considered. Lincoln cautioned Marylanders not to look to democracy as a license for majoritarian tyranny. He told the crowd that "the world has never had a good definition for the word *liberty*." Lincoln noted the irony that liberty is the most used and least understood value in the American republic: "We all declare for liberty, but in using the same word we do not all mean the same thing." Some think that liberty means "for each man to do as he pleases with himself." It is the difference between a license for unrestrained individual consumption or the consumption of others. "Here are two, not only different, but incompatible things, called the same name," Lincoln explained. The most powerful part of the speech is when Lincoln uses the analogy of a wolf to show how protecting the liberty of one can be viewed as imposing tyranny on the other:

> The shepherd drives the wolf from the sheep's throat, for which the sheep thanks the shepherd as a liberator, which the wolf denounces him for the same act as the destroyer of liberty. . . . Plainly the sheep and the wolf are not agreed upon a definition of the word liberty.

Lincoln does not expressly state which concept of liberty is the correct one. The rest of the speech strongly suggests the answer. Lincoln talks about the recent news of the massacre at Fort Pillow where Confederate forces killed hundreds of captured Black Union soldiers and their white officers. It was clear who the wolves were and the need of the good shepherd to deny them their wanton demands.

Lincoln's reference back to liberty as enshrined in the Declaration of Independence in his speech reinforces why it is important to consider that document as more than just a statement of severance from the British Empire or a list of grievances. It was first and foremost about liberty, not democracy. The shift from liberty to democracy as the emphasis of modern legal thought allowed for greater social and political reforms. The principles of the Declaration of Independence are often treated as aspirational at best. Yale law professor Akhil Amar spoke for many in describing the Constitution as "ringing words—but words that ring hollow today." The president of the Human Rights Campaign, Kelley Robinson, in 2024 dismissed the "little piece of paper" of the Founders and called for a "more revolutionary" system and a new type of democracy from what they envisioned. Of course, the republic was founded on the most revolutionary idea of its time. The view of the Founders was that liberty rights preexisted government. As Bradley Thompson has observed, "America's revolutionary founders viewed government as an artificial, man-made institution, the sole purpose of which was the protection of man's natural rights." Untethered from the values of individual liberty, a society has broader parameters for its "re-creation." At one time, society created itself into states allowing slavery or criminalizing homosexuality. Indeed, without these core values, society can re-create itself into ancient images of democratic despotism.

Where the Declaration was the ultimate expression of American values, the Constitution was the ultimate expression of American pragmatism. It was written not to inspire but to last. Madison took us for what we are and designed a system that could not only attain our loftiest values but also withstand our lowest impulses. It was (and remains) an article of faith. On the final day of the Constitutional Convention, there were still doubts among the delegates. That was when Benjamin Franklin signaled that he wanted to address the body. At eighty-one years of age and his body battered by gout and kidney stones, Franklin was greatly diminished and could no longer muster the strength to deliver his remarks. He turned to none other than James Wilson, his fellow Pennsylvania delegate, who had fought for his life in the Fort Wilson riot just eight years earlier. Franklin's comments were moving and telling, revealing his own physical fragilities and intellectual doubts. He started by acknowledging that "there are several parts of this Constitution which I do not at present approve." He then added that "the older I grow, the more apt I am to doubt my own judgment, and to pay more respect to the judgment of others." Franklin then told the fellow delegates: "I consent . . . to this Constitution, because I expect no better, and because I am not sure, that it is not the best." It was hardly a ringing endorsement, but it was a statement of faith in this republic and in each other.

Franklin was not alone in having doubts. Some doubts or disappointments would emerge among the framers even after the republic stabilized and grew. In his book *Fears of a Setting Sun: The Disillusionment of America's Founders*, Dennis Rasmussen details what he argues were profound disappointments of the Founders by the end of their lives. The one exception to this Founders' despair was Madison, who outlived them all. The reason for this distinction may have less to do with the reasons that Rasmussen suggests than with Madison's underlying philosophy. Some Founders, such as John Adams, were disappointed in what they saw as the avarice and lack of civic virtues in the populace. Adams had his doubts as early as January 1776 when he stated, "There is So much Rascallity, so much Venality and Corruption, so much Avarice and Ambition, such a Rage for Profit and Commerce among all Ranks and Degrees of Men even in America, that I sometimes doubt whether there is public Virtue enough to support a Republic." Those doubts only mounted with time. On December 31, 1817, Adams wrote his son John Quincy Adams that "the Selfishness of our Countrymen is not only Serious but melancholy, foreboding ravages of Ambition and Avarice which never were exceeded on this Selfish Globe . . . the distemper in our Nation is so general, and so certainly incurable." Madison made no such assumptions about human nature. Indeed, he created a system for the worst motivations to guarantee the best results. There were no "angels" in Madison's plan, so he was hardly surprised by those who proved to be devils. Moreover, Madison watched his system not only stress-tested in the United States and still flourish but he saw how nations like France performed poorly without these constitutional protections.

For two of the greatest American figures, a full appreciation of the "miracle of Philadelphia" would not come until the end of their lives. On January 1, 1812, Adams wrote a letter to Thomas Jefferson. It was an act that surprised many, not the least of which was Jefferson himself. The two bitterly estranged figures of the American Revolution had had virtually no contact in over a decade. In 1776, they had achieved what was viewed as a virtual impossibility in unifying thirteen colonies in a single Declaration of Independence. Once that independence was secured, the nation fell into poisonous and often violent political discord. Jeffersonians called him "the Duke of Braintree" and "His Rotundity" for his pomp and aggrandizement. He was mocked for such proposals as adding to the presidential title "His Highness, the President of the United States of America, and Protector of Their Liberties." Adams hardly fulfilled that title upon assuming the office himself. During his presidency, Adams allowed scores of Jeffersonians to be arrested for their criticism of him and his administration. A mutual disdain and distrust set in. Jefferson called the administration "the reign of the witches," and his supporters were equally unrelenting in their attacks on Federalists.

Then, without warning, the letter arrived at Monticello. Adams wished Jefferson a happy New Year and noted that Jefferson had long shown support for "American manufactures under proper restrictions, especially manufactures of the American kind." To that end, he enclosed a gift of "two pieces of homespun lately produced in this quarter by one who was honored in his youth with some of your attention and much of your kindness." It was a reference to two books by his son, and future fellow president, John Quincy Adams. The letter would lead to 158 such letters over fourteen years.

The Adams–Jefferson correspondence is at times moving and profound. Jefferson's response to Adams showed that he too longed for a rapprochement. He notably referred back to their most important work together on the Declaration of Independence:

> A letter from you calls up recollections very dear to my mind. It carries me back to the times when, beset with difficulties and dangers, we were fellow laborers in the same cause, struggling for what is most valuable to man, his right of self-government. Laboring always at the same oar, with some wave ever ahead threatening to overwhelm us and yet passing harmless under our bark, we knew not how, we rode through the storm with heart and hand, and made a happy port. . . .

That "happy port" was found not just after a revolutionary war but after the trauma that followed for the new nation struggling with its new identity and freedoms. The correspondence between Adams and Jefferson showed how the greatest political injuries could be healed by common articles of faith stemming from the Declaration. They came to appreciate how they shared in a uniquely American declaration of the inherent rights of all men, a new American voice. Adams touched on that voice in his August 24, 1815, letter wherein he explained what the American Revolution truly meant to them and the country:

> What do We mean by the Revolution? The War? That was no part of the Revolution. It was only an Effect and Consequence of it. The Revolution was in the Minds of the People, and this was effected, from 1760 to 1775, in the course of fifteen Years before a drop of blood was drawn at Lexington.

Where Adams referred earlier to Jefferson's love for the "manufactures of the American kind," the Declaration was the ultimate product of the American mind. The true revolution was found in the underlying rationale for "independency." The correspondence would continue until they both died on the same day of July 4, 1826—the fiftieth anniversary of the Declaration of Independence. The final words of Adams on his death bed in Quincy, Massachusetts, were "Jefferson still survives." He had again misjudged Jefferson. His renewed friend and former adversary had died just five hours earlier in Monticello, Virginia.

Jefferson and Adams finding a "happy port" in the American constitutional system was precisely what Tocqueville and other writers were seeking for years. Tocqueville insisted that "I cannot believe that God has for several centuries been pushing two or three hundred million men toward equality just to make them wind up under a Tiberian or Claudian despotism. Verily that wouldn't be worth the trouble. Why He is drawing us toward democracy, I do not know; but embarked on a vessel that I did not build. I am at least trying to use it to gain the nearest port." The voices today challenging core institutions and rights are the same voices that have echoed throughout our history. They are the voices of the faithless; citizens who believe that their grievances or fears are unprecedented and transcendent. In the twenty-first century, this country will have to deal with a crisis of faith that has few parallels since the founding. We can remain in the shelter of the "happy port" of the Founders, or we can set ourselves adrift in the tempest of democratic despotism.

That brings us back to where we began, with Thomas Paine. Even to this day, he is a figure that both draws and repels scholars. For those of us who have become engrossed in his life, our feelings are often as complex as the man himself. He is a man as difficult to entirely embrace in our times as he was in his own. Still, there is that unyielding brilliance to his life that fixates and inspires us. The feelings toward Paine may be best captured in a devastating line delivered by Robert Ryan to the ultimate femme fatale, Joan Fontaine, in the 1950 film noir *Born to Be Bad*. After Ryan learns that he was once again drawn in by her charms, he stops at the door and says, "I love you so much I wish I liked you." I love Thomas Paine. I just wish I liked him.

In many respects, our struggle is embodied in the struggles of Paine, a brilliant and flawed figure who became the voice of the American Revolution. His stout courage and conviction inspired a nation. He personified the national character described by Tocqueville as a nation exploding with creative energy, often moving in different directions but, almost by some miracle, heading to a true course. Paine's life was experiential and difficult as he advocated and then amended different approaches to governance. Yet he never lost a directional sense of the true north for a free people in this struggle for self-realization. He was the most revolutionary of the American Revolution and arguably the most selfless of his generation.

Paine's life also vividly showed how, within a single lifetime, a revolutionary could go out of style faster than a tricorn hat. In 1802, Paine returned to the United States. His arrival in Baltimore on October 30, 1802, was strikingly different from his first entry on November 30, 1774. He was no longer the unknown "Englishman" but one of the most famous living writers in the world. Both his admirers and his critics were waiting. His attacks on Washington only heightened the attacks on him as newspapers denounced the arrival of "a traitorous scribbler, saturated with brandy." Others called him the "archbeast" and a "loathsome reptile." Federalist papers labeled him "a lying drunken, brutal infidel, who rejoices in the opportunity of basking and wallowing in the confusion, devastation, bloodshed, rapine and murder, in which his soul delights." In Trenton, two coach drivers refused to drive him to New York City, one declaring that "My stage and horses were once struck by lightning, and I don't want them to suffer again." In New Rochelle, an official even refused to accept his ballot to vote in the federal and state elections. He insisted that Paine was not an American citizen and, in a terribly cruel argument, noted that neither Washington nor Morris would help him. He was never able to record his vote. Wherever he went, hostile crowds seemed to form against him.

Paine had long ago eschewed popularity for principles. Paine was not well but returned to his desire to advocate for his iron bridge and a new type of carriage wheel as well as to finish a third edition of *The Age of Reason*. Again, the world seemed to conspire against his efforts. On Christmas Eve, Paine's life almost came to an end when a drunk tenant living on his land, Christopher Derrick, stood outside the window of this cottage and shot at him sitting in a rear room. He missed, but Paine refused to press charges. One friend from England was shocked to see his condition in a pub after traveling to visit him. William Carver wrote:

> I found you at a tavern in a most miserable situation. You appeared as if you had not been shaved for a fortnight, and as to a shirt, it could not be said that you had one on, it was only the remains of one, and this likewise appeared not to have been off your back for a fortnight and was nearly the color of tanned leather; and you had the most disagreeable smell possible, just like that of our poor beggars in England.

Carver would personally bathe Paine, and friends would again find quarters and support for him in New York.

Being Paine, he was unbowed and unrelenting in observations that inflamed others. He continued to drink and argue heavily with anyone close enough to hold an opinion or buy a pint. For example, after celebrating the Fourth of July, Paine was injured in a fall down some stairs, though it is not clear if it was due to his age or alcohol or both. While he was recovering, he had a spirited argument on religion when the exasperated visitor told him: "Mr. Paine, here you sit, in an obscure, uncomfortable dwelling, powdered with snuff and stupefied with brandy; you, who were once the companion of Washington, Jay, and Hamilton, are now deserted by every good man, and even respectable deists cross the streets to avoid you." Paine pulled himself up and responded, "I care not a straw for the opinions of the world." When two clergymen later pushed into his room and demanded that he repent for his lifetime of sins, Paine tossed them out and yelled, "Let me have none of your Popish stuff, Get away with you."

In *The American Crisis*, Paine wrote years earlier a passage that could have been about himself rather than his countrymen:

> I love the man that can smile in trouble, that can gather strength from distress, and grow brave by reflection. 'Tis the business of little minds

> to shrink, but he whose heart is firm, and whose conscience approves his conduct, will pursue his principles unto death.

Paine was an honest man at a time of corruption, a principled man at a time of expediency. He was hated precisely because he did not compromise. He was the ultimate hard case, incorruptible and incorrigible. He had moments of doubt and weakness. The image of a frail Paine languishing in his cell in Luxembourg Palace was the perfect personification of the loss of innocence for many. Paine was an imperfect being, a man who often seemed intent to find his end at the bottom of a gallows or a bottle. It is a miracle that neither the Crown nor cirrhosis had not ended his life earlier. However, few could have shown his bravery and strength in pursuing "his principles unto death." He remains today, as he was then, a figure easier to admire from a distance. Still, it was his imperfections that always made Paine more real and authentic. Other men, like Washington, would ride from battle with the glories of victory, but it was Paine who brought his troops to the battle. It was Paine who gave them a reason to hold the line. It was always Paine who spoke not just to them but for them.

Many in the United States seemed to agree with Franklin's daughter that it would have been better for Paine to have died immediately after the publication of *Common Sense*. Recall, when he was eight years old, Paine wrote a poetic farewell for his pet crow that ended: "Ye brother Crows take warning all, For as you rise, so you must fall." It would prove a poignant epitaph for Paine himself, who would die with remarkably little fanfare and even fewer friends.

In his final will, Paine described his final resting place:

> The place where I am buried [should] be a square of twelve feet, to be enclosed with rows of trees, and a stone or post and a rail fence, with a headstone with my name and age engraved on it, author of *Common Sense*.

In his mind, his defining moment remained his first major work, which ignited a revolution. He added that "I have lived an honest and useful life to mankind; my time has been spent in doing good, and I die in perfect composure and resignation to the will of my Creator, God." As he lay dying, a friend told him that he had only a few hours and asked him if he wanted to profess his faith in Jesus Christ. Paine's final words were, "I have no wish to believe on that subject." It was in some ways the perfect summation of his life, not about his religion but his conviction. To the end, he refused to believe due to the exigency or popularity of the moment. Thomas Paine would not yield.

Paine would go to his grave at seventy-two years old with a small group of remaining friends, including Madame Marguerite Brazier Bonneville, her children, and a few others. His wish to be buried in a Quaker cemetery was denied. He was instead buried on his farm in New Rochelle, New York. (The tombstone would not be added for another thirty years.) Even in death, Paine was pursued by his critics. While largely ignored by the media, children sang a mocking song at his passing:

> *Poor Tom Paine! There he lies,*
> *Nobody laughs and nobody cries,*
> *Where he has gone or how he fares,*
> *Nobody knows and nobody cares.*

Paine has remained an enigma even to those he helped liberate. He seemed in death as he was in life: a man without a country who belonged to the world. Still, he truly belonged here. He was the perfect American. He was passionate, irreverent, and unafraid. In his *Letter to the Addressers*, Paine wrote about his own epitaph in a passage that lays out the values that remained constants in his life:

> If, to expose the fraud and imposition of monarchy, and every species of hereditary government; to lessen the oppression of taxes; to propose plans for the education of helpless infancy, and the comfortable support of the aged and distressed; to endeavor to conciliate nations to each other; to extirpate the horrid practice of war; to promote universal peace, civilization, and commerce; and to break the chains of

> political superstition, and raise degraded man to his proper rank—if these things be libelous, let me live the life of a libeller, and let the name of libeller be engraved upon my tomb.

He would never be given that or any lasting epitaph. His passing was given perfunctory and often derisive attention, with the *New York Evening Post* stating simply, "He had lived long, did some good and much harm."

Perhaps the most poignant fact of his life was that his body was ultimately lost to the world. Years later, English journalist William Cobbett felt that he belonged in England and decided to retrieve his body. He had no permission or permit. In September 1819, he found the grave in utter neglect and decided to reclaim Paine for England. A local constable was alerted but could not find a horse in time to stop the exhumation. There is no record of what happened to the body. Cobbett appears to have made it back to England with the body but died in 1835. His son took possession and reportedly wrote Paine's name on his skull and some bones. They then fell into the possession of Benjamin Tilly, Cobbett's secretary, and from there were lost to history. Some said they were tossed into the Thames and others that they were made into trinkets or buttons. Much like aspects of his own his life, Paine's whereabouts remain a mystery to everyone but himself.

In the end, Paine remains with us as do the voices of our founding. They should offer both solace and solidarity for a people that is still defining itself. At the start of this book, I described the American republic as embodied in two men: Paine and Madison, respectively the fathers of our Revolution and our Constitution. In his waning years, Madison wrote a moving essay titled "Advice to My Country." He noted ominously that "it may be considered as issuing from

the tomb where truth alone can be respected." Madison then offered this caution to the nation: "The advice nearest to my heart and deepest in my convictions is that the Union of the States be cherished & perpetuated. Let the open enemy to it be regarded as a Pandora with her box opened; and the disguised one, as the Serpent creeping with his deadly wiles into Paradise." The disguised enemy is tyranny from within. It is disguised in the cloak of democracy but seeks despotism. It is the lingering original sin of democracy that lurks within it and is never truly excised from it.

We now find ourselves facing another building crisis. We must again decide whether these times will define us or whether we will define our times. Looking back over the centuries that have passed since the Declaration, the miracle of Philadelphia has grown only more inspiring. The concept of republican government based on natural rights remains as revolutionary today as it was over two centuries ago. The "electric cord" described by Lincoln still ties this generation to the first generation. It is a powerful image. Indeed, it brings with it the image of Franklin with his key and kite trying to catch lightning. The Founders succeeded in catching that electricity in the atmosphere in their Declaration of Independence. It was a raw and natural form of power that they then sought to control and to direct. The success of that effort was evident in the stabilization of Philadelphia and, in the absence of those controls, it was equally evident in the destabilization of Paris.

Now, 250 years after the American Declaration of Independence, a new world seems again to be in the making, with transformative technological advancement, global economic shifts, and growing radicalism on the edges of our political debates. It is a situation not unlike that one described by Tocqueville, who warned that a new society may be forming where "time has not yet set its form." He observed that

> The world that is rising is still half caught in the ruins of the world that is falling, and amid the immense confusion presented by human affairs, no one can say which old institutions and ancient mores will remain standing and which will finally disappear. . . . I go back century by century to the most distant antiquity; I notice nothing that

> resembles what is before our eyes. Since the past no longer clarifies the future, the mind moves in shadows.

What will emerge from the current "shadows" is still unknown. What is clear is that there is great peril in assuming a purely pedestrian position in watching this revolutionary moment unfold. We do not have to fear the unknown so long as we are prepared to channel the tremendous energy and emotions that come from revolutionary periods. To do so, we must find what Paine referred to as that "happy something" found on these shores. That something is still with us even if the "ardor of seventy-six" has sometimes flagged under the pressures of the twenty-first century. Each generation must answer that Frenchman's question of "what then is the American?" From redcoats to robots, our challenges have changed. Yet we have remained. Our greatest danger is not forgetting the history detailed in this book but forgetting who we were in that history. For cen-

turies, that proved the difference between Philadelphia and Paris, between democracy and despotism. The fact is that we all carry the Saturn gene, but our appetite for liberty has proven greater than our appetite for each other. That was the true miracle that emerged 250 years ago. We emerged. We are that "happy something."

The twenty-first century will write the next chapter in the unfinished story of the American Revolution. It is a story that began in ancient Athens and has played out throughout the centuries. It was always a cautionary tale. When Athenians prayed for the future, they would gather at the central temple of Athena, where the goddess stood in the splendor of gold and ivory holding the image of Victory (Nike) in her hand. Athena's influence would shape much of the political and social debate in Athens. Beneath Athena's sandals is the image of Pandora. The story of Pandora's box is familiar to many, including Madison, who raised it in his own final advice to the nation that he shaped. It is a tale of how curiosity can unleash horrors on the reckless or incautious. The actual story is even more poignant. After Prometheus stole fire and gave it to humanity, Zeus was irate and sent Pandora with a jar (later described as a box) to Prometheus's brother, Epimetheus. (Prometheus was busy having his liver pecked out by an eagle in punishment.) Pandora's name literally means "the one who bears all gifts," but she was created as a punishment upon humanity. It was her very gifts that would bring disaster. She may have been the first femme fatale, created by Hephaestus from clay and given femininity by Aphrodite. She was taught crafts by Athena and deceit from Hermes. Despite being told not to open the jar, Pandora's curiosity got the better of her . . . and humanity. Indeed, Zeus made her too human. She opened the jar and unleashed an array of evils on the world, including sorrow, disease, vice, violence, greed, madness, old age, and death. What is rarely noted is that there was one more thing in the jar, and it may have been the thing Zeus least wanted released: hope. According to later versions of the story, it was hope that Pandora allowed to escape with the evils of humanity.

Perhaps Zeus knew us all too well. Humanity will always open Pandora's jar. We will continue to yield to violence, greed, and madness when conditions produce rage rather than reason. Some of those conditions are growing in the twenty-first century. However, the true story of democracy is one of hope. It is a shared hope that bound many of the figures in this book in the promise of humanity to be something greater as a people than we are as individuals. For Paine and the French, it was realization of the "general will." For Madison and the framers, it was the liberty that would unleash a golden age. It is the hope of every immigrant who comes to these shores seeking a future of their own making. We are not bound by generations in a country but a type of ancestry of ideas founded in liberty. We are bound by a faith that we have the capacity to be something greater. So, again, we ask, "What then is the American?" The answer is found at the moment of creation, when a people was defined by "certain inalienable rights, among which are life, liberty, and the pursuit of happiness." It is seen in an imperfect people of the insatiably curious, brash jar-openers who refuse to be denied new opportunities. We are bound by the revolutionary idea that government exists to allow every citizen to pursue one's own manifest destiny. As shown by Paine, we are our own greatest creations. What was true in 1776 is true today: These are revolutionary times, but we remain a revolutionary people.

Acknowledgments

I wish to thank George Washington University for its support for years of research as well as Harvard University, the Library of Congress, and other institutions for much of the art used in this book. I also wish to thank my assistant, Seth Tate, who has worked tirelessly for years to support me in my teaching, litigation, and research responsibilities.

I am also indebted to the extraordinary work of Simon & Schuster, Mia Robertson, and their brilliant team for getting this manuscript through the lengthy editing and production process. This book was vastly improved by your efforts.

Finally, I wish to thank my children, Benjamin, Jack, Aidan, and Madie, for tolerating years of unending and obsessive accounts on the progress of this book. The optimism found in these pages is due in no small part to you. Benjamin Franklin warned that every generation must fight to keep this republic. That will now be your fight.

Notes

INTRODUCTION

xv *"devours its children"*: Jacques Mallet du Pan, *Considérations sur la Nature de la Révolution en France* (1793).

xvi *"golden age of mortals"*: Samuel L. Macey, *Patriarchs of Time: Dualism in Saturn-Cronus, Father Time, the Watchmaker God, and Father Christmas* (University of Georgia Press, 2010), 24.

xvi *"connected them with another"*: Declaration of Independence (1776).

xvii *"liberation and freedom are not the same"*: Hannah Arendt, *On Revolution* (Viking Press, 1965), 22.

xviii *"struck as one"*: Wesley Frank Craven, *The Legend of the Founding Fathers* (New York University Press, 1956), 63.

xviii *born in rage*: Jonathan Turley, *The Indispensable Right: Free Speech in an Age of Rage* (Simon & Schuster, 2024).

xx *a stable government*: For further discussion, Richard Whatmore, *The End of Enlightenment: Empire, Commerce, Crisis* (Penguin Books Limited, 2023).

xx *"Noah until now"*: Thomas Paine, *Common Sense* (Dover Publications, 1997), 51.

xxi *handsome, and sophisticated*: Gaye Wilson, *Jefferson on Display: Attire, Etiquette, and the Art of Presentation* (University of Virginia Press, 2018).

xxi *"budding in leading minds"*: David Benner, *Thomas Paine: A Lifetime of Radicalism* (Life & Liberty Publishing Group, 2022), 205.

xxii *elements like bicameralism*: Benner, *Thomas Paine*, 205.

xxii *view of humanity*: See generally Harlow Giles Unger, *Thomas Paine and the Clarion Call for American Independence* (Grand Central Publishing, 2019).

xxii *a mere taxation dispute*: Benner, *Thomas Paine*, 139.

xxii *"England and her then colonies"*: Benner, *Thomas Paine*, 141.

xxii *"those we formerly used"*: C. Bradley Thompson, *America's Revolutionary Mind: A Moral History of the American Revolution and the Declaration That Defined It* (Encounter Books, 2019), 2.

xxiii *"has not appeared before"*: Thompson, *America's Revolutionary Mind*, 45.

xxiii *the source of those rights*: Benner, *Thomas Paine*, 71.

xxiii *natural rights and morality*: Benner, *Thomas Paine*, 72.

xxiii *"to bind themselves"*: Thompson, *America's Revolutionary Mind*, 11.

xxiii *"ignorance, indigence and oppression"*: H. A. Washington, *The Writings of Thomas Jefferson: Volume VII* (Outlook Verlag, 2018), 224.

xxiii *principles of the Enlightenment*: Robert P. George, "Natural Law, the Constitution, and the Theory and Practice of Judicial Review," *Fordham Law Review* 69, no. 6 (2001): 2269–70; Robert P. George, *In Defense of Natural Law* (Oxford University Press, 1999), 236.

xxiii *"act of independence"*: Thompson, *America's Revolutionary Mind*, 335.

xxiv *"legal provisions ineffectual"*: William Blackstone and William Draper Lewis, *Commentaries on the Laws of England: In Four Books* (Lawbook Exchange, 2007), 147.

xxiv *destabilizing decision*: Cynthia A. Bouton, *The Flour War: Gender, Class, and Community in Late Ancien Regime French Society* (Penn State University Press, 2010).

xxiv *"this new man?"*: Thompson, *America's Revolutionary Mind*, 345.

xxv *foundation for government*: Thompson, *America's Revolutionary Mind*, 286.

xxv *"supposed a knave"*: Mark G. Spencer, *David Hume: Historical Thinker, Historical Writer* (Penn State University Press, 2015), 219.

xxv *"government would be necessary"*: James Madison, Federalist 51, *The Federalist Papers*, ed. Clinton Rossiter (New American Library, 1961).

xxv *"our lost innocence"*: James T. Kloppenberg, *Toward Democracy: The Struggle for Self-Rule in European and American Thought* (Oxford University Press, 2016), 224.

xxvi *name of democracy*: Robert Roswell Palmer, *Twelve Who Ruled: The Year of the Terror in the French Revolution* (Princeton University Press, 1958), 4.

xxvi *a threat to the state*: Palmer, *Twelve Who Ruled*, 241.

xxviii *"an age of rage"*: Turley, *The Indispensable Right*, 1–2.

xxviii *"reclaim America from Constitutionalism"*: Ryan D. Doerfler and Samuel Moyn, "The Constitution Is Broken and Should Not Be Reclaimed," *New York Times*, August 19, 2022, https://www.nytimes.com/2022/08/19/opinion/liberals-constitution.html.

xxviii *the way of real change*: Zachary Rogers, "Mass Shootings Happen Because Americans Are 'Slaves' to the Constitution, MSNBC Guest Says," *National Desk*, July 6, 2022, https://thenationaldesk.com/news/americas-news-now/mass-shootings-happen-because-americans-are-slaves-to-the-constitution-msnbc-guest-says-rosa-brooks-reidout-joy-reid.

xxviii *the U.S. Constitution as "trash"*: Jonathan Turley, "America's Crisis of Faith," *Res Ipsa Loquitur* (blog), October 23, 2023, https://jonathanturley.org/2023/10/23/americas-crisis-of-faith-new-poll-reveals-more-americans-are-rejecting-the-constitution-and-embracing-violence/.

xxix *"All glory to God"*: Benjamin Lynch, "Jack Posobiec Hails 'End of Democracy at CPAC," *Newsweek*, February 23, 2024, https://www.newsweek.com/jack-posobiec-end-democracy-cpac-1872694.

xxix *threats to the nation*: Jonathan Turley, "The Return of the 'Reign of the Witches,'" *The Hill*, September 9, 2022, https://jonathanturley.org/2022/09/12/the-return-of-the-reign-of-the-witches-biden-and-trump-are-not-the-first-to-use-rage-rhetoric-for-political-gain/.

xxix *combating their efforts*: Turley, "America's Crisis of Faith."

xxix *elected to a second term*: For example, Michael Cohen stated that if Donald Trump wins the 2024 election, "there will never be another election thereafter." Michael Cohen, interview by Joy Reid, *The ReidOut*, MSNBC, March 29, 2024.

xxix *Vice President Kamala Harris*: Gabriel Hayes, "Kamala Harris Agrees 2024 Could 'Genuinely' Be the 'Last Democratic Election,'" Fox News, April 10, 2024, https://www.foxnews.com/media/kamala-harris-agrees-2024-could-genuinely-last-democratic-election.

xxx *"the epoch of incredulity"*: Charles Dickens, *A Tale of Two Cities* (London: Chapman & Hall, Limited, 1859), 1.

xxxi *on July 4, 1858*: John L. Haney, "Of the People, by the People, for the People," *Proceedings of the American Philosophical Society* 88, no. 5 (1944): 364.

xxxi *the Declaration of Independence*: Dennis C. Rasmussen, *Fears of a Setting Sun: The Disillusionment of America's Founders* (Princeton University Press, 2021), 117.

xxxii *"the rights of the minority"*: Rasmussen, *Fears of a Setting Sun*, 117.

xxxii *unlimited democratic governance*: Rasmussen, *Fears of a Setting Sun*, 68.

PART I. THE CAUSE OF INDEPENDENCY: THOMAS PAINE AND THE MAKING OF A REVOLUTIONARY

3 *twenty-seven injuries or grievances*: Thompson, *America's Revolutionary Mind*, 40.

3 *"divest their prosperity"*: Dan Edelstein, *On the Spirit of Rights* (University of Chicago Press, 2021), 168.

3 *in common use*: Thomas W. Benson, ed., *American Rhetoric: Context and Criticism* (Southern Illinois University Press, 1989), 124n50; Tom McMillan, *The Year That Made America: From Rebellion to Independence, 1775–1776* (Globe Pequot, 2025), 163–64.

3 *Bailey's New Universal Etymological English Dictionary: Robert A. Rutland, ed., The Papers of George Mason, 1725–1792* (University of North Carolina Press, 1970), 1:285; Benson, *American Rhetoric*, 124n50.

4 *"alienated or transferred to another"*: Rutland, *Papers of George Mason*, 1:285.

4 *social contract for the establishment of the state*: Edelstein, *On the Spirit of Rights*, 168.

4 *still claim such rights*: Edelstein, *On the Spirit of Rights*, 168; Robert Schehr, *The Political Economy of Plea Bargaining* (Taylor & Francis, 2024).

4 *alienable by the government*: Jonathan Turley, "UnNatural Speech," *George Washington University Law Review* (forthcoming 2026).

4 *they are inalienable*: Edelstein, *On the Spirit of Rights*, 168.

4 *"totally dissolved"*: Randy E. Barnett, *Our Republican Constitution: Securing the Liberty and Sovereignty of We the People* (HarperCollins, 2016), 32.

5 *Virginia Declaration of Rights by George Mason*: Barnett, *Our Republican Constitution*, 33.

5 *"obtaining happiness and safety"*: Barnett, *Our Republican Constitution*, 33.

6 *cause of "independency"*: Benner, *Thomas Paine*, 35.

6 *escaped most other people*: Walter Isaacson, *Benjamin Franklin: An American Life* (Simon & Schuster, 2004), 308.

7 *"I thought for myself"*: Harry Harmer, *Tom Paine: The Life of a Revolutionary* (Haus, 2006), 2.

7 *the way of democratic empowerment*: Benner, *Thomas Paine*, 41.

1. THE TRUE PAIN: FROM RUIN TO REVOLUTION

10 *spelled with an* e: John Keane, *Tom Paine: A Political Life* (Grove Press, 2003), xv.

10 *the daughter of a lawyer*: Harmer, *Life of a Revolutionary*, 4–5; Benner, *Thomas Paine*, 11.

11 *secured in part by her son*: Benner, *Thomas Paine*, 165.

11 *"tolerable stock of useful learning"*: Moncure Daniel Conway, *The Life of Thomas Paine*, vol. 1 (Outlook Verlag, 2018), 23.

11 *"so you must fall"*: Harmer, *Life of a Revolutionary*, 4; Benner, *Thomas Paine*, 13.

11 *"drab-colored creation"*: Benner, *Thomas Paine*, 12.

11 *his father's corset shop*: Michael Anthony Lawrence, *Radicals in Their Own Time: Four Hundred Years of Struggle for Liberty and Equal Justice in America* (Cambridge University Press, 2010), 72.

11 *war on France in 1756*: Harmer, *Life of a Revolutionary*, 7.

11 *the ship* Terrible: Harmer, *Life of a Revolutionary*, 7.

12 *the clandestine network of staymakers*: Harmer, *Life of a Revolutionary*, 8.

12 *a master staymaker in Covent Garden*: Harmer, *Life of a Revolutionary*, 8.

12 *"more remonstrance of a good father"*: Thomas Paine, *Rights of Man and Common Sense* (Knopf Doubleday Publishing Group, 1994), 187.

12 *officers named Ghost and Devil*: Jett Conner, "Thomas Paine Goes to Sea: A Pre-Revolutionary Tale," *Journal of the American Revolution*, November 6, 2018, https://allthingsliberty.com/2018/11/thomas-paine-goes-to-sea-a-pre-revolutionary-tale.

12 *flying British colors*: Edward Phillips Statham, *Privateers and Privateering* (J. Pott, 1910), 106.

12 *outmaneuvered the British vessel*: Conner, "Paine Goes to Sea"; Statham, *Privateers and Privateering*, 108.

12 *just 17 survivors*: Benner, *Thomas Paine*, 13.

13 *ample hunting grounds of the Caribbean*: Harmer, *Life of a Revolutionary*, 8.

13 *he did indeed join the crew*: Alyce Barry, "Thomas Paine, Privateersman," *Pennsylvania Magazine of History and Biography* 101, no. 4 (1977): 454, http://www.jstor.org/stable/20091202.

13 *the Caribbean for French takings*: Barry, "Thomas Paine, Privateersman," 455.

13 *twenty-four swivel guns*: Barry, "Thomas Paine, Privateersman," 457.

13 *overpower any merchant ship*: Barry, "Thomas Paine, Privateersman," 456.

13 *a remarkable haul for a privateer*: Benner, *Thomas Paine*, 14.

13 *"Ammunition, Soldiers Cloaths, &c"*: Barry, "Thomas Paine, Privateersman," 456.

13 *"Wine and Provisions"*: Barry, "Thomas Paine, Privateersman," 456.

14 *"gentleman volunteers"*: Barry, "Thomas Paine, Privateersman," 459.
14 *1 percent of the prize*: Barry, "Thomas Paine, Privateersman," 459.
14 *"kind of partial emigration"*: Barry, "Thomas Paine, Privateersman," 460.
14 *selling globes in the Strand*: Harmer, *Life of a Revolutionary*, 9.
14 *mathematician George Lewis Scott*: Benner, *Thomas Paine*, 24.
15 *thankless and hazardous job*: Benner, *Thomas Paine*, 16.
15 *"worthless, brutish man"*: Harmer, *Life of a Revolutionary*, 12.
15 *performing some inspections*: Harmer, *Life of a Revolutionary*, 12.
15 *"to restore me"*: Benner, *Thomas Paine*, 17.
15 *another position in Lewes*: Benner, *Thomas Paine*, 18.
15 *in spirited debate*: Benner, *Thomas Paine*, 19.
15 *"an Old Greek Homer"*: Amanda J. Thomas, *The Nonconformist Revolution: Religious Dissent, Innovation and Rebellion* (Pen & Sword History, 2020), 166.
15 *the Headstrong Club*: Harmer, *Life of a Revolutionary*, 13; Benner, *Thomas Paine*, 19.
16 *for political reforms*: Arthur H. Cash, *John Wilkes: The Scandalous Father of Civil Liberty* (Yale University Press, 2006), 102.
16 *as did his marriage*: Harmer, *Life of a Revolutionary*, 16.
16 *many toward corruption*: Benner, *Thomas Paine*, 17.
16 Insufficiency of the Present Salary: Harmer, *Life of a Revolutionary*, 16; Benner, *Thomas Paine*, 19–20.
16 *"too great distress of circumstances"*: Harmer, *Life of a Revolutionary*, 17.
16 *a supplemental printing*: Benner, *Thomas Paine*, 20.
17 *"he hath contracted"*: Benner, *Thomas Paine*, 21.
17 *Paine declared bankruptcy*: Harmer, *Life of a Revolutionary*, 17.
17 *according to acquaintances*: Benner, *Thomas Paine*, 21; Harlow Giles Unger, *Thomas Paine and the Clarion Call for American Revolution* (Grand Central Publishing, 2019), 15.
17 *married for the rest of their lives*: Benner, *Thomas Paine*, 21.
17 *"an ingenious, worthy young man"*: Harmer, *Life of a Revolutionary*, 18.
17 *"oblige your affectionate father"*: Benner, *Thomas Paine*, 25.
17 *arrival in the colonies*: Walter Isaacson, "Benjamin Franklin Joins the Revolution," *Smithsonian*, July 31, 2003, https://www.smithsonianmag.com/history/benjamin-franklin-joins-the-revolution-87199988/.
17 *friends of Franklin in Philadelphia*: Walter Isaacson, *Benjamin Franklin: An American Life* (Simon & Schuster, 2004), 308.
17 *120 other passengers*: Harmer, *Life of a Revolutionary*, 18.
17 *Franklin's physician, John Kearsley*: Benner, *Thomas Paine*, 25.
18 *Society for Political Inquiries*: Isaacson, *An American Life*, 439.

2. THE TRUE PAINE: THE "HAPPY SOMETHING" OF AMERICA

19 *"in the climate of America"*: Harmer, *Life of a Revolutionary*, 21.
20 *a biographical sketch of Voltaire*: Harmer, *Life of a Revolutionary*, 21.

20 *"a Wood Near Boston"*: Benner, *Thomas Paine*, 28.
20 *the New World*: Benner, *Thomas Paine*, 27.
20 *the scourge of slavery*: Benner, *Thomas Paine*, 31.
20 *"rum and water"*: Harmer, *The Life of a Revolutionary*, 22.
20 *detachment and anger toward England*: Benner, *Thomas Paine*, 26.
20 *"sullen-tempered Pharoh of England"*: Harmer, *Life of a Revolutionary*, 25.
20 *devouring its children*: Harmer, *Life of a Revolutionary*, 27.
21 *"weight and authority"*: David J. Bederman, *Custom as a Source of Law* (Cambridge University Press, 2010), 31.
21 *"no divinity in it"*: Thomas Paine, *Common Sense* (TheCapitolNet, 2011), 19.
21 *the "New World" could be discovered*: Benner, *Thomas Paine*, 44.
22 *"at its zenith"*: Benner, *Thomas Paine*, 45.
22 *greater rights, not revolution*: Benner, *Thomas Paine*, 49.
22 *"war upon their families"*: Benner, *Thomas Paine*, 53.
22 *"unmeaning names of parent and child"*: Benner, *Thomas Paine*, 58.
22 *engaging in "rebellious war"*: Benner, *Thomas Paine*, 59.
22 *just a year earlier*: Benner, *Thomas Paine*, 64.
22 *"unanswerable reasoning"*: Benner, *Thomas Paine*, 64.
22 *"the Continental Congress about?"*: Benner, *Thomas Paine*, 65.
22 *the third printing*: Harmer, *Life of a Revolutionary*, 35.
22 *"the science of government"*: Benner, *Thomas Paine*, 67–68.
22 *"manly and striking a style"*: Alfred F. Young et al., eds., *Revolutionary Founders: Rebels, Radicals, and Reformers in the Making of the Nation* (Knopf Doubleday Publishing Group, 2012), 87.
22 *"His Name is Paine"*: Young et al., *Revolutionary Founders*, 87.
22 *original publication of* Common Sense: Benner, *Thomas Paine*, 43.
23 *hereditary monarchy directly*: Benner, *Thomas Paine*, 43.
23 *identity of the author*: Harmer, *Life of a Revolutionary*, 24.
24 *Adams's house to confront him*: Harmer, *Life of a Revolutionary*, 36.
24 *"has genius in his eyes"*: Harmer, *Life of a Revolutionary*, 36.
24 *the "Flying Camp" near Staten Island*: Harmer, *Life of a Revolutionary*, 38; Benner, *Thomas Paine*, 74.
24 *20 percent of the population*: Harmer, *Life of a Revolutionary*, 39.
24 *maximum distribution*: Harmer, *Life of a Revolutionary*, 39.
24 *reinvigorate his troops*: Harmer, *Thomas Paine*, 79.
25 *"can never be brave"*: Harmer, *Life of a Revolutionary*, 39.
25 *"who is not?"*: Harmer, *Life of a Revolutionary*, 42.
25 *"simple and unassuming language"*: Benner, *Thomas Paine*, 3; Thompson, *America's Revolutionary Mind*, 312–13.
25 *ignited the nation*: Thompson, *America's Revolutionary Mind*, 312.
25 *"the world's first bestseller"*: Thompson, *America's Revolutionary Mind*, 338.
25 *living in North America*: Benner, *Thomas Paine*, 61–62.

3. THE BIRTH OF A NEW AGE: THE ENLIGHTENMENT AND THE CAUSE OF "INDEPENDENCY"

28 *a new constitution*: W. H. G. Armytage, "Thomas Paine and the Walkers: An Early Episode in Anglo-American Cooperation," *Pennsylvania History: A Journal of Mid-Atlantic Studies* 18, no. 1 (1951): 17.

28 *"the father of the American Revolution"*: Benner, *Thomas Paine*, 1.

28 *"the father of the American Constitution"*: Catherine Drinker Bowen, *Miracle at Philadelphia* (Perfection Learning Corporation, 2021); Jeff Broadwater, *James Madison: A Son of Virginia and a Founder of the Nation* (University of North Carolina Press, 2012). But see David O. Stewart, *The Summer of 1787: The Men Who Invented the Constitution* (Simon & Schuster, 2008), 105 (questioning this title).

28 *"the United States of America"*: Joseph M. Hentz, *The Real Thomas Paine* (iUniverse Books, 2010), 218.

28 *"crack-brained zealot for democracy"*: Benner, *Thomas Paine*, 63.

28 *"every evil work"*: Benner, *Thomas Paine*, 63.

28 *"so much credit"*: Harmer, *Life of a Revolutionary*, 52.

29 *setting it on fire*: Harmer, *Life of a Revolutionary*, 58.

29 *"pulling down than building"*: McMillan, *Year That Made America*, 89.

29 *figures like Madison*: Carine Lounissi, *Thomas Paine and the French Revolution* (Springer, 2018), 9.

29 *the American democracy*: Jonathan Scheick, "Roger Sherman's Draft Copy of the Declaration of Independence," Thomas Paine Historical Association, https://www.thomaspaine.org/the-sherman-copy/full.

30 *the fourth week of June 1776*: Scheick, "Roger Sherman's Draft Copy."

30 *"T.P." was Thomas Paine*: Scheick, "Roger Sherman's Draft Copy."

30 *"drew up the declaration"*: Harmer, *Life of a Revolutionary*, 37.

30 *by Paine*: Scheick, "Roger Sherman's Draft Copy."

30 *"uncontrollable, unlimited, despotic power"*: Timothy Sandefur, *The Conscience of the Constitution: The Declaration of Independence and the Right to Liberty* (Cato Institute, 2013), 38.

31 *"absolute and without control"*: Sandefur, *Conscience of the Constitution*, 38.

31 *alienable under the English Constitution*: Alison L. LaCroix, *The Ideological Origins of American Federalism* (Harvard University Press, 2011), 15.

31 *the sciences and philosophy*: Robert P. George, "Natural Law, the Constitution, and the Theory and Practice of Judicial Review," *Fordham Law Review* 69, no. 6 (2001): 2269.

31 *blind faith or fealty*: Edward Larkin, *Thomas Paine and the Literature of Revolution* (Cambridge University Press, 2005), 116.

31 *"in the Natural System"*: Thompson, *America's Revolutionary Mind*, 52.

31 *"All was Light"*: Alexander Pope, "Epitaph," in "Political Newtonianism: The Cosmic Model of Politics in Europe and America," by Richard Striner, *William and Mary Quarterly* 52, no. 4 (1995): 588.

31 *Copernican system of the universe*: I. Bernard Cohen, "Science and the Constitution," in *Science and the Founding Fathers: Science in the Political Thought of Jefferson, Franklin, Adams, and Madison* (W. W. Norton, 1995), 262–72.

31 *of other framers*: Jonathan Turley, "Madisonian Tectonics: How Function Follows Form in Constitutional and Architectural Interpretation," *George Washington University Law Review* 83, no. 2 (2015): 316–17, https://www.gwlr.org/wp-content/uploads/2015/05/83-Geo-Wash-L-Rev-305.pdf

31 *orbits like planets*: James Madison et al., *The Constitutional Convention: A Narrative History from the Notes of James Madison* (Random House Publishing Group, 2011), 35.

32 *"laws of nature"*: Bernard Cohen, *Science and the Founding Fathers: Science in the Political Thought of Jefferson, Franklin, Adams and Madison* (W. W. Norton, 1997), 114–21; Allen Mendenhall, "Jefferson's 'Laws of Nature': Newtonian Influence and the Dual Valence of Jurisprudence and Science," *Canadian Journal of Law & Jurisprudence* 23, no. 2. (2010): 319–42, https://doi.org/10.1017/S0841820900004951.

32 *Madison, Paine, Jefferson, James Wilson, and others*: Thompson, *America's Revolutionary Mind*, 12.

32 *"gain clear knowledge of the cosmic system"*: Striner, "Political Newtonianism," 589.

32 *the Newtonian Paine rejected*: Jana Šklíbová, "Newtonianism: How Thomas Paine Devalued the British Monarchy by Transforming John Locke's Empiricism and Social Contract Theory," *American & British Studies Annual* 9 (January 2016): 149–61.

32 *creators in their own right*: Turley, *The Indispensable Right*, 23–27.

33 *basis for rebellion*: Thompson, *America's Revolutionary Mind*, 288.

33 *"their own strength"*: Harmer, *Life of a Revolutionary*, 2.

33 *by the government*: Thompson, *America's Revolutionary Mind*, 289.

34 *up to the Revolution*: Thompson, *America's Revolutionary Mind*, 293.

35 *build on that foundation*: Turley, *The Indispensable Right*, 58–66.

35 *defines all humanity*: Thompson, *America's Revolutionary Mind*, 34.

35 *concepts of self-government*: Thompson, *America's Revolutionary Mind*, 47.

35 *"appealed to those of nature"*: Ellen Frankel Paul et al., eds., *Natural Rights Individualism and Progressivism in American Political Philosophy*, vol. 29, part 2 (Cambridge University Press, 2012), 118.

35 *"obscured by mortal power"*: Ron Chernow, *Alexander Hamilton* (Penguin Publishing Group, 2005), 60.

35 *"engraved on our hearts"*: Thompson, *America's Revolutionary Mind*, 69.

36 *"write what we pleased"*: Thompson, *America's Revolutionary Mind*, 69.

36 *history but in nature*: Thompson, *America's Revolutionary Mind*, 155.

36 *"cannot disjoin them"*: Thompson, *America's Revolutionary Mind*, 189.

37 *"maxims of reason and justice"*: Thompson, *America's Revolutionary Mind*, 170.

37 *"some fortunate Conqueror"*: John M. Murrin, *Rethinking America: From Empire to Republic* (Oxford University Press, 2018), 194.

37 *"reciprocal duties"*: Thompson, *America's Revolutionary Mind*, 179.

38 *"the right of personal freedom"*: Thompson, *America's Revolutionary Mind*, 188.

38 *"that is no mere human creation"*: George, "Natural Law, the Constitution, and the Theory and Practice of Judicial Review," 2269.

38 *many in academia*: Stuart Banner, *The Decline of Natural Law: How American Lawyers Once Used Natural Law and Why They Stopped* (Oxford University Press, 2021), 218–19.

38 *"at all times"*: Thompson, *America's Revolutionary Mind*, 55.

38 *"men and things"*: Thompson, *America's Revolutionary Mind*, 57.

38 *enjoyment of all mankind*: John Locke, *Second Treatise on Civil Governments*, ed. Lester DeKoster (London, 1690; repr., William B. Eerdmans, 1978), 26.

PART II. A TALE OF TWO CITIES: DEMOCRACY AND MOBOCRACY

44 "*America will be in magnitude*": *Thomas Paine, The Writings of Thomas Paine*, ed. Moncure Daniel Conway (AMS Press, 1967), 201.

4. OF DEMOCRACY AND DEMAGOGUES: ANCIENT ATHENS AND THE RISE OF THE DEMOS

46 *a model of democracy*: Loren J. Samons, *What's Wrong with Democracy? From Athenian Practice to American Worship* (University of California Press, 2007), 4.

46 *the size of Rhode Island*: Samons, *What's Wrong with Democracy*, 7.

46 *"the actual events of Athenian history"*: Samons, *What's Wrong with Democracy*, 11.

46 *a right of self-determination*: Bruce S. Thornton, *Democracy's Dangers & Discontents* (Hoover Institution Press, 2014), 10.

47 *took control of government*: Samons, *What's Wrong with Democracy*, 16.

47 *"the fourth and worst disorder of a State"*: Benjamin Jowett, trans., *The Dialogues of Plato* (Outlook Verlag, 2023) 432.

47 *"the vulgar are taught"*: Thornton, *Democracy's Dangers and Discontents*, 12.

47 *violence was rising*: Eli Sagan, *The Honey and the Hemlock: Democracy and Paranoia in Ancient Athens and Modern America* (Basic Books, 1991), 7.

47 *many of their captives*: Sagan, *The Honey and the Hemlock*, 13.

47 *"security of personal liberty"*: Sagan, *The Honey and the Hemlock*, 40.

47 *"themselves and their children"*: Sagan, *The Honey and the Hemlock*, 40.

47 *a council of aristocrats*: Sagan, *The Honey and the Hemlock*, 9.

48 *diffusion of political authority*: Sagan, *The Honey and the Hemlock*, 9.

48 *"leader of the demos"*: Samons, *What's Wrong with Democracy*, 43.

48 *"obscurity of his condition"*: Sagan, *The Honey and the Hemlock*, 64.

48 *exchange for their support*: Samons, *What's Wrong with Democracy*, 191.

48 *"by the first citizen"*: Sagan, *The Honey and the Hemlock*, 104.

48 *the Athenian economy*: Samons, *What's Wrong with Democracy*, 189.

49 *"establish a democracy"*: Vassiliki Frangeskou, "Tradition and Originality in Some Attic Funeral Orations," *Classical World* 92, no. 4 (1999): 325.
49 *more by mob than reasoned justice*: Frangeskou, "Tradition and Originality," 325.
49 *mete out popular justice*: Thornton, *Democracy's Dangers and Discontents*, 11.
49 *"profit by your disgrace"*: Thornton, *Democracy's Dangers and Discontents*, 20.
49 *misleading the public*: Thornton, *Democracy's Dangers and Discontents*, 39.
49 *"poor argument for popular rule"*: Samons, *What's Wrong with Democracy*, 50.
49 *"majority votes in the assembly"*: Samons, *What's Wrong with Democracy*, 50.
50 *shards on his behalf*: Sagan, *The Honey and Hemlock*, 171.
50 *name on the shard: Nicholas F. Jones, Politics and Society in Ancient Athens* (Praeger, 2008), 73.
51 *one side in a dispute*: Sara Forsdyke, *Exile, Ostracism, and Democracy: The Politics of Expulsion in Ancient Greece* (Princeton University Press, 2009), 146.
51 *fear of such a fate*: George Grote, *A History of Greece: From the Time of Solon to 403 BC* (Taylor & Francis, 2012), 707.
51 *pendulum back toward oligarchy*: Sagan, *The Honey and the Hemlock*, 136.
51 "*like a swollen river*": Sagan, *The Honey and the Hemlock*, 137.
52 *508 BC to 322 BC*: Victor Davis Hanson, *The Dying Citizen: How Progressive Elites, Tribalism, and Globalization Are Destroying the Idea of America* (Basic Books, 2021), 215.
52 *exchanges "with the young"*: I. F. Stone, *The Trial of Socrates* (Anchor Books, 1989), 158–59.
52 *a shopkeeper under the gag order*: Stone, *The Trial of Socrates*, 159.
53 *how they used it*: Stone, *The Trial of Socrates*, 162.
53 "*a golden age*": Stone, *The Trial of Socrates*, 162.
53 *neither an indictment nor a transcript*: Stone, *The Trial of Socrates*, 3.
53 *"when nobody answers"*: Stone, *The Trial of Socrates*, 135.
53 *"left-leaning politician"*: Stone, *The Trial of Socrates*, 174–75.
53 *his own property*: Stone, *The Trial of Socrates*, 175.
54 *passed legislation*: Samons, *What's Wrong with Democracy*, 30.
54 *"talking big"*: Stone, *The Trial of Socrates*, 185.
54 *the wisest man in Greece*: Stone, *The Trial of Socrates*, 185.
54 *the rest of his life*: Stone, *The Trial of Socrates*, 188.
55 *Athens might suggest*: Anthony D. Dayan, "Death of Socrates: A Likely Case of Poison Hemlock (*Conium maculatum*) Poisoning," *Clinical Toxicology* 62, no. 1 (2024): 56–60, https://doi.org/10.1080/15563650.2024.2309328.
55 *vomiting and seizures*: Philip Wexler, *History of Toxicology and Environmental Health: Toxicology in Antiquity*, vol. 1 (Elsevier Science, 2014), 79, https://doi.org/10.1016/C2013-0-09772-1.
56 *punishment for his role*: Wexler, *Toxicology in Antiquity*, 176.
56 *returned to Athens*: Wexler, *Toxicology in Antiquity*, 177.
56 *"free speech and free thought"*: Wexler, *Toxicology in Antiquity*, 197.
56 *the "collectivized monarch" of the demos*: Sagan, *The Honey and the Hemlock*, 193.

56 *"the ruled to obey"*: Stone, *The Trial of Socrates*, 16.

56 *translated Thucydides into English*: Sagan, *The Honey and the Hemlock*, 51.

5. PHILADELPHIA: THE AMERICAN REVOLUTION AND "THE INCLEMENCIES OF THE SEASON"

THE FORT WILSON RIOT AND THE "TAKING OF THE TORIES"

58 *"Get Wilson!"*: Paul Langston, "'A Fickle, and Confused Multitude': War and Politics in Revolutionary Philadelphia, 1750–1783" (PhD diss., University of Colorado, 2013), 202, https://scholar.colorado.edu/downloads/pg15bf02d.

60 *"too heavy to drag along"*: Morton to Anthony Wayne, Philadelphia, August 16, 1776, in "Letter of John Morton to Anthony Wayne, 1776," *Pennsylvania Magazine of History and Biography* 39, no. 3 (1915): 373–74.

60 *colonial government null and void*: Ruma Chopra, *Choosing Sides: Loyalists in Revolutionary America* (Rowman & Littlefield Publishers, 2013), 35.

60 *submitted to the grand jury*: Russell Frank Weigley et al., eds., *Philadelphia: A 300 Year History* (W. W. Norton, 1982), 145.

60 *knocked down by the mob*: C. Page Smith, "The Attack on Fort Wilson," *The Pennsylvania Magazine of History and Biography* 78, no. 2 (1954): 177, http://www.jstor.org/stable/20088567.

60 *made against Carlisle*: Carlton F. W. Larson, *The Trials of Allegiance: Treason, Juries, and the American Revolution* (Oxford University Press, 2019), 157–58.

60 *"certain enough"*: Larson, *The Trials of Allegiance*, 158.

60 *attack on his house*: Larson, *The Trial of Allegiance*, 151–153.

61 *supported independence*: Kloppenberg, *Toward Democracy*, 571.

61 *their own choosing*: Thompson, *America's Revolutionary Mind*, 166–67.

61 *none other than Thomas Paine*: Harmer, *Life of a Revolutionary*, 41.

61 *aristocrats resembling the House of Lords*: Benner, *Thomas Paine*, 75.

61 *radical Whig elements*: Benner, *Thomas Paine*, 77.

61 *"general principles of good government"*: Benner, *Thomas Paine*, 151.

61 *executive committee of twelve individuals*: Benner, *Thomas Paine*, 75.

62 *"passion of individual sovereignty"*: Benner, *Thomas Paine*, 151.

62 *widening wealth gaps, and rising debt*: John K. Alexander, "The Fort Wilson Incident of 1779: A Case Study of the Revolutionary Crowd," *William and Mary Quarterly* 31, no. 4 (1974): 589, 593. https://doi.org/10.2307/1921605.

62 *rose 45 percent in one month alone*: Harmer, *Life of a Revolutionary*, 47.

62 *a merchant and major in the militia*: Kevin Diestelow, "The Fort Wilson Riot and Pennsylvania's Republican Formation," *Journal of the American Revolution*, February 28, 2019 (quoting letter from Samuel Shaw to Winthrop Sargent, October 10, 177); Alexander, "The Fort Wilson Incident," 589, 593.

62 *work behind the scenes*: Diestelow, "The Fort Wilson Riot," 1.

63 *"fear of Vengeance"*: Alexander, "The Fort Wilson Incident," 589.

63 *"the blood of this county"*: Alexander, "The Fort Wilson Incident," 596.

63 *"affect themselves"*: Kenneth Owen, *Political Community in Revolutionary Pennsylvania, 1774–1800* (Oxford University Press, 2018), 64.

63 *"monopolizers and forestallers"*: Diestelow, "The Fort Wilson Riot," 3.

63 *well-known poverty*: Harmer, "Life of a Revolutionary," 49.

64 *finances for Congress*: Harmer, "Life of a Revolutionary," 44.

64 *"financier of the Revolution"*: Charles Rappleye, *Robert Morris: Financier of the American Revolution* (Simon & Schuster, 2010).

64 *support the institution*: Murray Newton Rothbard, *History of Money and Banking in the United States: The Colonial Era to World War II* (Ludwig von Mises Institute, 2002), 62–64.

64 *mocked public virtue with their profiteering*: John E. Ferling, *Apostles of Revolution: Jefferson, Paine, Monroe, and the Struggle Against the Old Order in America and Europe* (Bloomsbury, 2018), 86.

64 *possible commissions*: James J. Kirschke, *Gouverneur Morris: Author, Statesman, and Man of the World* (St. Martin's Press, 2005), 103.

64 *quickly turned on Paine*: Harmer, *Life of a Revolutionary*, 44–45.

65 *Paine resigned his post*: Harmer, *Life of a Revolutionary*, 45.

65 *"the scoundrel Paine declared him to be"*: Benner, *Thomas Paine*, 4.

65 *a resumption of ties to England*: Benner, *Thomas Paine*, 99.

65 *"reputation [was] totally ruined"*: Benner, *Thomas Paine*, 127.

65 *"America's aristocratic circles"*: Benner, *Thomas Paine*, 95.

65 *"ignorant even of grammar"*: Benner, *Thomas Paine*, 97.

65 *"labour, starve, and toil"*: Harmer, *Life of a Revolutionary*, 46.

66 *even afford a horse*: Harmer, *Life of a Revolutionary*, 47.

66 *a thriving shipping firm*: Roy C. Smith, *Adam Smith and the Origins of American Enterprise* (St. Martin's Griffin, 2004), 126.

66 *badly needed goods*: Hubertis Cummings, "Robert Morris and the Episode of the Polacre 'Victorious,'" *Pennsylvania Magazine of History and Biography* 70, no. 3 (1946): 239–57, http://www.jstor.org/stable/20087835; see also Alexander, "The Fort Wilson Incident," 595, https://doi.org/10.2307/1921605.

67 *pricing of the goods*: Cummings, "Robert Morris and the Episode of the Polacre 'Victorious,'" 239.

67 *reading the content*: Cummings, "Robert Morris and the Episode of the Polacre 'Victorious,'" 241.

67 *deaf ears in the city*: Cummings, "Robert Morris and the Episode of the Polacre 'Victorious,'" 241.

67 *"economic factionalism"*: Cummings, "Robert Morris and the Episode of the Polacre 'Victorious,'" 242; Sam Bass Warner, *The Private City: Philadelphia in Three Periods of Its Growth* (University of Pennsylvania Press, 1987), 37.

67 *"the great detriment of trade"*: Harmer, *Life of a Revolutionary*, 47.

67 *recurrence of an eye inflammation*: Cummings, "Robert Morris and the Episode of the Polacre 'Victorious,'" 245.

67 *"being untimely ignorant of the transaction"*: Cummings, "Robert Morris and the Episode of the Polacre 'Victorious,'" 245.

67 *"to be bidded for not to be bought"*: Cummings, "Robert Morris and the Episode of the Polacre 'Victorious,'" 243.

67 *spreading rumors of hoarding*: Cummings, "Robert Morris and the Episode of the Polacre 'Victorious,'" 245.

67 *flour was in his possession*: Cummings, "Robert Morris and the Episode of the Polacre 'Victorious,'" 249.

68 *force the lowering of prices*: Alexander, "The Fort Wilson Incident," 596.

68 *prove too unwieldy in size*: Alexander, "The Fort Wilson Incident," 600; Alice L. George, *Old City Philadelphia: Cradle of American Democracy* (Arcadia, 2004), 77.

68 *"become its destroyer"*: "The Address of the Committee of the City and Liberties of Philadelphia, William Bradford, Chairman, to Their Fellow Citizens Throughout the United States, Philadelphia," *Pennsylvania Evening Post*, June 29, 1779, quoted in Langston, "'A Fickle, and Confused Multitude,'" 190–91.

68 *restrain runaway prices*: Langston, "'A Fickle and Confused Multitude,'" 192.

69 *club-wielding thugs*: Smith, "The Attack on Fort Wilson," 180.

69 *the stage at meetings*: Smith, "The Attack on Fort Wilson," 180.

69 *self-advancing foreign business dealings*: Smith, "The Attack on Fort Wilson," 181.

69 *"the strong wine of freedom"*: Jowett, *The Dialogues of Plato*, 391.

69 *the concentration of power*: Diestelow, "The Fort Wilson Riot," 3.

69 *"the benefit of education"*: Diestelow, "The Fort Wilson Riot," 2.

69 *"a house of representatives"*: Rasmussen, *Fears of a Setting Sun*, 118.

70 *first Pennsylvania Constitution in March 1779*: Alexander, "The Fort Wilson Incident," 590.

70 *prices and arrest inflation*: Kloppenberg, *Toward Democracy*, 572.

70 *unfold in Philadelphia*: Harmer, *Life of a Revolutionary*, 88.

70 *the "ancient" families*: Alexander, "The Fort Wilson Incident," 590.

70 *life from the country*: Alexander, "The Fort Wilson Incident," 596.

70 *proposed by the Republicans*: Alexander, "The Fort Wilson Incident," 590.

70 *"fear and dejection"*: Diestelow, "The Fort Wilson Riot," 4.

71 *"a convulsion among the people"*: Laurens to John Adams, Philadelphia, October 4, 1779, in *The Works of John Adams*, vol. 9, Charles Francis Adams, ed. (Boston, 1854), 49, quoted in Alexander, "The Fort Wilson Incident," 589.

71 *keeping prices high*: Diestelow, "The Fort Wilson Riot," 3.

71 *"without transgressing this Line"*: "Notes of Debates in the Continental Congress, 13–15 May 1776," in The Adams Papers, Diary and Autobiography of John Adams, vol. 2, 1771–1781, ed. L. H. Butterfield (Harvard University Press, 1961), 238–41, https://founders.archives.gov/documents/Adams/01-02-02-0006-0007.

72 *"a community of angels"*: Smith, "The Attack on Fort Wilson," 180.

72 *"the last stages of consumption"*: Smith, "The Attack on Fort Wilson," 180; Alexander, "The Fort Wilson Incident," 593.

72 *depreciate as prices rose*: Alexander, "The Fort Wilson Incident," 593.
72 *"with Indignity and Contempt"*: Alexander, "The Fort Wilson Incident," 593–94.
72 *"the more virtuous part of the Community"*: Alexander, "The Fort Wilson Incident," 594.
72 *unable to pay their creditors*: Kloppenberg, "Toward Democracy," 365.
72 *greater anger from the Constitutionalists*: Smith, "The Attack on Fort Wilson," 177.
72 *an American aristocracy*: Smith, "The Attack on Fort Wilson," 177.
72 *"all desirous of becoming Lords?"*: Smith, "The Attack on Fort Wilson," 178.
72 *"every veering gale of politicks"*: Smith, "The Attack of Fort Wilson," 178.
73 *prison ships bound for New York*: Alexander, "The Fort Wilson Incident," 601.
73 *the Quaker Meeting House on Arch Street*: Diestelow, "The Fort Wilson Riot," 4.
73 *eat before being taken away*: Diestelow, "The Fort Wilson Riot," 4.
73 *"taking up Tories"*: Langston, "'A Fickle and Confused Multitude,'" 202.
73 *hunted down any Republicans and loyalists*: Smith, "The Attack on Fort Wilson," 182.
73 *remove all "unAmerican elements"*: Smith, "The Attack on Fort Wilson," 182.
73 *the outbreak of uncontrollable mob violence*: David C. Ward, *Charles Willson Peale: Art and Selfhood in the Early Republic* (University of California Press, 2004), 74.
73 *Joseph Reed, the president of the Supreme Executive Council of Pennsylvania*: Smith, "The Attack on Fort Wilson," 182.
73 *preparation for the coming battle*: Alexander, "The Fort Wilson Incident," 604.
74 *the militia followed at a distance*: Alexander, "The Fort Wilson Incident," 604.
74 *the home of Robert Morris*: Smith, "The Attack on Fort Wilson," 182.
74 *barricaded the doors*: Smith, "The Attack on Fort Wilson," 182.
74 *forced back at bayonet point*: Smith, "The Attack on Fort Wilson," 182.
74 *the mob and brandishing a pistol*: Larson, *The Trials of Allegiance*, 186.
74 *his pistols before being driven back*: Smith, "The Attack on Fort Wilson," 184.
74 *attack the house from the rear*: Smith, "The Attack on Fort Wilson," 184.
75 *retreated after firing wildly*: Smith, "The Attack on Fort Wilson," 184.
75 *stoned and fell back*: Langston, "'A Fickle and Confused Multitude,'" 202.
75 *the Articles of Confederation*: Aaron Sullivan, *The Disaffected: Britain's Occupation of Philadelphia During the American Revolution* (University of Pennsylvania Press, 2019), 221.
75 *one of the confiscated homes*: Harold Donaldson Eberlein and Horace Mather Lippincott, *The Colonial Homes of Philadelphia and Its Neighbourhood* (J. B. Lippincott, 1912), 128.
75 *the militia in the process*: Ennis Duling, *Thirteen Charges Against Benedict Arnold: The Accusations of Colonel John Brown Prior to the Act of Treason* (McFarland, 2021), 180.
75 *"now he cannot control it"*: Duling, *Thirteen Charges Against Benedict Arnold*, 180; Smith, "The Attack on Fort Wilson," 185.
75 *the corner of Walnut and Third Streets*: Alexander, "The Fort Wilson Incident," 606.
75 *they marched down the street*: Alexander, "The Fort Wilson Incident," 606.
75 *defenders would be charged*: Alexander, "The Fort Wilson Incident," 606.

76 *avoid extrajudicial execution*: Smith, "The Attack on Fort Wilson," 186.

76 *"the passions of men in a ferment"*: Smith, "The Attack on Fort Wilson," 186.

76 *to avoid detection*: Smith, "The Attack on Fort Wilson," 186.

76 *"hereafter condemn or their humanity regret"*: Smith, "The Attack on Fort Wilson," 187.

76 *"casual over-flowings of liberty"*: Smith, "The Attack on Fort Wilson," 608.

76 *undermining or unsupportive of the Revolution*: Alexander, "The Fort Wilson Incident," 607.

76 *clean the slate for many accused*: Alexander, "The Fort Wilson Incident," 608.

76 *John Cook, the Chief Justice of Ireland*: Andrew Boon, *Lawyers and the Rule of Law* (Bloomsbury Publishing, 2022), 44–45.

77 *"general disaffection thereunto"*: Alexander, "The Fort Wilson Incident," 608.

77 *"a rigorous pursuit of legal measures"*: Alexander, "The Fort Wilson Incident," 608.

77 *"an act of free and general pardon" to both sides*: Smith, "The Attack on Fort Wilson," 188.

77 *representative model after the Wilson riot*: Diestelow, "The Fort Wilson Riot," 2–3.

77 *"[Philadelphia] had ever felt"*: Valerius, *The Freeman's Journal: or, the North-American Intelligencer*, April 7, 1784, quoted in Alexander, "The Fort Wilson Incident," 590.

77 *political impulse on social order*: Diestelow, "The Fort Wilson Riot," 3.

77 *"the spirit of town meetings and porter shops"*: Diestelow, "The Fort Wilson Riot," 3.

77 *"one great and noble source: The People"*: Kloppenberg, *Toward Democracy*, 422.

FACTIONS AND FRATRICIDE: CONTROLLING THE "DEMOCRATICAL" FORCES IN REVOLUTIONARY PHILADELPHIA

79 *"deserved best of the state"*: Cicero, *The Orations*, vol. 2, trans. Charles Duke Yonge (Jazzybee Verlag, 2017), 331.

79 *"I will put an end to your sitting"*: Samuel Rawson Gardiner, *Oliver Cromwell* (Longmans, Green, and Co., 1901), 210–11.

79 *"the effusion of so much blood"*: Thomas Hobbes, *Leviathan*, ed. Richard Tuck (Cambridge University Press, 1991), 150; Moshe Berent, "Hobbes and the 'Greek Tongues,'" *History of Political Thought* 17, no. 1 (1996): 36–59, http://www.jstor.org/stable/26217121.

80 *"the equal rights of others"*: Sandefur, *Conscience of the Constitution*, 9.

80 *the Declaration of Independence*: "The Nevada Constitution," Utah-Nevada Territory, Nevada State Library, Archives & Public Records, updated January 3, 2024, https://nsla.nv.gov/utah-nevada-territory/nevada-constitution.

81 *"language of the slave"*: Alexis de Tocqueville, *Democracy in America*, eds. J. P. Mayer and Max Lerner, trans. George Lawrence (Harper & Row, 1966), 229–30.

81 *"I refuse to a single man"*: Tocqueville, *Democracy in America*, 229–30.

81 *"commonly mistaken for the general voice"*: Winton U. Solberg, ed., *The Constitutional Convention and the Formation of the Union* (University of Illinois Press, 1990), 138.

81 *"immediately degenerate into Democracy"*: Kloppenberg, *Toward Democracy*, 322.

82 *"despots, monarchs, aristocrats"*: John Adams, *The Works of John Adams*, vol. 6 (Jazzybee Verlag, 2015), 270.

82 *"always delight to call them"*: Kloppenberg, *Toward Democracy*, 315.

82 *the mixed government model*: Kloppenberg, *Toward Democracy*, 351.

82 *"what were their names?"*: Thornton, *Democracy's Dangers and Discontents*, 55.

83 *"a Remedy against a greater Evil"*: Rasmussen, *Fears of a Setting Sun*, 125.

83 *"every Athenian assembly would still have been a mob"*: James Madison, Federalist 55, *The Federalist Papers*, ed. Clinton Rossiter (New American Library, 1961), 342.

83 *"the major number of the constituents"*: Madison to Thomas Jefferson, New York, October 17, 1788, in *The Papers of Thomas Jefferson*, vol. 14, *8 October 1788–26 March 1789*, ed. Julian P. Boyd (Princeton University Press, 1958), 16–22, https://founders.archives.gov/documents/Jefferson/01-14-02-0018.

83 *"very ignorant of the Science of Government"*: Kloppenberg, *Toward Democracy*, 326.

83 *criticized him as someone who had just arrived in America*: Harmer, *Life of a Revolutionary*, 36.

84 *the moderating elements favored by Madison*: Thompson, *America's Revolutionary Mind*, 313.

84 *"I shall not live to see it—but you may"*: Kloppenberg, *Toward Democracy*, 326.

84 *"produce confusion and every evil work"*: Thornton, *Democracy's Dangers and Discontents*, 65.

84 *"circulated by designing men"*: Thornton, *Democracy's Dangers and Discontents*, 70.

85 *"sufficient checks against the democracy"*: Thornton, *Democracy's Dangers and Discontents*, 70.

85 *"overly democratic state government"*: Thornton, *Democracy's Dangers and Discontents*, 61; Turley, *The Indispensable Right*, 80–88.

85 *the Declaration of Independence*: Benjamin W. Redekop, *Common Sense and Science from Aristotle to Reid* (Anthem Press, 2020), 147.

85 *Common Sense Realism*: Kloppenberg, *Toward Democracy*, 380.

85 *any one person or one branch*: "The accumulation of all powers, legislative, executive, and judiciary, in the same hands, whether of one, a few, or many, and whether hereditary, self-appointed, or elective, may justly be pronounced the very definition of tyranny." James Madison, Federalist 10, *The Federalist Papers*.

85 *"was not the government we fought for"*: Kloppenberg, *Toward Democracy*, 356.

85 *"checked and restrained by the others"*: Kloppenberg, *Toward Democracy*, 356.

86 *the rights of citizens*: "In the compound republic of America, the power surrendered by the people is first divided between two distinct governments, and then the portion allotted to each subdivided among distinct and separate departments. Hence a double security arises to the rights of the people." Madison, Federalist 51.

86 *a type of unicameral body*: Kloppenberg, *Toward Democracy*, 334.

86 *"all of the vices, follies, and frailties of an individual"*: Kloppenberg, *Toward Democracy*, 326.
86 *"fidelity to the public"*: Kloppenberg, *Toward Democracy*, 321.
87 *a natural and a hereditary aristocracy*: Kloppenberg, *Toward Democracy*, 331.
87 *establishing a "Christian Sparta"*: Kloppenberg, *Toward Democracy*, 341.
87 *"fewer evils than frequent elections"*: Rasmussen, *Fears of a Setting Sun*, 126.
88 *powerful and fixed interests*: Alexander Jech, "What Has Athens to Do with Rome? Tocqueville and the New Republicanism," *American Political Thought* 6, no. 4 (2017): 555, https://doi.org/10.1086/694464.
88 *"permanent and aggregate interests of the community"*: Madison, Federalist 10.
88 *"different circumstances of civil society"*: Madison, Federalist 10.
88 *"the causes of factions cannot be removed"*: Madison, Federalist 10.
88 *"the rights of other citizens"*: Madison, Federalist 10.

THE MIRACLE OF PHILADELPHIA: THE RATIFICATION RIOT AND THE RETURN TO REASON

90 *"the engine of slavery"*: Daniel N. Finucane, "The Violent Peak of Anti-Federalism: The Riot in Carlisle, the Motives of the Mob, and Opposition to the Constitution in Cumberland County, Pennsylvania," *Gardner Digital Library* 33 (2016).
90 *"aristocratic delusion"*: Finucane, "The Violent Peak of Anti-Federalism."
90 *the model of popular government*: Kloppenberg, *Toward Democracy*, 337.
91 *"satiate their revenge"*: Pauline Maier, *Ratification: The People Debate the Constitution, 1787–1788* (Simon & Schuster, 2011), 121.
91 *not to otherwise speak*: Kloppenberg, *Toward Democracy*, 337.
91 *prosecutions under the Alien and Sedition Acts*: Turley, *The Indispensable Right*, 104–120.
91 *a familiar scene unfolded*: Finucane, "The Violent Peak of Anti-Federalism," 33.
91 *to fire thirteen times in celebration*: Finucane, "The Violent Peak of Anti-Federalism," 33.
91 *"reduced to a sort of vassalage"*: Finucane, "The Violent Peak of Anti-Federalism," 33.
91 *"appearance of harmony and good humor"*: James B. Whisker, "The Carlisle Anti-Constitutional Riot," *Bedford Gazette*, January 15, 2021, https://www.bedfordgazette.com/news/the-carlisle-anti-constitutional-riot/article_3e6461ce-511b-540f-8304-94a41466c7ef.html.
92 *"inspired by heaven"*: Whisker, "The Carlisle Anti-Constitutional Riot."
92 *"labels on their breasts"*: Whisker, *"The Carlisle Anti-Constitutional Riot."*
92 *"committed them to the flames"*: Whisker, *"The Carlisle Anti-Constitutional Riot."*
92 *warrants for twenty-three anti-Federalists*: Whisker, "The Carlisle Anti-Constitutional Riot."
92 *seven agreed to parole*: Whisker, "The Carlisle Anti-Constitutional Riot."
92 *"Fedrall conspiracy"*: Finucane, "The Violent Peak of Anti-Federalism."
92 *the Federalists were held*: Whisker, "The Carlisle Anti-Constitutional Riot."

92 *taxes and other grievances*: Turley, *The Indispensable Right*, 88–96.
93 *contingent on majoritarian whim*: Madison, Federalist 51.
94 *publication to avoid charges*: Benner, *Thomas Paine*, 196.
94 *opposition to Paine*: Benner, *Thomas Paine*, 228.
94 *selling the work*: Benner, *Thomas Paine*, 228.
94 *"from Satan to Citizen Paine"*: Benner, *Thomas Paine*, 228.
95 *"the metaphysics of barbers"*: Benner, *Thomas Paine*, 198.
95 *"raises indignation"*: Benner, *Thomas Paine*, 225.
95 *"prospect of plundering the rich"*: Benner, *Thomas Paine*, 225.
95 *demonizing him in publications*: Benner, *Thomas Paine*, 231.
95 *given the poisonous environment*: Benner, *Thomas Paine*, 233.
95 *"government of this kingdom"*: Harmer, *Life of a Revolutionary*, 82.
95 *spewing insults and threats*: Benner, *Thomas Paine*, 234.
96 *sold only 30,000 in two years*: Harmer, *Life of a Revolutionary*, 81.
96 *"promoted to the pillory"*: Harmer, *Life of a Revolutionary*, 78.
96 *a cockade on his hat*: Benner, *Thomas Paine*, 237.
96 *the Palace of Versailles*: Benner, *Thomas Paine*, 200.
96 *"here as in America"*: Benner, *Thomas Paine*, 117.
96 *Lafayette's intellectual and political circle*: Harmer, *Life of a Revolutionary*, 63.
96 *find Paine in France*: Harmer, *Life of a Revolutionary*, 64.
96 *honorary French citizenship*: Lounissi, *Thomas Paine and the French Revolution*, 118; Harmer, *Life of a Revolutionary*, 83.
96 *"the dangers and honors necessary to success"*: Benner, *Thomas Paine*, 239.
96 *"the great republic of man"*: Benner, *Thomas Paine*, 239.
97 *Grand Federal Edifice*: Jeffrey Rosen, *The Pursuit of Happiness: How Classical Writers on Virtue Inspired the Lives of the Founders and Defined America* (Simon & Schuster, 2024), 114.
97 *Wilson could finish his remarks*: Rosen, *The Pursuit of Happiness*, 114.
97 *the same fate as the ancient republics*: Rosen, *The Pursuit of Happiness*, 114.
97 *"if you can keep it"*: Neil Gorsuch, *A Republic, If You Can Keep It* (Crown Publishing Group, 2019), 8.

6. PARIS: THE FRENCH REVOLUTION AND THE RAZOR OF THE REPUBLIC

99 *"parasitic and illegitimate"*: Eli Sagan, *Citizens and Cannibals: The French Revolution, the Struggle for Modernity, and the Origins of Ideological Terror* (Bloomsbury, 2001), 67.
101 *the "Terror" that followed it*: Sagan, *Citizens and Cannibals*, 81.
101 *second revolution was Rousseauian*: Louis Blanc, *Histoire de la Révolution Française, 1847–1862* (Cambridge University Press, 2011), https://doi.org/10.1017/CBO9781139086448.
101 *"level with the rest of the Nation"*: Sagan, *Citizens and Cannibals*, 73.

101 *commoners prevailing over the bourgeoisie*: Joan McDonald, *Rousseau and the French Revolution, 1762–1791* (Bloomsbury Publishing, 2013), 11.

102 *the general will and, therefore, the people*: Sagan, *Citizens and Cannibals*, 138–39.

103 *a minority of leaders*: Sagan, *Citizens and Cannibals*, 139.

103 *"the original existence of healthy ones"*: Hannah Arendt, *On Revolution* (Viking Press, 1965), 75.

104 *"rotten fruit of Rousseauism"*: François Furet and Mona Ozouf, eds., *A Critical Dictionary of the French Revolution*, trans. Arthur Goldhammer (Belknap Press of Harvard University Press, 1989), 724; Sagan, *Citizens and Cannibal*, 93.

104 *his treatment as "divine man"*: Roland N. Stromberg, "The Philosophies and the French Revolution: Reflections on Some Recent Research," *History Teacher* 21, no. 3 (1988): 331, https://doi.org/10.2307/492999.

104 *"Christ-like magnitude"*: Holger Ross Lauritsen and Mikkel Thorup, eds., *Rousseau and Revolution* (Bloomsbury Publishing, 2011), 88.

104 *"the cause of justice and equality?"*: Gordon H. MacNeil, "The Cult of Rousseau and the French Revolution," *Journal of the History of Ideas* 6, no 2 (1945): 206, https://doi.org/10.2307/2707363.

104 *"domestic freedom with arms"*: Jean-Jacques Rousseau, *Confessions, in The Confessions and Correspondence, Including the Letters to Malesherbes*, ed. Christopher Kelly et al. (University Press of New England, 1995), 181.

105 *"escapes death's embrace"*: Lauritsen and Thorup, *Rousseau and Revolution*, 157.

105 *buried near his idol*: MacNeil, "The Cult of Rousseau," 201.

105 *a place of honor in the National Assembly*: MacNeil, "The Cult of Rousseau," 204.

105 *fight for the country*: MacNeil, "The Cult of Rousseau," 206.

105 property rather than liberty: Paul R. Hanson, *The Jacobin Republic Under Fire: The Federalist Revolt in the French Revolution* (Penn State University Press, 2010), 242.

105 *in the name of civil virtue*: Hanson, *Jacobin Republic Under Fire*, 13.

CITIZEN PAINE IN THE "AGE OF REVOLUTIONS"

106 *Luxembourg Prison during the French Revolution*: Benner, *Thomas Paine*, 276.

107 *private entities to enforce*: Graeme Fife, *The Terror: The Shadow of a Guillotine: France 1792–1794* (St. Martin's Press, 2016), 18–19.

107 *other basic items like tobacco*: Fife, *The Terror*, 19.

107 *bishops in conspicuous luxury*: Laura Mason, *The Last Revolutionaries: The Conspiracy Trial of Gracchus Babeuf and the Equals* (Yale University Press, 2022), 9.

107 *maintenance of the royal household*: Fife, *The Terror*, 21.

107 *failed efforts at price-fixing*: Fife, *The Terror*, 25.

107 *close to an economic meltdown*: William Doyle, *Origins of the French Revolution* (Oxford University Press, 1999). For further discussion, see Walter S. Zapotoczny Jr., "The Financial Crisis that Contributed to the French Revolution," *Essays* (2009), https://wzaponline.com/yahoo_site_admin/assets/docs/FrenchRevolution.292125815.pdf.

109 *"idea of downfall of despotism"*: Benner, *Thomas Paine*, 173.

109 *"the highest animation of liberty could inspire"*: Benner, *Thomas Paine*, 173.

109 *"the principles of America opened the Bastille"*: Lounissi, *Thomas Paine and the French Revolution*, 43.

109 *"living to some purpose"*: Benner, *Thomas Paine*, 174.

109 *"master and patron"*: Benner, *Thomas Paine*, 177.

110 "*Non, Sire, c'est une* révolution": Arendt, *On Revolution*, 40–41.

110 *seize weapons and powder*: Fife, *The Terror*, 25.

110 *"blow up the entire quarter and the garrison"*: Fife, *The Terror*, 26.

111 *covered in blood and wounds*: Fife, *The Terror*, 27.

111 *wine mixed with gunpowder to give him strength*: Fife, *The Terror*, 27.

111 *a medal for his courage*: Fife, *The Terror*, 27.

111 *"The people can eat grass"*: Fife, *The Terror*, 28.

111 *grass stuffed in his mouth*: Fife, *The Terror*, 28.

111 *brought their knitting and sat quietly*: Stromberg, "The Philosophies and the French Revolution," 330.

112 *"what will become of you then?"*: Jean-Jacques Rosseau, *Emile, Book III*, trans. Barbara Foxley (J. M. Dent, 1925), 194.

112 *eschew any moderation or mercy*: Palmer, *Twelve Who Ruled*, 19.

112 *prophetic wisdom of those words*: Palmer, *Twelve Who Ruled*, 257.

113 *"absolute poverty worse than death" of the Old World*: Arendt, *On Revolution*, 17.

113 *"conspicuously wretched individual of the whole United States"*: Arendt, *On Revolution*, 61–62.

113 *"the people constituting a government"*: Thomas Paine, *Common Sense, The Rights of Man and Other Essential Writings of Thomas Paine* (Penguin Random House, 2003), 173.

113 *"the revolution will be which replaces him"*: Arendt, *On Revolution*, 154.

114 *the executive, legislative, and judicial departments*: Benner, *Thomas Paine*, 238.

114 *"reaction of horror and indignation"*: Lounissi, *Thomas Paine and the French Revolution*, 189.

114 *the King's guilt was obvious and established*: Benner, *Thomas Paine*, 245.

114 *"the aristocracy of half-talented writers"*: Lounissi, *Thomas Paine and the French Revolution*, 118.

114 *a constitutional compromise with the Assembly*: Sagan, *Citizens and Cannibals*, 78.

114 *The second revolution was unfolding*: Sagan, *Citizens and Cannibals*, 81.

115 *the illusory safety of country homes*: Sagan, *Citizens and Cannibals*, 82.

115 *the Champ de Mars massacre in 1791*: Sagan, *Citizens and Cannibals*, 84.

115 *the guards fired directly into the crowd*: James R. Gaines, *For Liberty and Glory: Washington, Lafayette, and Their Revolutions* (W. W. Norton, 2008), 349.

115 *fifty lay dead in the streets*: Benner, *Thomas Paine*, 175, 207.

THE TERROR: THE RISE OF "THE SANGUINARY MEN"

118 *"a whole nation disturbed by the folly of one man"*: Benner, *Thomas Paine*, 202.

118 *possible invasion to restore the Bourbon reign*: Benner, *Thomas Paine*, 246.

118 *the oath of allegiance to the state*: Fife, *The Terror*, 47.
119 *"talent competing on the ballot with prelates"*: Sagan, *Citizens and Cannibals*, 102.
119 *"a joint reign over the same land"*: Sagan, *Citizens and Cannibals*, 211.
119 *the need to control the clergy*: Palmer, *Twelve Who Ruled*, 11.
119 *"we wish to save the body"*: Palmer, *Twelve Who Ruled*, 12.
120 *the Assembly would take the oath*: Sagan, *Citizens and Cannibals*, 82–83, 213.
120 *refractory priests at Saint-Cloud*: Sagan, *Citizens and Cannibals*, 83.
120 *the divisions in the country*: Sagan, *Citizens and Cannibals*, 213.
120 *they sat as a group*: Benner, *Thomas Paine*, 238.
120 *"the ordinary rites of collective action"*: Crane Brinton, *The Jacobins: An Essay in the New History* (Transaction Publishers, 2011), 20. For further discussion, see Sagan, *Citizens and Cannibals*, 101.
120 *"the Jacobin Club of Paris unopposed"*: Sagan, *Citizens and Cannibals*, 86, 87.
121 *declaring themselves the voice of the people*: Palmer, *Twelve Who Ruled*, 258.
121 *ample opposition to the Mountain, particularly outside of Paris*: Hanson, *The Jacobin Republic Under Fire*, 167.
121 *"the majority of the Convention"*: Hanson, *The Jacobin Republic Under Fire*, 21.
121 *"emanate from themselves"*: Furet and Ozouf, *Critical Dictionary of the French Revolution*, 724; Sagan, *Citizens and Cannibal*, 141.
121 *"transform men into what he wants them to be"*: Sagan, *Citizens and Cannibals*, 426.
121 *"the omnipotent king [with] the omnipotent nation"*: Sagan, *Citizens and Cannibals*, 219.
122 *"ruthlessly, fearlessly, favoring none, to the public good"*: Fife, *The Terror*, 35.
122 *"the regeneration of empires"*: Fife, *The Terror*, 74.
123 *a militia of armed citizens called the* Sans-Culottes: Soboul, *The Sans-Culottes: The Popular Movement and Revolutionary Government, 1793–1794* (Princeton University Press, 1980).
123 *their distinctive clothing as an article of faith*: Soboul, *The Sans-Culottes*, 2.
123 *The other added accessory was, of course, the pike*: Soboul, *The Sans-Culottes*, 228.
123 *one of the "pillars of freedom"*: Soboul, *The Sans-Culottes*, 102.
123 *"a heart gangrened with aristocratic sentiments"*: Soboul, *The Sans-Culottes*, 3.
124 *"anyone who has something"*: Soboul, *The Sans-Culottes*, 7.
124 *"reproduction of their species"*: Arendt, *On Revolution*, 55.
124 *"the rights of the Sans-Culottes"*: Arendt, *On Revolution*, 55.
124 *"refused to answer the call of unity"*: Soboul, *The Sans-Culottes*, 158.
124 *"emerge into the human character"*: Alexander Hamilton et al., *The Federalist Papers: 85 Articles and Essays on the United States Constitution* (Lulu Press, Incorporated, 2018), 291.
124 *spasms of religious intolerance*: Fife, *The Terror*, 37.
124 *a "Sans-Culotte democracy"*: Albert Soboul, "Robespierre and the Popular Movement of 1793–4," *Past and Present* 5 (May 1954), 63.
125 *"French bourgeois, non-noble society"*: Sagan, *Citizens and Cannibals*, 68.

125 *any agreement or prior law*: Soboul, *The Sans-Culottes*, 57.
125 *"to breathe or to complain"*: Soboul, *The Sans-Culottes*, 48.
125 *claims of merchants or citizens with property*: Soboul, *The Sans-Culottes*, 49.
125 *ransacked stores as a matter of right*: Soboul, *The Sans-Culottes*, 15.
125 *availability of capital and resources*: Soboul, *The Sans-Culottes*, 14.
125 *calls to limit land holdings and other measures*: Soboul, *The Sans-Culottes*, 61.
126 *the form of ships, merchandise, or cash*: Soboul, *The Sans-Culottes*, 62.
126 *"tentative measures help us"*: Soboul, *The Sans-Culottes*, 73.
126 *"toward a popular form of democracy"*: Soboul, *The Sans-Culottes*, 252.
126 *radicals and anarchists*: Fife, *The Terror*, 13.
126 *a friary of the Dominican order*: Fife, *The Terror*, 14.
127 *Robespierre was clearly wounded*: Sagan, *Citizens and Cannibals*, 504.
127 *"my lips brought a bitter response"*: Hanson, *The Jacobin Republic Under Fire*, 33.
128 *Royalists or counterrevolutionaries*: Hanson, *The Jacobin Republic Under Fire*, 39–40.
128 *fight for the republic*: Hanson, *The Jacobin Republic Under Fire*, 40.
128 *to kill the families of departing troops*: Hanson, *The Jacobin Republic Under Fire*, 40.
128 *a noble title during the monarchy*: Fife, *The Terror*, 43.
129 *"I am the rage of the people"*: Fife, *The Terror*, 60.
129 *laying the foundation for a dictatorship*: Sagan, *Citizens and Cannibals*, 110.
129 *"deluded by such a daydream"*: Lounissi, *Thomas Paine and the French Revolution*, 191.
129 *a clear threat to Paine*: Palmer, *Twelve Who Ruled*, 230.
129 *"murder, assassinations, and massacre"*: Benner, *Thomas Paine*, 257.
129 *many delegates were absent*: Hanson, *The Jacobin Republic Under Fire*, 53.
129 *226 voted in favor of the charges*: Hanson, *The Jacobin Republic Under Fire*, 54.
129 *the establishment of a dictatorship*: Sagan, *Citizens and Cannibals*, 124.
130 *"brave your fury!"*: Sagan, *Citizens and Cannibals*, 124.
130 *a unanimous verdict of acquittal*: Hanson, *The Jacobin Republic Under Fire*, 54.
130 *cultivated in bourgeois society*: Sagan, *Citizens and Cannibals*, 125.
130 *an estimated 10 percent of the population*: Sagan, *Citizens and Cannibals*, 157.
130 *the Sans-Culottes and the mob*: Sagan, *Citizens and Cannibals*, 182.
131 *"future assemblies at a distance from Paris"*: Sagan, *Citizens and Cannibals*, 119.
131 *"traitors, royalists, or fools"*: Sagan, *Citizens and Cannibals*, 128.
131 *being Royalist sympathizers*: Fife, *The Terror*, 68.
131 *"march off to face our enemies"*: Fife, *The Terror*, 68.
131 *other terrified prisoners*: Fife, *The Terror*, 69.
131 *made the good Samaritan kiss it*: Fife, *The Terror*, 72.
132 *"traitors lying hidden within the walls"*: Fife, *The Terror*, 73.
132 *the Girondins were gathered up and executed in droves*: Hanson, *The Jacobin Republic Under Fire*, 51.
132 *"the Gironde was no match for the Jacobins"*: Sagan, *Citizens and Cannibals*, 119.
132 *won them over to the side of the Mountain*: Sagan, *Citizens and Cannibals*, 119.
132 *an enraged basset hound*: Hanson, *The Jacobin Republic Under Fire*, 43.

132 *"this man must reign or die!"*: Benner, *Thomas Paine*, 244.
132 *"No one can reign innocently"*: Benner, *Thomas Paine*, 244.
132 *the promise of safe treatment*: Fife, *The Terror*, 61.
132 *the tyranny of the majority*: Hanson, *The Jacobin Republic Under Fire*, 19.
132 *"the factions that had preceded them"*: Sagan, *Citizens and Cannibals*, 112.
133 *to die as Constitutionalists*: Sagan, *Citizens and Cannibals*, 118–19.
133 *"their horrible tyranny"*: Hanson, *The Jacobin Republic Under Fire*, 13.
133 *the Montagnard Constitution of 1793*: Hanson, *The Jacobin Republic Under Fire*, 198.
133 *a twenty-four-member executive committee chosen by the deputies*: Hanson, *The Jacobin Republic Under Fire*, 198.
133 *before the national assembly*: Hanson, *The Jacobin Republic Under Fire*, 199.
133 *made popular referendums much more difficult*: Hanson, *The Jacobin Republic Under Fire*, 199.
133 *power handed over to the Committee of Public Safety*: Benner, *Thomas Paine*, 262.
134 *price limits combined with wage increases*: Soboul, *The Sans-Culottes*, 255.
134 *only magnified the economic disorder*: Soboul, *The Sans-Culottes*, 256.
134 *"Down with the veto, to hell with the veto"*: Fife, *The Terror*, 57.
134 *drink a toast to the Revolution*: Fife, *The Terror*, 58.
134 *"fair, equal, and honourable representation"*: Harmer, *Life of a Revolutionary*, 88.
135 *could not stomach capital punishment*: Harmer, *Life of a Revolutionary*, 88; Benner, *Thomas Paine*, 248.
135 *"without either prudence or morality"*: Benner, *Thomas Paine*, 255.
135 *speaking further to the crowd*: Fife, *The Terror*, 96.
138 *"shake the hand of the knife"*: Fife, *The Terror*, 164.
139 *"you will die when they recover it"*: Fife, *The Terror*, 165.
139 *"not enough blood is flowing"*: Soboul, *The Sans-Culottes*, 159.
139 *"I will not abide among sanguinary men"*: Harmer, *Life of a Revolutionary*, 88.
139 *a vote of no confidence*: Benner, *Thomas Paine*, 261.
139 *only eleven days earlier*: Unger, *Thomas Paine and the Clarion Call*, 107–9.
139 *eventually attempted suicide*: Benner, *Thomas Paine*, 257.
139 *the sole remaining inhabitant*: Benner, *Thomas Paine*, 266.
140 *"veneration and gratitude for the tyrant of France"*: Benner, *Thomas Paine*, 264–65.
140 *roughly forty thousand during the Terror*: Benner, *Thomas Paine*, 275.
140 *169 were taken away for execution*: Benner, *Thomas Paine*, 272.
140 *shake his hand one last time*: Harmer, *Life of a Revolutionary*, 93.
140 *go to the scaffold "gaily"*: Benner, *Thomas Paine*, 273.
140 *a chair, mattress, and box*: Harmer, *Life of a Revolutionary*, 92.
140 *"her government beholds my situation in silence"*: Paul Aron, *Founding Feuds: The Rivalries, Clashes, and Conflicts That Forged a Nation* (Sourcebooks, 2016), 180.
140 *"you must not leave me in [this] situation"*: William Hogeland, "Thomas Paine's Revolutionary Reckoning," HistoryNet, September 29, 2017, https://www.historynet.com/thomas-paines-revolutionary-reckoning/.

141 *"this epoch is out of my jurisdiction"*: Benner, *Thomas Paine*, 269.
141 *"a faction that [caused] this injustice"*: Benner, *Thomas Paine*, 277.
141 *report on his situation to Congress*: Benner, *Thomas Paine*, 270.
141 *"inexpedient and ineffectual"*: Benner, *Thomas Paine*, 270.
141 *"to procure him justice"*: Benner, *Thomas Paine*, 278.
141 *"the false friends of our revolution have invested it"*: Benner, *Thomas Paine*, 272.
141 *charged in France by Jacobins as a reactionary*: Lounissi, *Thomas Paine and the French Revolution*, 199.
141 *securing his release*: Harmer, *Life of a Revolutionary*, 93.
141 *"forgot your friend, and became silent"*: Harmer, *Life of a Revolutionary*, 97.
142 *a "distinguished patriot"*: Harmer, *Life of a Revolutionary*, 93.
142 *"the name of Thomas Paine"*: Benner, *Thomas Paine*, 280.
142 *ten months and nine days in crushing confinement*: Harmer, *Life of a Revolutionary*, 93.

SIC SEMPER TYRANNIS: THE FALL OF THE MOUNTAIN

143 *the Place des Victories in Paris*: Fife, *The Terror*, 1.
144 *a neat, green cardboard sheath*: Fife, *The Terror*, 3.
144 *the winding streets of the old Latin Quarter*: Fife, *The Terror*, 5.
144 *the knife secreted in her corsage*: Fife, *The Terror*, 5–6.
144 *he lay in a cooling bath*: Benner, *Thomas Paine*, 262.
144 *the words "LA MORT," or the death*: Fife, *The Terror*, 6.
144 *"I'll see them all to the guillotine in Paris"*: Fife, *The Terror*, 6.
145 *"'Citizen, help me, oh help me, help'"*: Fife, *The Terror*, 6.
145 *seemed to quiet the crowd*: Fife, *The Terror*, 8.
145 *"That was indeed my intention"*: Fife, *The Terror*, 9.
146 *"the courage to sacrifice themselves for their country"*: Fife, *The Terror*, 9.
147 *a name that rhymed with* machine *in French*: Fife, *The Terror*, 55.
147 *reduce any stress or pain at their executions*: Fife, *The Terror*, 55.
147 *they saw the face blush*: Fife, *The Terror*, 9.
147 *at least physiological responses in such cases*: Matthew D. Turner, "'The Most Gentle of Lethal Methods': The Question of Retained Consciousness Following Decapitation," *Cureus* 15, no. 1 (2023), https://doi.org/10.7759/cureus.33830.
148 *"Let's make terror the order of the day!"*: Elizabeth Duquette, *American Tyrannies in the Long Age of Napoleon* (Oxford University Press, 2023), 16.
148 *"the right to mount the tribune"*: Fife, *The Terror*, 166.
148 *they were now "killing intelligence"*: Fife, *The Terror*, 166.
148 *"friends of tyranny"*: Hanson, *The Jacobin Republic Under Fire*, 46.
148 *dissenting faction members*: Sagan, *Citizens and Cannibals*, 195.
148 *"guillotine the entire Republic"*: Fife, *The Terror*, 166.
149 *"ended up annihilating France"*: Sagan, *Citizens and Cannibals*, 109.
149 *unilaterally nullify laws*: Fife, *The Terror*, 206.
149 *the forced removal of children*: Sagan, *Citizens and Cannibals*, 470.

149 *confront their accusers*: Sagan, *Citizens and Cannibals*, 502.

149 *outrage from delegates*: Hanson, *The Jacobin Republic Under Fire*, 19.

149 *"formalities which stifle the conscience and hinder conviction"*: Sagan, *Citizens and Cannibals*, 502.

149 *"to pronounce sentence"*: Hanson, *The Jacobin Republican Under Fire*, 19–20; Sagan, *Citizens and Cannibals*, 502.

149 *"a man died in his bed"*: Fife, *The Terror*, 231.

149 *end the Terror*: Palmer, *Twelve Who Ruled*, 257.

149 *left in the Revolution*: Palmer, *Twelve Who Ruled*, 259.

150 *"they are afraid of ascending it"*: Sagan, *Citizens and Cannibals*, 425.

150 *"an exhausted volcano"*: Palmer, *Twelve Who Ruled*, 257.

150 *Martial Joseph Armand Herman sitting as judge*: Sagan, *Citizens and Cannibals*, 465.

150 *removed and tried in absentia*: Sagan, *Citizens and Cannibals*, 465.

150 *the president and the public prosecutor*: Sagan, *Citizens and Cannibals*, 466.

151 *executed on the guillotine*: Benner, *Thomas Paine*, 276.

151 *shriek in terror*: John Haycraft, *In Search of the French Revolution: Journeys Through France* (Secker & Warburg, 1989), 232.

152 *"I am the one who made that"*: Patrice L. R. Higonnet, *Goodness Beyond Virtue: Jacobins During the French Revolution* (Harvard University Press, 1998), 60.

152 *the long line of condemned persons that Robespierre had sent to that prison*: Benner, *Thomas Paine*, 271.

7. PAINE'S BRIDGE: REVOLUTION AND GOVERNANCE IN AN AGE OF RAGE

154 *An iron bridge to be specific*: Lounissi, *Thomas Paine and the French Revolution*, 11.

154 *invent a smokeless candle*: Harmer, *Life of a Revolutionary*, 60.

154 *"the greater emperor in it"*: Benner, *Thomas Paine*, 166.

155 *Sunderland Bridge in England*: Edward G. Gray, *Tom Paine's Iron Bridge: Building a United States* (W. W. Norton, 2016), 153–59.

155 *American rivers in the East*: Harmer, *Life of a Revolutionary*, 61.

155 *either wood or stone*: Benner, *Thomas Paine*, 152.

155 *greater foundation for his design*: Benner, *Thomas Paine*, 152.

155 *to display a model of the bridge*: Benner, *Thomas Paine*, 153.

155 *the stability of the arch*: Benner, *Thomas Paine*, 164.

155 *"His most Excellent Majesty King George the Third"*: Benner, *Thomas Paine*, 166.

155 *"principles new and different to anything hitherto practiced"*: Benner, *Thomas Paine*, 166.

156 *approval in Paris, though not funding*: Benner, *Thomas Paine*, 163.

156 *his house in Bordentown*: Benner, *Thomas Paine*, 176.

156 *social order and the rise of tyranny*: Yuval Levin, *The Great Debate: Edmund Burke, Thomas Paine, and the Birth of Right and Left* (Basic Books, 2013).

157 *he viewed the unfolding revolution*: Harmer, *Life of a Revolutionary*, 69.

157 *"whom has the National Assembly brought to the scaffold?"*: Harmer, *Life of a Revolutionary*, 70.

157 *accused of being an aristocrat*: Harmer, *Life of a Revolutionary*, 73.

157 *sign of the costs of nobility*: Benner, *Thomas Paine*, 202.

157 *explain to the mob who Paine was*: Benner, *Thomas Paine*, 202.

157 *tradition as the basis for legitimacy*: Lounissi, *Thomas Paine and the French Revolution*, 14.

157 *helped Paine look for patrons for his bridge*: Harmer, *Life of a Revolutionary*, 63.

158 *a just and legitimate representative of their interests*: Benner, *Thomas Paine*, 180.

158 *"rebels from principle"*: Harmer, *Life of a Revolutionary*, 68.

158 *both monarchial and democratic despotism*: Thompson, *America's Revolutionary Mind*, 274, 285.

158 *"an interested and over-bearing majority"*: Madison, Federalist 10, *The Federalist*, Benjamin F. Wright ed., 129–30.

158 *"absolute power of an individual"*: Madison, Federalist 10, *The Federalist*, 129–30.

158 *the absence of a stable political system*: Lounissi, *Thomas Paine and the French Revolution*, 54.

158 *an all-powerful single legislative body*: Benner, *Thomas Paine*, 208.

159 *aristocracy, monarchy, and democracy*: Thompson, *America's Revolutionary Mind*, 313.

159 *the extreme conditions created by the monarchy*: Lounissi, *Thomas Paine and the French Revolution*, 75.

159 *impulses to rule in the legislative process*: Lounissi, *Thomas Paine and the French Revolution*, 181.

159 *"more houses [as] . . . more parties"*: Lounissi, *Thomas Paine and the French Revolution*, 181.

159 *"at the threshold of the state house"*: Lounissi, *Thomas Paine and the French Revolution*, 181.

159 *too much power to minority factions*: Lounissi, *Thomas Paine and the French Revolution*, 153.

159 *the authority of "the sovereign people"*: Soboul, *The Sans-Culottes*, 97.

159 *"null and void"*: Soboul, *The Sans-Culottes*, 99.

159 *"laws will be those made by the people themselves"*: Soboul, *The Sans-Culottes*, 106.

159 *vote by acclamation, to pass measures*: Soboul, *The Sans-Culottes*, 252.

159 *any faction other than the majority faction was deemed counterrevolutionary*: Arendt, *On Revolution*, 54.

160 *"always avoided parties and factions"*: Lounissi, *Thomas Paine and the French Revolution*, 221.

160 *the most powerful faction, the Montagnards*: Harmer, *Life of a Revolutionary*, 86.

160 *no longer a safe place for him*: Harmer, *Life of a Revolutionary*, 89.

160 *execution, including Condorcet*: Harmer, *Life of a Revolutionary*, 89.

160 *"same danger was approaching myself"*: Harmer, *Life of a Revolutionary*, 90.

160 *"Thomas Paine be decreed of accusation"*: Harmer, *Life of a Revolutionary*, 89.

162 *linger alongside his painful memories*: Benner, *Thomas Paine*, 294.

162 *immediately seeking to meet Paine*: Turley, *The Indispensable Right*, 44.

162 *"Paine is now as odious in France as it is in England"*: Turley, *The Indispensable Right*, 44.

162 *the harm that he had caused France*: Lounissi, *Thomas Paine and the French Revolution*, 302.

162 *"a settled melancholy"*: Lounissi, *Thomas Paine and the French Revolution*, 302.

162 *dedicating the book to him*: Benner, *Thomas Paine*, 201.

162 *"those blessings to which they are entitled"*: Hogeland, "Thomas Paine's Revolutionary Reckoning."

163 *"whether you ever had any"*: Hogeland, "Thomas Paine's Revolutionary Reckoning."

163 *took the greatest toll*: Hogeland, "Thomas Paine's Revolutionary Reckoning."

163 *"I now relinquish that hope"*: Lounissi, *Thomas Paine and the French Revolution*, 200.

163 *Madisonian checks and balances*: Lounissi, *Thomas Paine and the French Revolution*, 229–30.

163 *early form of communist rule*: Mason, *The Last Revolutionaries*.

PART III. DEMOCRACY IN THE TWENTY-FIRST CENTURY AND THE "ART OF LIVING FREELY"

168 *"hard to tell it from a dictatorship"*: Edward F. Haas, ed., *The Age of the Longs: Louisiana, 1928–1960* (Center for Louisiana Studies, University of Louisiana at Lafayette, 2001), 63.

168 *"supposed government 'by the people'"*: Sagan, *Citizens and Cannibals*, 132.

168 *"another of Napoleon becomes inevitable"*: Sagan, *Citizens and Cannibals*, 123.

168 *the Jeffersonians were "our Jacobins"*: Rasmussen, *Fears of a Setting Sun*, 87.

169 *"even life are at stake"*: Rasmussen, Fears of a Setting Sun, 91.

169 *"rather than on institutions and constitutions"*: Arendt, *On Revolution*, 70.

169 *"American revolutionaries were not anarchists"*: Thompson, *America's Revolutionary Mind*, 262.

169 *"the most formidable enemies of the People mobilize themselves"*: Sagan, *Citizens and Cannibals*, 143.

169 *the American Revolution on later revolutionaries*: Arendt, *On Revolution*, 49.

170 *"the essence of Jacobinism"*: Sagan, *Citizens and Cannibals*, 459.

170 *Mensheviks likely represented more of the population*: Robert H. Donaldson and Joseph L. Nogee, *The Foreign Policy of Russia: Changing Systems, Enduring Interests* (Routledge, 2014), 38.

170 *an ice pick in Mexico City*: Enrique Soto-Pérez-de-Celis, "The Death of Leon Trotsky," *Neurosurgery* 67, no. 2 (2010): 417–23, https://doi.org/10.1227/01.NEU.0000371968.27560.6C.

170 *"a world completely new"*: Olivier Zunz, *The Man Who Understood Democracy: The Life of Alexis de Tocqueville* (Princeton University Press, 2023), 119.

171 *"their mathematical exactness false"*: Alexis De Tocqueville, *Recollections: French Revolution of 1848*, ed. J. P. Mayer and A. P. Kerr (Routledge, 1987), 62.

8. THE AMERICAN JACOBIN: THE RETURN OF THE BOURGEOIS REVOLUTIONARY

173 *George Washington University in Washington, D.C.*: Jonathan Turley, "'Guillotine! Guillotine! Guillotine!': GW Protesters Call for the Heads of President and Others to Be Cut Off," *Res Ipsa Loquitur*, May 6, 2024, https://jonathanturley.org/2024/05/06/guillotine-guillotine-guillotine-gw-protesters-call-for-the-heads-of-president-and-others-to-be-cut-off/.

173 *the inauguration and during later protests*: Jonathan Turley, "Heads Off: A Guillotine Makes Another Appearance in D.C. at the Hands Off! Protest Against Trump," *Res Ipsa Loquitur*, April 6, 2025, https://jonathanturley.org/2025/04/06/heads-off-guillotine-makes-another-appearance-in-d-c-at-a-hands-off-protest/.

173 *anti-ICE protestors in Portland*: Greg Norman, "Anti-ICE Rioters with Guillotine Clash with Police in War-Like Scenes," Fox News, September 2, 2025; Jonathan Turley, "The New Jacobins: Guillotines Return as Political Expression," *Res Ipsa Loquitur*, September 7, 2025, https://jonathanturley.org/2025/09/07/the-new-jacobins-guillotines-return-as-form-of-political-express/.

174 *"our piece of crap Constitution"*: Jonathan Turley, "The American Jacobin: How Some on the Left Have Found Release in the Rage," *Res Ipsa Loquitur*, April 7, 2025, https://jonathanturley.org/2025/04/07/the-american-jacobin-how-some-on-the-left-have-found-release-in-an-age-of-rage/.

175 *"They didn't take very kindly to the collaborators"*: Ashleigh Fields, "Carville: The Firms Making Deals with Trump Will Be Remembered as 'Collaborators,'" *The Hill*, April 4, 2025, https://thehill.com/homenews/administration/5233141-carville-trump-law-firms-nazi-collaborators/.

175 *rejecting messages of political reform*: Jonathan Turley, "'Have You Tried Gasoline?': Democrats Admit that Followers Are Embracing Violent Rhetoric," *Res Ipsa Loquitur*, April 8, 2025, https://jonathanturley.org/2025/07/08/have-you-tried-gasoline-democrats-admit-followers-are-embracing-violent-rhetoric.

175 *"a demand that we get ourselves arrested"*: Mike Bedigan, "Democratic Voters Are Demanding Reps Fight Dirty Against Trump and MAGA: 'There Needs to Be Blood,'" *Independent*, July 7, 2025, https://www.the-independent.com/news/world/americas/us-politics/democrats-voters-fight-trump-maga-b2784094.html.

175 *brandishing a baseball bat*: Jonathan Turley, "Fight in the Streets: Democratic House Leader Hakeen Jeffries Triggers Renewed Debate over Rage Rhetoric," *Res Ipsa Loquitur*, February 1, 2025, https://jonathanturley.org/2025/02/01/fight-in-the-streets-democratic-leader-hakeen-jeffries-triggers-renewed-debate-over-rage-rhetoric.

175 *"punch these sons of bitches in the mouth"*: Jonathan Turley, "The New Jacobins: Guillotines Return as Form of Political Expression," September 7, 2025, *Res Ipsa Loquitur*, https://jonathanturley.org/2025/09/07/the-new-jacobins-guillotines-return-as-form-of-political-express.

175 *reference to Trump supporters*: Jonathan Turley, "'When Must We Kill Them?' George Mason Student Captures the Growing Violent Ideation on the Left," *Res*

Ipsa Loquitur, April 19, 2025, https://jonathanturley.org/2025/04/19/when-must-we-kill-them-george-mason-phd-student-captures-the-growing-violent-ideation-on-the-left.

176 *"I can scrape a little off the top, too"*: Turley, "The American Jacobin."

176 *assassination of conservative activist Charlie Kirk*: Jonathan Turley, "'Prove Me Wrong': Charlie Kirk's Final Challenge on Free Speech, September 11, 2025, *Res Ipsa Loquitur*, https://jonathanturley.org/2025/09/11/prove-me-wrong-charlie-kirks-final-challenge-on-free-speech.

176 *political violence to increase in the United States*: Victor Nava, "More Than 33% of Young Americans Believe Political Violence Can Be Justified in Certain Cases: Poll," *New York Post*, November 3, 2025, https://nypost.com/2025/11/03/us-news/more-than-33-of-young-americans-believe-political-violence-can-be-justified-poll.

176 *anti–free speech groups in the United States*: Jonathan Turley, "The Naughty List: Former Obama Aides and Liberal Influencers Sell Antifa Line of Holiday Gifts," *Res Ipsa Loquitur*, December 16, 2024, https://jonathanturley.org/2024/12/06/the-naughty-list-former-obama-aides-and-liberal-influencers-sell-antifa-line-of-holiday-gifts/.

176 *throwing Molotov cocktails at police*: Jonathan Turley, "Two New York Attorneys Arrested for Throwing Molotov Cocktails at Police," *Res Ipsa Loquitur*, June 1, 2020, https://jonathanturley.org/2020/06/01/two-new-york-attorneys-arrested-for-throwing-molotov-cocktail-at-police/; Jonathan Turley, "Former Public Radio Reporter Among Those Charges in Molotov Cocktail Attack on Police," *Res Ipsa Loquitur*, December 30, 2020, https://jonathanturley.org/2020/12/30/former-public-radio-reporter-among-those-charged-in-molotov-cocktail-attack-against-police-vehicles/.

176 *"can only push people so far"*: Jonathan Turley, "Warren's 'Warning': Democratic Senator Explains Thompson was Murdered Because 'You Can Only Push People So Far,'" *Res Ipsa Loquitur*, December 12, 2024, https://jonathanturley.org/2024/12/12/warrens-warning-democratic-senator-explains-that-thompson-was-murdered-because-you-can-only-push-people-so-far/.

176 "an act of violence against [ordinary citizens]": Zoe Hussain, "AOC Sympathizes with Those Celebrating UnitedHealthcare CEO's Murder, Says Denied Claims Are 'Acts of Violence,'" *New York Post*, December 13, 2024, https://nypost.com/2024/12/13/us-news/aoc-sparks-criticism-defending-those-who-dont-have-sympathy-for-unitedhealthcare-ceo-brian-thompson-killing.

177 *two assassination attempts*: Jonathan Turley, "Age of Rage: 26 Million Americans Believe Political Violence Is Justified," *Res Ipsa Loquitur*, September 17, 2024, https://jonathanturley.org/2024/09/17/age-of-rage-26-million-americans-believe-political-violence-is-justified/.

177 *killing Donald Trump could be justified*: Jonathan Turley, "The American Jacobin."

177 *questioned the need for a Supreme Court*: Jonathan Turley, "Lebowitz Calls for Biden-Harris to 'Dissolve the Supreme Court,'" *Res Ipsa Loquitur*, September 29,

2024, https://jonathanturley.org/2024/09/29/lebowitz-calls-for-biden-harris-to-dissolve-the-supreme-court/.

177 *one of the most affluent student bodies*: Josh Freedman, "When Students Are Rejected for Being Poor: The George Washington University and the Roots of a Troubled System," *Forbes*, October 22, 2013, https://www.forbes.com/sites/joshfreedman/2013/10/22/when-students-are-rejected-for-being-poor-the-george-washington-university-and-the-roots-of-a-troubled-system/.

178 *a type of "bourgeois ideological terrorism"*: Sagan, *Citizens and Cannibals*, 183.

178 *traditional Democrats struggle to maintain control*: Victor Davis Hansen, "America's New Jacobins," *Hoover Institution*, October 2, 2018, https://www.hoover.org/research/americas-new-jacobins; Jonathan Turley, "Circling the Firing Squad: The Democratic Party Moves to Negate Earlier Election of David Hogg," *Res Ipsa Loquitur*, May 14, 2025, https://jonathanturley.org/2025/05/14/circling-the-fire-squad-the-democratic-party-moves-to-negate-earlier-election-of-david-hogg/.

178 *converting private housing into communes*: Jonathan Turley, "'The End Goal of Seizing the Means of Production': Yup, Mamdani Is a Hardcore Marxist," *Res Ipsa Loquitur*, July 2, 2025, https://jonathanturley.org/2025/07/02/the-end-goal-of-seizing-the-means-of-production-yup-mamdani-is-a-hardcore-marxist/.

178 *50 percent to 65 percent*: Abigail Tierney, "Share of Adults in the United States Who Have a Positive View of Socialism from 2010 to 2021, by Party Affiliation," Statista, July 5, 2024, https://www.statista.com/statistics/1078448/support-socialism-party-affiliation-us/.

178 *58 percent positivity response just two years earlier*: Laura Wronski, "Axios/SurveyMonkey Poll: Capitalism and Socialism," SurveyMonkey, June 2021, https://www.surveymonkey.com/curiosity/axios-capitalism-update/.

178 *34 percent of those under thirty*: Cato Institute, "Cato Institute 2025 Fiscal Policy National Survey," https://www.cato.org/sites/cato.org/files/2025-04/Tax%20Policy%20Survey_2025_2.pdf.

178 *little trust in the political system*: "Views of the U.S. Political System, the Federal Government and Federal-State Relations: 2. Americans' Dismal Views of the Nation's Politics," Pew Research Center, September 19, 2023, https://www.pewresearch.org/politics/2023/09/19/views-of-the-u-s-political-system-the-federal-government-and-federal-state-relations/.

178 *"hostile to liberal accommodationism"*: Jacobin, accessed July 12, 2025, https://jacobin.com/about.

THE POLITICIANS

180 *"leader of the rabble"*: James Fenimore Cooper, *The American Democrat and Other Political Writings* (Gateway Editions, 2001), 430.

180 *Aristophanes's play* Knights: Thornton, *Democracy's Dangers and Discontents*, 21.

180 *"the most powerful with The People"*: Thornton, *Democracy's Dangers and Discontents*, 21.

180 *"no thought for anything but the present"*: John Michael Moore, ed., *Aristotle and Xenophon on Democracy and Oligarchy* (University of California Press, 1975), 171.

180 *appease the mob*: Richard D. White, *Kingfish: The Reign of Huey P. Long* (Random House Publishing Group, 2009), x.

181 *crackdowns on suspected communists*: Larry Tye, *Demagogue: The Life and Long Shadow of Senator Joe McCarthy* (Houghton Mifflin Harcourt, 2020), 1–2.

181 *promises of prosperity*: Michael Lind, "Trump Was a Corrupt Populist Demagogue, Not a Would-Be Fascist Dictator," Opinion, *MarketWatch*, February 10, 2021, https://www.marketwatch.com/story/despite-the-capitol-insurrection-trump-was-never-a-would-be-fascist-dictator-11612889609.

181 *ignore opposing court rulings*: Tommy Christopher, "'Ignore This Ruling!' Alexandria Ocacio-Cortez Demands Biden Defy Federal Judge on Abortion Pill," *Mediaite*, April 8, 2023, https://www.mediaite.com/media/news/watch-aoc-lashes-out at-abortion-pill-decision-says-biden-should-ignore-this-ruling/.

181 *the start of the Trump administration*: Brad Polumbo, "Conservatives are Playing with Fire by Threatening Our Judicial System," Opinion, MSNBC, February 17, 2025, https://www.msnbc.com/opinion/msnbc-opinion/trump-conservatives-threatening-judicial-system-rcna192109.

181 *47 percent of Trump supporters say the same about Democrats*: Jonathan Turley, "America's Crisis of Faith: Poll Reveals More Americans Are Rejecting the Constitution and Embracing Violence," *Res Ipsa Loquitur*, October 23, 2023, https://jonathanturley.org/2023/10/23/americas-crisis-of-faith-new-poll-reveals-more-americans-are-rejecting-the-constitution-and-embracing-violence/.

181 *captured this "age of rage"*: Turley, *The Indispensable Right*, 335.

182 *a fire alarm in the middle of a major vote*: Solender and Cuneyt Dil, "Bowman Pleads Guilty to Pulling Capitol Hill Fire Alarm," Axios, October 25, 2023, https://www.axios.com/2023/10/25/jamaal-bowman-fire-alarm-charge.

182 *perpetuating racist and economic barriers*: Hannah Grossman, "Boston Council Member Calling for 'Revolution' Alarms Liberal Colleagues with Tirades, Threats," Fox News, May 24, 2024, https://www.foxnews.com/media/boston-council-member-calling-revolution-alarms-liberal-colleagues-wild-tirades-threats.

182 *"respect as a Black woman"*: Grossman, "Boston Council Member."

182 *"intimidation does work"*: Grossman, "Boston Council Member."

182 *public corruption and resigned*: Annie Jonas, "Tania Fernandes Anderson's Guilty Plea Has Readers Calling for an Ethics Committee," Boston.com, April 10, 2025, https://www.boston.com/community/readers-say/2025/04/10/tania-fernandes-andersons-guilty-plea-has-readers-calling-for-an-ethics-committee/.

183 *embraced violent groups such as Antifa*: Turley, *The Indispensable Right*, 175–79.

183 *patrons repeat slogans*: Jonathan Turley, "How 'Silence Is Violence' Can Become Compelled Speech," *Res Ipsa Loquitur*, August 31, 2020, https://jonathanturley.org/2020/08/31/how-silence-is-violence-can-became-compelled-speech/.

183 *an instant majority of liberal justices*: Jonathan Turley, "From Packing to Sacking, Democrats Pledge Politics 'By Any Means Necessary,'" *Res Ipsa Loquitur*, Decem-

ber 20, 2021, https://jonathanturley.org/2021/12/20/from-packing-the-supreme-court-to-sacking-the-senate-clerk-democrats-pledge-politics-by-any-means-necessary/.

184 *"policymakers drew consensus on"*: Turley, "From Packing to Sacking.

184 *"I don't think it does"*: Turley, "From Packing to Sacking."

184 *Barnes's belief in natural law*: Jonathan Turley, "Tim Kaine's Constitutional Blasphemy," *The Hill*, September 6, 2025, https://thehill.com/opinion/congress-blog/5489547-tim-kaines-embarrassing-constitutional-blasphemy.

185 *"obscured by mortal power"*: Richard B. Bernstein, *Hamilton: The Energetic Founder* (Oxford University Press, 2023), 33

185 *the government can taketh away*: Turley, "Tim Kaine's Constitutional Blasphemy."

185 *joined the Trump administration*: Jonathan Turley, "'I'm Thoroughly Disgusted': Democrats Attack Musk and Everything That They Once Believed In," *Res Ipsa Loquitur*, April 2, 2025, https://jonathanturley.org/2025/04/02/im-thoroughly-disgusted-democrats-attack-musk-and-everything-that-they-once-believed-in/.

185 *common in "an age of rage"*: Turley, *The Indispensable Right*, 14–19.

186 *his association with Trump*: Chase Difeliciantonio, "California Democrats Find New Ways to Resist Musk—Online and on the Road," *Politico*, March 28, 2025, https://www.politico.com/news/2025/03/28/california-democrats-elon-musk-00258203.

186 *greedy and privileged*: Jonathan Turley, "Eat the Rich: Warren Plan Would Impose Wealth Tax, Captivity Tax, and $100 Billion for Increasing Tax Audits," *Res Ipsa Loquitur*, March 20, 2021, https://jonathanturley.org/2024/03/20/eat-the-rich-warren-plan-would-impose-wealth-tax-captivity-tax-and-100-billion-for-increasing-tax-audits/.

186 *the bottom 90 percent combined*: Tax Foundation, updated March 13, 2024, https://taxfoundation.org/data/all/federal/latest-federal-income-tax-data-2024/.

187 *"by the people for the people"*: Jonathan Turley, "Warren's Wealth Tax: How a New Bill Would Convert the Tax Code into a Canned Hunt," *Res Ipsa Loquitur*, March 22, 2021, https://jonathanturley.org/2021/03/22/warrens-wealth-tax-how-a-new-bill-would-convert-the-tax-code-into-a-canned-hunt/; Owen Jones, "Eat the Rich! Why Millennials and Generation Z Turned Their Backs on Capitalism," *Guardian*, September. 20, 2021, https://www.theguardian.com/politics/2021/sep/20/eat-the-rich-why-millennials-and-generation-z-have-turned-their-backs-on-capitalism.

THE PROFESSORS

188 *libertarian faculty members*: Turley, *The Indispensable Right*, 306–308.

188 *unrelenting investigations and accusations*: Turley, *The Indispensable Right*, 289.

188 *seeking to defund the police*: Shai Davidai (@ShaiDavidai), "Lawmakers give police offers the ammunition which they then use disproportionately on Black men . . . ," Twitter (now X), April 16, 2021, https://twitter.com/ShaiDavidai/status/1383161107653726212.

188 *his presence on campus might trigger students*: Desheania Andrews, Isabel Keane, and Ronny Reyes, "Outspoken Jewish Professor Barred from Campus," *New York Post*, April 22, 2024, https://nypost.com/2024/04/22/us-news/columbia-professor-and-out spoken-israel-supporter-shai-davidai-says-hes-been-barred-from-the-main-campus/.

188 *"The time for this is over!"*: Jonathan Turley, "UW-EAU Claire Department Chair Allegedly Destroys College Republican Table," *Res Ipsa Loquitur*, April 3, 2025, https://jonathanturley.org/2025/04/03/uw-eau-department-chair-allegedly -destroys-college-republican-table/.

188 *trashed the tent and carried it off*: Jonathan Turley, "Leftist Mob on UC Davis Campus Destroys Conservative Group Display and Tent," *Res Ipsa Loquitur*, April 4, 2025, https://jonathanturley.org/2025/04/04/leftist-mob-on-uc-davis-campus-destroys-conservative-group-display-and-tent/.

189 *"hostility may be warranted"*: Jonathan Turley, "'Your Speech is Violence': How the Mob Is Using a New Mantra to Justify Campus Violence," *Res Ipsa Loquitur*, June 5, 2023, https://jonathanturley.org/2023/06/05/your-speech-is-violence-how -the-mob-is-using-a-new-mantra-to-justify-campus-violence/.

189 *political violence is justified*: Jonathan Turley, "A Quarter of Americans Now Believe Political Violence Is Justified," *Res Ipsa Loquitur*, November 4, 2025, https://jonathanturley.org/2025/11/04/a-quarter-of-americans-now-believe -political-violence-is-justified.

189 *pro-life students and destroyed their display*: Jonathan Turley, "Miller-Young and University of California Sued Over Campus Assault on Pro-Life Advocates," *Res Ipsa Loquitur*, November 10, 2014, https://jonathanturley.org/2014/11/10/miller-young -and-university-of-california-sued-over-campus-assault-on-pro-life-advocates/.

189 *supported Miller-Young after the violent attack*: Turley, "Miller-Young and University of California."

189 *a model of activism*: Jonathan Turley, "California Professor Who Assaulted Pro-Life Advocates Is Featured by Oregon to Help Students 'Embrace . . . The Radical Potential of Black Feminism in Our Everyday Lives,'" *Res Ipsa Loquitur*, October 17, 2018, https://jonathanturley.org/2018/10/17/california-professor-who -assaulted-pro-life-advocates-is-featured-by-oregon-to-help-students-embrace -the-radical-potential-of-black-feminism-in-our-everyday-lives/.

189 *"speech is violence"*: Jonathan Turley, "'Your Speech Is Violence.'"

189 *fired by Cooper Union for other reasons*: Jonathan Turley, "'This Is Fascism': Machete-Wielding Professor Fired Again," *Res Ipsa Loquitur*, February 4, 2024, https://jona thanturley.org/2024/02/04/this-is-fascism-machete-wielding-professor-fired-again/.

189 *shut down a display and was arrested*: "'She's a . . . Professor!': Albany Professor Arrested After Obstructing Pro-Life Display and Resisting Arrest," *Res Ipsa Loquitur*, May 4, 2023, https://jonathanturley.org/2023/05/04/shes-a-professor-albany -professor-arrested-after-obstructing-pro-life-display-and-resisting-arrest/.

189 *a growing movement against "constitutionalism"*: Jonathan Turley, "'Reclaim America from Constitutionalism': Law Professors Now Call to 'Pack the States' Rather than 'Pack the Court,'" *Res Ipsa Loquitur*, August 25, 2022, https://jonathanturley

.org/2022/08/25/reclaim-america-from-constitutionalism-law-professors-now-call-to-pack-the-states-rather-than-pack-the-court/.

190 *in the name of "popular constitutionalism"*: Mark Tushnet, "An Open Letter to the Biden Administration on Popular Constitutionism," *Balkinization*, July 19, 2023, https://balkin.blogspot.com/2023/07/an-open-letter-to-biden-administration.html.

190 *"cult of the Constitution"*: Mary Anne Franks, *The Cult of the Constitution* (Stanford University Press, 2019).

190 *advance "white male supremacy"*: Mary Anne Franks, "The Lost Cause of Free Speech," *Journal of Free Speech Law* 2 (2022): 337.

190 *"silencing of women and minorities"*: Mary Anne Franks, "Fearless Speech," *First Amendment Law Review* 17 (2018): 294.

190 *"more than they love anything"*: Dr. Mary Anne Franks (@ma_franks), X, November 7, 2024, https://x.com/ma_franks/status/1854610089212334179.

190 *denouncing "Constitution worship"*: Jennifer Szalai, "The Constitution Is Sacred. Is It Also Dangerous?" *New York Times*, August 31, 2024, https://www.nytimes.com/2024/08/31/books/review/constitution-secession-democracy-crisis.html.

190 *"slaves" to the U.S. Constitution*: Jonathan Turley, "Georgetown Law Professor Rosa Brooks: The Problem Is the Constitution Which Enslaves Us," *Res Ipsa Loquitur*, July 6, 2022, https://jonathanturley.org/2022/07/06/georgetown-law-professor-rosa-brooks-the-problem-is-the-constitution-which-enslaves-us/.

190 *"reclaim America from Constitutionalism"*: Jonathan Turley, "'Reclaim America from Constitutionalism.'"

191 *opposing views on the Constitution*: Jonathan Turley, "Georgetown Professor Denounces 'Lawless' and 'Actively Rogue' Justices, Lawyers, and Law Professors," *Res Ipsa Loquitur*, July 12, 2022, https://jonathanturley.org/2022/07/12/georgetown-professor-denounces-as-lawless-and-actively-rogue-justices-lawyers-and-law-professors/.

191 *"with and on behalf of law"*: Turley, "Georgetown Professor Denounces."

191 *too "aggressively individualistic"*: Jonathan Turley, "'Aggressively Individualistic': Miami Law Professor Proposes a 'Redo' of the First and Second Amendments," *Res Ipsa Loquitur*, December 20, 2021, https://jonathanturley.org/2021/12/20/aggressively-individualistic-miami-law-professor-proposes-a-redo-of-the-first-and-second-amendments/.

191 *"the attention of listeners"*: Tim Wu, "Is the First Amendment Obsolete?," Emerging Threats, The Knight First Amendment Institute at Columbia University, September 1, 2017, https://knightcolumbia.org/content/tim-wu-first-amendment-obsolete.

191 The New York Times *ran a column by Wu*: Tim Wu, "The First Amendment Is Out of Control," Opinion, *New York Times*, July 2, 2024, https://www.nytimes.com/2024/07/02/opinion/supreme-court-netchoice-free-speech.html.

191 *"now mostly protects corporate interests"*: Wu, "The First Amendment Is Out of Control."

192 *sweeping social reforms and greater wealth distribution*: Aziz Rana, *The Constitutional Bind: How Americans Came to Idolize a Document That Fails Them* (University of Chicago Press, 2024).

192 *"only intensified them"*: Daniel Steinmetz-Jenkins, "Aziz Rana Wants Us to Stop Worshipping the Constitution," *The Nation*, June 3, 2024, https://www.thenation.com/article/society/qa-aziz-rana/.

192 *"constitutions are often rules for governing"*: Steinmetz-Jenkins, "Aziz Rana."

193 *"before cold altars"*: Roberto Mangabeira Unger, *The Critical Legal Studies Movement: Another Time, A Greater Task* (Verso Books, 2015), 210.

194 *only two or three such faculty left*: Turley, *The Indispensable Right*, 306–307.

194 *identified as "very conservative"*: Jonathan Turley, "The Crimson Tide: Harvard Faculty Virtually Eliminated Conservative Faculty," *Res Ipsa Loquitur*, September 23, 2024, https://jonathanturley.org/2022/09/23/crimson-tide-harvard-faculty-has-virtually-eliminated-conservative-professors-but-apparently-that-is-not-a-problem/.

194 *relic from a prior age*: Jonathan Turley, "The Crimson Tide."

194 *the loss of intellectual diversity on campus*: Jonathan Turley, "The Crimson Tide."

194 *greater diversity is "downright reductive"*: Jonathan Turley, "The Crimson Tide."

194 *to debate professor Randall Kennedy at Harvard Law School*: Jonathan Turley, "The Harvard Debate: Professors Kennedy and Turley Debate Free Speech," *Res Ipsa Loquitur*, October 17, 2024, https://jonathanturley.org/2024/10/17/224418/.

195 *the massacre of Jews by Hamas terrorists*: Jonathan Turley, "The 'Exhilaration' of Massacre: Russell Rickford and the Radical Chic of Higher Education," *Res Ipsa Loquitur*, October 18, 2023, https://jonathanturley.org/2023/10/18/the-exhilaration-of-massacre-russell-rickford-and-the-radical-chic-of-academia/.

195 *"the Supreme Court's air conditioning budget"*: Rob Wolfe, "How to Fix the Supreme Court," *Washington Monthly*, January 16, 2024, https://washingtonmonthly.com/2024/01/16/how-to-fix-the-supreme-court/.

195 *"they should be completely normalized"*: Wolfe, "How to Fix the Supreme Court."

195 *"the mob is right"*: Jonathan Turley, "'When the Mob Is Right': Georgetown Law Professor Josh Chafetz Supports 'Aggressive' Protests at the Homes of Justices," *Res Ipsa Loquitur*, May 11, 2022, https://jonathanturley.org/2022/05/11/the-mob-is-right-georgetown-law-professor-calls-supports-aggressive-protests-at-the-homes-of-justices/.

196 *young children being inside*: Jonathan Turley, "Poetic License: How Press and Pundits Are Reframing Personalities to Fit Our Politics," *Res Ipsa Loquitur*, August 26, 2024, https://jonathanturley.org/2024/08/26/poetic-license-how-press-and-pundits-are-reframing-personalities-to-fit-our-politics/.

197 *"not in our stars, But in ourselves"*: Jonathan Turley, "The Left's Assault on the Constitution," Opinion, *Wall Street Journal*, September 12, 2024, https://www.wsj.com/opinion/the-lefts-assault-on-the-constitution-pack-the-court-attack-free-speech-kamala-harris-47a78eda?reflink=desktopwebshare_permalink.

THE PRESS

200 *out of receivership*: Elmer Holmes Davis, *History of the New York Times, 1851–1921* (New York Times, 1921), 185–86.

200 *the interests of social and racial justice*: Jonathan Turley, "'Leave Neutrality Behind': University of Texas at Austin Initiative Embraces Advocacy Journalism," *Res Ipsa Loquitur*, August 18, 2023, https://jonathanturley.org/2023/08/18/leave-neutrality-behind-university-of-texas-at-austin-initiative-embraces-advocacy-journalism/.

201 *widespread support for advocacy journalism*: Turley, *The Indispensable Right*, 242.

202 *the "racist" lab theory*: Jonathan Turley, "Silence of the Labs: How a Censorship Campaign Failed to Kill a COVID Origin Theory," *Res Ipsa Loquitur*, December 30, 2024, https://jonathanturley.org/2024/12/30/silence-of-the-labs-how-a-censorship-campaign-failed-to-kill-a-covid-origin-theory/.

202 *the story was unreliable*: Jonathan Turley, "America's State Media: The Blackout on Biden's Corruption Is Truly 'Pulitzer-Level Stuff,'" *Res Ipsa Loquitur*, May 15, 2023, https://jonathanturley.org/2023/05/15/americas-state-media-the-blackout-on-biden-corruption-is-truly-pulitzer-level-stuff/.

203 *the political and media establishment*: Jonathan Turley, "Yankee Doodling the Media: How 'Let's Go, Brandon' Became a Rallying Cry Against News Bias," *Res Ipsa Loquitur*, November 5, 2021, https://jonathanturley.org/2021/11/05/yankee-doodling-the-media-how-lets-go-brandon-became-a-rallying-cry-against-news-bias/.

204 *"I can't sugarcoat it anymore"*: Jonathan Turley, "'Let's Not Sugarcoat It . . . People are Not Reading Your Stuff': Publisher Drops Truth Bomb at *Post*," *Res Ipsa Loquitur*, June 4, 2024, https://jonathanturley.org/2024/06/04/lets-not-sugarcoat-it-people-are-not-reading-your-stuff-post-reporters-outraged-after-publisher-drops-truth-bomb/.

204 *"four White men running three newsrooms"*: Jonathan Turley, "Post Editor to Staff: Get on Board or Get Out," *Res Ipsa Loquitur*, July 12, 2025, https://jonathanturley.org/2025/07/12/washington-post-editor-to-staff-time-to-get-on-board-or-get-out/.

204 *"white male billionaire's self-interested agenda"*: Turley, "Post Editor to Staff."

9. WHY BIG, FIERCE RIGHTS ARE RARE: THE IMPORTANCE OF "RIGHTS TALK" IN CONFUSING TIMES

206 Why Big Fierce Animals Are Rare: Paul Colinvaux, *Why Big Fierce Animals Are Rare: An Ecologist's Perspective* (Princeton University Press, 1979).

208 *warning about such trade-offs*: "Ben Franklin's Famous 'Liberty, Safety' Quote Lost Its Context in Twenty-First Century," *All Things Considered*, National Public Radio, March 2, 2015, https://www.npr.org/2015/03/02/390245038/ben-franklins-famous-liberty-safety-quote-lost-its-context-in-21st-century.

209 *"charters and laws by Parliament"*: Benjamin Franklin, *Correspondence and Miscellaneous Writings, 1775–1779* (G. P. Putnam's Son, 1904), 58.

209 *"convert the constitutional Bill of Rights into a suicide pact"*: Terminiello v. Chicago, 337 U.S. 1, 37 (1949) (Jackson, J., dissenting).

210 *"trashing" the Constitution*: Turley, "America's Crisis of Faith."

210 *overthrowing the constitutional order*: Benjamin Lynch, "Jack Posobiec Hails 'End of Democracy' at CPAC," *Newsweek*, February 23, 2024.

210 *"rights talk"*: Mary Ann Glendon, *Rights Talk: The Impoverishment of Political Discourse* (The Free Press, 1991).

210 *fluid collective interests and responsibilities*: Glendon, *Rights Talk*, 44–45.

210 *"mere assertion over reason-giving"*: Glendon, *Rights Talk*, 14.

211 *"Rights are the commandments of our civic religion"*: Jamal Greene, *How Rights Went Wrong: Why Our Obsession with Rights Is Tearing America Apart* (Houghton Mifflin Harcourt, 2021).

211 *"No peace, no justice"*: Jill Lepore, foreword to *How Rights Went Wrong: Why Our Obsession with Rights Is Tearing America Apart*, by Jamal Greene.

212 *the "cult of the Constitution"*: Mary Anne Franks, *The Cult of the Constitution*, 105.

212 *state controls over speech as well as guns*: Turley, "'Aggressively Individualistic.'"

213 *"any religious belief or practice"*: Mary Anne Franks, "Redo the First Two Amendments," *Boston Globe*, December 1, 2021, https://apps.bostonglobe.com/ideas/graphics/2021/12/editing-the-constitution/redo-the-first-two-amendments.

213 *"responsibility for abuses"*: Franks, "Redo the First Two Amendments."

213 *to be fully human*: Turley, *The Indispensable Right*, 25–31.

213 *speak freely on the internet*: Brian Leiter, "Free Speech on the Internet: The Crisis of Epistemic Authority," *Daedalus* 153, no. 3 (Summer 2024): 91–104, https://doi.org/10.1162/daed_a_02091.

215 *refusing to censor more users on X*: Jonathan Turley, "Robert Reich Calls for the Arrest of Elon Musk for Resisting Censorship," *Res Ipsa Loquitur*, September 2, 2024, https://jonathanturley.org/2024/09/02/robert-reich-calls-for-the-arrest-of-elon-musk-for-resisting-censorship/.

215 *harmful, even lead to tyranny*: Jonathan Turley, "Freedom Is Tyranny: Robert Reich Goes Full Orwellian in Anti–Free Speech Screed," *Res Ipsa Loquitur*, April 13, 2022, https://jonathanturley.org/2022/04/13/187265/.

215 *demands for political censorship*: Greg Norman, "Tim Walz's AG Appears to Celebrate Brazil X Ban, Leading Musk to Say Dems Want to 'Destroy' First Amendment," Fox Business, September 3, 2024, https://www.foxbusiness.com/politics/tim-walzs-ag-appears-celebrate-brazil-x-ban-leading-musk-say-dems-want-destroy-first-amendment.

215 *national laws and countervailing "public interest"*: Turley, "Robert Reich Calls for the Arrest."

217 *retail grocery stores in the prior year*: Aswath Damodaran, "Margins by Sector (US)," Damodaran Online, NYU Stern, updated January 2025, https://pages.stern.nyu.edu/~adamodar/New_Home_Page/datafile/margin.html?nofollow=true.

217 *fallen significantly during that period*: Jason Miller and Ron Gordon, "Supermarket Chains Are Not Price Gouging," Sam M. Walton College of Business, January 3, 2022, https://walton.uark.edu/initiatives/supply-chain-research/posts/supermarket-chains-are-not-price-gouging.php.

217 *0.217 percent margin for Kroger's supermarkets*: Miller and Gordon, "Supermarket Chains Are Not Price Gouging."

218 *"form follows function"*: Jonathan Turley, "Madisonian Tectonics," 305.

218 *"structure only if necessary"*: Chris Chambers Goodman, "Constitutional Revolution: A Path Toward Equitable Representation," *Maryland Law Review* 81, no. 1 (2022): 366, 368.

218 *"render the Constitution too mutable"*: James Madison, Federalist 43, *The Federalist Papers*.

218 *just realign seats in a more equitable way*: Akhil Reed Amar, "Philadelphia Revisited: Amending the Constitution Outside Article V," *University of Chicago Law Review* 55, no. 4 (1988) 1043, 1071n98.

218 *"it scares me a little too"*: Amar, "Philadelphia Revisited," 1044.

218 *"not expressly provided for by Article V"*: Amar, "Philadelphia Revisited," 1044.

219 *their approach "Democratic Constitutionalism"*: Robert Post and Reva Siegel, "*Roe* Rage: Democratic Constitutionalism and Backlash," *Harvard Civil Rights–Civil Liberties Law Review* 42, no. 2 (2007): 373.

220 *"widely held public opinion"*: Elizabeth Warren, "Expand the Supreme Court," Opinion, *Boston Globe*, December 15, 2021, https://www.bostonglobe.com/2021/12/15/opinion/expand-supreme-court/.

220 *minority political interests*: Jonathan Turley, "Destroying the Supreme Court to Save It: Warren Calls for Packing the Supreme Court with a Liberal Majority," *Res Ipsa Loquitur*, December 16, 2021, https://jonathanturley.org/2021/12/16/destroying-the-court-to-save-it-warren-calls-for-packing-the-supreme-court-with-a-liberal-majority/.

220 *"will never win another election"*: Liz Mineo, "Do Justices Really Set Aside Personal Beliefs? Nope, Legal Scholar Says," *Harvard Gazette*, October 15, 2020, https://news.harvard.edu/gazette/story/2020/10/legal-scholar-warns-of-potential-supreme-court-changes/.

221 *flip control of the House of Representatives*: Martha McHardy, "What Susan Crawford's Wisconsin Means for Democrats," *Newsweek*, April 3, 2025, https://www.newsweek.com/wisconsin-supreme-court-race-democrats-susan-crawford-2054064.

222 *dangerous and destabilizing for our system*: Jonathan Turley, "No, The House Should Not Impeach Judge Boasberg," *Res Ipsa Loquitur*, March 16, 2025, https://jonathanturley.org/2025/03/16/no-the-house-should-not-impeach-judge-boasberg-over-his-tren-de-aragua-tro/.

223 *"under one word—Democracy"*: Patrick LaPierre, "The Disenchantment of American Liberalism: European Social Theory and the Travails of Mass Democracy, 1945–1962," (PhD diss., University of Rochester, 2007), 35, http://hdl.handle.net/1802/5882.

224 *"destructive of human happiness"*: Thompson, *America's Revolutionary Mind*, 281.
225 *"not by the way one breeds"*: Colinvaux, *Why Big Fierce Animals Are Rare*, 25.
225 *the availability of professorships*: Colinvaux, *Why Big Fierce Animals Are Rare*, 25.
225 *they must consume to survive*: Colinvaux, *Why Big Fierce Animals Are Rare*, 25.
225 *"the safety and privacy of its citizens"*: Colinvaux, *Why Big Fierce Animals Are Rare*, 25.
225 *the very personification of this "indispensable right"*: Turley, *The Indispensable Right*, 69.
226 *"never intended to be disaffected"*: Thomas Paine, *Collected Writings*, ed. Eric Foner (Library of America, 1995), 394.
226 *"shall it be preserved by an exceptional act?"*: Harmer, *Life of a Revolutionary*, 100.
226 *"the right of every man"*: Stephen A. Smith, *Freedom of Expression: Foundational Documents and Historical Arguments* (Oxbridge Research Associates, 2018), 86.
227 *Paine's writing could be banned as seditious*: Benner, *Thomas Paine*, 213.

10. ADAM SMITH AND THE LIBERTY-ENHANCING ECONOMY

229 *first and foremost able to pursue that freedom*: Bernard H. Siegan, *Economic Liberties and the Constitution* (Routledge, 2017), 59–87.
229 *price controls, monopolies, and market controls during the French Revolution*: Harmer, *Life of a Revolutionary*, 88.
229 *triggered rebellions in the United States after the Revolution*: Turley, *The Indispensable Right*, 80–104.
229 *the fate of being "overrun, ravaged, and ruined"*: Benner, *Thomas Paine*, 133.
229 *"the vast advantage of an open trade"*: Benner, *Thomas Paine*, 113.
229 *liberty and property was expressly drawn*: Barnett, *Our Republican Constitution*, 33.
230 *adopted in the Declaration of Rights*: Barnett, *Our Republican Constitution*, 39.
230 *Edmund Burke should read* The Wealth of Nations: Benner, *Thomas Paine*, 190.

ECONOMIC ENLIGHTENMENT AND THE AMERICAN REVOLUTION

231 *reasoned principles guided economies*: Athol Fitzgibbons, *Adam Smith's System of Liberty, Wealth, and Virtue: The Moral and Political Foundations of* The Wealth of Nations (Clarendon Press, 1995), 5.
231 *the "Newton of his subject"*: Fitzgibbons, *Adam Smith's System of Liberty*, 127.
231 *"lay down certain principles known or proved in the beginning"*: Fitzgibbons, *Adam Smith's System of Liberty*, 5.
231 *not open to such new concepts*: Fitzgibbons, *Adam Smith's System of Liberty*, 13.
231 *economic system on assumptions of virtue*: Fitzgibbons, *Adam Smith's System of Liberty*, 46.
232 *"a property in his rights"*: Thompson, *America's Revolutionary Mind*, 196.
232 *property within the "trinity of rights"*: Thompson, *America's Revolutionary Mind*, 195.
232 *"the means of production"*: Andrew Petter, *The Politics of the Charter: The Illusive Promise of Constitutional Rights* (University of Toronto Press, 2010), 84.
232 *the natural liberty of mankind*: Thompson, *America's Revolutionary Mind*, 199.

233 *"writer of reputation upon the subject"*: Thompson, *America's Revolutionary Mind*, 199.

233 *"a person has to a thing"*: Thompson, *America's Revolutionary Mind*, 195.

233 *no functioning banking system in the United States*: Roy C. Smith, introduction to *Adam Smith and the Origins of American Enterprise: How the Founding Fathers Turned to a Great Economist's Writings and Created the American Economy* (St. Martin's Griffin, 2004), ix.

233 *its foundations in feudal times*: Smith, *Adam Smith and the Origins of American Enterprise*, 7.

234 *"obliged to be oppressive and tyrannical"*: Ian Simpson Ross, *The Life of Adam Smith* (Oxford University Press, 2010), 106.

234 *a catalyst for the American Revolution*: Smith, *Adam Smith and the Origins of American Enterprise*, 18–19.

235 *"the social and religious power structure"*: Fitzgibbons, *Adam Smith's System of Liberty*, 70.

235 *"the futile interests of our merchants and manufacturers"*: Fitzgibbons, *Adam Smith's System of Liberty*, 174.

235 *manufacturing goods and developing its own markets*: Smith, *Adam Smith and the Origins of American Enterprise*, 30.

235 *government favoritism and protectionism*: Smith, *Adam Smith and the Origins of American Enterprise*, 32.

235 *barring imports from other countries*: Smith, *Adam Smith and the Origins of American Enterprise*, 35–36.

236 *dependent on British imports*: Smith, *Adam Smith and the Origins of American Enterprise*, 37.

236 *$12 billion today*: Smith, *Adam Smith and the Origins of American Enterprise*, 91.

236 *the British wanted to collect in taxes*: Smith, *Adam Smith and the Origins of American Enterprise*, 91.

236 *$1.3 billion today*: Smith, *Adam Smith and the Origins of American Enterprise*, 75.

236 *full and close trade relations with its mother country*: Smith, *Adam Smith and the Origins of American Enterprise*, 98.

236 *the crippling debt left in the aftermath of the Revolution*: Smith, *Adam Smith and the Origins of American Enterprise*, 115, 119.

236 *largely open to all citizens*: Smith, *Adam Smith and the Origins of American Enterprise*, 145.

236 *three hundred corporations were chartered*: Smith, *Adam Smith and the Origins of American Enterprise*, 159.

237 *second-greatest number were insurance companies*: Smith, *Adam Smith and the Origins of American Enterprise*, 159.

237 *By 1860, there were over 1,500*: Smith, *Adam Smith and the Origins of American Enterprise*, 160.

237 *"followed anyone else's policies except Hamilton's"*: Smith, *Adam Smith and the Origins of American Enterprise*, 160

ECONOMIC FACTIONALISM AND POLITICAL COLLECTIVISM

239 *roughly 35 percent of the household wealth*: Juliet Chung, "$1 Trillion of Wealth Was Created for the 19 Richest U.S. Households Last Year," *Wall Street Journal*, April 23, 2025, https://www.wsj.com/economy/1-trillion-richest-families-wealth-increase-bc13874a.

239 *just the nineteen wealthiest households in the United States*: Chung, "$1 Trillion of Wealth Was Created."

239 *controlling over 80 percent of the global wealth*: Tom Corley, "The 1 Percent Will Always Control the Wealth—and Here's How They Do It," CNBC, May 11, 2018, https://www.cnbc.com/2018/05/10/tom-corley-the-1-percent-will-always-control-the-wealth-heres-why.html.

240 *down from 60 percent in 1982*: Vanessa Sumo, "Most Billionaires are Self-Made, Not Heirs," *Chicago Booth Review*, August 22, 2014, https://www.chicagobooth.edu/review/billionaires-self-made.

240 *79 percent of millionaires were self-made*: Jeannine Mancini, "79% Of Millionaires Are Self-Made—Lessons from Those Who Built Wealth Without Inheritance," Yahoo Finance, May 8, 2023, https://finance.yahoo.com/news/79-millionaires-self-made-lessons-160025947.html.

240 *controlling laws or tax rules*: Ariel Zilber, "Elon Musk Blasts Robert Reich as 'Idiot, Liar' for Saying Self-Made Billionaires Are a 'Myth,'" *New York Post*, September 22, 2022, https://nypost.com/2022/09/21/elon-musk-blasts-idiot-and-liar-ex-clinton-labor-secretary-robert-reich/.

240 *74 percent for millennials*: Rainer Zitelmann, "If 70-80 Percent of the Rich are Self-Made—What About the Mass of 'Ordinary' Millionaires?," *International Business Times*, March 21, 2023, https://www.ibtimes.co.uk/if-7080-per-cent-rich-are-self-made-what-about-mass-ordinary-millionaires-1714394.

240 *democratic socialist agenda*: Andrew Mark Miller, "Absolutely a Communist": Mamdani Dodges Label, but His Record and Expert Say Otherwise," *Fox News*, October 6, 2025, https://www.foxnews.com/politics/absolutely-communist-mamdani-dodges-label-his-record-expert-say-otherwise.

240 *socialism is more popular than capitalism*: Noah Bressner and Mike Allen, "Jarring Generation Gap: America Is Divided on Values, Economics, Polices," Axios, May 21, 2024, https://www.axios.com/2024/05/21/us-generation-polls-economy-middle-east-politics.

240 *favor socialism over capitalism*: Jason Clemens and Steven Globerman, "New Poll Finds Strong Support for Socialism in the U.K.," Fraser Institute, March 23, 2023, https://www.fraserinstitute.org/commentary/new-poll-finds-strong-support-socialism-uk.

240 *"specifically a capitalist problem"*: Owen Jones, "Eat the Rich! Why Millennials and Generation Z Turned Their Backs on Capitalism," *Guardian*, September 20, 2021, https://www.theguardian.com/politics/2021/sep/20/eat-the-rich-why-millennials-and-generation-z-have-turned-their-backs-on-capitalism.

240 *67 percent want to live under a socialist economic system*: Jones, "Eat the Rich!"

241 *sweeping legal and economic changes*: Jonathan Turley, "Selling the Rope to Hang By: Clothing Giant Lululemon Launches Campaign to Resist Capitalism," *Res Ipsa Loquitur*, September 11, 2020, https://jonathanturley.org/2020/09/11/selling-the-rope-to-hang-by-clothing-giant-lululemon-launches-campaign-to-resist-capitalism/.

241 *"a colonized binary system of gender"*: Turley, "Selling the Rope to Hang By."

241 *Patrisse Cullors, to guide it on programming*: Jonathan Turley, "A 'Tragedy of Capitalism'? BLM Faces Growing Questions Over Millions in Donations," *Res Ipsa Loquitur*, February 23, 2022, https://jonathanturley.org/2022/02/23/the-tragedy-of-capitalism-blm-faces-growing-questions-over-millions-in-donations/.

241 *"We are super versed on, sort of, ideological theories"*: Turley, "A 'Tragedy of Capitalism'?"

242 *"the city's first oligarchic revolution"*: Samons, *What's Wrong with Democracy*, 90.

242 *the power for individual whim or advancement*: Samons, *What's Wrong with Democracy*, 93.

242 *the latter's support for free trade*: Hanson, *The Jacobin Republic Under Fire*, 48.

242 *in late February and early March 1791*: Hanson, *The Jacobin Republic Under Fire*, 48.

242 *"dedicated to humanity and to public education"*: Hanson, *The Jacobin Republic Under Fire*, 193.

242 *"there are no longer corporations in the State"*: Hanson, *The Jacobin Republic Under Fire*, 193.

243 *"the public interest by a spirit of corporation"*: Sagan, *Citizens and Cannibals*, 193–94.

243 *radicals turned to even more extreme philosophies*: Mason, *The Last Revolutionaries*.

243 *one of his greatest inspirations*: Mason, *The Last Revolutionaries*, 4.

244 *a universal basic income (UBI) for citizens*: Robert E. Wright and Aleksandra Przegalińska, *Debating Universal Basic Income: Pros, Cons, and Alternatives* (Palgrave Macmillan, 2022), 13.

245 *national debt will exceed $50 trillion by 2034*: Jacob Bogage, "National Debt Will Exceed $50 Trillion by 2034, Budget Watchdog Estimates," *Washington Post*, June 18, 2024, https://www.washingtonpost.com/business/2024/06/18/national-debt-budget-projections-cbo/.

245 *"high set in the aftermath of World War II"*: Bogage, "National Debt."

245 *still over $10,000*: Kimberly Adams, "Credit Card Delinquencies Are Up Year-Over-Year," *Marketplace*, June 19, 2024, https://www.marketplace.org/story/2024/06/19/credit-card-delinquencies-are-up-year-over-year-but-thats-not-the-whole-story.

245 *less than $1,000*: Jamela Adams, "American Savings by Generation: How Balances and Goals Vary by Age," *Forbes*, August 15, 2024, https://www.forbes.com/advisor/banking/savings/average-american-savings/.

245 *medical or another sudden problem*: Lorie Konish, "44% of Americans Can't Pay an Unexpected $1,000 Expense from Savings," CNBC, January 24, 2024, https://cnb.cx/3u80EUo.

245 *only 2.8 percent of the wealth*: Shehryar Nabi, "Charts That Explain Wealth Inequality in the United States," Aspen Institute, October 19, 2022, https://www.aspeninstitute.org/blog-posts/charts-that-explain-wealth-inequality-in-the-united-states/.

245 *all classes except for the top 20 percent*: Nabi, "Charts That Explain Wealth Inequality."

246 *the same constitutional barriers*: For example, see Jonathan Turley, "Bye and Bye: Washington Moves Toward a 'Wealth Tax' as the Wealthy Move to Leave the State," *Res Ipsa Loquitur*, December 22, 2024, https://jonathanturley.org/2024/12/22/bye-and-bye-washington-state-moves-to-toward-wealth-tax/.

248 *known to proclaim "F*** Capitalism"*: Hannah Grossman, "'F—king Angry' Marxist Teacher Calls for Urgent War Against Capitalism: 'Revolutions Involve Violence,'" Fox News, March 13, 2023, https://www.foxnews.com/media/maryland-teacher-calls-urgent-war-capitalism-revolutions-involve-violence.

248 *"money wouldn't be worth anything. Capitalism must go"*: Grossman, "'F—king Angry' Marxist Teacher."

248 *a rising number of Marxists and socialists*: Maxim Lott, "Socialism Rising: Universities and 'Radical' Profs Helping Steer Leftward Shift in Politics, Critics Say," Fox News, January 18, 2019, https://www.foxnews.com/politics/socialism-rising-universities-and-radical-profs-helping-steer-leftward-shift-in-politics.

248 *18 percent in social science departments*: Neil Gross and Solon Simmons, "The Social and Political Views of American Professors," Working Paper (2007), 40–41, https://www.researchgate.net/publication/228380360_The_Social_and_Political_Views_of_American_Professors/citation/download.

248 *increasingly identifying with socialism*: Rainer Zitelmann, "Anti-Capitalism on U.S. University Campuses: 'The Culture War Is Fought Dirty,'" *Forbes*, February 16, 2020, https://www.forbes.com/sites/rainerzitelmann/2020/02/16/anti-capitalism-on-us-university-campuses-the-culture-war-is-fought-dirty/. For further discussion, see "Gen Z Flirts with Socialism," Future View, *Wall Street Journal*, December 5, 2023, https://www.wsj.com/opinion/gen-z-flirts-with-socialism-economics-politics-generational-divide-3aa89ad7?reflink=desktopwebshare_permalink.

248 *"Marxist ideology in your papers, you will pass"*: Lott, "Socialism Rising."

248 *private property ownership is harmful for society*: Sean Salai, "U.S. Adults Increasingly Accept Marxist Views, Poll Shows," *Washington Times*, October 6, 2021, https://www.washingtontimes.com/news/2021/oct/6/us-adults-increasingly-accept-marxist-views-poll/.

248 *Sales of* The Communist Manifesto *and* Das Kapital *have surged*: Stuart Jeffries, "Why Marxism in on the Rise Again," *Guardian*, July 4, 2012, https://www.theguardian.com/world/2012/jul/04/the-return-of-marxism.

248 *the withering away of the state*: Jeffries, "Why Marxism Is on the Rise Again."

248 *42 percent want a return to socialism*: Jeffries, "Why Marxism Is on the Rise Again."

249 *"own excesses and confronts decline"*: Richard D. Wolff, preface to *Understanding Marxism* (Democracy at Work, 2021).

249 *"grotesque social inequalities and cutthroat economic competition"*: Terry Eagleton, *Why Marx Was Right* (Yale University Press, 2018), 89.

249 *a relatively small nation*: Johan Norberg, *The Mirage of Swedish Socialism: The Economic History of a Welfare State* (Fraser Institute 2023), https://www.fraserin

stitute.org/sites/default/files/mirage-of-swedish-socialism-economic-history-of-welfare-state.pdf

249 *a feature of other Scandinavian countries*: Daniel Bunn et al., "Insights into the Tax Systems of Scandinavian Countries," Tax Foundation, April 20, 2023, https://taxfoundation.org/blog/scandinavian-social-programs-taxes-2023/.

249 *one of the least progressive in Europe*: Norberg, *The Mirage of Swedish Socialism*, 2.

250 *the work took deep roots in Sweden*: Norberg, *The Mirage of Swedish Socialism*, 7.

250 *the third freest economy in the developed world*: Norberg, *The Mirage of Swedish Socialism*, 18.

250 *public welfare systems*: Bunn et al., "Insights into the Tax Systems."

250 "*It just didn't work*": David Schatz, "Bernie Sanders is Wrong on Democratic Socialism in Sweden, and Everywhere Else," NBC News, March 15, 2020, https://www.nbcnews.com/think/opinion/bernie-sanders-wrong-democratic-socialism-sweden-everywhere-else-ncna1158636.

250 *the common misunderstanding of Scandinavian policies*: Magne Mogstad et al., "Income Equality in the Nordic Countries: Myths, Facts, and Lessons," Working Paper No. 33444 (National Bureau of Economic Research, February 2025), https://doi.org/10.3386/w33444.

251 *"one of the most unequal distributions of wealth in the world today"*: Simon Torracinta, "Can Social Democracy Win Again," *Boston Review*, September 30, 2024, https://www.bostonreview.net/articles/can-social-democracy-win-again/; Kjell Östberg, *The Rise and Fall of Swedish Social Democracy* (Verso, 2024).

251 *"new VAT and higher social security contributions"*: Bunn et al., "Insights into the Tax Systems."

252 "*no possibility of becoming the majority*": Sagan, *Citizens and Cannibals*, 144.

252 "*illogical, unjustifiable and immoral*": Sagan, *Citizens and Cannibals*, 437 (quoting historian *Norman Hampson).*

THE LIBERTY-ENHANCING ECONOMY

253 *"people of fundamentally differing views"*: Poul F. Kjaer, ed., *The Law of Political Economy: Transformation in the Function of Law* (Cambridge University Press, 2020), 44.

253 *"a necessary condition for political freedom"*: David A. Reisman, *Democracy and Exchange: Schumpeter, Galbraith, T. H. Marshall, Titmuss and Adam Smith* (Edward Elgar Publishing, Incorporated, 2005), 99.

253 *"the benevolence of his fellow citizens"*: Fitzgibbons, *Adam Smith's System of Liberty*, 169.

254 *temper political discourse in society*: Kloppenberg, *Toward Democracy*, 446–47.

254 *"the ways of men are gentle"*: David L. Norton, *Democracy and Moral Development: A Politics of Virtue* (University of California Press, 1995), 33.

254 *the establishment of an aristocracy*: Kloppenberg, *Toward Democracy*, 446–47.

254 *"shaped by the hands of man"*: Kloppenberg, *Toward Democracy*, 217.

254 *Republicans favored market principles*: Diestelow, "The Fort Wilson Riot," 2.

254 *"the Republic should have preferred status"*: Palmer, *Twelve Who Ruled*, 225.
254 *France would push toward communism*: Mason, *The Last Revolutionaries*, 13.
255 *greater market forces*: Palmer, *Twelve Who Ruled*, 227.
255 *laws against hoarding*: Palmer, *Twelve Who Ruled*, 243.
255 *people executed under the law*: Palmer, *Twelve Who Ruled*, 244.
255 *with the price controls*: Palmer, *Twelve Who Ruled*, 244.
255 *in defiance of state controls*: Palmer, *Twelve Who Ruled*, 249.
255 *"irritating and inflaming most of the people"*: Palmer, *Twelve Who Ruled*, 252.
255 *take advantage of the chaos*: Palmer, *Twelve Who Ruled*, 253.
255 *"a minority many times subdivided"*: Palmer, *Twelve Who Ruled*, 255.
255 *could be bought or sold*: Palmer, *Twelve Who Ruled*, 227.
255 *the start of the Revolution*: Palmer, *Twelve Who Ruled*, 232.
255 *"to be exchanged for foreign copper, wool, wheat, and horses"*: Palmer, *Twelve Who Ruled*, 233.
256 *massive royal pensions*: Benner, *Thomas Paine*, 170.
256 *as an alternative to taxes*: Benner, *Thomas Paine*, 170.
256 *under opposition from aristocrats*: Benner, *Thomas Paine*, 170.
256 *the confiscation of church property*: Harmer, *Life of a Revolutionary*, 66.
256 *"seemed suddenly up for grabs"*: Mason, *The Last Revolutionaries*, 21.
256 *Bonaparte was brought to power*: Benner, *Thomas Paine*, 2.
256 *incompatible with democratic values*: Friedrich August Hayek, *The Road to Serfdom*, 2nd ed. (Routledge, 2001), 74.
256 *both libertarians and conservatives*: For example, see Mark R. Levin, *Liberty and Tyranny: A Conservative Manifesto* (Threshold Editions, 2010), 91.
257 *"it must become an arbitrary power"*: Hayek, *The Road to Serfdom*, 74.
257 *"extends itself to the lowest ranks of people"*: Fitzgibbons, *Adam Smith's System of Liberty*, 166–67.
257 *"their self-love"*: Adam Smith, *An Inquiry into the Nature and Causes of the Wealth of Nations* (Cosimo, Incorporated, 2010), 20.
257 *his work* The Theory of Moral Sentiments: Fitzgibbons, *Adam Smith's System of Liberty*, 90.
257 *large tracts of land to lie idle and unused*: Fitzgibbons, *Adam Smith's System of Liberty*, 102.
257 *produced from his land and animals*: Fitzgibbons, *Adam Smith's System of Liberty*, 101.
258 *"cause and apprehension of riots and tumults"*: Harmer, *Life of a Revolutionary*, 81.
258 *lodging and meals to work on public projects*: Benner, *Thomas Paine*, 123.
258 *"relieve a great deal of instant distress"*: Benner, *Thomas Paine*, 123.
258 *less relevant as robots replace workers*: Qing-Ping Ma, *Economics and Politics in the Robotic Age: The Future of Human Society* (Cambridge Scholars Publishing, 2024), 259.
258 *making inroads into the service industry*: Ma, *Economics and Politics*, 259.

258 *"called the zero-worker point"*: Ma, *Economics and Politics*, 259–60.

258 *operating without the need of lights or people*: Ma, *Economics and Politics*, 268.

259 *"in a moment crumble into atoms"*: Christopher Berry, *Social Theory of the Scottish Enlightenment* (Edinburgh University Press, 2020), 130.

259 *"the greatest and most effectual encouragement to every sort of industry"*: Fitzgibbons, *Adam Smith's System of Liberty*, 173.

260 *"chosen to have his actions immortalized on tape"*: Kurt Vonnegut Jr., *Player Piano* (Holt, Rinehart and Winston, 1966), 9–10.

260 *80 percent of all jobs from healthcare to sales to agriculture to manufacturing*: Vinod Khosla, "AI: Dystopia or Utopia," Khosla Ventures, September 20, 2024, https://www.khoslaventures.com/ai-dystopia-or-utopia/.

260 *20 percent in the next five years*: Jim Vandehei and Mike Allen, "Behind the Curtain: A White-Collar Bloodbath," Axios, May 28, 2025, https://www.axios.com/2025/05/28/ai-jobs-white-collar-unemployment-anthropic.

260 *positions like software engineers*: Kevin Okemwa, "OpenAI's Sam Altman Claims AI Will 'Gradually' Replace Software Engineers," MSN, March 24, 2025, https://www.msn.com/en-us/news/technology/openai-s-sam-altman-claims-ai-will-gradually-replace-software-engineers-creating-an-urgent-need-to-master-ai-tools/ar-AA1BxOPg.

261 *eliminated by robotic delivery systems*: Michael Sainato, "14-Hour Days and No Bathroom Breaks: Amazon Overworked Delivery Drivers," *Guardian*, March 11, 2021, https://www.theguardian.com/technology/2021/mar/11/amazon-delivery-drivers-bathroom-breaks-unions.

261 *robots with cognitive capability to work autonomously*: Dan Robinson, "Al-Driven 20-ft Robots Coming for Construction Workers' Jobs," *Register*, April 26, 2025, https://www.theregister.com/2025/04/26/aipowered_robots_construction/.

261 *prices for consumers*: "Midwest Mattress Chain HassleLess Mattress Introduces Employee-less Stores," McMillan Doolittle, April 13, 2022, https://www.mcmillandoolittle.com/midwest-mattress-chain-hassleless-mattress-introduces-employee-less-stores/.

261 *deportation of undocumented persons*: Jonathan Turley, "Your Latte and Lecture Is Ready: Starbucks Employees Pause Service to Protest Immigration Policies," *Res Ipsa Loquitur*, April 13, 2025, https://jonathanturley.org/2025/04/13/your-latte-and-lesson-is-ready-starbucks-employees-pause-service-to-protest-immigration-policies/.

261 *require them to wear uniforms*: Anthony Robledo, "Thousands of Starbucks Workers Walk Out in Protest of Uniform Policy," *Star Gazette*, May 16, 2025, https://www.stargazette.com/story/news/2025/05/16/thousands-of-starbucks-workers-walk-out-in-protest-of-uniform-policy/83669658007/.

261 *compliments customers on their beverage choices*: Alex Mitchell, "NYC Robot Barista Will Make You a Coffee in Minutes—But It Also Asks for a Tip," *New York Post*, March 19, 2024, https://nypost.com/2024/03/19/lifestyle/nyc-robot-barista-makes-you-coffee-but-it-also-demands-a-tip/#.

262 *21 percent reduction in workforce*: Rachel del Guidice, "Business Insider Embraces AI While Laying Off 21% of Workforce," Fox News, May 29, 2025, https://www.foxbusiness.com/media/business-insider-embraces-ai-while-laying-off-21-workforce.

262 *an AI-run government has occurred*: Anna Betts, "US Mayoral Candidate Who Pledged to Govern by Customized AI Bot Loses Race," *Guardian*, August 21, 2024, https://www.theguardian.com/us-news/article/2024/aug/21/wyoming-cheyenne-ai-bot-mayor.

262 *suicidal ideation and prior attempts*: Nadine Yousif, "Parents of Teenager Who Took His Own Life Sue OpenAI," BBC, August 26, 2025.

262 *interactions with ChatGPT*: Jonathan Turley, "OpenAI's Dark Side: ChatGPT Accused of Causing Suicide, Murder," *The Hill*, August 30, 2025, https://thehill.com/opinion/5478336-openais-dark-side-chatgpt-accused-of-causing-suicide-murder/.

263 *WebMD proved very popular*: Teddy Rosenbluth, "Dr. Chatbot Will See You Now," *New York Times*, September 11, 2024, https://www.nytimes.com/2024/09/11/health/chatbots-health-diagnosis-treatments.html.

263 *AI "doctor" was praised for being more accessible*: Daniel Akst, "I Finally Have a Physician Who's Available and Who Gets Me. Meet Dr. Grok," *Wall Street Journal*, October 29, 2025, https://www.wsj.com/health/wellness/ai-health-questions-chatbot-doctor-fa753c85.

263 *"multimodal conversational and visual assessment capabilities"*: Shreya Johri et al., "An Evaluation Framework for Clinical Use of Large Language Models in Patient Interaction Tasks," *Nature Medicine* 31, no. 1, (2025): 77–86, https://doi.org/10.1038/s41591-024-03328-5.

263 *a small dot on a mammogram*: M. A. Ansari et al., eds., *Artificial Intelligence in Biomedical and Modern Healthcare Informatics* (Academic Press, 2024), 383.

263 *absorbed by first-line jobs*: Xiaowen Wang et al., "How Artificial Intelligence Affects the Labour Force Employment Structure from the Perspective of Industrial Structure Optimisation," *Heliyon* 10, no. 5 (2024), https://doi.org/10.1016/j.heliyon.2024.e26686.

264 *adding one more robot reduced employment by six workers*: Daron Acemoglu and Pascual Restrepo, "Robots and Jobs: Evidence from U.S. Labor Markets," *Journal of Political Economy* 128, no. 6 (2020). For further discussion, see Sarah Brown, "A New Study Measures the Actual Impact of Robots on Jobs. It's Significant," MIT Sloan, July 29, 2020, https://mitsloan.mit.edu/ideas-made-to-matter/a-new-study-measures-actual-impact-robots-jobs-its-significant.

264 *"currently available for work"*: "How the Government Measures Unemployment," U.S. Bureau of Labor Statistics, updated October 8, 2015, https://www.bls.gov/cps/cps_htgm.htm.

265 *the use of automation or robotic technology*: Peter Eavis, "Will Automation Replace Jobs? Port Workers May Strike Over It," *New York Times*, September 2, 2024, https://www.nytimes.com/2024/09/02/business/economy/port-workers-robots-automation-strike.html.

265 *the establishment of state-run grocery stores*: Jonathan Turley, "Chicago Mayor Johnson Moves Toward City-Run Grocery Stores," *Res Ipsa Loquitur*, September 15, 2023, https://jonathanturley.org/2023/09/15/chicago-mayor-johnson-moves-toward-city-run-grocery-stores/.

265 *KC Sun Fresh is gushing money*: Annie Gowen, "Kansas City Poured Millions into a Grocery Store, It May Still Close," *Washington Post*, July 18, 2025.

265 *"government-owned, government-operated grocery stores"*: Bryce Covert, "One Way to Fight Rising Food Prices: Public Grocery Stores," *New Republic*, March 24, 2025, https://newrepublic.com/article/193056/food-egg-prices-public-grocery-stores.

266 *$535 million subsidy from the Obama Department of Transportation (DOT)*: Nick Pope, "One of America's Priciest Boondoggles May Be Going Offline After Sucking Up Subsidies and Incinerating Birds," MSN, January 3, 2025, https://www.msn.com/en-us/news/technology/one-of-america-s-priciest-green-boondoggles-may-be-going-offline-after-sucking-up-subsidies-and-incinerating-birds/ar-AA1ylZen?ocid=EMMX.

266 *sales slumped with consumers*: Jack Ewing, "Biden Offers $1.7 Billion to Help Factories Build Electric Vehicles," *New York Times*, July 11, 2024, https://www.nytimes.com/2024/07/11/business/biden-administration-electric-vehicles.html.

266 *a loss of $49,000 per EV*: Kevin Killough, "Ford Lost Nearly $49,000 on Each Electric Vehicle It Sold in 2024," *Just the News*, February 7, 2025, https://justthenews.com/politics-policy/energy/ford-lost-nearly-49000-each-electric-vehicle-it-sold-2024.

267 *reduced to £10*: Harmer, *Life of a Revolutionary*, 98.

267 *giving every citizen a monthly $1,000 payment*: Andrew Yang, *The War on Normal People: The Truth About America's Disappearing Jobs and Why Universal Basic Income Is Our Future* (Grand Central Publishing, 2018).

267 *Yang put the loss at 1 out of 3 jobs*: Katharine Miller, "Radical Proposal: Universal Basic Income to Offset Job Losses Due to Automation," HAI, Stanford University, October 20, 2021, https://hai.stanford.edu/news/radical-proposal-universal-basic-income-offset-job-losses-due-automation.

267 *69 percent of respondents between the ages of eighteen and thirty-four*: Gabriela Schulte, "Poll: Majority of Voters Now Say the Government Should Have a Universal Basic Income Program," *The Hill*, August 14, 2020, https://thehill.com/hilltv/what-americas-thinking/512099-poll-majority-of-voters-now-say-the-government-should-have-a/.

267 *the enormous costs became evident*: Hoover Institution, *The Human Prosperity Project: Essays on Socialism and Free-Market Capitalism from the Hoover Institution* (Hoover Institution Press, 2022).

268 *a UBI policy*: Milton Friedman, *Capitalism and Freedom* (University of Chicago Press, 1962); John F. Cogan and Daniel L. Heil, "The Economic Impact of a Universal Basic Income," Hoover Institution, January 14, 2021, https://www.hoover.org/research/economic-impact-universal-basic-income.

268 *Carter putting it higher at between 40 percent and 65 percent*: Cogan and Heil, "Economic Impact," 7.

268 *an income line equal to the poverty line*: Cogan and Heil, "Economic Impact," 8.

268 *elected to go on the dole rather than seek new positions*: Cogan and Heil, "Economic Impact," 7.

268 *greater educational and recreational pursuits*: Cogan and Heir, "Economic Impact," 2.

269 *enhance the lifestyles of citizens*: "A Minister of Free Time? Mais Oui!," *Christian Science Monitor*, August 27, 1982.

269 *the equal exchange of labor*: William Bailie, *Josiah Warren, The First American Anarchist: A Sociological Study* (Small, Maynard, 1906), 9.

270 *shedding the original collectivist principles*: Bailie, *Josiah Warren, the First American Anarchist*, 40.

270 *his typographical inventions*: Bailie, *Josiah Warren, the First American Anarchist*, 47.

270 *the lack of capital and employment soon led to failure*: Bailie, *Josiah Warren, the First American Anarchist*, 77.

270 *early democratic systems*: Samons, *What's Wrong with Democracy*, 23.

271 *the* thetes *(producing the least)*: Samons, *What's Wrong with Democracy*, 23.

271 archons, *or high officials*: Samons, *What's Wrong with Democracy*, 23–24.

272 *the top of their priorities: public education*: Soboul, *The Sans-Culottes*, 85.

272 *"none . . . remain uninstructed"*: Benner, *Thomas Paine*, 222.

272 *to cover "on the spot" educational opportunities*: Benner, *Thomas Paine*, 222.

272 *the same utilitarian grounds*: Benner, *Thomas Paine*, 123.

273 *unleashed fantastic production and wealth*: Ronald H. Coase and Ning Wang, "How China Became Capitalist," *CATO Policy Report* 35, no. 1 (January/February 2013).

273 *restoring market-based policies*: Geoffrey K. Fry, *The Politics of Decline: An Interpretation of British Politics from the 1940s to the 1970s* (Palgrave Macmillan, 2004), 236.

273 *worsening economic conditions in the 1990s*: Louis Rouanet, "The Persistent Failure of French Socialism," Working Paper No. 2024/04 (Center for Free Enterprise, University of Texas at El Paso, March 19, 2024).

274 *reduced inflation from 25 percent to 2.4 percent*: Jonathan Turley, "Afuera! Milei Administration Posts Record Reductions in Deficit and Inflation Numbers," *Res Ipsa Loquitur*, December 15, 2024, https://jonathanturley.org/2024/12/15/afuera-milei-administration-posts-record-reductions-in-deficit-and-inflation-numbers/.

274 *evidence of such progress*: Russell J. Dalton and Doh Chull Shin, *Citizens, Democracy, and Markets Around the Pacific Rim: Congruence Theory and Political Culture* (Oxford University Press, 2006), 222–24.

274 *resonate with many today*: Alexis de Tocqueville, *Tocqueville on America After 1840: Letters and Other Writings*, trans. and ed. Aurelian Craiutu and Jeremy Jennings (Cambridge University Press, 2009), 393–96.

275 *"education, work, and assistance"*: Daniel J. Mahoney, "Welfare Rights as Socialist Manqué," *Law & Liberty*, August 12, 2012, https://lawliberty.org/welfare-rights-as-socialist-manque/.

275 *"the significant use of freedom"*: Jech, "What Has Athens to Do with Rome?," 550.

275 *"usually imposes the least work"*: Tocqueville, *Tocqueville on America*, 395.

275 *"the principal means of supporting industry"*: Tocqueville, *Tocqueville on America*, 395.

275 *"the great and sole organizer of everything"*: Tocqueville, *Tocqueville on America*, 395.

11. LIVING FREELY IN THE TWENTY-FIRST CENTURY

278 *"indulgency"*: Palmer, *Twelve Who Ruled*, 259.

278 *a collectivized society without property and wealth inequalities*: Murray N. Rothbard, "Roots of Marxism: Messianic Communism," chap. 9 in *Classic Economics: An Austrian Perspective on the History of Economic Thought*, vol. 2 (Edward Elgar Publishing, 1995), 304–308.

278 *Babeuf worked as a feudal notary*: Mason, *The Last Revolutionaries*, 11.

279 *"an extralegal revolutionary conspiracy"*: James H. Billington, *Fire in the Minds of Men: Origins of the Revolutionary Faith* (Basic Books, 1980), 73.

ALL LIBERTY IS LOCAL

282 *"the great purposes of commerce, revenue, or agriculture"*: Rasmussen, *Fears of a Setting Sun*, 67.

283 *"each will be controlled by itself"*: Madison, Federalist 51, 323.

284 *"no special interest in their welfare"*: Ralph A. Rossum, *Federalism, the Supreme Court, and the Seventeenth Amendment: The Irony of Constitutional Democracy* (Lexington Books, 2001), 191.

285 *"the most important task of those who care for liberty"*: Walter Lippmann, "The Teacher and the Rule of Majorities," chap. 3 in *American Inquisitors* (Routledge, 2017), 111.

286 *the Supreme Court overturned* Chevron *in* Loper Bright Enterprises v. Raimondo *in 2024: Loper Bright Enterprises v. Raimondo*, 603 U.S. 369 (2024).

287 *created only forty years earlier*: For example, see Tim Noah, "The Supreme Court's War on Regulation Is Going to Tank the Economy," *New Republic*, July 3, 2024, https://newrepublic.com/article/183416/supreme-court-chevron-endangers-economy.

288 *every aspect of the sprawling territories*: Ali Farazmand, ed., *Bureaucracy and Administration* (Taylor & Francis, 2009).

288 *wielding control over the sultans themselves: Aysel Yildiz, Crisis and Rebellion in the Ottoman Empire: The Downfall of a Sultan in the Age of Revolution* (Bloomsbury Publishing, 2017), 142.

289 *"institutions replacing individual rulers" in governance*: Ali Farazmand, ed., *Handbook of Bureaucracy* (Routledge, 2018), 663.

INDIVIDUAL LIBERTY AND TRANSNATIONAL GOVERNANCE

290 *"the people can eat grass"*: Fife, *The Terror*, 28.

292 *combat Trump and nationalistic movements*: United States Senate, Committee on the Judiciary, Subcommittee on the Constitution, "The Censorship Industrial

Complex," March 25, 2025 (testimony of Jonathan Turley); Jonathan Turley, "'A New World Order with European Values': The Unholy Union of Globalism and Anti–Free Speech Measures," *Res Ipsa Loquitur*, March 24, 2025, https://jonathanturley.org/2025/03/24/a-new-world-order-with-european-values-the-unholy-union-of-globalism-and-anti-free-speech-measures/.

292 *failing to censor users to meet EU demands*: Jon Bordkin, "EU May 'Make an Example of X' by Issuing a $1 Billion Fine to Musk's Social Network," *ArsTechnica*, April 4, 2025, https://arstechnica.com/tech-policy/2025/04/eu-may-make-an-example-of-x-by-issuing-1-billion-fine-to-musks-social-network/.

292 *decried the orders as lawfare by the ruling elite*: Christian Edwards, "Marine Le Pen Verdict Fuels Debate Over That Europe's 'Rule of Law' Is Throttling the 'Will of the People,'" CNN, April 5, 2025, https://www.cnn.com/2025/04/05/europe/le-pen-georgescu-judiciary-banning-candidates-intl.

292 *comply with European ESG regulations*: Kevin Killough, "European Union Directive Will Require American Companies to Adhere to ESG Policy Goals: Report," *Just the News*, April 4, 2025, https://justthenews.com/politics-policy/energy/european-union-directive-will-require-american-companies-adhere-esg-policy.

292 *supplier farms in the United States*: Jack McPherrin and Justin Haskins, "CSDDD: The European Union's Corporate Sustainability Due Diligence Directive Is a Direct Threat to U.S. Sovereignty, Free Markets, and Individual Liberty," Policy Study, Heartland Institute, March 31, 2025, https://heartland.org/wp-content/uploads/2025/03/Mar-25-CSDDD-final.pdf.

293 *"all crimes and follies of the past"*: Beatrice Heuser, *Brexit in History: Sovereignty or a European Union?* (Hurst, 2019), 192.

294 *one area would lead to "spillover" in other areas*: Herman Lelieveldt and Sebastiaan Princen, *The Politics of the European Union*, 3rd ed. (Cambridge University Press, 2023), 30.

294 *coordinate national regulations to achieve greater uniformity*: Ivan T. Berend, *The Economics and Politics of European Integration: Populism, Nationalism and the History of the EU* (Routledge, 2020), 54.

295 *"competence post-Lisbon has been entrenched"*: N. Peršak, "Criminalising Hate Crime and Hate Speech at EU Level: Extending the List of Eurocrimes Under Article 83(1) TFEU," *Criminal Law Forum* 33, no. 2 (2022): 85–119, https://doi.org/10.1007/s10609-022-09440-w.

295 *its 2021 European Climate Law (ECL)*: Parliament and Council Regulation 2021/1119 of 30 June 2021 Establishing the Framework for Achieving Climate Neutrality and Amending Regulations (EC) No 401/2009 and (EU) 2018/1999 ("European Climate Law") 2021 O.J. (L 243) 1.

295 *cuts across national policies and programs*: 2021 O.J. (L 243) 1.

295 *"the empowerment of the individual across borders and cultures"*: "About Us," Global Governance Institute, accessed July 13, 2025, https://www.globalgovernance.eu/about-us.

296 *EU's pro-immigration policies and countervailing national policies*: "Italy, Other EU States Urge Rethink on European Rights Convention," France24, May 22, 2025, https://www.france24.com/en/live-news/20250522-italy-other-eu-states-urge-rethink-on-european-rights-convention.

296 *interviews with former president Donald Trump*: Jonathan Turley, "'We Are Monitoring': EU Censor Threatens Musk Ahead of the Trump Interview," *Res Ipsa Loquitur*, August 13, 2024, https://jonathanturley.org/2024/08/13/we-are-monitoring-eu-censor-threatens-musk-ahead-of-the-trump-interview/.

297 *their attacks on free speech in the West*: Jonathan Turley, "'The Threat from Within': J. D. Vance Delivers Historic Defense of Free Speech," *Res Ipsa Loquitur*, February 17, 2025, https://jonathanturley.org/2025/02/17/the-threat-from-within-j-d-vance-delivers-a-historic-defense-of-free-speech/.

298 *how to protect the "New World Order"*: United States Senate, *Committee on the Judiciary, Subcommittee on the Constitution, "The Censorship Industrial Complex,"* March 25, 2025 (testimony of Jonathan Turley); Turley, "A New World Order."

298 *she called a world threat*: Jonathan Turley, "Back with a Vengeance: Nina Jankowicz Calls on Europeans to Oppose the United States," *Res Ipsa Loquitur*, April 23, 2025, https://jonathanturley.org/2025/04/23/back-with-a-vengeance-former-biden-disinformation-governance-board-chief-chief-nina-jankowicz-tells-european-union-to-oppose-the-united-states/.

298 *"a menace to peaceful people everywhere"*: Jonathan Turley, "Hit Us Please—America's Left Issues Broken 'Arrow Signal' to Europe," *Res Ipsa Loquitur*, July 7, 2025, https://jonathanturley.org/2025/07/07/hit-us-please-americas-left-issues-a-broken-arrow-signal-to-europe/.

298 *"restitution, compensation and satisfaction"*: Ian Swanson, "UN Top Court: Failure to Act Against Climate Change Could Violate International Law," *The Hill*, July 23, 2025, https://thehill.com/policy/energy-environment/5415989-icj-climate-law-obligation/.

299 *supporting global censorship efforts*: Jonathan Turley, "WHO Head Tedros Supports Corporate Censorship to Combat the 'Infodemic,'" *Res Ipsa Loquitur*, January 28, 2022, https://jonathanturley.org/2022/01/28/who-head-tedros-supports-corporate-censorship-to-combat-the-infodemic/.

299 *an unacceptable barrier to achieving progress*: Jonathan Turley, "'Curbing' Free Speech: John Kerry Criticizes the First Amendment as 'a Major Block' for Censorship," *Res Ipsa Loquitur*, October 3, 2024, https://jonathanturley.org/2024/10/03/curbing-free-speech-john-kerry-denounces-the-first-amendment-as-a-major-block-to-removing-disinformation/.

299 *subordinated to exceptions*: Anne M. Cohler et al., eds., *Montesquieu: The Spirit of the Laws* (Cambridge University Press, 1989 [1748], 124); see also Ola Olsson and Gustav Hansson, "Country Size and the Rule of Law: Resuscitating Montesquieu," *European Economic Review* 55, no. 6 (2011): 613–29.

301 *the revolution was designed to end feudalism*: Sagan, *Citizens and Cannibals*, 51.

305 *"repeated the false claim about Turley"*: Jonathan Turley, "Ghosted by ChatGPT: How I Was First Defamed and Then Deleted by AI," *Res Ipsa Loquitur*, December 16, 2024, https://jonathanturley.org/2024/12/16/ghosted-by-chatgpt-how-i-was-first-defamed-and-then-deleted-by-ai/.

"WHAT THEN IS THE AMERICAN" IN THE TWENTY-FIRST CENTURY?

308 *a jump of 75 percent over the past ten years*: Elizabeth Dickinson, "Double Booked," *Foreign Policy*, September 30, 2009, https://foreignpolicy.com/2009/09/30/double-booked/.

308 *easier travel and living conditions abroad*: Whizzy Kim, "The Ultimate Score for Rich People? 'Golden' Passports," *Vox*, June 25, 2023, https://www.vox.com money/23762537/golden-passports-wealthy-explained.

309 *a return to an agrarian existence*: Edward Kissi, *Revolution and Genocide in Ethiopia and Cambodia* (Lexington Books, 2006), 61.

309 *"that race now called Americans have arisen"*: J. Hector St. John Crèvecoeur, *Letters from an American Farmer* (Applewood Books, 2003), 55.

310 *"This is an American"*: Crèvecoeur, *Letters from an American Farmer*.

311 *"both deceived and oppressed it"*: David McNally, *Political Economy and the Rise of Capitalism: A Reinterpretation* (University of California Press, 1988), http://ark.cdlib.org/ark:/13030/ft367nb2h4/.

312 *"not necessarily attached to any particular country"*: McNally, *Political Economy*, 224.

312 *"guarantee liberty of work and investment, and security of property"*: McNally, *Political Economy*, 251.

313 *the American democracy and character to agrarian values*: Elizabeth Anderson, "Thomas Paine's '*Agrarian Justice*' and the Origins of Social Insurance," chap. 3 in *Ten Neglected Classics of Philosophy*, ed. Eric Schliesser (Oxford University Press, 2016), https://doi.org/10.1093/acprof:oso/9780199928903.003.0003.

314 *a metaphor for American individuality and industry*: Paul B. Thompson and Thomas C. Hilde, eds., *The Agrarian Roots of Pragmatism* (Vanderbilt University Press, 2000).

315 *receiving state support*: Robin E. McGee and Nancy J. Thompson, "Unemployment and Depression Among Emerging Adults in 12 States, Behavioral Risk Factor Surveillance System, 2010," *Preventing Chronic Disease* 12, no. 3 (2015), http://doi.org/10.5888/pcd12.140451.

315 Paddle Your Own Canoe *in 1887*: Horatio Alger, *Strong and Steady; Or, Paddle Your Own Canoe: Finding Success and Self-Reliance in a Classic American Tale* (Good Press, 2023).

315 *a communal town called New Harmony in Indiana*: For further discussion, see Turley, *The Indispensable Right* at 257–58; William Bailie, "Relations with Robert Dale Owen," chap. 3 in *Josiah Warren, the First American Anarchist: A Sociological Study* (Small, Maynard, 1906); George B. Lockwood and Charles Allen Prosser, *The New Harmony Movement* (D. Appleton, 1905; repr., Augustus M. Kelley, 1970), 69–71.

315 *Warren was a committed anarchist*: Bailie, *Josiah Warren, the First American Anarchist*, 1.

315 *such items as a lard-burning lamp*: Bailie, *Josiah Warren, the First American Anarchist*, 2.

316 *"the foundation of society"*: Bailie, *Josiah Warren, the First American Anarchist*, 5.

316 *a type of democratic despotism*: Bailie, *Josiah Warren, the First American Anarchist*, 6.

316 *famous figures like John Stuart Mill*: Turley, *The Indispensable Right*, 257–64.

317 *based on individuality to succeed*: Bailie, *Josiah Warren, the First American Anarchist*, 99.

317 *the outgrowth of Jefferson and Paine*: Bailie, *Josiah Warren, the First American Anarchist*, 122.

318 *"Arsenal of Democracy"*: Albert J. Bairne, *The Arsenal of Democracy: FDR, Detroit, and an Epic Quest to Arm an America at War* (Houghton Mifflin Harcourt, 2014), 157.

CONCLUSION

329 *liberty, not democracy*: Sandefur, *Conscience of the Constitution*, 5.

329 *"ring hollow today"*: Akhil Reed Amar, "The Consent of the Governed: Constitutional Amendment Outside of Article V," *Columbia Law Review* 94, no. 2 (1994): 457.

329 *from what they envisioned*: Jonathan Turley, "Human Rights Campaign President Calls for Rejection of 'the Little Piece of Paper' of the Founders," *Res Ipsa Loquitur*, August 30, 2024, https://jonathanturley.org/2024/08/30/human-rights-campaign-president-calls-for-rejection-of-the-little-piece-of-paper-of-the-founders/.

329 *"the protection of man's natural rights"*: Thompson, *America's Revolutionary Mind*, 273.

330 *"I do not at present approve": Rasmussen, Fears of a Setting Sun*, 1.

330 *"it is not the best": Rasmussen, Fears of a Setting Sun*, 1.

330 *Madison, who outlived them all*: Rasmussen, *Fears of a Setting Sun*, 4.

330 *"there is public Virtue enough to support a Republic"*: Rasmussen, *Fears of a Setting Sun*, 9.

331 *"miracle of Philadelphia"*: Rasmussen, *Fears of a Setting Sun*, 9.

331 *until the end of their lives*: Bowen, *Miracle at Philadelphia*.

331 *his pomp and aggrandizement*: Rasmussen, *Fears of a Setting Sun*, 124.

331 *"Protector of Their Liberties"*: Rasmussen, *Fears of a Setting Sun*, 124.

331 *their attacks on Federalists*: Turley, *The Indispensable Right*, 104–125.

332 *"made a happy port"*: Jefferson to John Adams, Monticello, January 21, 1812, in *The Adams-Jefferson Letters: The Complete Correspondence Between Thomas Jefferson and Abigail and John Adams*, ed. Lester J. Cappon (University of North Carolina Press, 1959), https://nationalhumanitiescenter.org/pds/livingrev/religion/text3/adamsjeffersoncor.pdf.

332 *five hours earlier in Monticello, Virginia*: Jonathan Turley, "E Pluribus Unum: What We Can Learn from Jefferson and Adams on this Fourth of July," *Res Ipsa Loquitur*,

July 4, 2024, https://jonathanturley.org/2024/07/04/e-pluribus-unum-what-we-can-learn-from-jefferson-and-adams-on-the-fourth-of-july/.

334 *"a traitorous scribbler, saturated with brandy"*: Benner, *Thomas Paine*, 311.

334 *the "archbeast" and a "loathsome reptile"*: Benner, *Thomas Paine*, 334.

334 *"in which his soul delights"*: Harmer, *Life of a Revolutionary*, 102.

334 *"I don't want them to suffer again"*: Benner, *Thomas Paine*, 345.

334 *neither Washington nor Morris would help him*: Harmer, *Life of a Revolutionary*, 105.

334 *hostile crowds seemed to form against him*: Harmer, *Life of a Revolutionary*, 104.

334 *finish a third edition of* The Age of Reason: Benner, *Thomas Paine*, 341, 343.

335 *Paine refused to press charges*: Benner, *Thomas Paine*, 359.

335 *"our poor beggars in England"*: Benner, *Thomas Paine*, 361.

335 *his age or alcohol or both*: Benner, *Thomas Paine*, 363.

335 *"cross the streets to avoid you"*: Harmer, *Life of a Revolutionary*, 104.

335 *"the opinions of the world"*: Harmer, *Life of a Revolutionary*, 104.

335 *"Get away with you"*: Harmer, *Life of a Revolutionary*, 106.

336 *the loss of innocence for many*: Sagan, *Citizens & Cannibals*, 5.

336 *"For as you rise, so you must fall"*: Harmer, *Life of Revolutionary*, 4.

336 *"author of* Common Sense*"*: Benner, *Thomas Paine*, 377.

337 *"the will of my Creator, God"*: Harmer, *Life of a Revolutionary*, 105; Benner, *Thomas Paine*, 377.

337 *"I have no wish to believe on that subject"*: Benner, *Thomas Paine*, 380.

337 *The tombstone would not be added for another thirty years*: Benner, *Thomas Paine*, 377.

337 *"Nobody knows and nobody cares"*: Harmer, *Life of a Revolutionary*, 106.

338 *"engraved upon my tomb"*: Thomas Paine, *The Life and Works of Thomas Paine*, ed. William Manley Van der Weyde (Thomas Paine National Historical Association, 1925), 292–93.

338 *"some good and much harm"*: Benner, *Thomas Paine*, 381.

338 *decided to reclaim Paine for England*: Benner, *Thomas Paine*, 383.

338 *what happened to the body*: Harmer, *Life of a Revolutionary*, 106.

338 *made into trinkets or buttons*: Benner, *Thomas Paine*, 383.

338 *"Advice to My Country"*: Rasmussen, *Fears of a Setting Sun*, 224.

339 *"his deadly wiles into Paradise"*: Rasmussen, *Fears of a Setting Sun*, 224.

341 *the image of Victory (Nike) in her hand*: Samons, *What's Wrong with Democracy*, 55.

Image Credits

PHOTOS THROUGHOUT

Page xv: Courtesy of Muzeum Narodowe w Warszawie

Page xx: Thomas Paine, Library of Congress

Page 10: Courtesy of Thetford Town Council, Norfolk

Page 27: Thomas Paine, Library of Congress; James Madison, Library of Congress

Page 39: Bibliothèque nationale de France

Page 66: Harvard Art Collection

Page 78: Library of Congress

Page 82: National Gallery of Art

Pages 90 and 94: Library of Congress

Page 98: Musée du Louvre

Page 100: Rousseau, Musée Antoine-Lécuyer; Voltaire, Musée Carnavalet

Page 108: By H. Jannin, Musée de la Révolution française, Vizille

Page 115: Library of Congress

Page 119: Helen Regenstein Collection

Page 130: Library of Congress

Page 143: Courtesy of National Gallery of Art, Washington, D.C.

Page 144: Royal Museums of Fine Arts of Belgium, Brussels

Pages 180, 199, 206, and 243: Library of Congress

Page 280: Image generated by the author using artificial intelligence

Page 308: The Art Institute of Chicago / Art Resource, NY

Page 318: © Norman Rockwell

Page 338: *Encyclopaedia Britannica*

PHOTO INSERT

Images 2 and 3: Harvard Art Museums / Fogg Museum, Bequest of Grenville L. Winthrop © President and Fellows of Harvard College

Image 4: Harvard University Portrait Collection, Bequest of Ward Nicholas Boylston to Harvard College, 1828 © President and Fellows of Harvard College

Image 5: Harvard Art Museums / Fogg Museum, Bequest of Grenville L. Winthrop © President and Fellows of Harvard College

Image 6: Historical Society of Pennsylvania

Image 8: Library of Congress

Images 9 and 10: Harvard Art Museums / Fogg Museum, Bequest of Grenville L. Winthrop © President and Fellows of Harvard College

Image 11: Musée du Louvre

Image 12: Harvard Art Museums / Fogg Museum, Bequest of Grenville L. Winthrop © President and Fellows of Harvard College

Image 13: By H. Jannin, Musée de la Révolution française, Vizille

Image 17: Library of Congress

Image 18: © RMN-Grand Palais / Art Resource, NY

Image 19: Jacques-Louis David, *Marat Assassinated*, Royal Museums of Fine Arts of Belgium (Brussels), inv. 3260, photo: J. Geleyns

Image 22: Erik Cornelius / Nationalmuseum

Image 23: Bibliothèque nationale de France

Image 24: Harvard Art Museums / Fogg Museum

Images 25 and 26: Library of Congress

Image 27: St. Johnsbury History & Heritage Center

Image 28: Asher B. Durand, *James Madison (1750/51–1836)*, 1833, oil on canvas, 24¼ × 20¼ in., Gift of P. Kemble Paulding, The New York Historical Society

Image 30: © Rockwell Foundation

Image 31: Library of Congress

Image 32: National Portrait Gallery, Smithsonian Institution

Image 34: The Art Institute of Chicago / Art Resource, NY

Image 35: Photo still from *Star Trek: The Next Generation*, courtesy of CBS Studios

Image 36: Image generated by the author using artificial intelligence

All other images are in the public domain.

Index

Page numbers in italic refer to illustrations.

About the Author

JONATHAN TURLEY is a law professor, columnist, television analyst, and litigator. Since 1998, he has held the Shapiro Chair for Public Interest Law at George Washington University Law School. He has served as counsel in some of the most notable cases in the last two decades, including representing members of Congress, judges, whistleblowers, five former attorney generals, celebrities, accused spies and terrorists, journalists, protesters, and the workers at the secret facility Area 51. Turley has testified before Congress more than one hundred times, including during the impeachments of Presidents Bill Clinton and Donald Trump. He was also lead counsel in the last judicial impeachment in U.S. history. He has written for *The New York Times*, *The Wall Street Journal*, *The Washington Post*, the *Los Angeles Times*, and *USA Today*. Called the "dean of legal analysts" by *The Washington Post*, Turley has worked as a legal analyst for CBS, NBC, BBC, and Fox. In a study by Judge Richard Posner, Turley was found to be thirty-eighth in the top one hundred most cited "public intellectuals" (and the second most cited law professor).